canadian
microeconomics

problems and policies

seventh edition

canadian microeconomics

problems and policies

seventh edition

brian lyons Sheridan Institute of Technology and Advanced Learning

PEARSON

Prentice
Hall

Toronto

National Library of Canada Cataloguing in Publication

Lyons, Brian
      Canadian microeconomics: problems and policies/Brian Lyons—7th ed.

Includes index.
ISBN 0-13-120124-7

1. Microeconomics. 2. Canada—Economic conditions. I. Title.

HB172.L96 2004   338.5′0971   C2003-901415-0

0-13-120124-7

Vice President, Editorial Director: Michael J. Young
Acquisitions Editor: Gary Bennett
Marketing Manager: Deb Meredith
Developmental Editor: Meaghan Eley
Editorial Coordinator: Marisa D'Andrea
Copy Editor: Susan Marshall
Proofreader: Laurel Sparrow
Production Coordinator: Andrea Falkenberg
Page Layout: Christine Velakis
Art Director: Julia Hall
Interior and Cover Design: Amy Harnden
Cover Image: Digital Vision

Statistics Canada information is used with the permission of the Minister of
Industry, as Minister responsible for Statistics Canada. Information on the availability of the wide range of data from Statistics Canada can be obtained from Statistics
Canada's Regional Offices, its World Wide Web site at http://www.statcan.ca, and its
toll-free access number 1-800-263-1136. The Statistics Canada CANSIM II database
can be accessed at http://cansim2.statcan.ca/cgi-win/CNSMCGI.EXE.

2 3 4 5   08 07 06 05 04

For Barb, Amber, Marnie,
Brent, Dylan, and Liam

BRIEF TABLE OF CONTENTS

TABLE OF CONTENTS

Chapter 3 Business Organization in Canada   38

Chapter 4 The Demand Side of Markets   58

Chapter 5   The Supply Side of Markets   79

Chapter 6   The Dynamics of Competitive Markets   97

Chapter 7   Market Structures   116

Chapter 8   The Costs and Revenues of the Firm   143

Chapter 12   The Government Sector   243

Chapter 13   The Politics of Economics   264

Chapter 14   Environmental Economics   276

"In the News" Boxes

"You Decide" Boxes

Preface

Introduction

This book is an introductory microeconomics text that addresses itself to the key economic issues and problems facing Canada and Canadians today. It is not oriented toward rigorous, elegant or abstract theory, nor to a mathematical approach to economics—students of introductory economics neither want nor need these. Rather, its approach tends to be practical and "real-world" based, using economic theory to develop an understanding of the issues and problems being discussed, and the policy choices facing governments in dealing with these matters. It is ideally suited for a student's first course in economics and has been used in this role at the secondary-school, community-college, and university levels.

New to This Edition

In addition to updating some of the sixth edition's material, the revisions for the seventh edition were undertaken with the following goals in mind:

1. Improve the flow of the material, within chapters and between chapters.

2. Add current and interesting material, through:

   - various new *In the News* and *You Decide* boxes.
   - new end-of-chapter questions that add interest and relevance to the material.
   - many new margin boxes with examples and colourful facts.
   - increased coverage of ebusiness (including the growth of high-tech manufacturing and the "dot-com, dot-bomb, dot-gone" phenomenon), as well as Chapter 8's questions on how the costs and revenues of ebusiness firms differ from conventional firms, and the problems and opportunities that this creates.

3. Increase interactivity of students with the text, not only through new *In the News* and *You Decide* boxes, but also through more references to websites and questions that invite students to use websites to update information in the text. Along the way, various sections were updated and improved as opportunities presented themselves. Chapter 11 has been improved with updated coverage of poverty—particularly the use of the new after-tax Low Income Cut-Offs that were recently introduced and which change estimates of the number of poor Canadians by 27 percent. The result is coverage that is updated, more relevant, clearer, and more concise.

Chapters 11 and 12 benefit from the use of Statistics Canada's data from the Survey of Labour and Income Dynamics (SLID), and the clarification that is provided by the three definitions of "income" used in these data.

In Chapter 12, there is reorganized and streamlined coverage of government finances, the result of which is an updated and concise presentation of the issues that flows more smoothly from start to finish.

The revisions to Chapter 14 provide improved coverage of the evolution of government farm policy over the years in the context of the changing economic environment.

The most up-to-date coverage of the Kyoto agreement and its implications as of the time of writing has been added to Chapter 15.

Finally, Chapter 16 has been updated to provide the broadest possible context for a recap of the past and glimpse into the future.

Overall, the intended result of these changes is a text that is more current and that flows more effectively, providing additional opportunities for students to interact with the material.

Features

According to both students and teachers, a major feature of this book is its readability, which helps considerably in the learning and teaching of a subject that has an (undeserved) reputation of being rather formidable. Other aspects of the text include:

- **Coverage of "the basics"** Chapters 1, 2, and 5 through 7 provide good coverage of the microeconomics basics of markets and market structure.

- **Flexibility** In addition to these "basics," a variety of topics can be covered, including marginal cost/marginal revenue analysis (Chapter 8), competition policy (Chapter 9), labour markets and unions (Chapter 10), trends concerning jobs and incomes (Chapter 11), the role of government in the economy (Chapter 12), the economics of the environment (Chapter 14), and agriculture (Chapter 15).

- **Interactiveness** The boxes described below, together with the discussion questions at the end of each chapter and the Study Guide, provide extensive opportunities for students to interact with the material, both in groups and on their own.

- **Pedagogical Tools** Learning Objectives, *You Decide* boxes, *In the News* boxes, and end-of-chapter questions all help students focus on and apply the important points in each chapter.

Organization

To a considerable extent, the text consists of two sections, with the section through Chapter 8 covering mostly the basic elements of microeconomics and the second half of the book presenting specific topics, most of which involve data pertaining to Canada's current economic situation. Following the discussion of the basic problems and questions of economics and an examination of the Canadian economy, the text presents the basic tools of microeconomics—demand and supply—and how these interact to determine output and prices under a variety of conditions, ranging from highly competitive to monopolistic industries. In the second half of the book various topics are covered, including government policy toward business, labour markets and labour unions, trends in employment and incomes, government programs, financial problems and policy choices, and economic issues related to the environment and agricultural sector. The text concludes with a short chapter that ties the text together with a review of Canada's past economic directions and a discussion of future trends.

Supplements

The following supplements are available for this text:

- **Instructor's Resource CD-ROM**:
  - Instructor's Resource Manual: includes the answers to all end-of-chapter questions, assignment questions and answers for each chapter, answers to boxed questions in the text, and Transparency Masters for all figures and tables in the text.
  - Pearson TestGen: includes all the contents of a test item file in a computerized format, which enables instructors to view and edit the existing questions, add questions, generate tests, and print the tests in a variety of formats. The Pearson TestGen is compatible with both Windows and Macintosh systems.
- **Study Guide**: includes a review of central themes, self tests with multiple-choice, true/false, fill-in-the-blank, short-answer, problem, and case-study questions, and answers for all self-test questions.
- **Companion Website**: includes valuable student resources, such as self-assessment quizzes, links to related websites, and more. Visit the site at **www.pearsoned.ca/lyons**.

Acknowledgments

Anyone undertaking a project of this magnitude and duration feels indebtedness to many people. In particular, I would like to express my gratitude to Bill Trimble, who said I should do it, Len Rosen, who refused to let me say I wouldn't, and all those teachers and students who used the first six editions and offered helpful comments and suggestions. I would also like to thank the people whose reviews of all seven editions of the manuscript were so helpful: for the first edition, Ray Canon, Gord Cleveland, Ward Levine, Jim Thompson, and Ian Wilson; for the second, Alan Idiens and Chuck Casson; for the third, Linda Nitsou, Bo Renneckendorf, Gord Enemark, L.W. Van Niekerk, Stephen Wise, and Ann Dunkley; for the fourth, Carol Ann Waite, Izhar Mirza, John Parry, and Byron Eastman; for the fifth, Valerie Beckingham, Michael Loconte, Pauline A. Lutes, Peter J. MacDonald, Karen Murkar, John Parry, Don Pepper, Judith Skuce, Don Wheeler, and Peter Young; for the sixth edition, Peter Peters, Karen Murkar, Ian Wilson, Don Wheeler, Martin Moy, Bill Gallivan, Terri Anderson, and Jane Taylor; and for this seventh edition, Worku Aberra of Dawson College, Frances Ford of New Brunswick Community College (Moncton), Carl Graham of Assiniboine Community College, Donald Howick of St. Clair College, Al Idiens of College of New Caledonia, Peter J. MacDonald of Cambrian College, Raimo Marttala of Malaspina College, Martin Moy of University College of Cape Breton, A. Gyasi Nimarko of Vanier College, John Pirrie of St. Lawrence College, and Charles Walton of Nova Scotia Community College.

Finally, I want to express my appreciation to my family—Barb, Marnie, and Amber—who have provided support and understanding over unduly long periods of time.

I have no doubt that there are many improvements that can be made to this book, and welcome suggestions from teachers and students. Please write to me at Sheridan College, 7899 McLaughlin Road, Brampton, Ontario L6V 1G6, or email me at **brian.lyons@sheridanc.on.ca**.

Brian Lyons
2003

A Great Way to Learn and Instruct Online

The Pearson Education Canada Companion Website is easy to navigate and is organized to correspond to the chapters in this textbook. Whether you are a student in the classroom or a distance learner you will discover helpful resources for in-depth study and research that empower you in your quest for greater knowledge and maximize your potential for success in the course.

[www.pearsoned.ca/lyons] Enter

PEARSON
Prentice
Hall

Jump to... http://www.pearsoned.ca/lyons   ⇅ Home | Search | Help | Profile

Companion Website

Home >

Companion Website

Canadian Microeconomics: Problems and Policies, Seventh Edition, and *Canadian Macroeconomics: Problems and Policies,* Seventh Edition, by Lyons

Student Resources

The modules in this section provide students with tools for learning course material. These modules include:

- Chapter Objectives
- Destinations
- Quizzes
- Net Search
- Glossary

In the quiz modules students can send answers to the grader and receive instant feedback on their progress through the Results Reporter. Coaching comments and references to the textbook may be available to ensure that students take advantage of all available resources to enhance their learning experience.

Instructor Resources

The modules in this section provide instructors with additional teaching tools. A downloadable Instructor's Manual will be available in this section. Where appropriate, this section will be password protected.

Chapter 1

What Is Economics?

Learning Objectives

After studying this chapter, you should be able to:

1. Describe the three basic types of economic inputs and explain the role played by each in the economy.

2. State the basic "economic problem" of scarcity.

3. Define the terms *productivity*, *efficiency*, and *effectiveness*.

4. Identify the three basic questions of economics.

5. Estimate the opportunity cost of an economic decision.

What is "economics"? To the householder, economics is the difficult task of balancing the family budget so that there is not too much month left over at the end of the money. To the business leader, economics is the problem of producing a product at a sufficiently low cost to be sold profitably in competition with the products of other producers. To a government leader, economics means making difficult policy choices between goals that often conflict with each other, making it impossible to please everyone and difficult to ensure re-election. To the general public, economics is usually associated with vague, incomprehensible, and often contradictory pronouncements by people called "economists," who many people suspect were created in order to make weather forecasters look good.

Each viewpoint, representing a particular group (householders, business leaders, and government leaders), is only one aspect of the real meaning of economics. To the economist, however, economics deals with the broader question of how well a society's economic system satisfies the economic needs and wants of its people. Since the basic task of an economic system is to produce goods and services and to distribute them among the people of a society, the most common definition of **economics** is "the study of the decisions a society makes concerning the production of goods and services and how the society distributes these goods and services among its members."

economics The study of the decisions a society makes concerning the production of goods and services and the division of these among its people.

This somewhat dry definition will lead us into considering much more interesting questions about Canadian society, employment, incomes, and government policy, such as:

- How many Canadians are really poor?
- Would a big increase in the minimum wage rate help to reduce poverty?
- How big is the male–female "pay gap," and what should be done about it?
- In what occupations will job opportunities be greatest in the future?
- Are strikes severely damaging to the Canadian economy?
- Should the government limit the rents charged by landlords?
- Why have governments reduced the services they provide to the public?
- Can we have economic growth without destroying our environment?
- Why does Mats Sundin earn $7 500 000 per year while some people only earn $10 000?

Some aspects of economic matters, such as those above, raise *philosophical* questions; for instance, is it proper for the government to control apartment rents, or people's wages, or workers' strikes? Other aspects of economics, however, involve more *technical economic analysis*. For example, if the government increased the minimum wage rate by 10 percent, would unemployment consequently increase by 5 percent or not at all, that is, by 0 percent? Often, economics also becomes involved with *value judgments*. For example, suppose experts agreed that a 10-percent increase in the minimum wage rate would cause youth unemployment to increase by 25 000. *Should* the government increase the minimum wage rate by 10 percent? Some people would favour increasing the minimum wage because of the expected benefits for the *employed*. Others would oppose the wage increase because it would reduce job opportunities for the *unemployed*. There is no "right" answer to this question because the response to the question depends on the respondent's value judgment.

Folklore Versus Economic Analysis

Probably the greatest obstacle to the effective learning (and teaching) of economics is the fact that many people already think that they know a great deal about the subject. In fact, much of this "knowledge" consists of widely believed but not necessarily accurate ideas such as the following:

- Producers' profits add 20 percent to 40 percent to the prices we pay for products.
- Canadian companies cannot compete with foreign producers.
- Companies locate wherever wages are lowest.
- The more benefits and services their governments provide, the more economically prosperous Canadians will be.
- A major increase in the minimum wage rate would reduce poverty considerably.
- If the rich paid higher taxes, the rest of us could pay much lower taxes and receive many more government services and benefits.
- A government ban on strikes by labour unions would bring Canada major economic benefits.

None of the above statements are true, but many people believe them to be true. One key objective of this book, and its companion text, *Canadian Macroeconomics: Problems and Policies*, is to replace such folklore about economics with the tools for accurate analysis of economic issues of importance to Canadians.

The Limitations of Economic Analysis

Because economics deals with the behaviour of people (consumers, businesspeople, government policy-makers), economics cannot be a precise science such as mathematics. Similarly, economic analysis does not provide clear and simple answers to important questions, such as whether the government should reduce taxes. However, economic analysis can greatly clarify the choices to be made. For example, it's possible through economic analysis to estimate the consequences of reducing (or not reducing) taxes. So, while economic analysis does not provide us with *decisions*, it does provide us with a much better *basis for making decisions*.

Then What Is Economics About?

Economics is about many matters both small and large. On a large scale, *macroeconomics* (after the Greek word *macro* meaning big) deals with broad aspects of the performance of the economy as a whole—such as recession, inflation, unemployment, and international trade and finance. These are the subjects of the companion text *Canadian Macroeconomics: Problems and Policies*.

On a small scale, *microeconomics* (after the Greek word *micro* meaning small) focuses on particular aspects of the economy such as consumer demand, supply, demand, and prices under various conditions, and the role of big business, labour unions, and government in the economy, as well as the economics of specific industries (such as agriculture) or specific issues (such as the environment). The purpose of this book is to develop an understanding of these microeconomic matters, which are important to all Canadians. Before examining these issues, however, we will consider the basic problems of economics in general. Then, in Chapter 2, we will examine the nature of Canada's economic system.

The "Economic Problem": Too Many Wants, Not Enough Resources

The fundamental problem of economics—so basic that it is known as *"the economic problem"*—is the simple fact that we cannot have everything that we would like. And this reality forces us to make some difficult decisions.

All too often, however, this and other simple but key economic realities become lost in the confusing complexity of our modern economy. And a modern industrial or post-industrial economy can seem very bewildering because it consists of a myriad of factors, such as consumers, small businesses, big businesses, and ebusinesses. In addition, there are labour unions, governments, exports, imports, and the level of output. And to make matters more complicated, there is employment, unemployment, the money supply, interest rates, prices, the international value of the nation's currency, government tax revenues, government spending, consumer spending and saving, banks, profits, stock markets, and many other factors. Furthermore, each of these factors is related to the others in ways that are often subtle and complex. Such complexities often make understanding an issue difficult because they obscure the basic economic principles involved in the issue.

In order to better understand an economic issue, it is helpful to eliminate the many complexities associated with a modern economy so that we can focus on the basic economic principles involved. As an example of eliminating complexities, suppose that a group of people has been stranded on a deserted island. With none of the complexities of a modern economy to distract us, our group must come to grips with the single most basic economic problem: the people in the group have *economic needs and wants*, but there are only certain *economic resources* available to this particular group. The group needs and wants things such as food, shelter, clothing, security, and so on. To produce these things, the group can use the three basic types of economic resources, or **inputs**—the skills of the people in the group, the equipment they have, and the natural resources of the island.

The Skills of People ("Labour")

The largest and most important single economic resource of any society is the skills of its people, which economists refer to collectively as **labour**. Labour includes all the skills possessed by a wide range of people, from manual labourers and skilled workers to managers and research scientists. In our island mini-society, people would have various useful and necessary skills such as hunting, fishing, farming, building, planning, and managing.

Capital Equipment

Another vitally important economic resource is society's stock of **capital equipment** (also simply called **capital**), by which we mean its factories, equipment, machinery, computers, tools, and so on. Capital equipment is crucially important because it increases *output per worker per hour*, or **productivity**. And when each worker produces more, the society can enjoy more economic prosperity, or a higher **standard of living**—more goods and services per person. Figure 1-1 illustrates the importance of capital equipment.

FIGURE 1-1 The Importance of Capital Equipment

Capital Equipment		Higher Output per Worker per Hour (productivity)		Higher Potential Standard of Living (goods per person)

While a modern industrial economy possesses a vast array of factories, machinery, equipment, and tools, our island mini-society will have only a few basic tools, such as spears, fishnets, and plows. So productivity will be low, and the people of the mini-society will have relatively few goods available to them. This scarcity of goods could interest the people in increasing their stock of capital equipment in order to increase their productivity and their standard of living.

Natural Resources ("Land")

The third economic resource available to a society is natural resources, which economists refer to as **land**. In our island mini-society, these natural resources would likely be few and simple—waterways, fish, land, trees, plants, and so on.

People tend to think of natural resources as depletable (and depleting), which is not always the case. Some natural resources, such as forests and fish, can be renewable if managed effectively, while technology is capable of

inputs Economic resources, such as labour, capital equipment, and natural resources, that are used to produce goods and services.

labour The largest single productive input available to any economy, labour includes all of the productive talents of the people of a society, mental as well as physical.

capital (equipment) The tools, equipment, machinery, and factories used to increase production per person per hour and thus living standards.

productivity Output per worker per hour; a measure of efficiency.

standard of living A measure of the economic prosperity of the people of a society, usually expressed in terms of the volume of consumer goods and services consumed per household or per person per year.

land Short form for all the natural resources available to a society's economy as economic inputs.

output The goods and services produced by a society using its productive inputs.

creating entirely new resources, such as oil, natural gas, and nuclear power. In a similar way, improvements in technology are making the Athabasca Tar Sands of Northern Alberta a viable energy resource. Thus, while some natural resources are depletable, it is also true that new resources can be developed through technology.

The Task of an Economic System

The task of the economic system of any society is to organize and use these economic resources, or productive inputs, to produce goods and services (**output**) of the types and quantities that will best satisfy the needs and wants of the people of the society. This process is shown in Figure 1-2.

In our island mini-society, the process shown in Figure 1-2 would be quite simple: people with different skills would use simple tools, such as spears, nets, and plows, to produce products to satisfy basic needs, such as food, shelter, and security. In a modern economy, this process is much more sophisticated, involving a wide range of skills and "high-tech" equipment and resources to produce a tremendous volume and variety of both goods and services. However, the basic task is the same in both economies: to try to use our economic resources to our best advantage.

FIGURE 1-2 The Basic Operation of Any Economic System

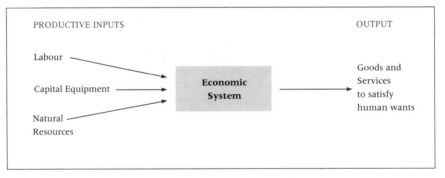

The Basic "Economic Problem" of Scarcity

scarcity The problem that, while economic inputs (and thus potential output) are limited in availability, people's wants and needs are apparently unlimited.

How to use our economic resources to our best advantage is a particularly important question because we do not have enough economic resources to produce everything that we would like to have. This is the basic "economic problem" of **scarcity**: the economic resources (inputs) on the left side of Figure 1-2 are in *limited* supply, while the amount of goods and services wanted by people on the right side of Figure 1-2 seems to be *unlimited*. Since we cannot have everything that we want, we are forced to *make choices*, some of which might be difficult.

The island mini-economy illustrates this reality particularly clearly because the choices are so limited. Suppose we have ten people available for work and decide to use five of them for getting food, three for getting fuel, and two for taking care of security by maintaining fences and guarding against certain threatening creatures that roam the island. If we find that we don't have enough food, we can increase food production by 20 percent by *adding* a sixth person to the "food team." However, this addition would require *removing* that person from either the group getting fuel or the group providing security. While we would be better fed, we would have either less comfort or less security. And more of any one of these items means less of another, forcing us to make difficult choices. This forgoing of one thing in order to enjoy more of another is called **opportunity cost** by economists; this concept is explained more fully in Appendix 1A at the end of this chapter.

opportunity cost The concept that the real economic cost of producing something is the forgone opportunity to produce something else that could have been produced with the same inputs.

YOU DECIDE

THE SCARCITY PROBLEM ON A PERSONAL LEVEL

On a personal level, the problem of scarcity manifests itself in the form of your income. If your take-home pay is $2000 per month, then you have only $2000 (at most) to spend on consumer goods and services each month. If you spend $200 more this month on new clothes, you will have $200 less to spend on, say, restaurant dinners. Just like on the deserted island, enjoying more of one thing means that you must accept less of something else.

Or must you accept less of something else if you enjoy more of one thing? Unlike the unfortunate people on the deserted island, you have a credit card! You can put the $200 for the new clothes on the credit card, and enjoy $2200 of consumer spending this month. Better yet, put the restaurant dinners on the credit card too, and then you can enjoy $2400 of consumer spending—an increase of 20 percent from your monthly take-home pay of $2000.

Questions

1. Would you recommend this credit strategy to a good friend? Why?
2. If you would not recommend this credit strategy, how *would* you suggest that credit cards be used?

These are the same issues that Canadian households face in managing their budgets. Since your income can't buy everything that you would like, you have to *make choices* as to what you will have and what you will forgo. Taking that dream vacation would be wonderful, but it will mean that you cannot buy that car that you really want.

And an entire nation, through its government, must come to grips with the same problems. The public wants the best health care and education systems as well as other government services, but governments lack the tax revenues to provide the ideal levels of all services. Since using more tax resources for one service would leave less for other services, the public must accept that each service will not be provided at an ideal level.

"THERE'S NO SUCH THING AS A FREE LUNCH"

In popular language, the phrase "There's no such thing as a free lunch" refers to the concept of opportunity cost as it applies to things that are said to be "free," such as samples of products.

Questions

1. Explain how this phrase relates to seemingly "free" items such as samples.

Another popular phrase is that something is "as free as the air."

2. Is there any opportunity cost in your breathing of air?

3. Does this phrase mean that we should consider our breathing of air to be completely "free"?

So the basic economic problem of scarcity is a universal one, affecting all societies. This problem is illustrated in more detail by something called a *production-possibilities* curve in the appendix to this chapter. In the following sections, let's consider some of the implications of the problem of scarcity.

Effectiveness and Efficiency

Because we cannot have everything that we would like, it is very important that we use our scarce economic resources wisely by producing as much as we can of things that are needed and wanted. These goals are expressed by the terms *effectiveness* and *efficiency*, which are the two most basic measures of the performance of any economic operation, from an individual business to a nation's entire economy.

Effectiveness refers to achieving certain goals, in this case, producing goods and services that are *needed and wanted*. If an economic system can achieve these goals, it is "effective." **Efficiency** refers to using the economic resources available to you to produce a *high volume of output* at a *low production cost per unit*. One common measure of efficiency is "productivity," or output per worker per hour. Societies with efficient economies that produce a high volume of goods and services per worker tend to have a high standard of living, or consumption per person.

To recap, it is important that an economy be *both* effective *and* efficient. The more efficiently and effectively a society uses its economic resources, the more successful it will be in making available to its people larger volumes of goods and services that are needed and wanted and at lower prices. As a result, its people will enjoy a higher standard of living.

effectiveness A measure of how well an economy performs in terms of producing goods and services that are needed and wanted.

efficiency A measure of how well an economy performs in terms of producing high volumes of goods and services at a low cost per item.

The Three Basic Questions of Economics

As we have seen, the task of any economic system is to use its scarce economic resources efficiently and effectively so as to best satisfy the needs and wants of its people. Since economic resources are scarce and we cannot have everything that we want, we are forced to make certain very basic choices:

- What goods and services should we produce?
- How should we produce goods and services?
- How should we divide up our output of goods and services among ourselves?

These are the three most basic economic decisions that must be made by every society, regardless of its stage of development or its economic system.

What to Produce?

Because economic resources, or productive inputs, are scarce, no society can have all the goods and services it would like to have. Instead, it must make choices or set priorities. For example, the people in our island mini-society would have to decide whether to produce fish, vegetables, shelter, fuel, or equipment such as spears and plows to help them to be more productive.

What makes such choices difficult is that they involve deciding not only what *will* be produced, but also what *will not* be produced. If we decide to use six people to farm vegetables, those six people will not be available to catch fish or build shelter. So a decision to produce *more* of one thing necessarily means accepting *less* of other things. This type of decision forces us to set priorities, or decide what is most important to us. Obviously, making decisions relates to the goal of *effectiveness*, as discussed in the previous section, because the priorities we set will reflect our needs and wants, or how much we value each product.

Consumer Goods or Capital Goods?

One of the most basic "what-to-produce" decisions that must be made is whether consumer goods or capital goods will be produced. Consumer goods (such as food and fuel) can be enjoyed now, but are used up quickly and do not contribute to longer-term economic prosperity. Capital goods (such as tools and equipment), on the other hand, cannot be consumed and enjoyed today, but they will increase our productive efficiency in the future. In this way, capital goods will contribute to our production and prosperity in the longer term, by increasing our productivity for the many years that they will last. Figure 1-3 illustrates this choice.

These decisions will have a crucial influence on the prosperity of a society both in the present and in the future. If our island mini-society emphasizes the production of *consumer goods*, its people will enjoy a higher

FIGURE 1-3 Consumer Goods and Capital Goods: The Choice

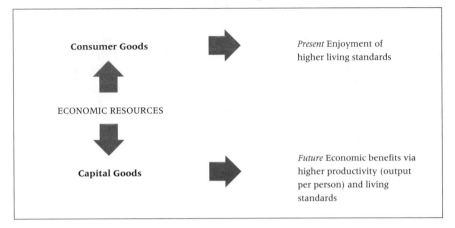

standard of living *in the present*. However, if they emphasize consumer-goods production to the point of neglecting capital-goods production, they will enjoy less prosperity in the future. On the other hand, if its people are willing to do with fewer consumer goods in the present in order to build more *capital goods,* they can look forward to higher levels of economic prosperity *in the future.* In the second half of the twentieth century, the greatest economic improvement was experienced by nations such as Japan and Germany that stressed the production of capital goods.

How to Produce It?

Once we have decided *what* we want to produce, we must decide *how* each product or service is to be produced. These decisions are a question of production methods: How should we combine our scarce inputs of labour, capital equipment, and natural resources to produce a product or service?

As a simple example, suppose our island mini-society has decided to produce (cultivate) vegetables. The next question is, How should it do this? Should the vegetables be cultivated by hand? Or should people use simple tools such as hoes? Or more sophisticated equipment such as plows? Before the vegetables that the group wants can be produced, the group will have to decide how to produce them.

Generally speaking, our goal will be to develop production methods that result in *higher efficiency* so as to increase our economic prosperity. However, the decision becomes more complicated if we need to use economic resources to build capital equipment in order to increase output per worker. If the amount of capital equipment we can build is limited, would it be better to build a plow for cultivating vegetables or a net for fishing? This decision would be easier to make if we could find a way to measure the *costs* of building the plow and the net (in terms of the hours needed to build each of them) against the *benefits* of each (in terms of the increased output each would bring).

Obviously, in deciding the answer to this question, we are pursuing the goal of *efficiency* as discussed earlier. By being efficient, we avoid wasting our scarce economic resources, and thus increase our economic prosperity.

Who Gets How Much? (Dividing the "Economic Pie")

The last of our three basic questions is, How will we divide up our output of goods and services among our people? Who will receive what share of the output?

Should everyone receive an equal share? Or should some people receive more than others? If some are to receive a larger share, why should they get more, and how much more should they get?

We have seen that a society will prosper economically if the work of its people is *effective* and *efficient*. This consideration argues in favour of inequality, with a larger "piece of the pie" providing incentives for people to work more effectively and efficiently. If everyone knew that they were going to receive the same share as everyone else, why should anyone make an extra effort or contribution?

In addition to effectiveness and efficiency, however, there is the goal of *fairness*. How wide a gap between the rich and the poor are we prepared to accept? What if some people cannot produce enough to live decently without help from others? Should the most productive people give up some of what they have produced (earned) in order to help the less productive ones? And if our answer to this question is yes, how much should the better-off people give up in order to help the less fortunate (or less capable)?

This question of how to divide up the economic pie is certainly the most controversial of the three basic economic questions. In a modern economy such as Canada's, a person's share of the "economic pie" depends on his or her *income*. If an accountant's income (*after taxes*, a factor that we will consider in Chapter 12) is twice as large as a labourer's, the accountant's share of the economic pie will be twice that of the labourer.

But by what standards should we *decide* who gets higher incomes and a larger share of the pie? Should hockey players receive a larger share than doctors? Should lawyers have a larger share than social workers? Should firefighters get a larger share than day-care workers? Somehow, every society has to work out the question of how to divide up the economic pie.

Answering the Three Questions

In this chapter we have considered the three basic questions of economics that every society must answer—what to produce, how to produce it, and how to divide it up. Different societies answer these questions in very different ways. In the next chapter we will begin to examine how Canada's economic system deals with these most basic questions.

Chapter Summary

1. The basic task of an economic system is to use its productive inputs (labour, capital equipment, and land) to produce goods and services so as to satisfy the wants and needs of the people of the society. (L.O. 1)

2. This task involves the problem of *scarcity*: whereas society's economic resources are limited in quantity, people's wants and needs are apparently unlimited; thus, not all wants and needs can be satisfied. (L.O. 2)

3. Scarcity makes it important that economic resources be used both effectively (so as to produce goods and services that are needed and wanted) and efficiently (with high productivity, or output per worker). (L.O. 3)

4. The task of an economic system is to make the best possible use of its scarce economic resources by providing answers to the following three questions:

   (a) what to produce,

   (b) how to produce it, and

   (c) how to divide it among the people in order to best satisfy the needs and wants of the society. (L.O. 4)

5. The opportunity cost of producing one good is the other goods that could have been produced with the same resources. (L.O. 5)

Questions

1. In some societies, elderly people who are unable to work any longer are left to die. What might explain such a custom?

2. How does the custom referred to above compare to Canada's attitudes toward those who are unable to support themselves? What might explain this difference?

3. It has been suggested that the highest paid people in industry and government should receive no more than two-and-a-half times as much take-home pay as the lowest-paid workers. Do you agree with this suggestion? Why? What do you believe would happen if such a policy were implemented?

4. Suppose that in an island mini-economy, there were four people working: two people catching a total of 6 fish per day and two others picking a total of 8 kg of fruit per day. If they decided that they wanted to have three more fish each day, what would be a reasonable estimate of the opportunity cost of that decision?

5. Suppose that you have only $150 and your mother is expecting a Mother's Day gift (tickets to a Rolling Stones concert) that will cost $150; however, your car has just broken down and it will cost $150 to repair it.

(a) What would be the opportunity cost of buying your mother the gift?

(b) What would be the opportunity cost of getting your car fixed?

6. Explain how each of the following decisions would be intended to affect *effectiveness* and/or *efficiency*:

(a) A plan whereby a company's sales representatives provide feedback and suggestions to management based on their experience with customers.

(b) The introduction of a piece rate incentive plan under which workers are paid according to the number of products they produce.

(c) A quality-control program under which finished products are inspected more thoroughly in order to ensure that they meet quality standards.

(d) A profit-sharing plan, under which a portion of the company's profits above a certain level will be shared with the employees.

(e) The use of industrial robots that are programmed to perform production tasks repetitively and with great precision.

(f) A company lays off some of its employees in order to cut costs.

7. In some of the situations in Question 6, a conflict could arise between effectiveness and efficiency; that is, a decision that increased efficiency would decrease effectiveness, or vice versa. Which are these decisions, and why could such a conflict occur?

8. How could having a website improve the *effectiveness* and the *efficiency* of a firm's operations?

9. Fred's Furniture Ltd. can produce chairs using either of two production methods: manual or mechanized. Under the manual production method, ten employees are required, working 8 hours per day at $10 per hour. Overhead costs (rent, office, etc.) are $200 per day and material costs are $5 per chair. The manual method produces 50 chairs per day.

Under the mechanized production method, five employees are required, working 8 hours per day at $10 per hour. Overhead costs (rent, office, etc.) are $200 per day and material costs are $5 per chair. Depreciation expenses on the machinery are $300 per day and the machinery uses $150 of energy per day. The mechanized production method also produces 50 chairs per day.

(a) Use the table below to calculate the cost of producing one chair, under each of these two production methods.

	Manual Method	*Mechanized Method*
Labour cost per chair	$ _____	$ _____
Material cost per chair	_____	_____
Overhead cost per chair	_____	_____
Depreciation cost per chair	_____	_____
Energy cost per chair	_____	_____
Total cost per chair	$ _____	$ _____

According to the above figures, which production method is the most efficient?

(b) Suppose wage rates increased to $12 per hour. What effect would this increase have on:

  (i)   production cost per unit under the manual method?

  (ii) production cost per unit under the mechanized method?

  (iii) the choice of production methods?

  (iv) the number of workers employed?

(c) Suppose wage rates were still $10 per hour and energy prices declined by 40 percent. What effect would this change have on:

  (i)   production cost per unit under the manual method?

  (ii) production cost per unit under the mechanized method?

  (iii) the choice of production methods?

  (iv) the number of workers employed?

(d) Suppose new machinery is developed which still requires five workers, costs twice as much as the old machinery (making depreciation expenses $600 per day), uses $320 of energy per day (compared with $150 for the old machine), and produces 80 chairs per day. Would it be economical for the company to introduce the new machine?

(e) Sections (b), (c), and (d) show that the most efficient production method depends on _____, _____, and _____.

Appendix 1A

Production-Possibilities Curves and Opportunity Costs

Learning Objectives

After studying this appendix, you should be able to:

1. Construct a production-possibilities curve from given data concerning production possibilities for two products.

2. Show on the curve the effect of a given change, such as an increase or decrease in the efficiency of producing one or both products.

3. Calculate the opportunity cost of a decision to produce more of one of the products.

One way of illustrating the problem of scarcity is with a **production-possibilities curve.** Suppose our islanders can only produce two items—vegetables and fish. If all their economic inputs were devoted to producing vegetables, they could produce 15 kg of vegetables daily, but no fish. This option is shown as combination **A** in Figure 1A-1,

which indicates vegetable production of 15 kg and fish production of 0 kg. If the islanders went to the opposite extreme and used all their productive inputs to produce fish, the result would be fish production of 5 kg and vegetable production of 0 kg, as shown by combination **F** in Figure 1A-1.

Of course, it is more likely that the

FIGURE 1A-1 Production-Possibilities Curve

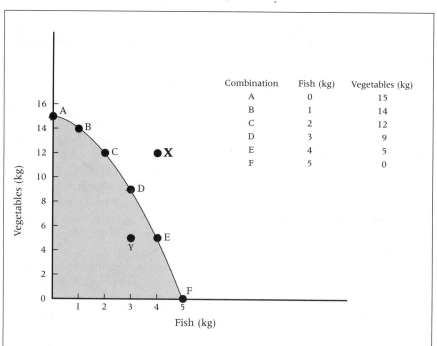

Combination	Fish (kg)	Vegetables (kg)
A	0	15
B	1	14
C	2	12
D	3	9
E	4	5
F	5	0

islanders would choose to produce some combination of vegetables and fish, such as combination **B** (14 kg of vegetables and 1 kg of fish), **C** (12 kg and 2 kg), **D** (9 kg and 3 kg), or **E** (5 kg and 4 kg). In making their choice, however, they will be restricted by the limitations of the production-possibilities curve: since their economic resources are limited, *producing more of one product necessarily means being able to produce less of the other*. The islanders may *want* 4 kg of fish and 12 kg of vegetables (combination **X**), but they will not be able to *have* this combination. Resource scarcity dictates that if they want 4 kg of fish, they can only have 5 kg of vegetables, and if they are to have 12 kg of vegetables, fish production can only be 2 kg. So while it is possible to produce 4 kg of fish or 12 kg of vegetables per day, it is not possible to produce this much of both on the same day. The islanders must choose among various combinations of products, and the production-possibilities curve reflects the limitations that resource scarcity imposes upon their choices.

However, the combinations shown by the production-possibilities curve are based on two important assumptions—that the islanders use all of their available productive inputs and that they utilize them as efficiently as possible. If some of their productive inputs were not used (if, for instance, some of the workers were sick, or one of their fish spears was broken), output would be below the potential level shown by the production-possibilities curve. Point **Y**, at which fish production is 3 kg and vegetable production is 5 kg, reflects such a situation. With fish production at 3 kg, vegetable production could be as high as 9 kg rather than 5 kg, and with vegetable production at 5 kg, fish production could be as high as 4 kg rather than 3 kg. However, if the islanders do not employ all of their productive inputs, their production will be below its potential. In fact, even if all inputs are employed, production may fall short of its potential. If the islanders' inputs (labour and capital equipment) were not producing fish and vegetables as efficiently as possible, production could be *below* its potential level and the islanders could still wind up at point **Y**.

It is important to recognize that the production-possibilities curve indicates the economy's *potential* output, assuming that economic inputs are fully employed and efficiently utilized. Production can be at any point *on* the production-possibilities curve (if inputs are fully and efficiently utilized) or *within* the shaded area (if they are not), but cannot be *outside* the curve.

However, the islanders need not live forever within the limitations imposed by the curve shown in Figure 1A-1. This curve represents the situation at a particular point in time, given the economic resources available to the islanders at that time. If, in the future, they were to add to their economic resources, say, by building new capital equipment or developing new technologies, their potential output of *both* fish *and* vegetables could increase. Figure 1A-2 shows the new production-possibilities curve that could be created by additions to or improvements in the islanders' economic resources.

The inquisitive reader may wonder why the production-possibilities curve is bowed outward as it is, rather than following a straight line. The shape of the curve reflects the changing efficiency of resources as they are shifted from one use to another. For instance, the table in Figure 1A-1 shows that to increase fish production from 0 kg to 1 kg, we must sacrifice only 1 kg of vegetable production, which falls from 15 kg to 14 kg. But as we push fish production higher, we must forgo ever higher amounts of vegetable production to achieve the same increases in fish production. The second kilogram of fish costs 2 kg of vegetables, the third kilogram of fish requires the forgoing of 3 kg of vegetables, and so on.

To produce the first kilogram of fish, we would shift resources (labour and capital) out of their *least efficient use* in vegetable production (say, from the least productive land or using

FIGURE 1A-2 Economic Progress: Shifting the Production-Possibilities Curve Outward

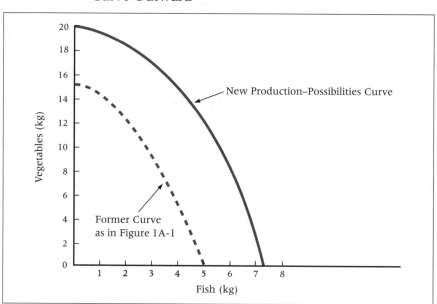

the least efficient capital equipment) into their most efficient use in fishing (say, using the best available equipment to fish the most productive waters). However, as we push fish production higher and higher, the trade-off between fish and vegetable production becomes less attractive. Increasingly, we have to shift labour and capital out of more efficient uses in vegetable production and into less efficient uses in fishing. The fifth kilogram of fish production is particularly costly in terms of vegetable production lost (5 kg of vegetables), as it requires that we shift labour and capital out of our last (and most efficient) use in vegetable production and into our least efficient use in fish production. As a result of these factors, the production-possibilities curve is not a straight line, which would reflect a constant trade-off between fish and vegetable production, but rather a curve that reflects changing efficiencies and trade-offs.

We have used a very simple situation, involving a production-possibilities curve for only two products, to illustrate the basic nature of the problem of scarcity. While the real world is much more complex, involving many more inputs and outputs, the basic reality shown by our simple production-possibilities curve still exists. Because economic resources are limited, society must somehow make choices between various goods and services. We cannot have as much of everything as we would like; enjoying more of one thing means having less of something else.

Opportunity Cost

The trade-offs between fish and vegetable production as shown by the production-possibilities curve are called **opportunity costs** by economists. The opportunity cost of using economic resources to produce any item is the amount of any other item that those same economic resources could have produced instead. The production-possibilities curve in Figure 1A-1 provides a good illustration of this concept.

The opportunity cost of producing the first kilogram of fish is the loss of 1 kg of vegetable production, which declines from 15 kg to 14 kg. The opportunity cost of the second kilogram of fish is the 2 kg of vegetable production lost when their production falls from 14 kg to 12 kg, and so on, as shown in Table 1A-1.

We can express opportunity cost in terms of vegetable production forgone for *each additional kilogram* of fish, as shown in the table. Alternatively, we can calculate the opportunity cost of *any given amount* of fish production. For instance, the table shows that the opportunity cost of the third kilogram of fish production is 3 kg of vegetables, while the opportunity cost of 3 kg of fish production is 6 kg of vegetables, because if the entire 3 kg of fish had not been produced, vegetable production could have been 15 kg rather than 9 kg.

To calculate the opportunity cost of anything, ask yourself, What could have been produced instead of it? For instance, the

TABLE 1A-1 Opportunity Cost

Combination	Fish Production (kg)	Vegetable Production (kg)	Opportunity Cost of:
A	0	15	
B	1	14	The 1st kg of fish = 1 kg vegetables
C	2	12	The 2nd kg of fish = 2 kg vegetables
D	3	9	The 3rd kg of fish = 3 kg vegetables
E	4	5	The 4th kg of fish = 4 kg vegetables
F	5	0	The 5th kg of fish = 5 kg vegetables

opportunity cost to society of $3 billion of military equipment is not the $3 billion, but rather the consumer and capital goods that could have been produced by the inputs used to produce the military equipment. And, to a student, the opportunity cost of riotous living on the weekend could be viewed as the 16 extra marks that he or she could have obtained on the economics test if the time had been spent studying.

Key Terms

Production-possibilities curve
Opportunity cost

Questions

1. Following is a table showing the production possibilities for fish and vegetables.

Combination	Fish (kg)	Vegetables (kg)
A	0	20
B	1	18
C	2	14
D	3	8
E	4	0

What is the opportunity cost of producing:
(a) the first kilogram of fish?
(b) the second kilogram of fish?
(c) 2 kg of fish?
(d) the third kilogram of fish?
(e) 3 kg of fish?
(f) the fourth kilogram of fish?
(g) 4 kg of fish?

2. The following table shows production possibilities for two items—chairs and tables.

Combination	Chairs	Tables
A	0	6
B	8	5
C	15	4
D	21	3
E	26	2
F	30	1
G	33	0

(a) What is the opportunity cost of producing

    (i)   the first table?

    (ii) the second table?

    (iii) the third table?

    (iv) the fourth table?

    (v) the fifth table?

    (vi) the sixth table?

(b) Draw the production-possibilities curve for chairs and tables on a graph, placing tables on the vertical axis and chairs on the horizontal axis.

(c) If the economy achieved greater efficiency in the production of tables, how would the production-possibilities curve change?

(d) If a more efficient method of producing chairs were developed, how would the curve change?

(e) Suppose more economic resources (labour, materials, and capital) became available. How would the curve change?

Chapter 2

Canada's Economic System

Learning Objectives

After studying this chapter, you should be able to:

1. Demonstrate how a market system economy provides answers to each of the three basic questions of economics.

2. Explain how profits and the profit motive contribute to the effective and efficient use of economic resources.

3. Explain how competition contributes to the effective and efficient use of economic resources.

4. Identify three types of problems that tend to occur in market system economies.

5. Explain why Canada's economic system is appropriately described as a mixed free-enterprise system.

6. Describe three major types of roles played by government in the Canadian economy.

In Chapter 1 we saw that the basic economic problem of scarcity forces every society to address three questions: what to produce (and not produce), how to produce it, and how to divide it up among the people of the society. To deal with these questions, a society has to use its economic resources (labour, capital equipment, and natural resources) *effectively* (produce things that are needed and wanted) and *efficiently* (produce them in high volume and at low cost and price), thereby generating economic prosperity for its people.

This goal is no small task. The Canadian economy—the eighth largest in the world—comprises over 31 million consumers with their own wants and needs, more than two million business enterprises using a vast array of capital equipment and producing millions of different goods and services, and a labour force of about 17 million people who have a wide variety of skills. How, then, does the Canadian economy organize all these economic resources to produce over $1 trillion ($1 000 000 000 000) of goods and services, and in the process succeed in providing its people with one of the highest standards of living in the world?

The Market System

Most of Canada's economic system is organized according to a *market system*. In the **market system** (also known as the *free-enterprise system*), privately owned businesses (*free enterprises*) produce goods and services in response to the demand of buyers and for a profit. Nearly 80 percent of the total output of the Canadian economy is produced by such businesses, which are collectively known as the *private sector*. In the private sector, the key economic decisions are made by consumers and businesses.

> **market system** An economic system in which economic decisions are made mainly by consumers and privately owned producers, in a decentralized manner.

In addition to its private sector, the Canadian economy has a substantial *government sector*, in which the key decisions are made by governments. The government sector accounts for over 20 percent of the output of the economy, consisting mostly of public services such as health care, education, and public security. In addition, governments play a number of other important roles in the economy, which we will examine later.

First let's examine what a market is and how it operates, and how a market system functions.

What Is a "Market"?

Simply stated, a *market* is where buyers and sellers come together to exchange goods and services for money, or to buy and sell things. Figure 2-1 illustrates this concept a little more formally, using the market for pizza as an example.

FIGURE 2-1 The Market for Pizza

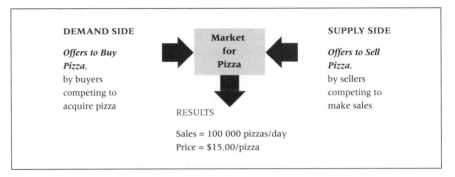

Figure 2-1 shows that the market for pizza consists of:

(a) a number of sellers offering to sell pizzas, in competition with each other (economists call this the *supply side* of the market), and

(b) a number of buyers offering to buy pizzas, in competition with each other (economists call this the *demand side* of the market).

In Figure 2-1, the interaction between buyers and sellers in the marketplace determines that the price of one pizza is $15.00 and 100 000 pizzas are sold each day. But if the willingness of buyers to buy pizzas (demand) or the willingness of sellers to sell them (supply) were to change, the price and sales of pizza would also change.

How Do Markets Work?

Markets respond to changes in buyers' demand. For instance, if the demand for pizza increased (because there were more buyers, or buyers had more money, or they just liked pizza better than before), the increased demand would cause the price of pizza to increase, say, from $15 to $18 per pizza. This higher price, together with higher sales, would make it more profitable to make pizzas. Because of the potential for higher profit, more pizzas would be made and offered for sale, perhaps 110 000 pizzas per day instead of 100 000 pizzas.

In the same way, if the demand for pizza were to fall, then the price would fall, making it less profitable to make pizza. With lower prices and lower sales, producers would make fewer pizzas, in response to the lower demand of consumers.

The "classic" form of market is a farmers' market or a flea market, where many producers and consumers come directly together to buy and sell various products. However, markets take many other forms. To most people, the most familiar market is at the retail level, where consumers buy goods and services from retailers. In addition, there are wholesale markets and commodity markets (where the buyers are businesses that bid for the products in an auction environment), labour markets (where people's time and skills are purchased and the price paid is a wage rate or salary), capital markets (or markets for loans, where the use of someone else's money is purchased and the price paid is the interest rate), and stock markets (where the shares of corporations are bought and sold).

Some markets, such as the market for baby-sitters, are extremely local in nature, while others, such as the market for wheat or oil, are worldwide in scope. In many markets buyers and sellers deal face to face, while in e-markets they deal over the internet without ever seeing each other. Regardless of its particular form, however, each market consists of a supply side and a demand side, as shown in Figure 2-1. In Chapters 4 to 6 we will examine the operation of markets in more detail.

> Some markets are conducted over the internet. For examples, visit www.autotrader.ca and www.expedia.ca.

Because demand is the most basic force in markets, the market system is sometimes said to be *demand-driven*. And because of the key role played by prices and price changes in adjusting production to demand, the market system is sometimes referred to as the *price system*.

How a "Market System" Type of Economy Is Organized

Figure 2-2 illustrates the operation of a market system. The upper flows in Figure 2-2 represent consumers buying goods and services from businesses. These flows represent many thousands of markets for specific goods and services, in which millions of consumers buy these items at the prices and in the quantities determined in the marketplace.

FIGURE 2-2 A Market Economy

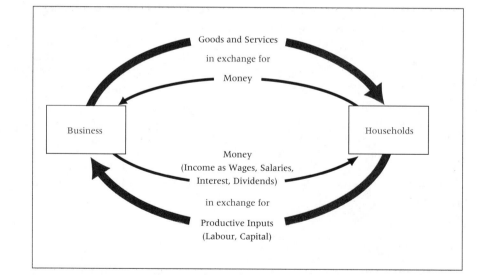

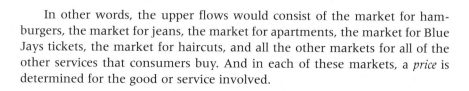

In other words, the upper flows would consist of the market for hamburgers, the market for jeans, the market for apartments, the market for Blue Jays tickets, the market for haircuts, and all the other markets for all of the other services that consumers buy. And in each of these markets, a *price* is determined for the good or service involved.

The lower flows in Figure 2-2 represent a different side of the economy in which businesses buy the inputs for producing the goods and services shown in the top flows.

So the lower flows would include markets for factory workers, for retail clerks, for computer programmers, for professional athletes, and for all of the other job skills that the economy needs. And in each of these markets, a *price*—in the form of a wage rate or salary level for that type of skill—is established. Also, the lower flows would include markets for the capital needed by businesses; for instance, funds being loaned by people to businesses, for a *price*, or an interest rate.

The operation of a market system such as that shown in Figure 2-2 involves billions of individual decisions by consumers, business firms, and workers about consumer purchases, production levels, prices, the numbers of workers to be employed, wage rates, capital investment, and so on. It is through these decisions, made in countless markets, that the answers are developed to the three basic questions of what to produce, how to produce it, and how to divide it up.

How the Market System Answers the Three Questions

What to Produce?

Consumers play the largest role in deciding what will be produced. Since the basic goal of business is to earn a profit, businesses will produce those goods and services that are in demand. This process is described by the phrases "consumer sovereignty" (meaning that the consumer is "king of the marketplace") and "dollar votes" (meaning that, by purchasing a product, a consumer is in effect casting a vote in the marketplace for the production of that product).

Prices provide an important link between what buyers want and what businesses produce. For instance, if the demand for golfing increases, the price of golfing will rise. The increase in price will make operating golf courses potentially more profitable, creating an incentive for businesses to provide more golfing. In a similar way, a reduction in the demand for red meat would depress its price, making its production less profitable and creating an incentive to reduce production. "Price signals" such as these are also transmitted through the labour markets shown at the bottom of Figure 2-2. For instance, if the higher demand for golfing led to an increase in the demand for golf professionals, the wages of golf professionals would rise, attracting more people into working as golf professionals.

How to Produce It?

The decision of how to produce the product is made by producers, or private businesses, who will strive for the most efficient possible production method. Lower production costs not only mean higher profits; in a highly competitive industry, they may be the key to survival.

Prices also help to determine the methods for producing goods and services. In determining the most efficient production methods, it makes obvious economic sense to minimize the use of the most scarce inputs. Prices help to minimize using scarce inputs because the more scarce an input is, the more costly it will be for producers to buy. For instance, if lumber is scarce, its price will be high. Since it is such a costly input, producers will minimize waste and will substitute other less costly materials, if possible. Thus, to maximize their profits, businesses have to manage society's scarce economic resources carefully, economizing the most on the use of the most scarce resources.

How to Divide up the Economic Pie?

As we saw in Chapter 1, a person's share of the economic pie depends on his or her income. For instance, if computer programmers take home (after taxes) five times as much pay as day-care workers, their share of the economic pie will be five times as large as that of day-care workers.

And since your income is really the price of your productive skills, *prices* play a major role in deciding the question of how to divide up the economic pie. Like other prices, people's incomes (or salaries or wages) are mostly determined by the interplay of supply and demand—in this case, the supply of and the demand for your productive skills. For example, if tool-and-die makers are in short supply but in great demand, their incomes (and their share of the economic pie) will be quite high. On the other hand, if there is a large supply of low-skilled workers relative to the demand for them, they will have low incomes and a small share of the economic pie.

How Does the Market System Organize the Use of Economic Resources?

As we have seen, organizing the vast and varied economic resources of an economy such as Canada's into the effective and efficient production of millions of goods and services is an enormous task. On the face of it, the market system might appear to be ill-suited to such a complex task. The market system seems to lack any organizing or coordinating forces; rather, it looks more like an economic "free-for-all" in which people buy whatever they want to, produce whatever they want to, and work wherever they want to. Millions of consumers and producers make economic decisions, which are decentralized and apparently uncoordinated, rather than organized according to a centralized plan. Nevertheless, the market system has in practice proven to be the best system for achieving both effectiveness and efficiency in the use of economic resources and in providing a high standard of living for its people.

Then what are the forces within the market system that enable it to mobilize economic resources so effectively and efficiently? The two key features of the market system that promote effectiveness and efficiency are the *profit motive* and *competition*.

The Profit Motive

Profits are those funds from a business's sales revenues that are left after all expenses and taxes have been paid. Profits are therefore available for

profits Those funds left from a business's sales revenues after all expenses have been paid; such funds are therefore available (after taxes have been paid) for dividends to shareholders and reinvestment in the business.

reinvestment in the business or to be paid out as dividends to the shareholders who own the business.

The *profit motive* plays two vital roles in the operation of a market system. First, profits provide incentives for businesses to use economic resources both effectively and efficiently. By producing goods and services that consumers will buy—that is, by using economic resources *effectively*—a business will increase its sales and profits. And by producing those goods and services at the lowest possible production cost—that is, by using economic resources *efficiently*—a business will also increase its profits.

The second important role of profits is that they provide funds for the *purchase of capital equipment*. Each business purchases capital equipment to improve its own efficiency and profitability. But when many businesses do this, the result is improved productivity across the economy, which is the basic source of higher living standards for society generally. Thus, the reinvestment of profits by businesses makes an important contribution to a society's economic prosperity.

In addition, many Canadians have a large stake in the profitability of corporations. In 2002, 46 percent of adult Canadians owned shares of corporations, many in registered retirement savings plans. In addition, about three dollars of every eight in *pension funds* in Canada are invested in corporate shares, so many people who do not think of themselves as shareholders have a stake in the success of Canadian corporations. In fact, millions of Canadians have billions of dollars invested in shares. These people not only receive part of corporate profits as dividends but also depend on the prosperity of those corporations for financial security in their retirement.

Despite the financial importance of profits, there is a great deal of misunderstanding and even hostility among the public concerning profits. The very word "profit" evokes for many people images of exploitation of workers and consumers, or "profiteering." One misconception concerns the level of profits. According to surveys, the public believes that manufacturers' profits amount to 30 cents or 40 cents per dollar of sales, whereas before-tax profits are actually about 7 cents to 10 cents per dollar of sales, and after taxes, most manufacturers' profits amount to only 4 cents or 5 cents per dollar of sales. Ironically, the public believes 20 cents per dollar of sales to be a "fair" profit, indicating that there is a great deal of confusion regarding this matter.

The public also has misconceptions concerning the *uses* of profits, which are widely regarded as being hoarded away in corporate coffers or being paid out in lavish dividends to vulgarly wealthy shareholders. In fact, between two-fifths and one-half of business profits goes to taxes and most of the remainder is reinvested by businesses in capital equipment. Dividends to shareholders generally amount to a modest return on their investment, and these "capitalist" shareholders

---

There are different ways of looking at profits.

Suppose a corporation has annual sales of $600 million, profits after taxes of $24 million, 4000 employees, and $300 million of shareholders' capital invested in the company.

From the viewpoint of the *employees*, it might seem that they are being underpaid. If the $24 million of profits were divided among them, each would receive $6000 more ($24 million ÷ 4000).

From the viewpoint of *consumers*, $24 million in profits might seem to indicate that they are being overcharged for this company's product. .Realistically though, the total elimination of the manufacturer's profits would only reduce prices by 4 percent ($24 million ÷ $600 million).

From the viewpoint of the *shareholders* of the company, their capital invested in the company is earning a rate of return (after tax) of only 8 percent ($24 million ÷ $300 million). Compared to other investments, this rate of return is not attractive.

Thus, while employees and consumers and politicians might be complaining about this company's high profits, investors could very well be deciding to sell their shares in the company.

include not only the wealthy but also ordinary Canadians. Because of the public's misconceptions about profits and the negative emotional overtones attached to the word, many companies prefer to call their profits "earnings."

Competition

Competition, which is the other key element in a market system, plays three vitally important roles in a market economy. First, competition forces businesses to provide consumers with what they want in order to increase their sales and profits. In this sense, competition *promotes effectiveness* in the use of economic resources. Second, competition *promotes efficiency* in the use of economic resources. To prosper in a competitive marketplace, a producer must be as efficient as possible. And third, competition forces producers to *keep prices as low as possible*, in order to compete successfully for business. Thus, competition ensures that the advantages of higher efficiency/lower production costs are passed along to the consumer, allowing the maximum possible number of people to enjoy them.

Competition is closely linked with *information* in the effective functioning of markets. A free marketplace provides a wide variety of goods and services, of various qualities and at different prices. If consumers are well-informed about what items are available and at what prices, they will be better able to take advantage of the opportunities offered by a free and competitive marketplace. By contrast, poorly informed consumers will be more likely to pay higher prices and/or wind up with lower-quality products.

In summary, a highly competitive marketplace pushes private profit-making producers to serve the interests of consumers by being effective and efficient and by keeping prices down. By contrast, in situations in which there is little or no competition, producers tend to be less responsive to consumers' preferences (less effective), to be less efficient than they could be, and to charge consumers excessive prices.

Together, the two incentives of profits and competition tend to push producers to use economic resources both effectively and efficiently. The ability of the market system to coordinate the decisions of millions of businesses and individuals automatically in response to changes in consumer demand has been referred to as "the miracle of the market." As long ago as 1776, in *The Wealth of Nations*, Adam Smith, the earliest advocate of this economic system, described businesspeople as being led by an "invisible hand" (the profit motive) "to promote (the interest of) the society more effectually than when they really intend to promote it."

Figure 2-3 summarizes the market system's powerful incentives for efficiency and effectiveness, which contribute greatly to productivity and prosperity.

Figure 2-3 also shows how the basic concepts of effectiveness and efficiency relate to the income statement and the profits of a business. A business that is *effective* in the sense of producing what buyers want will enjoy a *high sales income*. If that business is also *efficient*, it will have *low production costs* and other expenses. Thus, the more effective and efficient a business is, the higher its profits will be.

FIGURE 2-3 Incentives in a Market System

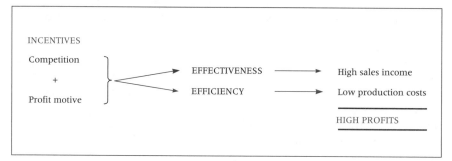

Assessment of the Market System

We have seen that about four-fifths of the Canadian economy—the private sector—is organized as a market system. How well does this sector of the economy perform?

According to the criteria of *effectiveness* and *efficiency*, the market system performs very well. With respect to effectiveness, there is no economic system that is more responsive to consumer demand than the market system, which is marvelously flexible in adjusting its production automatically in response to changes in consumer preferences. And with respect to efficiency, no system provides greater incentives for efficient use of economic resources than the combination of the profit motive and competition.

However, the market system also has certain weaknesses. For instance, there is good reason to doubt that private enterprise is the best way to deliver certain *public services*, such as health care and education. For example, social policy may say that all Canadians should have open access to health care and education. These services might then be provided by government-controlled schools and hospitals, funded by the taxpayers in order to keep costs low and make them accessible to everyone.

market power The ability to raise one's prices; usually associated with a dominant or monopolistic position in the market.

A problem that can develop in a market system is **market power**, or monopoly-like power in some markets. Sometimes, producers may be able to band together and agree to limit competition among themselves, resulting in higher prices and profits. In the same way, some workers may be able to band together into labour unions that achieve essentially the same result—less competition and higher prices (wages) for their members. In both cases, an organized group (of businesses or workers) reduces competition in the marketplace for its own benefit at the expense of others.

And while free markets for labour provide strong incentives for people to acquire skills that are in demand and to work efficiently, it is also true that in a market system there is a tendency for great *inequality in incomes*, as some people enjoy very high incomes, while others live in poverty.

While the profit motive provides strong incentives to be effective and efficient, it also provides incentives to do some things that are less beneficial to society. These things include unfair competitive practices, the misleading of consumers, the unfair treatment of vulnerable employees, and pollution of the environment.

On a larger macroeconomic scale, another fundamental problem with the market system is *economic insecurity*. Market economies tend to slump into periodic **recessions**, during which the economy's output falls and unemployment rises. During a typical recession in Canada, the number of unemployed people rises by more than half a million.

recessions Situations in which the economy is producing considerably less than its potential output, and unemployment is high.

The Command System

The major alternative to the market system is known as the **command system**. In a market system, we have seen that the key economic decisions are made by millions of consumers and businesses in a very *decentralized* manner. However, in a command system, all major economic decisions are made in a *centralized* manner by the government. Government economic planners draw up a central economic plan that maps out all major economic activity for the nation. The economic planners decide what products will be produced and give detailed instructions to plant managers, telling them what to produce. Since the government owns all major production facilities, the planners also choose the production technology and methods. And since the government is the only employer, the planners also can decide the incomes of various groups, and thus how the economic pie is divided. The most famous example of a command system was, of course, the economy of the former Soviet Union.

command system An economic system in which economic decisions are made mainly by the government in a centralized manner.

The command system seems simple in principle, and organizing all of society's economic resources according to a central economic plan sounds attractive. But this system ultimately proved to be a failure. By the time of the collapse of the Soviet Union in the late 1980s, its command system was failing miserably to produce goods and services efficiently and effectively, and the standard of living of the people had been falling for some time. Since then, the countries of the former communist bloc have mostly abandoned their command systems in favour of the market system approach.

Probably the most serious shortcoming of the command system was its lack of incentives. Without competition and the profit motive, producers tended to be both ineffective and inefficient in their use of economic resources. As a result, shortages of many goods were common, and most of the goods that were available were of low quality and of limited usefulness.

Ultimately, the command system proved incapable of organizing and coordinating through a central planning process the millions and millions of decisions needed to run a complex modern economy. The central planning process was simply unable to deal with the gigantic task of organizing the resources of such a vast economy. As one Soviet economic planner said near the collapse of the system, "The latest index of products has 20 million articles. The plan can't detail that amount."

The Ubiquitous Nature of the Market System

A strong argument can be made that markets are a natural aspect of human behaviour. People have different abilities, needs, and wants, so it is only natural for them to exchange (buy and sell) what they produce. For instance, when the former Soviet Union's command system failed to produce the goods wanted by consumers, an illegal but very active black market for many such goods developed. Some of these were smuggled into the Soviet Union from Western nations—for instance, a Sony Walkman would sell for over US$600 on the street in Moscow. Other goods were produced illegally by Russians themselves in secret plants and sold to consumers through the underground economy. In both cases, the unfulfilled demand of Soviet consumers created a market opportunity for enterprising (and risk-taking!) Soviet "entrepreneurs."

"Unofficial" markets also developed in the industrial sector of the Soviet economy. Often, the central planning system would fail to deliver the materials needed by plant managers for their operations—sometimes managers would get too little or none at all, while at other times they would receive more materials than they needed. In order to meet their production quotas, plant managers set up a "parallel market," through which managers would trade surplus materials with each other, receiving in return materials that were needed or credits for future materials when these became available.

Markets can develop under quite unlikely circumstances. The article in the "You Decide" box describes how, as a prisoner in a German prisoner of war camp during the Second World War, R.A. Radford watched the spontaneous development within the camp of a miniature "market system." During its operation, this small-scale, primitive "price system" displayed many of the characteristics and encountered many of the problems of the more sophisticated and complex price systems of modern economies.

YOU DECIDE | THE ECONOMIC ORGANIZATION OF A PRISONER OF WAR CAMP

By R.A. Radford

One aspect of social organization is to be found in economic activity, and this, along with other manifestations of a group existence, is to be found in any P.O.W. camp. Everyone receives a roughly equal share of essentials; it is by trade that individual preferences are given expression and comfort increased. All at some time, and most people regularly, make exchanges of one sort or another.

Our supplies consisted of rations provided by the detaining power and (principally) the contents of Red Cross food parcels—tinned milk, jam, butter, biscuits, bully, chocolate, sugar, etc., and cigarettes. So far the supplies to each person were equal and regular. Private parcels of clothing, toilet requisites and cigarettes were also received, and here equality ceased owing to the different numbers despatched and the vagaries of the post. All these articles were the subject of trade and exchange.

The Development and Organization of the Market

We reached a transit camp in Italy about a fortnight after capture and received 1/4 of a Red Cross food parcel each a week later. At once exchanges, already established, multiplied in volume. Starting with simple direct barter, such as a non-smoker giving a smoker friend his cigarette issue in exchange for a chocolate ration, more complex exchanges soon became an accepted custom.

In this camp we did not visit other bungalows very much and prices varied from place to place. By the end of a month, when we reached our permanent camp, there was a lively trade in all commodities and their relative values were well known, and expressed not in terms of one another—one didn't quote bully in terms of sugar—but in terms of cigarettes. The cigarette became the standard of value. In the permanent camp people started by wandering through the bungalows calling their offers—"cheese for seven" (cigarettes)—and the hours after parcel issue were Bedlam. The inconveniences of this system soon led to its replacement by an Exchange and Mart notice board in every bungalow, where under the headings "name," "room number," "wanted" and "offered" sales and wants were advertised. When a deal went through, it was crossed off the board. The public and semipermanent records of transactions led to cigarette prices being well known and thus tending to equality throughout the camp, although there were always opportunities for an astute trader to make a profit from arbitrage. With this development everyone, including non-smokers, was willing to sell for cigarettes, using them to buy at another time and place. Cigarettes became the normal currency, though, of course, barter was never extinguished.

The permanent camps in Germany saw the highest level of commercial organization. In addition to the Exchange and Mart notice boards, a shop was organized as a public utility, controlled by representatives of the Senior British Officer, on a no profit basis. People left their surplus clothing, toilet requisites and food there until they were sold at a fixed price in cigarettes. Only sales in cigarettes were accepted—there was no barter. Of food, the shop carried small stocks for convenience; the capital was provided by a loan from the bulk store of Red Cross cigarettes and repaid by a small commission taken on the first transactions. Thus the cigarette attained its fullest currency status, and the market was almost completely unified.

Actually there was an embryo labour market. Even when cigarettes were not scarce, there was usually some unlucky person willing to perform services for them. Laundrymen advertised at two cigarettes a garment. Battledress was scrubbed and pressed and a pair of trousers lent for the interim period for twelve. A good pastel portrait cost thirty or a tin of "Kam." Odd tailoring and other jobs similarly had their prices.

⇨

There were also entrepreneurial services. There was a coffee stall owner who sold tea, coffee or cocoa at two cigarettes a cup, buying his raw materials at market prices and hiring labour to gather fuel and to stoke; he actually enjoyed the services of a chartered accountant at one stage. After a period of great prosperity he overreached himself and failed disastrously for several hundred cigarettes. Such large-scale private enterprise was rare but several middlemen or professional traders existed. The more subdivided the market, the less perfect the advertisement of prices, and the less stable the prices, the greater was the scope for these operators.

The Cigarette Currency

Although cigarettes as currency exhibited certain peculiarities, they performed all the functions of a metallic currency as a unit of account, as a measure of value and as a store of value, and shared most of its characteristics. They were homogeneous, reasonably durable, and of convenient size for the smallest or, in packets, for the largest transactions.

Machine-made cigarettes were always universally acceptable, both for what they would buy and for themselves. It was this intrinsic value which gave rise to their principal disadvantage as currency, a disadvantage which exists, but to a far smaller extent, in the case of metallic currency;—that is, a strong demand for non-monetary purposes. Consequently our economy was repeatedly subject to deflation and to periods of monetary stringency. While the Red Cross issue of 50 or 25 cigarettes per man per week came in regularly, and while there were fair stocks held, the cigarette currency suited its purpose admirably. But when the issue was interrupted, stocks soon ran out, prices fell, trading declined in volume and became increasingly a matter of barter. This deflationary tendency was periodically offset by the sudden injection of new currency. Private cigarette parcels arrived in a trickle throughout the year, but the big numbers came in quarterly when the Red Cross received its allocation of transport. Several hundred thousand cigarettes might arrive in the space of a fortnight. Prices soared, and then began to fall, slowly at first but with increasing rapidity as stocks ran out, until the next big delivery. Most of our economic troubles could be attributed to this fundamental instability.

More interesting than changes in the general price level were changes in the price structure. Changes in the supply of a commodity, in the German ration scale or in the make-up of Red Cross parcels, would raise the price of one commodity relative to others. Tins of oatmeal, once a rare and much sought after luxury in the parcels, became a commonplace in 1943, and the price fell. In hot weather the demand for cocoa fell, and that for soap rose. A new recipe would be reflected in the price level: the discovery that raisins and sugar could be turned into an alcoholic liquor of remarkable potency reacted permanently on the dried fruit market.

As soon as prices began to fall with a cigarette shortage, a clamour arose, particularly against those who held reserves and who bought at reduced prices. Sellers at cut prices were criticised and their activities referred to as the black market. In every period of dearth the explosive question of "should non-smokers receive a cigarette ration?" was discussed to profitless length. Unfortunately, it was the non-smoker, or the light smoker, with his reserves, along with the hated middleman, who weathered the storm most easily.

Source: Adapted from *Economica*, November 1945, pp. 189–201.

Questions

The Radford article illustrates some of the most basic problems in economics, and how societies utilize markets to deal with these. It also provides some interesting insights into the day-to-day functioning of a market system, including problems that can arise. Consider the following:

1. Why was it inevitable that a market system would develop in the POW camps?

2. Using examples from the POW camps, explain the importance to the effective operation of a market system of:

    (a) information (as through the bulletin boards);

    (b) the ability of buyers and sellers to move freely from place to place.

3. Why was it inevitable that a form of currency would be developed, and why were cigarettes suitable as a currency?

4. What caused the prices of goods *in general* to rise or fall substantially?

5. What caused the prices of particular goods to fluctuate *relative to the prices of other goods?*

The Market System in Perspective

Perhaps the most outstanding feature of the market system is the high degree of *economic freedom* for both consumers and businesses. This freedom underlies the key strengths of the market system, such as the ways in which its incentives of the profit motive and competition drive producers to be both efficient and effective managers of economic resources. The result is that market economies tend to be the best at generating high levels of productivity and a high standard of living.

Ironically, this freedom also underlies the most serious weaknesses of the market system. If producers are free to dominate industries and markets, the problem of market power (or monopoly power) will tend to arise in some situations. Because individuals and groups are free to earn (take?) as big a share of the pie as they can get, some can wind up with a very large share of the pie, while others get only crumbs. And because consumers and businesses are free to spend—and not spend—as they see fit, there are times when spending is inadequate and the economy slides into recessions and high unemployment. These weaknesses of the market system have led governments to take corrective action in various ways, as we will see when we look at Canada's "mixed" economic system.

The "Mixed" Economic System of Canada

Canada's economic system can best be described as a *mixed free-enterprise system* because, while this type of system is basically a market system, it also includes a large government sector and a great deal of government involvement in its private sector.

The Private Sector

As we have seen, nearly 80 percent of the total annual output of the Canadian economy is produced by the private sector. In this sector, in which the vast majority of Canadians are employed, businesses produce goods and services in response to market demand and for a profit. In the private sector of the economy, households (or consumers) and businesses make the key economic decisions.

The Government Sector

In the government sector, the key economic decisions are made by governments. The government sector accounts for about 21 percent of the annual output of the economy, most of which consists of public services such as health care and education. In broad terms, governments play three major roles in the economy.

First, governments are major *providers of public services*. From health care, education, and law enforcement, to traffic control, public transit, and postal service, Canadian governments provide the public with a wide range of services in various ways. In most cases, such as health care, police protection, and elementary and secondary education, the public pays for these services with its tax revenues. In effect, then, the government is buying these services collectively on the public's behalf from the government's own employees (such as teachers) and from others (such as doctors) who provide the services. In some cases, governments *operate enterprises* that provide services, including Crown corporations (such as Canada Post and the Canadian Broadcasting Corporation) and public commissions that provide services (such as public transit and hydroelectricity). In many cases, such as public transit and post-secondary education, governments *subsidize public services*. **Subsidies** use tax revenues to pay part of the cost of the service, making the cost to the user lower. The grand total of these government-provided services is impressive—when the services of all government employees are counted as government purchases, Canadian governments account for about 21 percent of all the goods and services produced by the economy. In 2002 this portion amounted to over $243 billion, or over $7700 for every Canadian man, woman, and child.

Second, governments *regulate* in many ways the operations and practices of businesses. For example, government laws or agencies set standards for many products, regulate advertising practices, set employment standards (such as minimum wage rates and safety standards), set rules for the conduct of employer–employee/union relations, regulate the competitive practices of businesses (including the prohibition of monopolistic practices), and set environmental protection standards. In the case of some farm products, government marketing boards regulate the amount that farmers can produce. In addition, many prices are regulated by government, including electrical rates, tobacco and alcohol prices, some transportation rates, and apartment rents in some areas.

subsidies Payments by the government of part of the cost of a service in order to reduce the cost to the user of the service.

The third major area of government involvement in the economy is the *redistribution of income* through programs that transfer income from people with higher incomes to those with lower incomes. Such programs include Employment Insurance, welfare, old age security allowances, assistance to farmers and other groups, and various features of the income-tax system (tax credits) that reduce the taxes payable by those with lower incomes. In 2001 government transfer payments to persons (mostly through Employment Insurance, welfare, and pensions) amounted to $120 billion, or nearly $3900 for every Canadian. This figure includes only government payments to people; in addition to these, there is government assistance to lower-income Canadians through tax credits that reduce the income taxes that they pay or entitle them to tax refunds, such as the GST credits received by many students.

Taken together, these government programs amount to a great deal of government involvement in the Canadian economy. In 2001–02 the grand total of spending by Canadian governments (on goods and services, transfer payments to persons, and interest on government debt) amounted to 41 percent of Canada's **Gross Domestic Product (GDP)**, which measures the total of goods and services produced and incomes earned in Canada in any one year. When the many government regulations of economic activity as described earlier are added, the Canadian economy is accurately called a "mixed" system—still mostly "market" in nature, but with a large amount of government involvement.

Gross Domestic Product (GDP) A measure of the total value of goods and services produced and incomes earned in a country in one year.

A Preview of Microeconomics

In Chapter 3 we will take a closer look at parts of the Canadian economy, particularly the various forms of business organization, as well as the "small business" and "big business" sectors of the economy. In Chapters 4 through 6 we will cover the basics of demand and supply, and examine how prices are determined in markets. In the ensuing chapters, we will see how demand and supply interact to determine prices and incomes in a wide variety of markets under a wide range of conditions. In Chapters 7 and 8 we will examine how the prices of goods and services are determined in various types of industries, ranging from highly competitive industries in which there is a large number of small firms to industries with only a few firms, to monopolies. In Chapter 9 we will consider government policy regarding these various types of industries. In Chapters 10 and 11 we will consider markets for labour and trends in the distribution of income and employment, and in Chapter 12 we will examine the role of government in the economy in more detail. The remaining chapters deal with specific industries or economic issues. At the end of Chapter 16, we will have completed our microeconomic study of the four major sectors of the economy—consumers, business, labour, and government.

Chapter Summary

1. A market system type of economy (also called the price system and the free enterprise system) operates through markets. In these markets, what to produce is decided by consumer demand, how to produce it is decided by producers, and the division of the economic pie is decided by people's incomes. (L.O. 1)

2. Profits play a vital role in the operation of a market system. Profits provide incentives for the efficient and effective use of economic resources and are a major source of funds for capital investment, which contributes to economic prosperity by increasing output per worker. (L.O. 2)

3. Competition is essential to the effective operation of a market economy. Competition keeps prices and profits down and forces producers to be both efficient and responsive to consumers. (L.O. 3)

4. The main strength of the market system is its high living standards, which are the result of the strong incentives this system provides for efficient and effective use of resources. (L.O. 2, 3)

5. The main weaknesses of the market system are its tendency toward periodic recessions, a lack of competition in some markets, and a tendency for incomes to be distributed very unevenly. (L.O. 4)

6. Canada's economic system is called a "mixed" or "mixed free enterprise" system: while it is basically a market or free-enterprise system, it includes significant elements of government involvement in the economy. (L.O. 5)

7. Major aspects of government involvement in the Canadian economy are the provision of various public services, the regulation of economic activity, and the redistribution of income from those with higher incomes to those with lower incomes. (L.O. 6)

Questions

1. Suppose that a manufacturer is selling two products (product A and product B) for $100 each, and is making a profit (before taxes) of 7 percent of the selling price of each product.
   (a) If strong demand increases the price of product A by 2 percent, by what percentage will the profits on product A rise?
   (b) If weak demand for product B causes its price to fall by 1 percent, by what percentage will the profits on product B decline?
   (c) Given these facts, what would be the logical decision for the management of the company to make?

2. Suppose there were a shortage of apartments.
   (a) How would the market correct this situation?
   (b) How would a law that made it illegal to increase rents affect the operation of the market for apartments?

3. Three of the following are essential to the operation of a free-enterprise market economy; one is not essential. Which one might such an economy operate *without*?
   (a) the profit motive
   (b) markets
   (c) corporations
   (d) prices

4. Explain how a development in communications technology such as the internet could improve the way in which some markets function.

5. When the government subsidizes a service, it uses tax revenues to reduce the cost of that service to the people who use it. What justification might there be for using tax revenues to subsidize:
   (a) users of the Toronto Transit Commission?
   (b) students taking post-secondary education?
   (c) users of campsites at provincial parks?
   (d) a city's symphony orchestra?

6. Suppose that, due to an interruption of international crude oil supplies, gasoline became so scarce that its price would become too high for many people to afford. Suppose that the government decided that instead of letting the marketplace decide through very high prices who would—and would not—get gasoline, it would be fairer to low-income households to *ration* gasoline, by selling coupons to each household, where the coupons could only be redeemed for gasoline.
   (a) If you were administering such a rationing system, how would you decide who gets how many gas coupons and at what price?
   (b) Suppose that some people received more gas coupons than they needed, while others received fewer than they needed. How would such an imbalance probably be dealt with?

7. The sixteenth-century philosopher Michel de Montaigne asserted that "No man can profit except by the loss of others, and by this reasoning all manner of profit must be condemned." Do you agree with his position? Does every economic transaction necessarily involve a winner and a loser?

8. What is the thing that you dislike the most about the performance of Canada's economic system? What would you do to correct this problem? Would this action to correct the one problem have the side effect of causing any other problems?

Chapter 3

Business Organization in Canada

Learning Objectives

After studying this chapter, you should be able to:

1. Summarize the advantages and disadvantages of the sole proprietorship, the partnership, and the corporation.

2. Describe the importance of small business in the Canadian economy, particularly in terms of providing employment.

3. Identify three of the most serious problems facing small businesses in Canada.

4. Describe the importance of the "big business" sector of the Canadian economy, in terms of output, employment, and exports.

5. Define the terms *multinational enterprise* and *corporate concentration*, and describe the significance of each for the Canadian economy.

6. Explain why control of the modern large corporation usually does not lie in the hands of its shareholders.

7. Summarize and evaluate the arguments in favour of retaining government enterprises in the Canadian economy and the arguments in favour of privatizing them.

We have seen that prices are determined by supply and demand, a process that we will examine in detail in Chapters 4 and 5. In this chapter we will examine some of the structural aspects of the supply side of the economy— the various forms of business enterprise in Canada—to gain more insight into the business sector that supplies most goods and services.

The most common forms of business enterprise are the sole proprietorship, the partnership, and the corporation, each of which has certain characteristics, advantages, and disadvantages. Rather than listing and describing these forms, which tends to be quite dull, we will illustrate the pros and cons of the different forms of business organization through the story of Dan's Doughnut Den.

Dan's Doughnut Den

Dan, an enterprising young man employed by a large multinational corporation, decided that he was tired of working for someone else and would go into business for himself. He found it quite simple to start up his own business—after obtaining a licence from the municipal government, he rented an appropriate building and purchased equipment and supplies with $25 000 of capital obtained from his own savings, a small inheritance, and some loans from his relatives. Before long, "Dan's Doughnut Den" opened. The business was a **sole proprietorship**; that is, it was totally owned by Dan.

At first, things went exceptionally well: enjoying his newfound freedom and independence, Dan worked harder than he ever had, and the results showed, as sales were good and the business seemed headed for success. As the business grew more complex, Dan was working very long hours, many of which were spent recruiting, training, and supervising staff, and dealing with his bank manager. Dan found financial matters a continual hassle—his bank manager was reluctant to provide the kind of credit Dan felt he needed, and was always pestering Dan for financial information, which Dan was too busy to prepare carefully. Keeping the books for the business was a constant and time-consuming chore, and one at which Dan was not too skilled. Partly as a result of this problem, preparing his income tax return was a nightmare that tied up much of his time for about a month each year. Finally, he hired an accountant to sort it out, and was horrified to learn that he owed nearly $4000 in taxes, most of which he didn't have: he had plowed practically all of the earnings back into the business, including the opening of another Doughnut Den across town. The sales at the new location were good, too, but having two outlets put an even greater strain on Dan's limited time and talents. For Dan, the crunch came when some of his suppliers and the Canada Customs and Revenue Agency (CCRA) threatened to sue him for unpaid debts and taxes. Upon consulting his lawyer, Dan learned, to his dismay, that as the sole proprietor of a business he was subject to *unlimited liability*. That is, if the business went bankrupt, he could lose not only the assets of the business but also his personal assets, such as his house.

Still, Dan thought, the business had a lot of promise, with strong sales at both locations. What was required, he concluded, was more than just hard

sole proprietorship
A business firm owned (and usually managed) by a single person who bears full legal liability for the firm's debts.

partnership A business firm owned by two or more persons, with each person bearing full legal liability for the firm's debts.

limited partner A partner who invests in a business but takes no active part in the management of it, and whose liability is limited to the amount invested.

general partners Partners who take an active part in the management of the business and who have unlimited personal liability for its debts.

work; he needed more management experience and more capital. So Dan decided to change the business from a sole proprietorship to a **partnership**. One of his new partners was Sally, an old high-school friend of Dan's who had a diploma in Business Administration from Sheridan Institute of Technology and Advanced Learning. Due to the untimely accidental death of her uncle, Sally had $25 000 to contribute to the capital of the business. Perhaps more important, Sally brought a more systematic approach to the management of the business, which soon began to show up in the profit figures. These figures were calculated (much more proficiently) by the other new partner, Ed, who contributed $50 000 to the capital of the business. Ed kept the books, working on weekends and in the evening after working at his regular job in an accountant's office. Unlike Dan and Sally, Ed took no active part in the management of the business and was therefore a **limited partner**: if the business went bankrupt, his liability was limited—all he could lose was the $50 000 he had invested. Dan and Sally, on the other hand, were **general partners** who had unlimited liability and could therefore lose their personal assets if the business went bankrupt. As is customary in partnerships, all of the partners took out life insurance policies on each other's lives, so that if one died, the others would have sufficient cash from the insurance to buy the deceased partner's share from his or her heirs. This practice ensured that the death of a partner would not force the business to dissolve. The three partners signed an agreement outlining their respective rights and responsibilities and the proportions of the profits that each would receive.

The infusion of new capital and managerial expertise improved the business's operations considerably, and things went quite well for a while. However, after a period of time, disagreements began to develop among the partners. Dan continued to work almost as hard as before, and began to resent the share of the profits taken by the others who, he felt, weren't working as hard as he was. He found this particularly hard to accept because he was the one who had undertaken the effort and risk necessary to start the business originally. Sally felt that, if anything, she was contributing more to the business than Dan, due to her superior business knowledge. Sally's increasingly frequent reminders to Dan that her capital and know-how had saved the business only aggravated the situation (Sally's grade in Human Relations at Sheridan had been a well-deserved low "D," and she had fought with the teacher over it). Ed was annoyed by these attitudes on the part of his partners: while he didn't work full-time at the business, his after-hours accounting tasks on their behalf made for a long day for him. Furthermore, he knew that without the accounting data and analysis that he prepared, Sally couldn't manage the business nearly as effectively as she did. Also, he had contributed more money to the business than either of the other two (the $50 000). The disagreements came to a head when, after a heated exchange with Ed, Dan learned that Sally had signed certain long-term contracts on behalf of the business, which Dan believed to be unwise. Since Sally was a partner, there was no way Dan could cancel these contracts—he was bound by Sally's decisions. Worse yet, as a partner, he was personally liable for the debts of the business. Dan was furious that unilateral decisions by someone else could possibly cause the bankruptcy of the business and the loss of Dan's personal assets. The other two partners threatened to pull out of the partnership, which would almost certainly mean the end of the business. Dan went home that night wishing that there were some way that he could collect on the insurance on the lives of his partners.

Finally, Dan decided that too much was enough; the partnership just couldn't work over the long term. On the advice of his lawyer, Dan decided to change the form of the business into a **corporation**. As his lawyer explained to him, the corporation would be owned and controlled by **shareholders**, and would be a separate legal entity from the shareholders, whose liability in the event of bankruptcy would be limited to their investment in the corporation's stock. Control of the corporation would lie with its **board of directors**, which would be selected by the shareholders, who would have one vote per share held. As the lawyer pointed out, Dan could control the board of directors, and thus the corporation, by owning (or controlling the votes of) 51 percent of the shares of the company.

The corporation was set up so that Dan and his wife held 85 percent of the shares, with Dan owning 45 percent and the other 40 percent being registered in his wife's name, in order to split their dividend income and reduce their total personal income taxes. A few family friends bought the other 15 percent of the shares. The friends were attracted not only by the prospects for the success of the business but also by the limited liability of shareholders and the tax treatment of the gains from their investments, since both dividend income from their shares and any capital gains realized from sale of their shares for a profit would be subject to favourable tax rates. In addition, as the lawyer pointed out, if the business were ever to expand, the corporate form of organization would prove very advantageous for raising the necessary capital, because the corporation could sell shares to the public.

The incorporation process was complex and quite costly, but it seemed like an excellent idea. The two partners were bought out, improved equipment was purchased, and the facilities were renovated. A qualified manager was hired, a website and online purchasing system was implemented, and a sophisticated sales promotion campaign was undertaken. Sales and profits rose, and there were bonuses for the managers and substantial dividends for the shareholders. Dan found that incorporation brought tax advantages to the business, too. When the business was first a sole proprietorship and then a partnership, its income (profit) was taxed as personal income, at personal income tax rates, which became quite high as the income of the owners rose. However, the profits of the corporation were taxed at *corporate income tax rates*, which were lower unless profits were quite low. (On the other hand, the shareholders were somewhat disappointed to find that they were subject to "double taxation": not only were the profits of the corporation taxed, but the dividends they received out of after-tax profits were also taxed, although at reduced rates, as their personal income.) Bank credit became more available as the business prospered, with the opening of three more outlets. After talking to his investment advisor, Dan also considered selling an issue of shares to the public to raise capital to finance expansion into other provinces.

corporation A business firm that is a separate legal entity from its owners, or shareholders, each of whose liability is limited to the amount of his or her investment in the firm.

shareholders The owners of shares (stocks) in a corporation; shareholders may or may not have voting rights and their liability is limited to the amount invested.

board of directors A group of people elected by the shareholders of a corporation to provide direction to the management of the corporation.

While Dan found being president of a successful and rapidly growing corporation exciting (not to mention financially rewarding), he also found that, as president, he seemed to spend all of his time in his office, working on paperwork and meeting with managers, committees, and lawyers to talk about financing arrangements, short-, medium-, and long-range plans, reorganization plans, controls systems, and seemingly endless government regulations that had to be followed. At times, Dan longed for the days when he worked in the shop, where he had spent time talking with his customers, and when life was simple.

Dan's wishes were soon to be answered. Fed up with Dan's heavy responsibilities and long working hours (as well as impressed by the assets he had accumulated), his wife established a relationship with the manager of Dan's largest outlet (an ambitious young man anxious to get ahead in the organization) and divorced Dan. She then teamed up with the other shareholders (her friends) against Dan at a shareholders' meeting. While Dan's 45 percent of the shares made him the largest single shareholder, the other shareholders (including his ex-wife) were able to outvote him and remove him from the presidency. The new board of directors was kind enough to offer Dan a job as manager of the company's largest outlet (an opening created by the promotion of its former manager to the presidency of the company), but Dan had lost interest in the business. He declined the offer and went to work for Canada Post, where he had been told he wouldn't ever have to worry about anything. As a shareholder in Dan's Doughnut Dens, Ltd., Dan is entitled to any dividends per share that are paid to the other shareholders, and he lives quite comfortably on this income, plus his Canada Post salary. While he still owns 45 percent of the company shares, he does not attend shareholders' meetings of the company. Now see the "You Decide" box below for an update to Dan's story.

UPDATE TO THE SAGA OF DAN'S DOUGHNUT DENS

Recently, Dan has been spending an increasing amount of time with Ermyntrude, a former old friend of his ex-wife, who Dan never did like very much at all. Ermyntrude is the owner of 5.1 percent of the shares of Dan's Doughnut Dens, Ltd.

Questions

1. From the story about Dan's Doughnut Dens, compile a list of the advantages and disadvantages of each of the three forms of business organization: the sole proprietorship, the partnership, and the corporation.
2. What accounts for Dan's new interest in Ermyntrude?
3. What advice would you give Dan if he were just starting his business?
4. Why do you think that virtually all medium- and large-sized businesses are corporations?

Small Business in Canada

Small business in Canada includes such a wide range of enterprises that no simple definition can cover it. According to one definition used by Industry Canada, a small business is any manufacturing firm employing fewer than 100 workers and any nonmanufacturing firm employing fewer than 50 workers. For tax purposes, the size of the firm is less important than its profits: all Canadian-controlled private corporations pay a lower tax rate on the first $200 000 of active business income per year. According to the Canadian Federation of Independent Business (CFIB), any independently owned firm with less than 50 employees is "small." CFIB classifies a firm with 50 to 499 employees as "medium-sized."

The Extent of Small Business

The vast majority of businesses in Canada are small businesses. At the start of 2001, there were 2 024 508 businesses in Canada. Of these, over 78 percent (1 586 749) had less than 5 employees, over 97 percent (1 969 811) had less than 50 employees, and nearly 99 percent (2 000 892) had less than 100 employees.

www.industrycanada.ca
www.cfib.ca

Small business includes a tremendous variety of individuals, firms, and economic activities: professionals such as doctors and lawyers; farmers; small-scale manufacturers producing toys, boats, clothing, furniture, and a host of other products; retailers such as drug stores, gift shops, grocery stores, clothing stores, bookstores, music stores, and variety stores; service industry operations such as dry cleaning, hairdressing, restaurants, motels, real estate, insurance, services to business, employment agencies, repairs, and landscaping; and construction, which is characterized by large numbers of small contractors and subcontractors.

Small businesses use all the forms of business organization: while over half are sole proprietorships or partnerships, many are corporations. Many of these corporations are **private corporations**, meaning that they have fewer than 50 shareholders. By becoming a private corporation, a small business can gain the income tax advantages of incorporation without having to comply with the regulations governing public corporations. Because they can sell shares and bonds to the general public to raise capital, **public corporations** are required to publish considerable financial information in order to protect the investing public. Private corporations are not required to publish such financial data.

private corporation A private corporation has fewer than 50 shareholders.

public corporation A public corporation has 50 or more shareholders.

It is estimated that the small business sector accounts for over 80 percent of net new job creation in Canada, and in 2002 it was estimated that small businesses created 250 000 new jobs. A 1996 study by the CFIB highlighted the qualities that employers look for in young employees. As Figure 3-1 shows, the four most important qualities are, in fact, related to character: discipline, reliability, adaptability, and the will to stay at the job. Basic education and good communication skills are other important factors.

FIGURE 3-1 The Qualities Business Owners Look for
When Hiring Youths

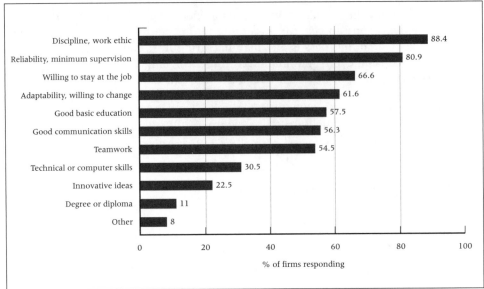

Source: Canadian Federation of Independent Business, results of *Job* survey, part 2, August 1996.

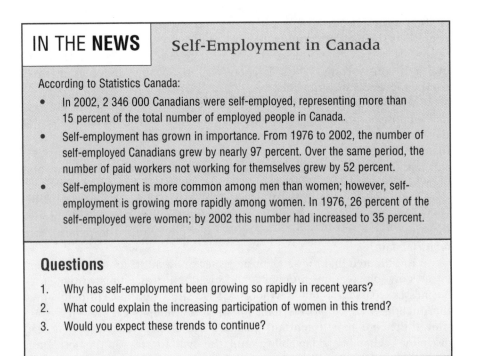

IN THE **NEWS**   Self-Employment in Canada

According to Statistics Canada:

- In 2002, 2 346 000 Canadians were self-employed, representing more than 15 percent of the total number of employed people in Canada.
- Self-employment has grown in importance. From 1976 to 2002, the number of self-employed Canadians grew by nearly 97 percent. Over the same period, the number of paid workers not working for themselves grew by 52 percent.
- Self-employment is more common among men than women; however, self-employment is growing more rapidly among women. In 1976, 26 percent of the self-employed were women; by 2002 this number had increased to 35 percent.

Questions

1. Why has self-employment been growing so rapidly in recent years?
2. What could explain the increasing participation of women in this trend?
3. Would you expect these trends to continue?

Problems of Small Business

While some 150 000 new businesses start each year, the failure rate is high, especially in the first year of operation. About 15 percent of new firms do not make it through their first year.

One of the main reasons for failures of small businesses is that management is often stretched too thinly. In many small businesses, a single owner–manager is required to perform more functions than time or expertise permit; as a result, the business often suffers from inadequate management.

According to an ongoing survey by the CFIB (see Figure 3-2), taxation and government regulation are the major impediments to the operations and growth of small and medium-sized businesses in Canada.

FIGURE 3-2 Small Business Priorities

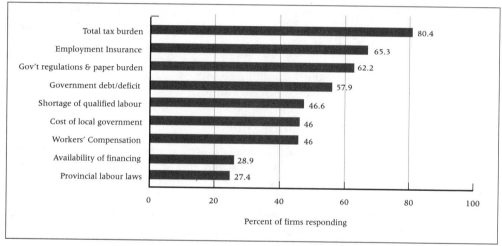

Source: Canadian Federation of Independent Business, results of *Our Members' Opinion* survey no. 49, July to December 2001.

In a 2001 survey of over 22 000 CFIB members, over 80 percent of the respondents cited the total *tax burden* as the most important issue facing smaller firms. CFIB research has shown that the burden of the Canadian tax system falls particularly heavily on labour-intensive small businesses and that small firms actually pay a *higher* percentage of their profits to taxes than larger firms pay. This heavier tax burden is largely due to **payroll taxes**, which are calculated as a percentage of a firm's payroll. For a large high-technology manufacturing corporation whose payroll is a relatively small percentage of its sales income, payroll taxes are not too burdensome. But for small businesses in service industries whose payroll is a high percentage of their sales income, payroll taxes can cut significantly into profits. So payroll taxes such as premiums for Canada Pension Plan, Employment Insurance, and Workers' Compensation, and taxes for health care create a heavier burden for smaller, more labour-intensive businesses than for large corporations.

payroll taxes Taxes paid by employers based on the number of their employees or the amount of their payroll.

Another major concern of small business is *government regulation and paper burden,* as cited by 62 percent of the respondents. For small business owners who spend a great deal of time managing their enterprise, the time required to fill out government forms relating to statistical information and tax collection (which in many cases consumes five hours to ten hours per week) can be a real burden.

Shortages of qualified labour are another problem for many small businesses. Small firms have traditionally given young entrants into the workforce their first job. However, for a number of years, small business owners have identified a shortage of qualified labour as a serious problem for their firms. In 2001 small businesses reported that they had 265 000 vacant jobs, of which 185 000 had been open for at least four months. And, as noted earlier, the burden of payroll taxes adds significantly to the cost to small business of hiring employees.

Financing problems often create serious handicaps. Small firms face considerable problems in attempting to raise sufficient equity and risk capital, and also tend to lack the access that larger businesses have to banks and other credit sources. Not only are small businesses considered by lenders to be a greater risk than larger firms, but also owner–managers of small firms often have difficulty identifying sources of funds.

Ebusiness and Small Business

Use of the internet by small business more than tripled between 1996 and 2000. A CFIB survey in 2000 showed that almost 70 percent of small businesses were actively using the internet. Virtually all firms with more than 100 employees each were on the internet, and even among the "micro" businesses with fewer than five employees each, the internet usage rate was 60 percent. By far, the most common internet application is email, which is used by virtually every online business.

ebusinesses Businesses using processes and activities based on electronic information and data exchanges via the internet and the World Wide Web.

Firms that have a website, where consumers can buy their products or services online or sell online, are called **ebusinesses**. The most common ebusiness application is a website for the business. "Business-to-business" (B2B) transactions, where businesses buy from one another via the internet, are becoming more common. Firms that sell to consumers online—known as "business-to-consumer" (B2C) firms—are much less common. In fact, B2B accounts for about 90 percent of all business transactions on the web, even though B2C activity gets much more media attention.

Canadian Federation of Independent Business

Until the early 1970s, small business owners in Canada felt that they lacked a voice in the policy-making process of federal and provincial governments. As a result, they believed, government policies were often formed without consideration of their effects on small business, which was being threatened by the expansion of taxation and regulations, and the proliferation of "red tape." In response to these problems, several small business organizations were created, the most important of which is the Canadian Federation of Independent Business (CFIB).

The CFIB was formed in 1971, and by 2002 it included 103 000 small and medium-sized Canadian-owned businesses in its membership. With offices located across the country, the federation employs a staff of about 300, including legislative specialists, economists, and field staff engaged in selling memberships nationwide. A major function of the CFIB's staff is conducting surveys and other research with the small business membership. The analysis of this information on the views of the small business community provides the basis for the CFIB's presentations to governments.

www.cfib.ca

The CFIB acts as the small business lobby with government, raising issues concerning taxation, financing, government regulations, and red tape. It claims to have saved small business several billions of dollars through its influence on government decisions. The CFIB's stated objective is to promote and protect a system of free competitive enterprise in Canada and to give the independent business owner a greater voice in the laws governing business and the nation. With its sizable cross-country membership base and its lines of communication with each provincial government as well as the federal government, the CFIB is by far the most important and influential of the groups representing small business in Canada.

Big Business in Canada

As Table 3-1 shows, big business in Canada is a very different world from the small business sector, a world dominated by corporate giants that are household names. All such large businesses are incorporated, mostly in the form of *public corporations* that have the ability to raise capital through the sale of stocks and bonds to the public. Public corporations shares are traded on stock exchanges such as the Toronto Stock Exchange and the TSX Venture Exchange. Through these stock exchanges, corporations can issue new shares to raise capital, and the investing public can buy and sell shares. The ability to buy and sell corporate shares freely, together with the limited liability of shareholders, makes it possible for public corporations to raise the vast amounts of capital they need, not only from the general public but also from large institutional investors such as pension funds and mutual funds.

www.tsx.ca

The 25 corporations shown in Table 3-1 play a major role in the Canadian economy, with sales amounting to over $392 billion in 2001. This amount represents 36 percent of all the goods and services produced in Canada that year. The column showing each firm's sales outside of Canada indicates that several of these largest Canadian firms are major exporters.

In 2001 the Ontario Lottery and Gaming Corp. had the 48th–largest sales revenues in Canada, up from 98th place in 2000.

Table 3-1 also shows that the ownership of these large enterprises is quite diverse. In 2001, about four-fifths of Canada's largest 25 companies were public corporations. Of these public corporations, about one-third were

www.olgc.ca

TABLE 3-1 Canada's 25 Largest Non-Financial Corporations by Sales, 2001

Rank by Revenue 2001	Company	Sales Revenue $'000s	% Sales Outside Canada	Profits $'000s	Major shareholder(s)	% Foreign
1	General Motors of Canada Ltd.	37 000 000	n.a.	n.a.	General Motors, US	100
2	Nortel Networks Corp.	21 137 988	95	(42 486 408)	Widely held	
3	George Weston Ltd.	24 661 000	n.a.	582 000	W. Galen Weston 62%	
4	Onex Corp.	23 803 000	81	798 000	Gerald W. Schwartz 67%	11
5	BCE Inc.	21 711 000	15	523 000	Widely held	
6	Bombardier Inc.	21 633 800	93	390 000	Bombardier family 63%	100
7	Ford Motor Co. of Canada, Ltd.	21 581 900	68	n.a.	Ford, US	100
8	DaimlerChrysler Canada Inc.	20 404 000	n.a.	n.a.	DaimlerChrysler, US	
9	Alcan Inc.	19 545 048	95	7 740	Widely held	
10	Power Corp. of Canada	18 360 000	n.a.	618 000	Paul Desmarais & Associates 65%	
11	Imperial Oil Ltd.	17 153 000	13	1 244 000	Exxon Mobile, US	70
12	Magna International Inc.	17 068 248	67	897 840	Stronach Trust 58%	
13	Hydro-Québec	12 578 000	29	1 108 000	Quebec government	
14	Westcoast Energy Inc.	11 897 000	n.a.	572 000	Widely held	
15	Quebecor Inc.	11 633 300	70	(241 700)	Les Placements Péladeau 62%	
16	Empire Co. Ltd.	11 538 600	n.a.	580 000	D.R. Sobey 27%; D.F. Sobey 21%	
17	The Thomson Corp.	11 202 876	98	1 159 452	The Woodbridge Co. 73%	100
18	Honda Canada Inc.	10 900 000	65	n.a.	Honda, Japan	
19	PanCanadian Energy Corp.	10 098 000	50	1 304 000	Widely held	
20	Air Canada	9 611 000	n.a.	(1 254 000)	Widely held	
21	Petro-Canada	8 582 000	1	904 000	Federal government 19%	
22	British Columbia Hydro & Power	7 889 000	n.a.	446 000	British Columbia government	
23	Shell Canada Ltd.	7 658 000	n.a.	1 010 000	Shell, Netherlands	78
24	Hudson's Bay Co.	7 445 813	n.a.	72 750	Widely held	
25	TELUS Corp.	7 202 600	n.a.	453 500	Verizon Communications, US 26%	33

n.a.—Not available/not applicable.
Source: The ranking by revenue is adapted. Reprinted with permission from National Post Business, *The Financial Post 500, 2001*.

widely held, meaning that ownership is spread among a large number of relatively small shareholders. In more than half the corporations, control was in the hands of another corporation or a family.

Nearly one-fifth of these largest firms were private corporations. A private corporation has fewer than 50 shareholders and is not required to publish nearly as much financial information as a public corporation. Family-owned firms and subsidiaries of foreign companies often take the form of private corporations, because this form provides greater privacy. About one-quarter of Canada's largest 25 nonfinancial corporations were foreign-owned, mostly by U.S.-based parent companies.

Table 3-2 lists the 25 largest employers in Canada in 2001. Each of these firms employs an average of over 55 000 people. Altogether, these enterprises accounted for nearly 8 percent of all jobs in Canada.

Table 3-3 shows that most of Canada's ten largest banks and financial institutions are widely held, and none are foreign-owned. Foreign banks have been establishing a growing presence in Canada, and in 2001, twelve of the largest 50 financial institutions were foreign-owned. However, most of

TABLE 3-2 Canada's 25 Largest Employers, 2001

Rank by Employees 2001	Company	Number of Employees	Revenues per Employee $	Assets per Employee $	Profile per Employee $
1	George Weston Ltd.	126 000	195 722	129 183	4 619
2	Onex Corp.	87 300	272 658	239 061	9 141
3	Bombardier Inc.	79 000	273 846	351 299	4 948
4	McDonald's Restaurants of Canada Ltd.	77 000	29 093	21 381	n.a.
5	BCE Inc.	75 000	289 480	724 467	6 973
6	Hudson's Bay Co.	71 730	103 803	63 212	1 014
7	Magna International Inc.	67 000	254 750	187 974	13 401
8	Canada Post Corp.	65 767	90 349	55 545	1 277
9	Royal Bank of Canada	58 000	440 029	6 194 138	41 569
10	Quebecor Inc.	54 000	215 431	361 356	(4 476)
11	Nortel Networks Corp.	52 600	515 931	613 305	(807 726)
12	Alcan Inc.	52 000	375 866	534 543	149
13	Sears Canada Inc.	51 000	131 890	76 078	1 845
14	The Bank of Nova Scotia	46 804	449 827	6 076 938	46 342
15	The Toronto-Dominion Bank	45 565	459 092	6 317 085	30 352
16	The Thomson Corp.	44 500	251 750	658 750	26 055
17	Canadian Imperial Bank of Commerce	42 315	505 407	6 793 667	39 844
18	Canadian Tire Corp., Ltd.	41 000	131 092	106 614	4 309
19	Air Canada	39 535	243 101	225 142	(31 719)
20	Le Mouvement des caisses Desjardins	38 816	166 504	2 073 707	n.a.
21	Extendicare Inc.	38 800	43 931	44 852	(938)
22	Empire Co. Ltd.	34 000	339 371	125 126	17 059
23	Bank of Montreal	33 842	508 894	7 074 316	43 467
24	Canada Safeway Ltd.	30 000	177 943	52 490	n.a.
25	Fairmont Hotels & Resorts Inc.	30 000	27 033	100 741	48 014

n.a.—Not available/not applicable.

Source: Reprinted with permission from National Post Business, *The Financial Post 500*, 2001.

TABLE 3-3 Canada's 10 Largest Financial Institutions, 2001

Rank by Revenue 2001	Company	Revenues $'000s	Assets $'000s	Profit as % of Shareholders' Equity	Major Shareholder(s)
1	Royal Bank of Canada	25 521 659	359 260 000	20.06	Widely held
2	Canadian Imperial Bank of Commerce	21 386 289	287 474 000	16.39	Widely held
3	The Bank of Nova Scotia	21 053 718	284 425 000	17.15	Widely held
4	The Toronto-Dominion Bank	20 918 505	287 838 000	11.28	Widely held
5	Power Financial Corp.	17 889 000	67 069 000	n.a.	Power Corp. of Canada 67%
6	Bank of Montreal	17 222 000	239 409 000	13.99	Widely held
7	Le Mouvement des caisses Desjardins	6 463 000	80 493 000	n.a.	Members
8	Fairfax Financial Holdings Ltd.	6 125 700	35 438 700	(11.51)	V. Prem Watsa 56%
9	National Bank of Canada	5 170 000	75 763 000	15.17	Widely held
10	Caisse de dépôt et placement du Québec	3 750 000	121 808 000	n.a.	Quebec government

n.a.—Not available/not applicable.
Source: Reprinted with permission from National Post Business, *The Financial Post 500*, 2001.

them were small compared to those listed in Table 3-3. Foreign banks mainly do commercial lending to businesses, and are therefore not very visible to the general public.

Multinational Enterprises

Many of the corporations listed in Table 3-1 are what are known as *multinational enterprises*, or corporations that conduct business internationally. Multinational corporations first attracted attention in the 1960s and 1970s; however, following the shift in the 1980s toward freer international trade, their growth became spectacular. Worldwide, there are estimated to be more than 37 000 multinationals with more than 170 000 affiliates, and more than one-third of world trade is conducted between related companies. Over half of all Canada–U.S. trade takes place between multinational affiliates.

The strategic significance of these firms is great—it is estimated that North America's largest 1000 multinationals employ 30 million people and account for about 25 percent of all the goods and services produced in Canada and the United States. Most of the largest multinationals are U.S.-owned; however, approximately 12 percent of the top North American firms are Canadian-controlled, providing Canada with a good presence in this large and growing aspect of business enterprise.

Corporate Concentration

In Canada, much business activity is concentrated in the hands of relatively few very large corporations. In broad terms, the largest 25 enterprises (ranked by sales) have tended to control about one-third of all corporate nonfinancial assets in Canada. In particular industries, such as automobile manufacturing, steel, and breweries, concentration is especially high. This corporate concentration is the result of various factors, including the growth of the sales and assets of the most successful corporations and the tendency of corporations to purchase control of, or merge with, other corporations. As a result, as we will see in Chapter 7, some industries and markets in Canada have come to be dominated by a few large corporations, and to a greater degree than in the United States. When a few firms dominate an industry, concerns are raised about whether there is sufficiently strong competition in the industry. The handful of "competitors" may tend to agree among themselves not to compete too strongly, especially with respect to prices, so that all of them can live together more comfortably and profitably. In these cases, it is viewed as necessary for the government to set down rules for corporate behaviour that, in effect, prohibit anticompetitive practices, a matter that will be considered further in Chapter 9.

The High-Tech Manufacturing Sector

Table 3-4 shows the top ten high-tech manufacturers in Canada, ranked by sales revenue. In the late 1990s, investors become very excited about upstart dot-com companies and other internet-related businesses, pouring billions of dollars into new stock issues by these companies. When these funds were spent on electronic equipment and information technology, the sales and profits of high-tech manufacturers soared spectacularly. However, most of the dot-com firms had failed to develop business models that would generate sales and earn profits, so when they had used up their investors' funds, their purchases of technology and equipment plunged drastically. To make matters worse for the high-tech equipment manufacturers, over-investment had created a surplus of bandwidth that killed off spending in that area. As can be seen from Table 3-4, these events had extremely serious effects on the profits of high-tech manufacturers in 2001.

TABLE 3-4 Canada's Top 10 High-Tech Manufacturers, 2001

Rank by Revenue	Company	Rank in FP 500	Revenues $'000s	Profits $'000s
1	Nortel Networks Corp.	2	27 137 988	(42 486 408)
2	Bombardier Inc.	7	21 633 800	390 900
3	Celestica Inc.	4 (sub)	15 486 492	(61 920)
4	IBM Canada Ltd.	51	5 300 000	n.a.
5	JDS Uniphase Canada	58	4 910 623	(85 249 166)
6	Hewlett-Packard (Canada) Ltd.	138	1 800 000	n.a.
7	Xerox Canada Inc.	145	1 725 000	n.a.
8	Cisco Systems Canada Co.	177	1 440 000	n.a.
9	Honeywell Ltd.	184	1 393 200	n.a.
10	CAE Inc.	197	1 191 400	108 100

n.a.—Not available/not applicable.
Source: Reprinted with permission from National Post Business, *The Financial Post 500*, 2001.

Who Controls the Modern Large Corporation?

In theory, this is a simple question, since the shareholders of a corporation vote to elect the board of directors, which in turn selects top management and directs them as to the corporation's objectives and the policies to be followed. In reality, however, the matter is often not so simple. In many large corporations, the shares are so widely held that the shareholders are too numerous and too dispersed to exercise any effective control. A typical shareholders' meeting of a large corporation attracts only a handful of shareholders, few of whom ever seriously question or challenge the executive officers of the corporation.

If the small shareholders are often not in a position to exercise control over the large corporation collectively, then who does control it? Given the importance of large corporations in the economy, this is an important question. Unfortunately, the answer is not always clear since it depends on the circumstances.

If the corporation's stock is so widely held that there is no major shareholder or organized group of shareholders, it will be impossible for the shareholders to exercise control through their meetings. Rather, control will often fall to the *top management* of the corporation, which can control the shareholders' meetings through **proxies**. (A proxy is a legal instrument whereby a shareholder, in effect, delegates to another person authority to vote on his or her behalf.) Under these circumstances, the top management of a corporation can control the firm, even to the point of nominating and selecting the members of the board of directors to which top management reports. In such cases, the management of the corporation can usually retain control as long as the corporation performs well enough to keep the shareholders content. Those shareholders who disagree strongly with management's decisions will generally sell their shares rather than engage in a struggle for control that will probably prove futile.

proxies Legal instruments that allow a shareholder's right to vote at shareholders' meetings to be delegated to another person, either with or without specific instructions as to how that vote will be exercised.

In Canada it is widely accepted that, in many large corporations, the *board of directors* takes a more active part in company policies and decisions than is suggested in the preceding paragraphs. Sometimes such control is exercised through boards of directors by majority shareholders, such as family interests or other corporations that own a majority of the shares. However, the situation is not always so clear-cut: under certain conditions, a group of shareholders (individuals or other corporations) can maintain control of a corporation's board of directors even though it holds only a small percentage of the total shares outstanding; such control can be achieved through proxy votes or simply through personal relationships between the people involved.

While corporate directorships have in the past been thought of as sinecure positions involving status and perks but relatively little responsibility, the situation has changed. Directors now face significantly increased responsibilities due to changes in the law that place much more liability upon them for their companies' actions. Under a variety of laws (by one count, more than 100 in Ontario alone), directors of companies are now exposed to a wide range of both civil and criminal penalties including claims for employees' wages and infractions of environmental laws. In fact, during the

1990s there was growing concern that governments had taken the concept of directors' liability too far. In several cases directors of companies that were in difficulty resigned when the possibility arose that they could be held personally liable for millions of dollars of claims. This event raised the concern that the laws relating to directors' liability could discourage Canada's most capable people from serving on the boards of corporations.

Partly as a result of this concern, and partly in response to increasing concerns that board members be impartial and independent in providing shareholders with information about their companies, corporations are seeking directors with more expertise and dedication than ever before, and are increasingly going outside their own companies for them. Thus, the question of who controls the large corporation is not a simple one. What can be said is that large corporations play a very important role in the Canadian economy, even greater relative to the size of the economy than in the United States, and that in these large corporations, *control is often separated from ownership*. Widespread small shareholders are not in a position to exercise active control. As a result, control tends to shift, depending on the circumstances, to the top management of the corporation or to groups of influential members of the board of directors. Generally, neither top managers nor directors are major shareholders in their corporation; their claim to control over the corporation is based on their expertise rather than on ownership.

Government Enterprises

No discussion of big business in Canada would be complete without reference to government-owned enterprises. Comprising roughly 10 percent of Canada's very large corporations, government enterprises often take the form of **Crown corporations.** Crown corporations, like other corporations, are legally independent, separate entities. However, their shares are owned by a government, and they are ultimately responsible to the government through a cabinet minister. In addition to Crown corporations, government enterprises often take the form of *boards* or *commissions*, such as hydroelectric commissions.

Crown corporations
Corporations owned by a government and that are ultimately responsible, through a cabinet minister, to that government.

Whatever legal forms they take, government enterprises constitute an important part of big business in Canada. Their largest single activity is the *provision of electricity*: the combined sales of the ten provinces' electricity utilities would make them the largest enterprise in Canada. Traditionally, government enterprises have also been important in the fields of *transportation and communications* in Canada, including, at various times, Canadian National Railways, Air Canada, Pacific Western Airlines, British Columbia Railway, and Nordair. More recently, government enterprises, such as PetroCan, Atomic Energy of Canada, Eldorado Nuclear, the Canada Development Corporation, and the Potash Corporation of Saskatchewan, have established a presence in the *energy and resources* sector of the Canadian economy. While government enterprises play a smaller role in the *manufacturing sector*, some provincial governments have acted as partners in manufacturing firms in attempts to stimulate growth and employment in their regions. Table 3-5 lists the ten largest Crown corporations in Canada, ranked by sales in 2001.

TABLE 3-5 Canada's 10 Largest Crown Corporations, 2001

Rank by Revenue	Company	Rank in FP 500	Revenues $'000s	Owned by
1	Hydro-Québec	20	12 578 000	Quebec government
2	British Columbia Hydro & Power Authority	30	7 889 000	British Columbia government
3	Ontario Power Generation Inc.	41	6 239 000	Ontario government
4	Canada Post Corp.	45	5 942 000	Federal government
5	Ontario Lottery and Gaming Corp.	48	5 339 336	Ontario government
6	Canadian Wheat Board	62	4 227 675	Federal government
7	Caisse de dépôt et placement du Québec	70	3 750 000	Quebec government
8	EPCOR Utilities Inc.	71	3 723 900	City of Edmonton
9	Hydro One Inc.	76	3 466 000	Ontario government
10	Workplace Safety & Insurance Board	96	2 909 000	Ontario government

Source: Reprinted with permission from National Post Business, *The Financial Post 500*, 2001.

The question of government enterprises has been a controversial one in Canada. Supporters argue that government enterprises have contributed enormously to the economic development and unity of the nation. They point out that in a far-flung country such as Canada, the costs of operating such enterprises are so great that it is necessary for the government to subsidize their operation in order to provide a reasonable level of service to all Canadians. Critics of government enterprises stress the fact that their numbers have increased greatly over the years and have come to include money-losing businesses that the government acquired mainly for political reasons, that is, to "save jobs." They point out that many government enterprises pay above-market wages to their employees and/or operate inefficiently, losing money regularly and falling back on taxpayers for subsidies. As the federal government's budget deficits mounted in the 1980s and 1990s, pressures to re-assess the government's commitment to many of its money-losing enterprises grew.

In 1985 the federal government undertook a critical review of the performance of its Crown corporations. It decided to sell some of them to private interests, or **privatize** them. The privatization program started with the high-profile sale of De Havilland Aircraft of Canada Ltd. to Boeing Corp. of the United States. In 1989, the sale of Air Canada to private interests was completed, and in the 1990s Petro-Canada and Canadian National were privatized.

privatize The process of selling government enterprises (usually Crown corporations) to private interests.

Governments have also generally owned and operated most educational institutions at all levels. Some people have suggested, however, that this government "monopoly" should be changed to a situation in which schools have to compete for customers in the same ways as other businesses do (see the "You Decide" box on the next page).

To summarize, government enterprises are big business in Canada, many of them being household names and major forces in the economy. The objectives of these enterprises are not only profits—some of them, such as the Canadian Broadcasting Corporation, are intended to provide particular services throughout the country whether doing so is profitable or not, or to aid in the development of particular industries, products, or regions. The matter of government enterprises has always been a controversial one; critics argue that such operations tend to be inefficient and costly because of political interference and the absence of the profit motive, and supporters argue that they are an essential component of the Canadian economy, performing functions that private enterprise would not or could not.

A COMPETITIVE MARKET FOR EDUCATION?

In most elementary and secondary school systems, students have no choice as to which school they will attend—they are assigned to the school in the area in which they live. Some critics would like to see competition introduced into the education "industry." They want the government to give students (or their parents) vouchers for each year's education and allow them to "spend" these vouchers at any school they wish. In such a system, schools would function partly like businesses—the more students (and vouchers) a school attracted, the more revenue it would have. The theory is that this competition would put pressure on schools to improve the quality of their education.

Questions

1. What advantages do you see in such a system?
2. What disadvantages or potential dangers do you see in it?
3. What would be required for such a system to operate effectively and improve the quality of education?

Market Structure

In this chapter we have considered the nature of the "business sector" of the economy, which produces most of the supply of goods and services. In Chapters 4 through 7, we will see how supply and demand interact to determine prices. This task is complicated somewhat by the fact that supply—the production of goods and services by business—occurs under various conditions ranging from industries comprising large numbers of small firms to industries dominated by a few large firms to industries in which there is only one producer (a monopoly). These different conditions— referred to as *market structures* by economists—have a significant impact on the supply of goods and services. If there is only one firm in an industry (a monopoly), it is in a position to control the supply of the product, thereby raising the price of the product and increasing its profits. In industries dominated by a few large firms, it is sometimes possible for these firms to get together to avoid competing on prices and thus increase their profits. On the other hand, in industries in which there are many small firms, such collective action is very difficult or impossible to achieve. As a result, competition in such industries tends to be more intense, and prices and profits are lower than in either of the first two cases. In Chapter 4, we will examine the concept of demand, and then in Chapter 5, we will begin our examination of supply (and its interactions with demand) in those industries that have a large number of small firms—industries that economists call *competitive*.

Chapter Summary

1. The advantages of the sole proprietorship and the partnership are that they are easily formed and provide strong motivation and a high degree of independence. Disadvantages include lack of access to financing, lack of managerial expertise, the unlimited personal liability of the owner(s), and higher tax rates once the income of the business exceeds a certain amount. An added disadvantage of the partnership is the possibility of disagreements among the partners. (L.O. 1)

2. One advantage of the corporation, the typical form taken by larger businesses, is that it can raise larger amounts of capital due to the limited liability of its shareholders. Another advantage is the lower tax rates on income above a certain level. Disadvantages include the initial costs of incorporation and a greater degree of government regulation, especially with respect to public corporations. (L.O. 1)

3. Small business is an important and dynamic sector of the Canadian economy, consisting of many hundreds of thousands of firms and providing over one-third of all private sector employment and a high proportion of new private sector job creation in recent years. (L.O. 2)

4. Major problems faced by small business include high tax rates, lack of management expertise, financing problems, government regulations and paperwork, and difficulties attracting and retaining skilled employees. (L.O. 3)

5. Big business is another major component of the Canadian economy, accounting for particularly high proportions of the country's output and exports. Multinational enterprises are an increasingly important aspect of Canada's big business sector. (L.O. 4, 5)

6. While these large corporations are important to the Canadian economy, the domination of some industries by a few large corporations raises questions as to whether such corporate concentration is in the public interest. (L.O. 5)

7. Control of the modern large corporation is not usually in the hands of the shareholders as a group; rather, it tends to rest with top management and/or the board of directors, neither of which are usually major shareholders. (L.O. 6)

8. A significant number of Canada's large corporations are government-owned, particularly in the areas of electrical utilities, transportation and communications, and energy and resources. (L.O. 7)

Questions

1. In 2001 General Motors was ranked 1st in sales revenue and 32nd in number of employees. McDonald's was ranked 108th in sales revenue and 4th in number of employees. What might explain these differences?

2. Check the most recent Financial Post 500 listing of the largest Canadian corporations, ranked by sales revenue. What changes in the rankings have occurred since 2001, and what might explain these changes?

3. Check the most recent Financial Post 500 listing of the largest Canadian high-tech manufacturers, ranked by sales revenue. What changes have occurred since 2001 in the rankings and profitability of these firms? What might explain these changes?

www.nationalpost.com

4. Following are the income statements for a manufacturing company with sales of $500 million per year and a service firm such as a restaurant with sales of $500 thousand per year:

	Manufacturing Company	Restaurant
Sales revenue	$ 500 million	$ 500 thousand
Nonlabour costs	370	320
Labour costs	100	150
Profit	30	30
Payroll taxes (10% of payroll)	_____	_____
Profit after payroll taxes	_____	_____

(a) Why are the manufacturing company's labour costs 20 percent of sales revenue while the restaurant's labour costs are 30 percent of sales revenue?

(b) Finish the table by calculating the payroll taxes and the profits after payroll taxes for each firm.

(c) By what percent do payroll taxes reduce the profit of each firm?

5. Small-business "incubators" are one way to help small businesses to get started. Incubators provide mentoring to nurture start-up businesses through the fledgling stage to become successful enterprises. In 1980, there were only 12 business incubators in North America; by 2001, there were about 900. For more information on incubators, visit the Toronto Business Development Centre at www.tbdc.com or the Hamilton Technology Enterprise Centre at www.ghtec.com.

6. Divide your class into teams of three or four students. Each team has $10 000 to invest in shares listed on the Toronto Stock Exchange. Over the remainder of your course, keep track of the changing value of the stocks purchased by each team.

Chapter 4

The Demand Side of Markets

Learning Objectives

After studying this chapter, you should be able to:

1. Draw a demand curve for a product from a demand schedule showing the quantity demanded at various prices.

2. Explain whether a given event would increase or decrease the demand for a particular product, and show how the event would affect the demand curve.

3. Explain the difference between *elastic* and *inelastic* demand.

4. Calculate whether the demand for a product is elastic or inelastic over a specific price range, given the demand schedule for that product.

5. Determine whether a given event would make the demand for an item more elastic or more inelastic.

FIGURE 4-1 An Illustration of a Market

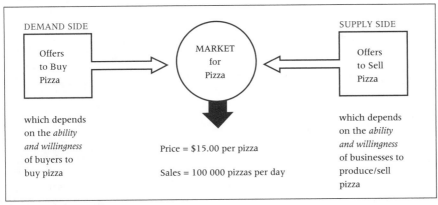

In Chapter 2, we saw how markets consist of:

- a demand side, or offers by buyers to purchase products, and
- a supply side, or offers by sellers to sell products.

Figure 4-1 illustrates in a general way how, in a market, the supply side and demand side interact to determine the price and sales of a particular item.

In this chapter, we will consider the "demand side" of markets, or factors that affect the ability and willingness of buyers to *purchase* particular goods or services. In the next chapter, we will cover the "supply side" of markets, or factors that affect the ability and willingness of businesses to *produce and sell* particular goods or services.

Part A: What Is Demand?

Generally, people will buy more of a product if its price is lower, all other things being equal. Suppose we took a survey of all the households in Cantown to determine how many pizzas people would buy each week in March 2003 if the price were $20 per pizza, $16 per pizza, $12 per pizza, $8 per pizza, and $4 per pizza, respectively. While surveys such as this one are an imprecise way of gathering information, especially when they ask people to estimate what they *might* do under different circumstances, we would expect that the results of the survey would show that people would buy more pizza at lower prices than at higher prices, as shown in Table 4-1.

Table 4-1 shows the relationship between the price of a pizza and the quantity of pizzas sold (bought): as the price *rises*, the quantity demanded *falls*. This drop occurs for two reasons: higher prices cause some people to become *unwilling* to buy pizza and others to become *unable* to buy pizza. Those who do not buy pizza at the higher prices can either substitute another product (such as submarine sandwiches) for pizza, or they can do without some pizza (that is, buy pizzas less often, or not at all).

TABLE 4-1 Demand Schedule for Pizza in Cantown, March 2003

If the price per pizza were	The quantity sold (bought) per week would be
$20	20 000
16	30 000
12	50 000
8	80 000
4	120 000

demand The entire relationship between the various possible prices of a product or service and the quantity demanded at each price, expressed through either a schedule or a graph.

This relationship between price and quantity demanded, known as **demand**, can be shown in a table, or *demand schedule* as in Table 4-1, or a *demand curve* as in Figure 4-2. The demand curve is simply another way of showing the same information in the demand schedule. The demand curve also shows that as the price rises, the quantity demanded falls (assuming that no other factor affecting demand changes).

FIGURE 4-2 Demand Curve for Pizza in Cantown, March 2003

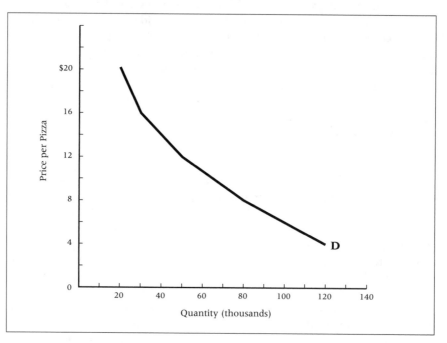

What Demand Is Not

Suppose that, in the example discussed above, the *actual* price of a pizza was $12, and that the *actual* quantity sold was 50 000 pizzas. Under these circumstances, it is tempting to conclude that the demand for pizza is 50 000 pizzas, but this conclusion would be incorrect. Demand refers to much more than the *actual* price and quantity bought; it also includes the idea that *if* the price of pizza *had been* higher, less *would have been* sold, and that lower prices would have generated higher sales. When we say "demand," we mean the entire relationship between the *various possible prices* and the quantity demanded at each price. Think of "demand" as the entire results of our hypothetical survey, or as the entire demand schedule or curve, as shown in Table 4-1 and Figure 4-2, respectively.

Shifts in the Demand Curve

In Figure 4-3 the information in the second column of the demand schedule and the demand curve labelled D is the same as that in our previous example. But suppose that some time after we did the original survey, we did another similar survey.

FIGURE 4-3 Demand Schedule and Curve Showing an Increase in Demand

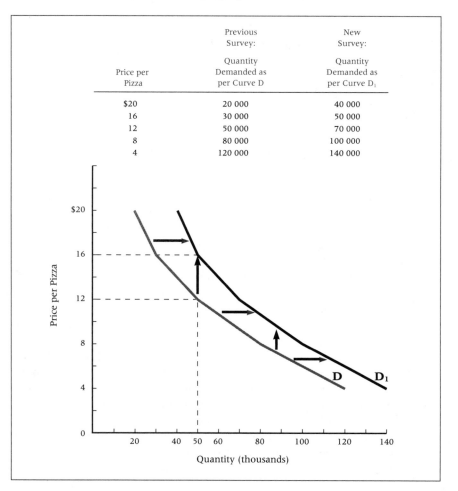

Price per Pizza	Previous Survey: Quantity Demanded as per Curve D	New Survey: Quantity Demanded as per Curve D_1
$20	20 000	40 000
16	30 000	50 000
12	50 000	70 000
8	80 000	100 000
4	120 000	140 000

This new survey reveals certain changes in the demand for pizza, which are shown in the third column of the demand schedule. This information shows that, at every possible price, consumers *will buy more* pizza than before. At a price of $20 per pizza, people used to buy 20 000 pizzas but will now buy 40 000; at a price of $16, people will increase their purchases from 30 000 to 50 000 pizzas; at a price of $12, sales used to be 50 000 pizzas but will now be 70 000, and so on. The demand for pizza has *increased*.

On the graph, this increase in demand causes the demand curve to move to the position shown by the new demand curve D_1. This shift in the demand curve can be seen in two ways. First, as the horizontal arrows show, the demand curve has shifted *to the right*. This shift reflects the fact discussed in the previous paragraph: at every possible price, consumers are prepared to *buy more* pizza than before. Second, as the vertical arrows show, the demand curve has shifted *upward*. This reflects the fact that consumers are prepared to *pay higher prices* for pizza. For instance, to get 50 000 pizzas, they will now pay $16 per pizza, whereas before they would only pay $12.

So demand curve D_1 shows that consumers are prepared both to buy more pizza and to pay higher prices for it. Clearly, there has been an increase in demand.

Causes of an Increase in Demand

For buyers' behaviour to change in these ways, there has to have been an increase in their *ability* and/or their *willingness* to buy pizza. What could cause such changes?

One possible explanation could be an *increase in consumer income*. Total incomes in the marketplace could increase either because the average incomes of consumers had risen or because there were more buyers in the market. Such an increase in income would increase the demand for pizza.

Another possible explanation is a *change in people's tastes*. If people's preferences changed so that they prefer pizza to other foods more strongly now than in the past, their willingness to buy pizza would increase and the demand for it would increase, shifting the demand curve to the right.

Another explanation for such an increase in demand could be an *increase in the price of substitutes* for pizza. For example, an increase in the price of submarine sandwiches, hamburgers, or tortillas would make pizza a better buy by comparison, causing an increase in the demand for pizza that would shift the demand curve for pizza to the right. The demand for pizza could also be increased by a *decrease in the price of a complementary good* that is bought along with pizza, such as garlic bread.

Another explanation for an increase in the demand for a product is a *change in consumer expectations* concerning its price or availability. If consumers expect that a product will be in shorter supply and/or become more expensive, some of them will buy it *now*, before its price increases. In the case of pizza, this is unlikely; however, in some markets such as housing, the prospect of rising prices can—and does—cause an increase in demand, as some buyers try to beat the price increases.

In summary, the causes of an *increase* in demand include changes in:

- buyers' incomes,
- buyers' tastes,
- the prices of substitutes,
- the prices of complementary goods, and
- buyers' expectations.

Causes of a Decrease in Demand

Everything discussed in the preceding sections about increases in demand can be reversed for the purpose of discussing decreases in demand. As Figure 4-4 shows, when the demand for pizza decreases, less pizza is bought at every possible price (as shown by the demand schedule), and the demand curve shifts to the left (as shown by the horizontal arrows) to the new location D_2. The change can also be interpreted as a downward shift of the demand curve, as shown by the vertical arrows. This downward shift means that consumers are not prepared to pay as high a price for pizza as they were before.

FIGURE 4-4 Demand Schedule and Curve Showing a Decrease in Demand

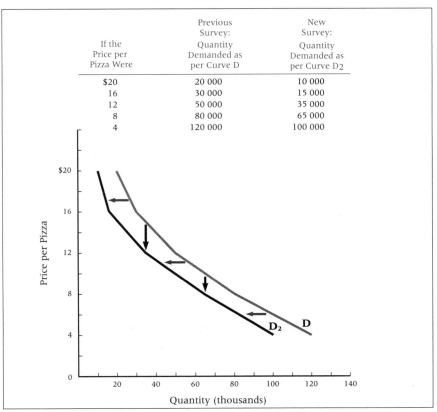

If the Price per Pizza Were	Previous Survey: Quantity Demanded as per Curve D	New Survey: Quantity Demanded as per Curve D2
$20	20 000	10 000
16	30 000	15 000
12	50 000	35 000
8	80 000	65 000
4	120 000	100 000

A shift of the demand curve to the left and down indicates that the factors underlying the demand for pizza have changed in such a way that the demand for pizza has decreased. Such a change can be explained by reference to the same factors discussed earlier. Perhaps people's *incomes have fallen*, leaving them less able to buy as much pizza as before, or perhaps their *tastes have changed,* and they find pizza less attractive than before. Or, perhaps the *prices of substitute products* have fallen—if other foods became less costly, consumers would buy more of them, causing a decrease in the demand for pizza. An increase in the *price of complementary* goods could also cause a decrease in the demand for pizza. Finally, a *change in people's expectations* could cause a decrease in the demand for a product. If people expect lower prices in the future, they may reduce their purchases now, and wait for the lower prices that are anticipated. The housing market provides a better example than the pizza market of the role of expectations. In the housing market, both house prices and mortgage interest rates (the prices of the loans used to buy houses) periodically rise to very high levels, then fall again. When house prices and mortgage rates are believed to be near one of their periodic peaks, many house buyers postpone purchases, expecting that the future will bring lower prices and interest rates.

Whatever the cause, the decrease in demand shown by the shift in the demand curve from D_1 to D_2 reflects the fact that buyers are not as *able* and/or *willing* to buy as much pizza and pay as much for it as before.

In summary, the causes of a *decrease* in demand include changes in:

* buyers' incomes,
* buyers' tastes,
* the prices of substitutes,
* the prices of complementary goods, and
* buyers' expectations.

"Changes in Demand" Versus "Changes in Quantity Demanded"

We have seen that, if the tastes, incomes, or expectations of consumers change, or the prices of other products change, the demand for a product will change—the demand curve will *shift,* either to the left or to the right.

But what if the *price* of that product changes—will the *demand* for the product also change? Certainly, the quantity demanded (or sales) will change, as Figure 4-5 shows: an increase in the price from $1 to $3 causes a reduction in quantity demanded (sales) from 400 to 200.

But "demand," as we have explained it in this chapter, has *not* changed—there has been no *shift* of the demand curve as occurs when demand changes, only a *movement along* the demand curve, from point A to point B. So while a change in price does cause a change in *quantity demanded* (sales), it does not alter *demand,* by shifting the demand curve to the right or to the left. Instead, there is merely a movement to a different point on the same demand curve.

FIGURE 4-5 Demand Curve Showing an Increase in Price

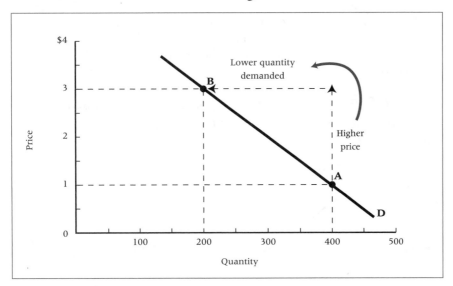

Factors Underlying Demand

In summary, demand is the relationship between the *price* of a product and the *quantity demanded* by buyers. This relationship can be expressed numerically, in a demand schedule, or graphically, in a demand curve. The location of the demand curve for a product depends on such factors as buyers' tastes and incomes, the prices of other products, and buyers' expectations of future price changes. Should these factors change so as to increase the demand for the product, the demand curve will shift to the right and up, whereas changes that reduce the demand for the product will cause the demand curve to shift to the left and down.

Part B: Elasticity of Demand

In Part A of this chapter, we saw that at higher prices buyers will purchase less of a product than at lower prices. A very important question, which we will consider later in this chapter, is *how much will sales fall* when the price rises? Since the answer to this question will depend on the nature of a specific product or service, we will examine two different cases.

"Elastic" Demand

Figure 4-6 shows a hypothetical demand schedule and demand curve for chicken. As the price rises, consumers reduce their purchases of chicken considerably—for instance, an increase in price from $0.35 to $0.65 per 100 g will reduce sales from 500 kg to only 100 kg. We could also say that if the price of chicken were to decrease, consumers would increase their purchases of it a great deal.

When changes in price cause buyers to make large changes in the amount they purchase, the demand for the product or service is said to be **elastic demand.** Another way to describe this situation is to say that buyers are *price-sensitive.*

elastic demand The term used to describe demand if a price increase causes a reduction in total sales revenue.

FIGURE 4-6 Elastic Demand: A Hypothetical Demand Schedule and Curve for Chicken

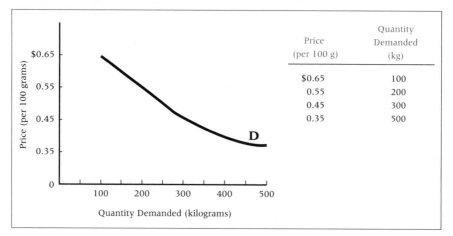

Price (per 100 g)	Quantity Demanded (kg)
$0.65	100
0.55	200
0.45	300
0.35	500

"Inelastic" Demand

Figure 4-7 shows a hypothetical demand schedule and demand curve for gasoline. The demand for gasoline is different: as the price rises, buyers do not reduce their purchases of gasoline by that much. For instance, an increase in price from $0.35 to $0.65 per litre would reduce sales from 325 000 L to 250 000 L—a much smaller decrease than in the case of chicken. And if the price of gasoline were to fall, consumers would not increase their purchases of it by very much.

When changes in price do not cause buyers to change the amount that they purchase by much, the demand for the product or service is said to be "inelastic." An **inelastic demand** means that buyers are not price-sensitive.

inelastic demand The term used to describe demand if a price increase causes an increase in total sales revenue.

What Makes Demand Elastic?

For demand to be elastic, buyers have to be able and willing to reduce their purchases substantially if the price rises by a small percentage. Two things could make this situation possible:

(a) a reasonably close substitute could be available, making it easy for buyers to switch to the substitute, or

(b) buyers could readily do without the product because it is not a necessity or treated as such.

FIGURE 4-7 Inelastic Demand: A Hypothetical Demand Schedule and Curve for Gasoline

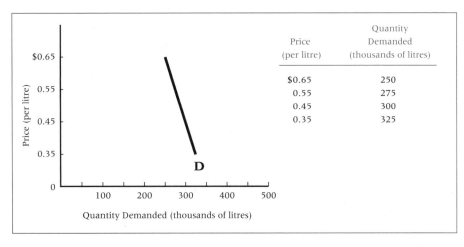

Price (per litre)	Quantity Demanded (thousands of litres)
$0.65	250
0.55	275
0.45	300
0.35	325

For the demand for chicken to be elastic, buyers do not need to *completely* do without chicken or *completely* switch to a substitute. Instead, they could buy smaller cuts of chicken, and buy it less frequently (and other meats more often). By combining these two responses, they could reduce their purchases of chicken considerably if its price rises by a small percentage, making the demand elastic. But buyers do not necessarily need to make *both* of these adjustments—by *either* substituting *or* cutting back (partially doing without), they can reduce their purchases considerably.

What Makes Demand Inelastic?

If demand is inelastic, buyers will not reduce their purchases by much even if the price increases considerably. They would behave this way because:

(a) there are no close substitutes available, and

(b) they are unable or unwilling to do without the product because it is a necessity or is treated as such.

Both of these conditions need to exist in order for demand to be inelastic. For instance, there may be no substitutes for a product, but if buyers can and will do without it, the demand for it would be elastic rather than inelastic.

Also, a product need not *be* a physical necessity for its demand to be inelastic; it need only be *treated* as a necessity. For instance, consumers may be able to survive without colour television sets, but if they *want* them strongly enough, the effect will be the same as if they were a necessity—if the price goes up, people will still buy them.

It is important to be very specific about the product in question when analyzing elasticity of demand. If the price of gasoline *in general* increased, the demand would be inelastic, because buyers need gasoline and there is no ready substitute. However, if the price of a *particular brand* of gasoline rose (and other brands did not), the demand for that brand would be very elastic, because buyers could readily switch to other brands as substitutes.

Defining "Elastic" and "Inelastic"

The preceding examples provide an *illustration* of the concepts of elastic and inelastic demand, but they do not give precise *definitions* of these terms. To define elastic and inelastic more precisely, we will use as an example the demand for Supersmooth Shaving Cream, as illustrated in Table 4-2.

TABLE 4-2 Demand Schedule and Total Revenue for Supersmooth Shaving Cream

Price per Can	Quantity Demanded (thousands of cans per week)	Total Revenue ($ thousands) (price × quantity demanded)
$1.80	60	$108
1.60	70	112
1.40	80	112
1.20	90	108
1.00	100	100

In Table 4-2, we have added a third column—*total revenue*, which is the total sales revenue, or price times quantity demanded. If we assume that the Supersmooth Shaving Cream Company is presently selling 90 000 cans per week at a price of $1.20 per can, Table 4-2 provides some interesting information.

First, while a price cut from $1.20 to $1.00 would increase sales from 90 000 cans to 100 000 cans, it would actually reduce the company's total revenue from $108 000 to $100 000, making such a price reduction an unattractive decision.[1] On the other hand, a price increase from $1.20 to $1.40 would have the opposite effect: while it would *reduce sales* from 90 000 to 80 000 cans, it would *increase the total revenue* of the company from $108 000 to $112 000.

So increases in price within the $1.00 to $1.40 price range cause total revenue to rise. Within this price range buyers are not particularly sensitive to price changes—when the price rises, purchases are not reduced by so much that total revenue falls. We have said that when buyers are relatively unresponsive to price changes, demand is said to be *inelastic*. Our formal definition, then, is that

if a price increase causes total revenue to rise, demand is **inelastic**.

....

1. Note that we say *total revenue*, not *profits*. The effect on profits is more complex—it depends on the combined effect of the increased sales and output on total sales revenue *and* total production costs, respectively. This concept is covered in Chapter 8; however, at this point we can simply assume that higher total revenue means higher profits, and vice versa.

However, increases in the price of Supersmooth Shaving Cream beyond a certain point cause total revenue to *fall*. An increase in price from $1.60 to $1.80 causes total revenue to decrease from $112 000 to $108 000, as this higher price cuts more deeply into sales. In this price range, where buyers are quite sensitive to changes in price, demand is *elastic*. Our definition then is that

if a price increase causes total revenue to fall, demand is **elastic**.

In summary, elasticity of demand refers to the responsiveness of buyers to changes in price. Demand is said to be elastic if a price increase causes total revenue to fall, and inelastic if a price increase causes total revenue to rise.[2] Similar rules can be worked out for the effects of price reductions, but these tend to be confusing. A simple rule of thumb is that if the *price* and the *total revenue* move in the same direction (up or down), demand is inelastic. These definitions are illustrated in the Supersmooth Shaving Cream demand schedule in Table 4-3.

TABLE 4-3 Elasticity of Demand for Supersmooth Shaving Cream Over Various Price Ranges

Price per Can	Quantity Demanded (thousands of cans per week)	Total Revenue ($ thousands) (price × quantity demanded)	Elasticity of Demand (over price range shown)
$1.80	60	$108	
			elastic from $1.60 to $1.80
1.60	70	112	
			unitary[a] elasticity from $1.40 to $1.60
1.40	80	112	
			inelastic from $1.20 to $1.40
1.20	90	108	
			inelastic from $1.00 to $1.20
1.00	100	100	

[a] Unitary elasticity means there is no change in total revenue as a result of a price increase.

----

2. When the price rises from $1.40 to $1.60, total revenue remains unchanged at $112 000. In this borderline case, when the effects of the higher price per unit sold are exactly offset by effects of the reduced number of units sold so that total revenue remains unchanged, we say that the demand has "unitary elasticity."

In the Supersmooth Shaving Cream example, demand is inelastic over the lower price ranges, presumably because at low prices buyers are not very sensitive to price increases. Beyond a certain price, however, the demand becomes elastic, as such high prices drive away more and more buyers. So the elasticity depends on the price range we are discussing. In the real world, when we say that the demand for a product is elastic or inelastic, we are implicitly referring to the price range around its *present actual price*.

Real-World Elasticity

Elasticity of demand is a very important factor in many business and economic decisions. One obvious area is that of *business pricing policies* since the elasticity of demand will determine whether a price change will increase or reduce the firm's total revenue. Suppose, for instance, that the Canmore Ice Turkeys hockey team is presently pricing tickets to its games at an average price of $4 each, and that average ticket sales per game are 2400, which is well below the arena's capacity of 3000. Should the Ice Turkeys' management seek to increase ticket sales to 3000 and fill the arena for their games? The answer is not as simple as it seems if increasing attendance requires the kind of price reductions shown in the demand schedule in Table 4-4. If the demand for tickets is as shown, ticket prices will have to be cut to $3 to lure 3000 people to support the Ice Turkeys—a price that would *reduce* the club's total revenue by $600 per game, or more than 6 percent.

TABLE 4-4 Hypothetical Demand Schedule for Tickets to Canmore Ice Turkeys' Home Games

Average Price per Ticket	Quantity of Tickets Demanded per Game	Total Revenue per Game
$3	3000	$ 9000
4	2400	9600
5	2000	10 000
6	1650	9900

In fact, the schedule indicates that, financially, the Ice Turkeys would be better off if they *raised* the ticket price to $5, as the loss of sales would be more than offset by the higher price per ticket. Even at a price of $6 per ticket, there are still enough die-hard Ice Turkeys fans to make a nearly half-empty arena more profitable for the club than one with 2400 fans paying $4 each.

On the other hand, suppose the demand schedule is as shown in Table 4-5. In this case, it would pay the club to *reduce* the ticket price. A price reduction would increase total revenue as well as attendance, whereas price increases would have the opposite effect.

Obviously, the Ice Turkeys' management would like to know the elasticity of the demand for their tickets. However, in the real world, sellers

TABLE 4-5 Another Hypothetical Demand Schedule for Tickets to Canmore Ice Turkeys' Home Games

Average Price per Ticket	Quantity of Tickets Demanded per Game	Total Revenue per Game
$3.25	3000	$9750
4.00	2400	9600
5.00	1900	9500
6.00	1500	9000

do not have neat and precise demand schedules to guide them in their pricing decisions. While the market research departments of larger corporations may expend considerable effort in attempts to estimate the elasticity of demand for their products,[3] many smaller businesses operate on a trial-and-error basis, gaining a rough idea of the elasticity of demand by testing the market with small price increases or reductions. But this lack of a reliable method for determining elasticity of demand does not mean that sellers operate in the dark in their pricing decisions. Large corporations might sense that their position in the market is so dominant that the demand for their product is quite inelastic. And small retailers sense that if their prices rise above those of their competitors, the demand for their products will prove to be quite elastic. For similar reasons, discount retailers operate on the basis that at least a certain segment of consumers is quite sensitive to prices.

In a similar way, elasticity of demand influences the *ability of workers to increase their wages*. For instance, the demand for certain highly skilled workers, such as computer programmers, is inelastic. Such work has to be done, and there is no alternative way of doing it. Consequently, such workers are in an excellent position to bargain for higher wages—which they do. By contrast, people in the lawn-mowing industry probably face a more elastic demand since their service is not essential and buyers have the alternative of mowing their own lawns. As a result, the demand for lawn mowing would be more elastic, making it more difficult for people who mow lawns to raise their prices and incomes.

Elasticity of demand is also an important consideration underlying the *taxation policies* of governments. Three of the most heavily taxed products are alcohol, tobacco, and gasoline. Moral, health, and ecological considerations aside, a major reason for these products being singled out for exceptionally high taxes is that the demand for all three is inelastic: sales (and tax

---

3. Usually, the elasticity is expressed numerically as a **coefficient of elasticity**. For instance, a coefficient of 1.2 means that a 1-percent increase in price causes a 1.2-percent reduction in quantity demanded, while a coefficient of 0.4 means that if the price rises 1 percent, quantity demanded declines only 0.4 percent. Demand is *elastic* if the coefficient is greater than 1.0 and *inelastic* if the coefficient is less than 1.0. For example, the coefficient of elasticity for food has been estimated at 0.4, while for durable goods the coefficient has been estimated at 1.1.

coefficient of elasticity
The percentage change in quantity demanded that results from a 1-percent change in price.

revenues) hold up quite well even after tax increases have raised these products' prices considerably. There is little point in imposing heavy taxes on products whose demand is elastic as sales would fall drastically, devastating those industries (not to mention reducing government tax revenues).

Elasticity of demand is also a factor underlying certain social problems, a good example of which is the low incomes of many farmers over the years. Farmers have advanced technologically, raising productivity and the total output of farm products, but most still find themselves in a difficult position economically. While the increased output has depressed farm prices, the lower prices have not led to increased sales of farm products because the demand for food is inelastic: people do not buy much more food just because it is a bargain. Farmers receive lower prices for their crops, but are unable to sell more crops to offset the lower prices, leaving them with low incomes. Largely as a result of these problems, many groups of farmers have had to rely upon various types of government programs to support their prices and/or incomes, as we will examine in Chapters 9 and 15.

Conclusion

This chapter has considered demand—the first part of the demand-and-supply process that determines prices in markets. In Chapter 5 we will consider supply, and how supply and demand interact to determine prices.

Chapter Summary

1. A demand schedule or curve reflects the fact that, as the price of a good or service increases, the quantity demanded generally decreases, other things being equal. (L.O. 1)

2. If consumer tastes, incomes, or expectations change, or the prices of other products change, the demand for a product will increase (in which case the curve shifts to the right) or decrease (in which case the demand curve shifts to the left). (L.O. 2)

3. If buyers can do without a product or find a close substitute, a price increase will cause the seller's total sales revenue to fall, and demand will be elastic. (L.O. 3, 4, 5)

4. If buyers cannot or will not do without a product and cannot find a close substitute, a price increase will cause the seller's total sales revenue to rise, and demand will be inelastic. (L.O. 3, 4, 5)

Questions

1. State how each of the following would affect the demand curve for steak:

(a) increases in family income

(b) a decrease in the prices of pork and chicken

(c) medical research showing that eating red meat increases the risk of certain health problems

(d) reports that a railway strike may interrupt shipments of beef to your market area

(e) an increase in the price of steak

2. In recent years, the high value of the Japanese yen has caused the price of cars made in Japan to increase. How would this development affect the demand curve for cars made in North America?

3. For each of the following pairs of goods, state which one of the pair has the more *elastic* demand, and state the reason for your choice.

(a) air conditioners/furnaces

(b) new automobiles/licences for automobiles

(c) telephone service/electricity

(d) beef/meat in general

4. Explain whether each of the following will make the demand for the product or service involved more elastic or more inelastic, and *why* it would do so.

(a) Rising consumer incomes should make the demand for restaurant dinners more _____.

(b) At Christmas, the demand for turkey should become more

_____.

(c) The opening of a new pizzeria in town would make the demand for the existing pizzerias' products more _____.

(d) The use of freezers in more homes should make the demand for foods that can be frozen more _____.

5. Place the following in order of elasticity of demand, the most elastic coming first.

____ chocolate ice cream

____ dairy products

____ Neilson's chocolate ice cream

____ ice cream

6. For the 2002–03 season, the Toronto Maple Leafs, already the team with the highest ticket prices in the National Hockey League, increased ticket prices for the fifth consecutive year. The most expensive tickets increased to $175, while the cheapest seats increased to $35 apiece. The Leafs last won the Stanley Cup in 1967.

(a) What makes it possible for the Maple Leafs to charge such high prices and to increase them even further?

(b) Could a team such as the Edmonton Oilers do the same thing? Why or why not?

(c) Could a team such as the Los Angeles Kings do the same thing? Why or why not?

7. In the winter, would Canadians' demand for vacation packages to the Caribbean become more elastic or more inelastic? Why?

8. A customer is about to buy four shirts at $20 each. When she finds that they have just gone on sale for $15, she buys five shirts instead. Is her demand for these shirts elastic or inelastic?

9. It has been estimated that a 10-percent increase in the price of tobacco leads to a reduction in consumption of 3 percent to 4 percent for adults and about 8 percent for youths. What explains the difference in elasticity of demand for the two groups?

10. If you were selling a product with an *inelastic* demand, what would you emphasize and not emphasize in your advertising?

11. If you were selling a product with an *elastic* demand, what would you emphasize in your advertising?

12. "The dilemma posed by the demand curve is that, to increase *sales*, you must lower your *price*. This means that you will have to charge *less* to some buyers than they would have been prepared to pay, thus forgoing some sales revenue." Is there any way for a seller to get around this dilemma?

13. Many economists (and merchandisers) believe that the demand curve for some products is the type of curve shown in the following graph rather than the simple downward-sloping demand curve discussed in Part A of this chapter.

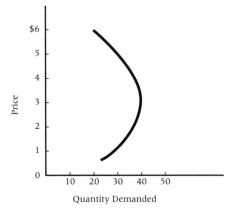

(a) What is the relationship between price and quantity demanded as shown by this curve?

(b) What could explain this peculiar type of consumer behaviour?

(c) How could merchandisers use this type of consumer behaviour to their advantage?

APPENDIX 4A

Graphs as Tools

In economics, graphs are frequently used, not only to illustrate statistical data but also as tools of analysis. This appendix is intended to introduce students who are not familiar with graphs to the types of graphs we will use in the remainder of this text.

The simplest and most common graph, and the one with which most people are quite familiar, is the *historical series graph*, which shows the behaviour of a statistic over a period of time. Figure 4A-1 is an example of such a graph. It shows the fluctuations in

FIGURE 4A-1 Historical Series Graph

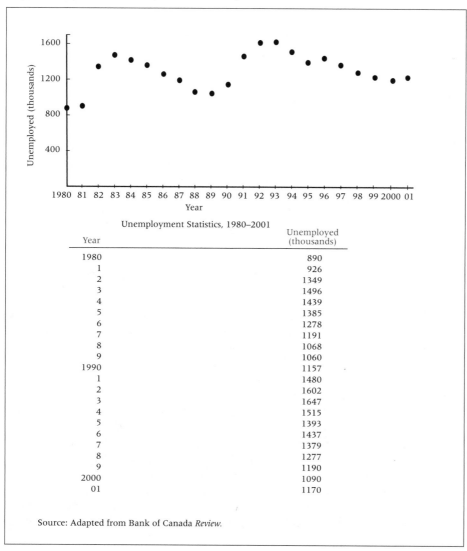

Unemployment Statistics, 1980–2001

Year	Unemployed (thousands)
1980	890
1	926
2	1349
3	1496
4	1439
5	1385
6	1278
7	1191
8	1068
9	1060
1990	1157
1	1480
2	1602
3	1647
4	1515
5	1393
6	1437
7	1379
8	1277
9	1190
2000	1090
01	1170

Source: Adapted from Bank of Canada *Review*.

the number of Canadians unemployed in each year from 1980 to 2001.

The actual statistics on which the graph is based are shown in the table below the graph. Since we have only one figure for each year, only the dots can be drawn on the graph with certainty. However, to allow the graph to give us a better visual presentation of the trends it shows, we usually join the dots together as a line, as shown in Figure 4A-2. Because such a time series graph simply describes a trend in a visual manner, it can be called a *descriptive graph*.

There is, however, another type of graph that we use in economics, particularly in microeconomics. Such a graph partly *describes* a situation, but can also be used to help to *analyze* the situation. Suppose that we wish to show how many coats Kathy's Coat Shop could sell at various prices. This information could be shown in a *table*, as in the first part of Figure 4A-3. This table tells us that at low

FIGURE 4A-2 Descriptive Graph

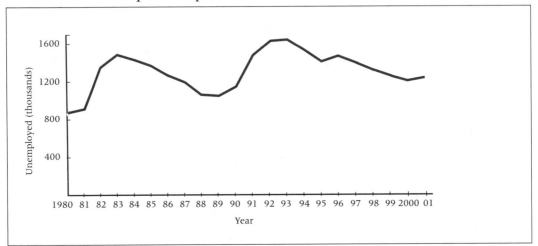

prices, Kathy can sell more coats per week than she can sell at higher prices. The same information can also be shown on a graph, as in the second part of Figure 4A-3. This graph shows the same information as the table does, but this graph shows the information visually. (Again, we have only the five specific pieces of information as shown by the dots, but have joined the dots together as a line to provide a better visual presentation of the information.)

It is important to understand the nature of graphs such as the one in Figure 4A-3, because it is quite different from graphs such as the one in Figure 4A-2. Figure 4A-2 shows the behaviour of unemployment *over a period of time*—the 1980–2001 period, as shown on the horizontal axis. Figure 4A-3, by contrast, shows the relationship between the price of coats and coat sales *at a particular point in time* (January 2003 in our example). As time changes and the behaviour of buyers changes, so will this relationship change—for instance, in July we would expect coat sales to be much lower at each price shown on the graph.

The most important function of graphs such as the one in Figure 4A-3 is to show the relationship between two variables—the price

FIGURE 4A-3　Analytical Table and Graph

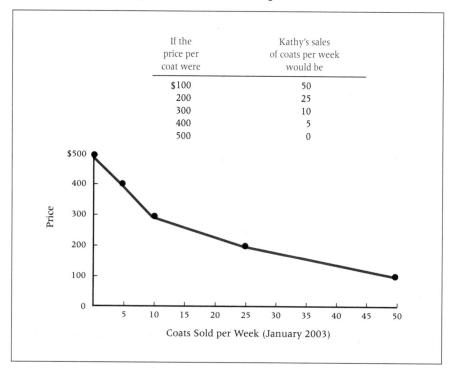

If the price per coat were	Kathy's sales of coats per week would be
$100	50
200	25
300	10
400	5
500	0

of coats (on the vertical axis) and sales of coats (on the horizontal axis). The two basic types of relationships that can be shown on such a graph are *inverse* and *direct*. Figure 4A-4 shows an inverse relationship—the higher the price goes, the lower the sales go and vice versa. When higher amounts of one variable are associated with lower amounts of the other variable in this way, the line on the graph slopes down to the right, and we say that the two variables are *inversely related.*

Conversely, if higher quantities of one variable are associated with higher quantities of the other, the two variables are said to be *directly related.* An example of a direct relationship in economics would be the relationship between the wage rate offered for part-time student help by a college's athletic department and the number of hours of

work offered by students—the higher the wage rate, the greater the number of hours the students will be prepared to work. Such a relationship is shown in Figure 4A-5.

Finally, while graphs such as Figure 4A-4 and 4A-5 can describe a relationship between two variables, they can also help to analyze, or explain, that relationship. That is, the graph can portray a *cause-and-effect relationship* between two variables such as the price of coats and sales of coats. If Kathy raises her price from $200 to $300, the increase will *cause* sales to decline from 25 coats to 10 coats per week. Because they can be used to analyze relationships in this way, graphs such as Figure 4A-4 and Figure 4A-5 are sometimes referred to as *analytical graphs*, as distinct from the simpler descriptive graphs, such as Figure 4A-3.

FIGURE 4A-4 An Inverse Relationship

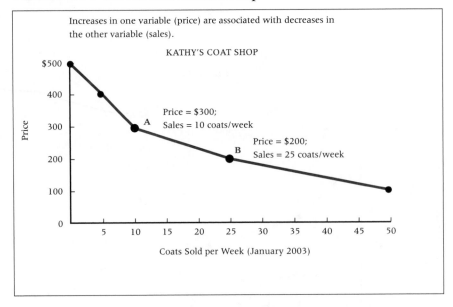

Increases in one variable (price) are associated with decreases in the other variable (sales).

KATHY'S COAT SHOP

A Price = $300;
   Sales = 10 coats/week

B Price = $200;
   Sales = 25 coats/week

Coats Sold per Week (January 2003)

FIGURE 4A-5 A Direct Relationship Between Two Variables

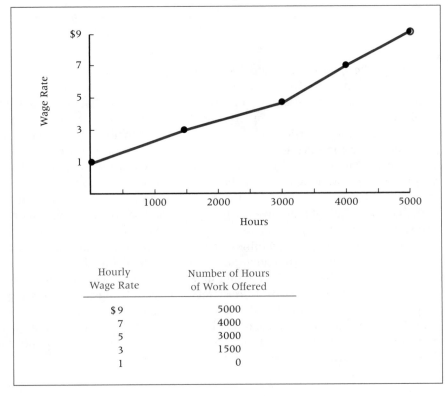

Hourly Wage Rate	Number of Hours of Work Offered
$9	5000
7	4000
5	3000
3	1500
1	0

Chapter 5

The Supply Side of Markets

Learning Objectives

After studying this chapter, you should be able to:

1. Differentiate between the nature of supply in competitive and concentrated industries, using the terms *price-taker*, *price-maker*, and *market power* in your explanation.

2. Draw a supply curve for a product from a supply schedule showing the quantity supplied at various prices.

3. Explain whether a given event would increase or decrease the supply of a particular product, and show how this would affect the supply curve.

4. Explain the difference between *elastic* and *inelastic* supply.

5. Determine whether a given event would make the supply of an item more elastic or more inelastic.

6. Draw the demand and supply curves for an item and show the equilibrium price and quantity, given the demand schedule and the supply schedule for that item.

FIGURE 5-1 An Illustration of a Market

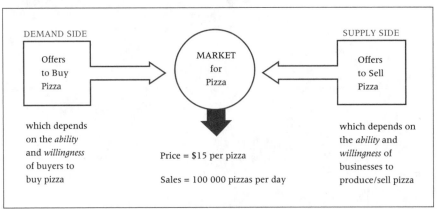

As we have seen, markets consist of:

- a demand side, or offers by buyers to purchase products, and
- a supply side, or offers by sellers to sell products, as shown in Figure 5-1.

In Chapter 4, we saw how, on the demand side of the market, the demand for particular products is determined by the ability and willingness of buyers to *purchase* those products. In this chapter, we will consider the supply side of markets and factors that affect the ability and willingness of businesses to *produce and sell* particular goods and services.

Competitive Conditions

Before we examine how demand and supply interact to determine prices, we must take a closer look at the supply side of the market—the right panel of Figure 5-1. In particular, we need to examine how different types of industries and firms[1] are organized and operate.

As we saw in Chapter 3, the process that we call "supply" takes place under different conditions. Some industries have many small firms, while other industries are dominated by a few large firms, and in a few markets there is only one producer (a monopoly). These different conditions—which economists refer to as **market structures**—have a significant effect on the supply of various products. There is a great deal of difference between the ways in which a small vegetable farmer and a huge automobile manufacturer make their decisions as to how much output to produce and what price to charge for it.

market structure Term used to describe the organization and nature of a market or an industry, particularly whether it is competitive or concentrated in nature.

---

1. The term "firm" refers to a business; the term "industry" refers to the group of business firms producing a particular product or service. For example, Ford is one *firm* in the North American automobile *industry*.

Competitive Industries

One basic market structure consists of what economists call **competitive industries**. Competitive industries have the following two basic characteristics:

* they consist of a large number of small firms, and
* it is easy for new firms to enter (and exit) the industry.

competitive industry An industry that consists of many small firms and is easily entered by new competitors.

As a result, competition among producers is strong, and the strong competition holds prices and profits down to relatively low levels. If prices and profits *were* to increase to higher levels, new producers would be attracted into the industry, which would increase supply and push prices and profits back downward. While this situation is not to the advantage of the producers in the industry, they are unable to do anything about it—because they are so numerous, it is impossible for them to get together and agree to restrict competition among themselves. Examples of competitive industries include much of the small business sector described in Chapter 3, such as small-scale retail stores, many small agricultural producers, small-scale manufacturing, and many service industries, such as restaurants, barbershops, repair shops, home renovations, lawn care, and so on.

Figure 5-2 summarizes and illustrates the characteristics of competitive industries. In the left panel of the diagram, each circle represents one of the many firms in a competitive industry. The arrow pointing down into the industry shows the "births" of newly established firms entering the industry. The arrow at the bottom illustrates another aspect of a competitive industry—the "deaths" of some firms that fail to survive in such a competitive environment.

Concentrated Industries

Not all industries are competitive in this sense—in some industries, a few large firms dominate the market. In these industries, it is much more difficult for newcomers to enter the market, due to obstacles such as the amount of capital required and the established position of the existing firms in the market. Such obstacles put these established firms at a greater advantage than firms in competitive industries. First, because they are few in number, the dominant firms will be in a better position to agree among themselves not to compete vigorously on prices. As a result, profits in such **concentrated industries** are often higher than those in competitive industries. Second, because it is so difficult for new firms to enter the industry, there is much less risk that the industry's high profits will attract newcomers who would increase competition and erode their high profits. Examples of concentrated industries include banking, steel, breweries, and petroleum refining, as well as government monopolies such as Canada Post.

concentrated industry An industry that is dominated by a few large firms and is not easily entered by new competitors.

FIGURE 5-2 Characteristics of Competitive and
Concentrated Industries

Competitive Industries	*Concentrated Industries*
Producers have very little control over prices and profits	Producers are sometimes in a better position to influence prices and profits
because:	*because:*
1. there are many small firms in the industry; and 2. it is easy for new firms to enter (and exit) the industry;	1. there are only a few firms in the industry; and 2. it is difficult for new firms to enter;

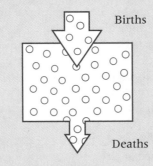 Births

Deaths

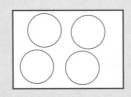

so that:	*so that:*
the producers are unable to control the supply—if profits become high, new firms start up, causing supply to rise and prices and profits to fall;	existing producers may be able to reach agreements to limit supply and increase prices;
with the result that:	*with the result that:*
prices and profits tend to be held down to low levels.	prices and profits tend to be maintained at above-competitive levels.

The panel on the right side of Figure 5-2 shows the characteristics of concentrated industries. The industry is dominated by a few large firms, and there are few if any "births" of new entrants or "deaths" of firms.

Price-Makers, Market Power, and Price-Takers

price-maker Term used to describe the position of the dominant firm(s) in a concentrated industry, which can influence the price of the product.

market power The ability to raise one's prices; usually associated with a dominant or monopolistic position in the market.

Prices are determined by demand and supply. If a group of producers/sellers in a "concentrated" industry can restrict the supply of their product by agreeing to restrict their production of it, they can increase its price. Sellers who possess the ability to influence the supply of their products are called **price-makers**, because they have the ability to determine (or at least influence) the price of the product. Another way of describing this situation is to say that such producers have **market power**. In this way, organized groups have been able to maintain high price levels, at various times, for a wide variety of products, including diamonds, oil, coffee, and eggs.

By contrast, in an industry that is "competitive," there are many disorganized sellers and new producers can enter the industry easily, which makes it impossible for producers to control the supply or the price. Such producers are described as **price-takers**, because the market, not the producers, determines the price, and each producer must accept that price. Since each individual producer cannot control the price, the economic incentive is for each producer to produce as much as possible, as efficiently as possible, and sell it for the going price.

Because the production and pricing decisions associated with "supply" in concentrated industries are different from those in competitive industries, we will consider the two separately. In this chapter, our first look at supply will be limited to the case of competitive industries, which includes a wide range of industries, from farming to small-scale manufacturers to a vast array of services such as restaurants, home repair contractors, barbershops, and so on. Later, in Chapter 7, we will consider the case of concentrated industries.

price-taker Term used to describe the position of the individual small firm in a competitive industry, which is unable to influence the price of its product and is forced to accept (take) whatever price is determined in the market.

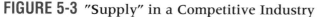

Supply Under Competitive Conditions

As a general rule, in a competitive industry, an increase in the *price* of the product will lead to an increase in the *quantity supplied*. By making it more profitable to produce the product, higher prices will generate higher output by

- leading existing firms to increase their output, and also
- attracting new firms into the industry, which will also increase output.

This important characteristic of competitive industries is illustrated in Figure 5-3, in which a price increase from $6 to $8 causes the quantity supplied (offered for sale) to increase from 50 000 units per week to 80 000 units per week.

FIGURE 5-3 "Supply" in a Competitive Industry

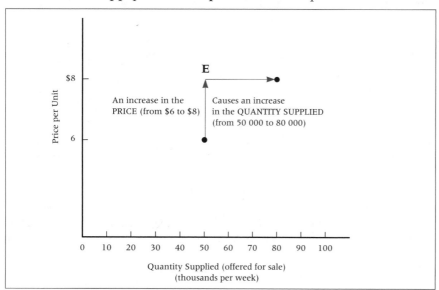

Finally, it should be clarified that the concept of *supply* does not refer to the physical *quantity* of a product in existence but rather to the quantity of it that is *offered for sale*. For instance, the "supply" of used 10-speed bicycles in a city is not the 300 000 such bicycles that *exist* there but rather the number that would be *offered for sale* at various possible prices. And the 1000 used 10-speed bicycles that are presently on the market (offered for sale) is the *quantity supplied* at the current market price of, say, $85.

Back to the Pizza Example

Now let's revisit the market for pizza that we used in Chapter 4 to illustrate the demand side of markets. Suppose that the supply side of the pizza market is a "competitive" industry consisting of a large number of pizzerias (and their suppliers) in competition with each other, and that it is easy to enter the industry. Now suppose that pizza prices *increase*. What effect will this increase have on the amount of pizza offered for sale?

We should expect the higher prices to induce producers to offer *more* pizzas for sale by making it more profitable to sell pizzas. Existing pizzerias will increase their output, and new pizzerias will start up, attracted by the industry's higher profits.

supply schedule A table depicting the relationship between the price of a product and the quantity supplied (offered for sale).

supply curve A graphical representation of a supply schedule.

The supply of pizzas is illustrated in the **supply schedule** in Table 5-1, and graphically in a **supply curve** in Figure 5-4. Both the supply schedule and the supply curve reflect the fundamental fact that we have stressed: in a competitive market, increases in price will tend to cause increases in the quantity that producers will supply. At a price of $6 per pizza, no one could make a profit selling pizza. But higher prices would cause increasing amounts to be produced and offered for sale. At very high prices such as $20 per pizza, the quantity of pizzas supplied would increase greatly.

TABLE 5-1 Supply Schedule for Pizza in Cantown, March 2003

If the price per pizza were	The quantity supplied (offered for sale) would be
$20	100 000
16	80 000
12	50 000
8	20 000
6	0

As with demand, the concept of supply includes the entire supply schedule or curve—that is, "supply" refers to the amounts that would be offered for sale at every possible price. If the actual price were $12 per pizza and the actual quantity supplied were 50 000 pizzas, the supply would not

FIGURE 5-4 Supply Curve for Pizza in Cantown, March 2003

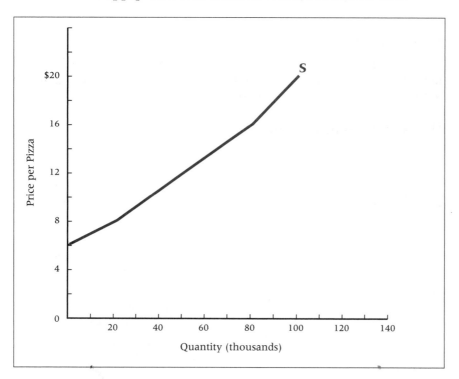

just be 50 000 pizzas—supply also includes the amounts that *would have been offered* for sale if the price had been higher or lower. See the "In the News" box below for a look at the relationship between price and supply.

IN THE **NEWS**   Price and Supply

The market for wheat provides an excellent illustration of how price affects the quantity supplied. When wheat prices were very low in the 1980s, Western Canadian farmers reduced their production of wheat in favour of other crops. However, when wheat prices increased again in the mid-1990s, farmers increased their planting of wheat again. In a similar way higher oil prices prompt increases in oil exploration and development, while declining prices have the opposite effect.

Question

1.   In what way can these events be considered to be illustrations of markets working effectively?

Changes in Supply

An Increase in Supply

In Chapter 4, we saw that, if demand increased, the demand curve shifted to the right. In a similar way, increases in supply cause the supply curve to shift to the right, as shown by the new supply curve S_1 in Figure 5-5.

FIGURE 5-5 An Increase in Supply

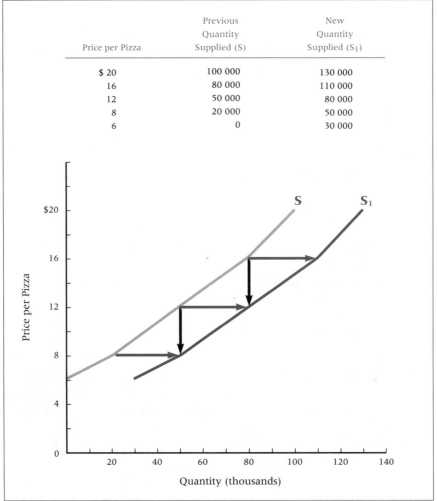

Price per Pizza	Previous Quantity Supplied (S)	New Quantity Supplied (S_1)
$ 20	100 000	130 000
16	80 000	110 000
12	50 000	80 000
8	20 000	50 000
6	0	30 000

There are two ways of looking at the changes shown in Figure 5-5:

(a) *Sellers are offering more pizza for sale.* The supply schedule at the top of Figure 5-5 shows that at a price of $20, sellers used to offer 100 000 pizzas for sale, but will now put 130 000 pizzas on the market; at a price of $16, 110 000 pizzas will be offered for sale as compared to 80 000 pizzas before, and so on. At every possible price, sellers are offering 30 000 more pizzas for sale than they did before. On the graph, this relationship is shown by the shift of the supply curve to the right, to its new location, as shown by the new curve S_1. The horizontal arrows pointing in the direction of higher output show this change.

(b) *Sellers are willing to sell pizza at lower prices.* The supply schedule shows that when 80 000 pizzas are offered for sale, sellers used to charge $16 for each pizza, but will now charge only $12. Similarly, for 50 000 pizzas, they used to charge $12, but now their price is $8. On the graph, the vertical arrows pointing in the direction of lower prices show this change.

Causes of Increased Supply

What could *cause* producers to offer more pizzas for sale, and at a lower price than before? One likely reason is *an increase in efficiency*, which would enable producers to *produce more pizza*. Increased efficiency would also *reduce production costs per pizza*, enabling producers to offer pizza for sale at a *lower price* than before. These two effects of increased efficiency are shown in Figure 5-6.

Technology often generates increases in supply both by making it possible to produce more of a product and by reducing production costs per unit. Technology was an especially strong force in increasing productivity in various industries in the period following the mid-1990s.

FIGURE 5-6 Higher Efficiency as a Cause of Increased Supply

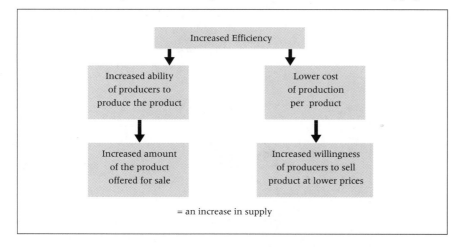

There are various other possible causes of an increase in supply. If *new producers* (either domestic or foreign) were to enter the market, the increased *competition* would bring both a higher supply of the product and lower prices, as has happened recently with freer trade between nations. If the government paid *subsidies* to producers such as public transit commissions, they could afford to expand and charge lower prices, both of which represent an increase in supply. In the case of farm products, weather is a factor as a *good harvest* causes an increase in supply. *Expectations* can also affect supply—if higher sales and profits were expected in the near future, existing producers might produce more, and new producers might enter the industry.

In general, anything that increases the ability and willingness of producers to offer more of their product for sale and/or reduce prices will cause an increase in supply. Such factors include the following:

*   increases in efficiency,

*   improvements in technology,

*   increased competition, such as from new firms or imports,

*   subsidies from governments,

*   weather, in the case of agricultural products, and

*   producers' expectations.

A Decrease in Supply

A decrease in supply is shown in Figure 5-7. This figure shows the opposite of everything that is covered in the previous section, in terms of what happens and the causes of these changes.

FIGURE 5-7 A Decrease in Supply

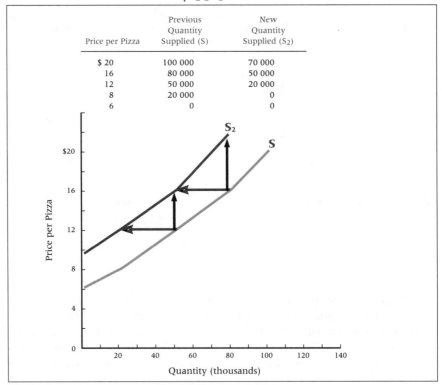

Price per Pizza	Previous Quantity Supplied (S)	New Quantity Supplied (S₂)
$ 20	100 000	70 000
16	80 000	50 000
12	50 000	20 000
8	20 000	0
6	0	0

As the supply schedule shows, less pizza is offered for sale at each possible price. This relationship is shown on the graph by the horizontal arrows pointing in the direction of lower output. Also, as the supply schedule and the vertical arrows show, sellers will only sell their pizza at higher prices than before. As a reflection of these changes, the supply curve shifts to the left, to its new location S_2.

Causes of Decreased Supply

Such a decrease in supply would be caused by the same factors that cause an increase in supply, but operating in the opposite direction. For instance, a *decrease in efficiency* in the industry would decrease supply by reducing the amount produced and offered for sale and by increasing production costs per unit of the product and thus prices, as shown in Figure 5-8. Also, *higher production costs* (for labour or materials) would push the supply curve upward to S_2 in Figure 5-7, by forcing producers to increase their prices.

FIGURE 5-8 Lower Efficiency as a Cause of Decreased Supply

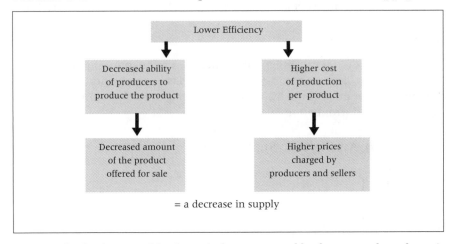

A *reduction in competition* in an industry, caused by factors such as the exit of some firms or government restrictions on imports, would cause a decrease in supply. *Taxes* can decrease supply, by forcing producers to require higher prices for their products (for instance, cigarettes), and may even reduce their ability to produce as much. *Government regulations* can also decrease supply; for example, some agricultural marketing boards can actually limit how much farmers produce. In the case of farming, bad weather will decrease the supply of affected crops. And *expectations* can generate a decrease in supply. If lower sales and profits were expected, supply might be reduced as firms cut back on output or as some of them even leave the industry.

In general, anything that reduces the ability and/or willingness of producers to produce the product and/or increases their production costs will reduce the supply of the product, and shift the supply curve to the left or upward. These factors include the following:

- reductions in efficiency and increases in production costs per unit,
- reductions in competition, such as restrictions on imports or firms leaving the industry,
- taxes on the product or the producers,
- government regulations that limit output and/or increase costs per unit, and
- producers' expectations.

Elasticity of Supply

We have seen that, as the price of a product produced in a competitive industry rises, the quantity supplied will rise. What we must consider now is the question of *how much* the quantity supplied will rise in response to a higher price. In some cases, the higher price will cause prompt and large increases in the quantity supplied, while in other cases, even very large increases in price will not cause the quantity supplied to change significantly, at least in the short run.

Inelastic Supply

inelastic supply A situation in which quantity supplied does not increase readily when the price rises.

If rising prices do not cause significant increases in quantity supplied, supply is said to be **inelastic**. Figure 5-9 shows an inelastic supply: here, even a five-fold increase in price (from $2 to $10) only causes the quantity supplied to rise by one-half (from 40 to 60 units).

FIGURE 5-9 An Inelastic Supply Curve

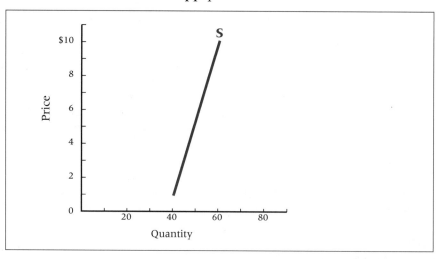

Such a high degree of inelasticity usually means that there are obstacles to increasing production of the product, at least in the short run. These obstacles could include shortages of labour or materials, limited plant capacity, or rising costs such as overtime wage rates. For instance, the supply of strawberries in January would be inelastic—while an increased volume of them could be obtained, the amount would be limited and the cost of importing them over long distances would add greatly to their cost.

The most extreme case of inelasticity of supply—*perfectly inelastic supply*—is illustrated in Figure 5-10: here, despite very large price increases, *no* increase in the amount offered for sale takes place. The best example of such a situation would be a unique item such as an original work of art—no matter how high the price goes, there can only be one of it.

FIGURE 5-10 A Perfectly Inelastic Supply Curve

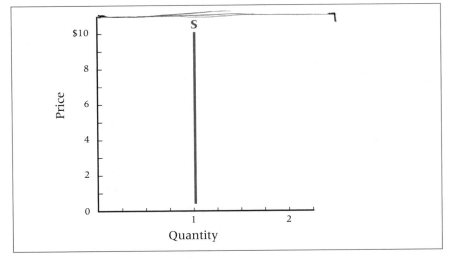

Elastic Supply

If an increase in price brings forth onto the market a large increase in the quantity supplied, supply is referred to as **elastic supply**.

Figure 5-11 shows an elastic supply curve. Here, tripling of the price (from $2 to $6) causes a fivefold increase in the quantity supplied (from 20 to 100). An example of such a situation could be the production of pencils or compact discs—with the machinery already in existence and the labour and materials readily available, it is a simple and low-cost matter to increase production of pencils or CDs if price increases warrant doing so.

elastic supply A situation in which the quantity supplied increases readily when the price rises.

Elasticity of Supply Over Time

Finally, as with elasticity of demand, elasticity of supply tends to increase with the passage of time. When the price of the product first increases, limited amounts of equipment or trained labour may make it impossible (or quite costly) to increase the quantity supplied by much for a while. However, given more time, producers can often overcome these obstacles by obtaining

FIGURE 5-11 An Elastic Supply Curve

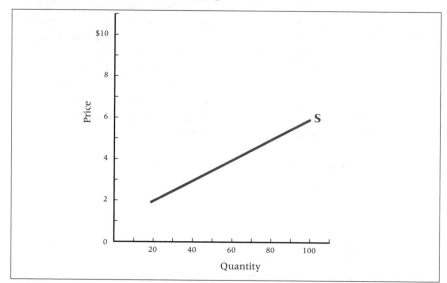

equipment and training workers to increase the quantity supplied in response to price increases. How elasticity of supply can change from the short run to the long run is illustrated in Figure 5-12, which shows the supply becoming much more elastic as time passes.

FIGURE 5-12 Elasticity of Supply in the Short Run and in the Long Run

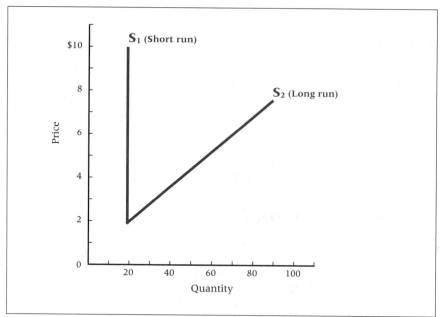

What is the actual difference between the "short run" and the "long run"? For the production of pencils or CDs, it may just be a matter of days before production can be increased significantly; for annual agricultural products, up to a year. For higher oil prices to stimulate increased exploration, development, and production of oil on a large scale, 10 to 15 years may be required.

The Market: Supply, Demand, and Prices

We have now examined both demand (in Chapter 4) and supply under competitive conditions (in this chapter); these two concepts are summarized in Table 5-2. We are now ready to consider how demand and supply interact, by combining them, as in Table 5-3.

TABLE 5-2 Supply and Demand Schedules for Pizza in Cantown, March 2003

DEMAND		SUPPLY	
The relationship between the price of the product and the number of units buyers will offer to buy		The relationship between the price of the product and the number of units producers will offer to sell	
Price per Pizza	*Quantity Demanded*	*Price per Pizza*	*Quantity Demanded*
$20	20 000	$20	100 000
16	30 000	16	80 000
12	50 000	12	50 000
8	80 000	8	20 000
4	120 000	4	0

As the supply and demand schedules in Table 5-3 show, the price of pizza will tend to stabilize at $12 each. This price is called the **equilibrium price**. It is not possible for the market to clear at any other level, because all other prices lead to either a shortage or a surplus, which would cause the price to change. For instance, at a price of $20, the quantity supplied exceeds the quantity demanded, generating a surplus of 80 000 pizzas on the market. Under these circumstances, competition among sellers will drive the price down toward the equilibrium level of $12. Similarly, prices below $12 discourage production but encourage demand, causing shortages on the market. As buyers compete for the limited supply, the price will be bid up toward the equilibrium level of $12. Only at a price of $12 are the actions of both buyers and sellers in harmony so that there is neither a surplus nor a shortage. As a result, the price will tend to settle at the equilibrium level of $12.

equilibrium price A price determined in the marketplace by the interaction of supply and demand.

TABLE 5-3 Supply and Demand Interacting to Determine the Price of Pizza in Cantown, March 2003

Price per pizza	Quantity Demanded	Quantity Supplied	Balance	Price Will Tend to
$20	20 000	100 000	Surplus of 80 000	Fall
16	30 000	80 000	Surplus of 50 000	Fall
12	50 000	50 000	No surplus/no shortage	Remain stable
8	80 000	20 000	Shortage of 60 000	Rise
4	120 000	0	Shortage of 120 000	Rise

The interaction of supply and demand can also be shown on a graph, as in Figure 5-13. On the graph the equilibrium price of $12 is determined by the intersection of the supply curve and the demand curve at the *equilibrium point* (E). The intersection of the curves also determines the quantity that will be bought (and sold), that is, the **equilibrium quantity** of 50 000 pizzas.

equilibrium quantity The quantity sold (bought) at the equilibrium price.

To summarize, the way in which supply and demand interact to determine the price of a product or service can be represented on a schedule such as Table 5-3, or on a graph such as Figure 5-13. Both the schedule and the graph depict the behaviour of buyers (demand) and sellers (supply) in the

FIGURE 5-13 Supply, Demand, and the Price of Pizza in Cantown, March 2003

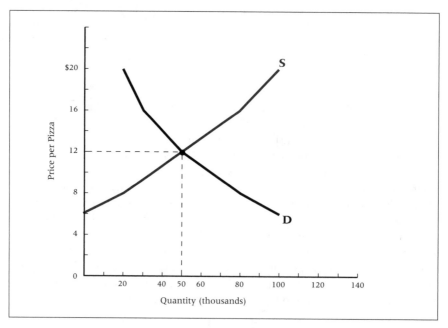

market for a particular good or service, and the equilibrium price and quantity that will emerge in that market.

Figure 5-13 is a very *static* representation of a market, showing the demand for and supply of pizza *at a particular point in time* (March 2003). In reality, however, markets are very *dynamic,* with constant changes in supply and demand occurring, causing continual changes in equilibrium prices and quantities. In effect, then, Figure 5-13 is a *snapshot* of a dynamic, changing situation at a particular point in time. In the next chapter, we will consider the more realistic situation of how markets change and adjust in response to changes in both supply and demand.

Chapter Summary

1. Competitive industries consist of many small firms and are easy to enter; in concentrated industries, a few large firms are dominant and it is difficult for new firms to start. (L.O. 1)

2. In competitive industries, the nature of supply is such that increases in the price of a product will cause increases in the quantity supplied. (L.O. 2)

3. Increases in supply will shift the supply curve to the right, while decreases in supply will shift the curve to the left. (L.O. 3)

4. If the quantity supplied does not increase significantly in response to a small increase in price, supply is *inelastic,* while supply is *elastic* if small price increases cause large increases in the quantity supplied. (L.O. 4)

5. In competitive markets, supply and demand interact freely to determine the equilibrium price and quantity, which will change as supply or demand changes. (L.O. 5)

Questions

1. State whether each of the following would cause the supply curve for shoes to shift to the right or to the left.

    (a) an increase in imports of shoes from South America

    (b) an increase in the cost of the materials from which shoes are made

    (c) large inventories of unsold shoes in the hands of retailers and wholesalers

    (d) new shoe-making equipment that increases the efficiency of manufacturers

2. At 8:00 p.m., one hour before closing, your local supermarket cuts the price of its fresh barbecued chickens by half. How does this affect the "supply" (supply curve) of barbecued chicken?

3. Which would be more inelastic:

    (a) the supply of crude oil or the supply of paper clips?

    (b) the supply of professional hockey players or the supply of retail clerks?

4. The following are the supply and demand schedules for candles.

Price	Quantity Demanded	Price	Quantity Supplied
$6	20	$6	50
5	40	5	40
4	60	4	30
3	80	3	20
2	100	2	10

(a) On a graph, draw the supply and demand curves for candles, and indicate the equilibrium price and quantity.

(b) Suppose that improvements in efficiency cause the supply of candles to increase by 30 at each price shown. Plot the new supply curve on the graph you drew in part (a) and indicate the new equilibrium price and quantity.

5. In the following graphs, the demand curves are identical and the equilibrium price is $2 in each case. However, the supply curves have different shapes.

(a) What might explain the different shapes of the two supply curves?

(b) How would this affect the price of the products if the demand were to increase? (Hint: Draw a new demand curve on each graph showing an identical increase in demand.)

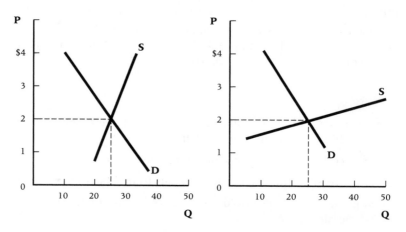

6. A good example of government subsidizing a service is *public transit*. In this case, subsidies keep public transit fares low with the objective of encouraging the public to use public transit in order to reduce automobile traffic congestion and pollution. These social benefits are the justification for using taxpayers' money to subsidize transit riders.

Another example of a subsidized public service is *college and university education*. How is post-secondary education subsidized, and what are the social benefits that the public is intended to derive from these subsidies?

Chapter 6

The Dynamics of
Competitive Markets

Learning Objectives

After studying this chapter, you should be able to:

1. Explain with the aid of a graph how a market will adjust to factors that cause an increase in demand, a decrease in demand, an increase in supply, and a decrease in supply.

2. Use a graph to illustrate and explain why a change in supply will have a larger effect on price if demand is inelastic rather than elastic.

3. Use a graph to illustrate and explain why a change in demand will have a larger effect on price if supply is inelastic rather than elastic.

4. Estimate the changes in demand and/or supply that are occurring in a market, given data on changes in price and sales, plus other market information.

5. Explain with the aid of a graph the effects on a market of a government price support that holds the price above its equilibrium level.

6. Explain with the aid of a graph the effects on a market of a government-imposed price control that holds the price below its equilibrium level.

In Chapter 5, we considered how supply and demand interact in competitive markets to determine equilibrium prices and quantities, using as our example the market for pizza, reproduced in Figure 6-1.

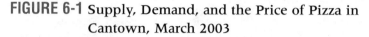

FIGURE 6-1 Supply, Demand, and the Price of Pizza in Cantown, March 2003

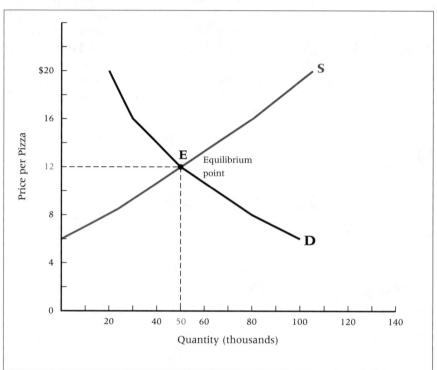

The equilibrium price ($12) and equilibrium quantity (50 000 pizzas) in Figure 6-1 must be interpreted carefully. They do not mean that the "proper" price is $12, or that the price will necessarily *stay* at $12. All they mean is that, given the behaviour of sellers (supply) and buyers (demand) *at that time* (March 2003), the equilibrium price will be $12. However, the behaviour of buyers and sellers does not remain static; rather, it continually changes. As a result, the supply and demand curves in Figure 6-1 are best viewed as a "snapshot" of a dynamic, changing situation. As supply or demand changes, the supply and demand curves will shift, causing changes in the equilibrium price and quantity. In the following sections, we will consider a few such changes, and in doing so, we will see how competitive markets actually operate.

Changes in Supply and Demand

An Increase in Demand

The demand curve in Figure 6-1 depicts buyer behaviour in March 2003. Suppose that a change in consumers' tastes leads to an increase in demand so that the demand curve shifts to the right, as shown in Figure 6-2. Assuming no change in supply, the new demand curve, labelled D_1, intersects the supply curve at a higher point, resulting in a higher equilibrium price of $14 per pizza. This higher price creates an incentive for pizza-makers to offer more pizzas for sale. As a result, there is an increase in quantity supplied, to 65 000 pizzas. So an increase in demand (without a change in supply) will cause increases in both the equilibrium price and quantity as the market responds to the higher demand.

FIGURE 6-2 An Increase in Demand

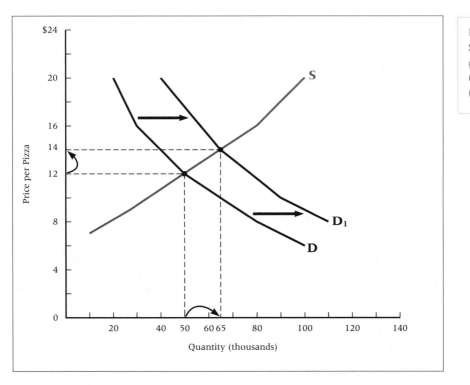

In 2002, golfers paid $235 for 18 holes of golf at Glen Abbey Golf Club in Oakville, Ontario.

A Decrease in Demand

Figure 6-3 shows the results of a decrease in demand for pizza, such as might occur if consumers switched to buying other types of food that had become more popular. As the graph shows, such a decrease in demand will shift the demand curve to the left (to D_2), causing the equilibrium price to decline (from $14 to $12), and leading pizza-makers to reduce the quantity supplied (from 65 000 pizzas to 50 000 pizzas). Thus, the market responds to a decrease in demand by reducing both the equilibrium price and quantity.

FIGURE 6-3 A Decrease in Demand

The decrease in the volume of passenger train service provides a good example of a long-term decrease in demand.

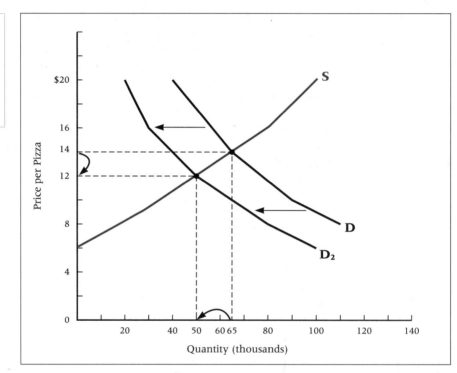

Quantity (thousands)

An Increase in Supply

Suppose that, for some reason such as the establishment of new pizzerias, the supply of pizzas increased. Such an increase in supply would cause the supply curve to shift to the right, as shown by curve S_1 in Figure 6-4. This increase in supply would decrease the equilibrium price from $12 to $9, and this price reduction would induce an increase in the quantity demanded, from 50 000 pizzas to 70 000 pizzas. Then the market's response to an increase in supply is to reduce the equilibrium price and increase the equilibrium quantity.

A Decrease in Supply

If factors such as increases in production costs led to a decrease in the supply of pizzas, the supply curve would shift to the left, as shown by curve S_2 in Figure 6-5. With the lower supply, the equilibrium price would increase from $12 to $14 and this price increase would induce a reduction in the quantity demanded from 50 000 pizzas to 40 000 pizzas. When the supply of a product

FIGURE 6-4 An Increase in Supply

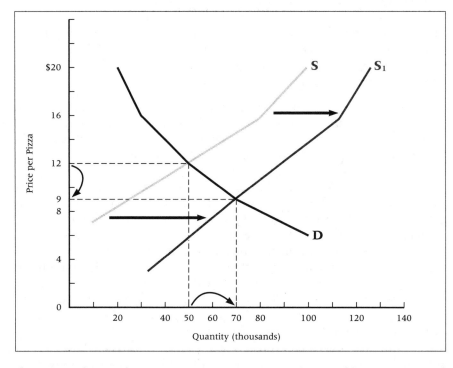

In 2001, excess production capacity and fierce competition in the computer chip industry led to price cuts as large as 30 percent at one time.

decreases, the market's response is to increase the equilibrium price and to reduce the equilibrium quantity.

FIGURE 6-5 A Decrease in Supply

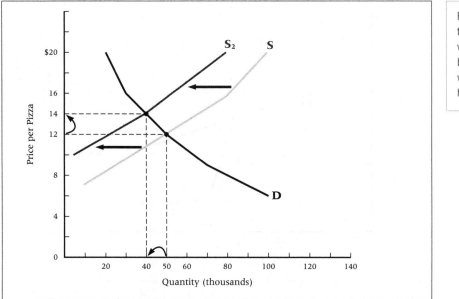

From 1994 to 1997, the price of coffee on world markets doubled due to bad weather that reduced harvests.

....

Elasticity

Elasticity—the responsiveness of buyers and sellers to changes in prices—greatly affects how markets respond to changes in supply and demand.

Elasticity of Demand

The importance of elasticity of demand is shown in Figure 6-6. When the market is faced with a reduction in supply, the supply curve shifts from S to S_1. If the demand for the product is *inelastic*, as shown by curve D, the equilibrium point shifts from E_1 to E_2, and the equilibrium price rises a great deal, from $5 to $8. The price increase is so large because demand is inelastic—buyers are unable or unwilling to substitute or do without this product, so they bid actively for the reduced supply, forcing the price up sharply. If, on the other hand, the demand were *elastic*, as shown by curve D_1, the situation would be quite different, with the equilibrium point shifting to E_3 instead of E_2. The same reduction in supply would cause a much smaller price increase, to only $6, because the demand is elastic—since buyers are able to substitute for this product or do without it, they do not bid up its price nearly as much when it is in short supply. So how a change in supply will affect price depends to a great extent on the elasticity of demand—the more inelastic demand is, the larger the price changes will be.

FIGURE 6-6 How Elasticity of Demand Affects Price Changes

In the market for crude oil, inelastic demand is a major contributor to the sharp fluctuations in prices that often occur.

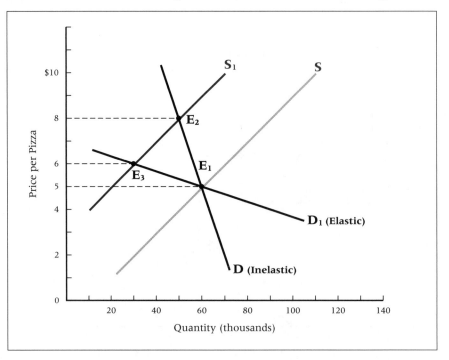

Elasticity of Supply

Elasticity of supply also has a large effect on how changes in demand affect prices (see the "In the News" box on the following page for an interesting example). Figure 6-7 shows the effect of an increase in demand (from curve D to D_1) on the price of the product when supply is inelastic and when supply is elastic. If supply is perfectly inelastic, as shown by curve S, the increase in demand causes the equilibrium point to shift from E_1 to E_2 and the price to increase greatly from $5 to $8. An example of such an inelastic supply would be an agricultural product: the harvest (60 000 units) is in, and the quantity supplied cannot be increased beyond 60 000 units, regardless of how high demand and prices go. However, if the supply had been elastic, as shown by curve S_1, the equilibrium point would have shifted to E_3 instead of E_2 so that the price increase would have been much smaller, rising to only $6. The reason for the smaller price increase is that supply is elastic—as the price rises, producers increase the quantity supplied, holding the price increase down. To continue the example of the agricultural product, curve S_1 could represent the supply curve after a period of one year, when farmers have had time to respond to the $8 price by planting and harvesting more of the product. Generally, price fluctuations are likely to be most extreme in the short run, when supply is inelastic, and more moderate over the longer run, when supply has had sufficient time to become more elastic.

> **Space tourists**
> The first two "space tourists" each paid US$20 million for a week in space. Plans were underway to offer a one-hour economy excursion package for only $100 000 sometime after 2004.

FIGURE 6-7 How Elasticity of Supply Affects Price Changes

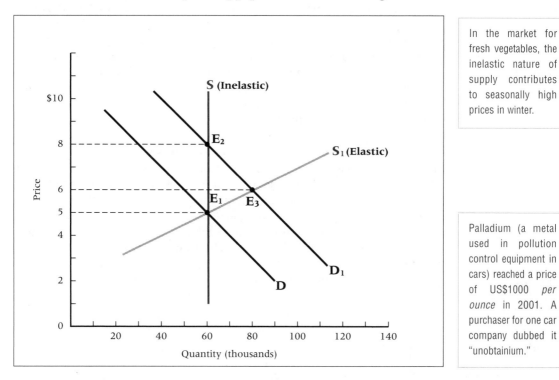

> In the market for fresh vegetables, the inelastic nature of supply contributes to seasonally high prices in winter.

> Palladium (a metal used in pollution control equipment in cars) reached a price of US$1000 *per ounce* in 2001. A purchaser for one car company dubbed it "unobtainium."

IN THE **NEWS**   The Market for World Series Tickets

For World Series games, ticket prices are approximately triple the prices for the same seats during the regular season. These price increases are decided by Major League Baseball (the Commissioner's Office), in consultation with the players' association.

Questions

1. Why do prices rise so much for post-season games? Consider not only changes on the demand side of this market but also the nature of the supply side. Draw a graph of the market, showing the demand and the supply for regular-season games, and how the market changes during the play-offs.

2. Do you agree with those who say that it is "highway robbery" to increase prices for these games? If prices were not increased by the clubs, what would happen?

3. What could prevent prices from increasing in this manner?

How Markets Adjust: An Example

www.opec.org

World oil markets provide a good example of how markets adjust over time to changed circumstances.

The first major increase in oil prices by the Organization of Petroleum Exporting Countries (OPEC) in 1973–74 caught consumers unaware. Because many were unprepared to cut back on their consumption of gasoline, demand was quite inelastic. This inelastic demand made it possible for OPEC to impose a major price increase that generated the greatest international transfer of wealth in the history of the world.

Following the 1973–74 price increases, consumers gradually adjusted to higher prices through energy conservation measures that held down the demand for oil—demand was slowly becoming more elastic. However, after the second major OPEC price increase in 1979 (a further doubling of prices), conditions in world oil markets changed more rapidly on both the demand side and the supply side of the market.

On the *demand side* of the world oil market, demand for oil in the non-communist world decreased by 11 percent from 1979 to 1985. This decrease in demand represented a cut in oil purchases of roughly six million barrels per day, leaving OPEC producing more oil than consumers were willing to buy at the current price. Developments on the *supply side* of the world oil market compounded this situation. High oil prices had attracted into world oil markets a number of new producers, including the United Kingdom, Mexico, and Norway. As a result of these developments, there were considerable surpluses of oil on world markets, and prices fell sharply, from about US\$34 per barrel to US\$12–20 after 1985.

These price adjustments reflect the elasticity of both demand and supply. They also show why it is naive to project that because a price *has increased* sharply, it will *continue to increase* rapidly. If anything, it is more likely that it will *not* continue to rise rapidly (and may actually fall) as the higher prices cause more of the product to be supplied and less to be demanded.

Summary

It can be said that, in many markets, equilibrium prices and quantities are constantly changing in response to changes in supply and demand (see the "In the News" boxes below and on the following page for two interesting examples). In those cases where supply and demand are elastic, the market's adjustment to changing conditions occurs quite completely and quickly, while in cases where supply or demand is inelastic, the adjustments will be less complete and/or will take longer. In any case, it is through these markets, and through price adjustments in these markets, that the economy adjusts to fluctuations in consumer demand, the cost and availability of products, and other changes.

IN THE **NEWS**   Commercials During the Super Bowl

For Super Bowl games, advertisers pay over US*\$2 million (more than Cdn\$3 million)* for *30 seconds* of commercial time.

Questions

1. What factors on the demand side of this market would help to explain such a high price?

2. What factors on the supply side of this market would help to explain such a high price? (Hint: Define exactly what it is that advertisers buy from television networks.)

IN THE **NEWS**   The Monday Effect

One example of unusual market behaviour is the so-called "Monday effect" that occurs in the stock market. Typically, share prices fall somewhat on Mondays, whereas they rise during the rest of the week. Also, over a 25-year period, seven of the 15 worst one-day declines in stock prices occurred on Mondays. Two additional facts are that four of every five share-price declines on Mondays happened after a fall on the previous Friday, and the "Monday effect" is really a Monday-morning effect: after 1:00 p.m., share prices tended to edge up. Finally, most of the selling on Mondays that caused stock prices to decline was by small shareholders.

Questions

1.   Why would stock prices have a greater tendency to fall on Mondays?
2.   Why would a decline in stock prices on Monday apparently often be related to a decline on the previous Friday?
3.   After falling on Monday morning, why would stock prices tend to recover after 1:00 p.m.?

Real-World Supply and Demand: Interpreting Signs from Markets

In the "real world" (as distinct from textbooks), we do not have neat supply and demand curves that show us the *causes* of changes in the prices of products and the quantities of them bought and sold in markets. Instead, what we have are certain facts concerning changes in prices and quantities bought and sold, together with other information relevant to demand and supply in those markets. From such information, it is usually possible to interpret what *has happened* concerning demand and supply in those markets. More interestingly, it is sometimes possible to use such information to predict *what will happen* concerning demand, supply, prices, and sales volumes. In the following sections, we will consider a few examples of how this can be done.

Rising Sales and Prices

In the late 1980s, both *sales* of houses (the quantity demanded) and the *prices* of houses increased very sharply. What would likely have caused these two trends? It is logical to conclude that rising demand was driving both sales and prices up. And, indeed, that is what happened—in the late 1980s, many of the "baby boomers" (the very large group of Canadians born between 1946 and 1966) reached the age at which people tend to buy homes, driving the demand for houses to unprecedented levels.

But what happened next to house prices? Many people assumed that prices would continue to rise, but the information in the previous paragraph could be used to predict that the opposite would happen. Once the baby boomers had bought their homes, the demand for housing would fall considerably. When this happened, housing prices would also fall—as they in fact did. People who understood these market dynamics were able to take advantage of them by selling or buying at the right time. Those who did not understand the market might buy or sell a home at the wrong time—an error that in that market could cost them $100 000 or more.

Rising Sales and Falling Prices

If the *sales* of an item were higher than usual but its *price* were falling, the logical conclusion would be that the supply of that product had increased. For example, large harvests sometimes lead to high inventories of unsold wheat that depress prices.

Does this mean that prices will continue to fall even lower? Not likely—the lower prices will lead farmers to plant less wheat, and they will help to increase sales and reduce inventories. Eventually, it can be expected that this combination of forces will cause prices to recover.

Falling Sales and Prices

If *both* the *sales* of an item and its *price* fall, the logical conclusion is that falling demand is pulling both down. This situation happened in the early 1990s in the housing market, when demand fell not only because the baby boomers had purchased their homes but also because of very high interest rates on mortgage loans. In some markets, the prices of homes fell by as much as 40 percent.

Does this mean that housing prices would continue to fall? Again, not likely—such low prices would discourage not only new home construction but also resales of homes, as homeowners would wait for the market to improve before selling. And, as buyers returned to the market (encouraged, in part, by low prices), sales and prices would begin to recover.

Falling Sales and Rising Prices

A combination of *falling sales* and *rising prices* would indicate that the supply of the item had decreased. For instance, if weather conditions or disease caused a low supply of broccoli, the volume sold would fall and the price would rise. Again, however, it is not likely that the price would continue to rise. The higher price would not only curb demand but also would create an incentive for farmers to increase their production of broccoli.

In summary, from the information available concerning the sales and the price of an item, together with other information concerning the demand for and/or supply of that item, it is possible to determine what has caused the changes in the sales volume and price (see the "You Decide" box on p. 108). More importantly, it is often possible to forecast future trends in the market for that item. And finally, it is often the case that due to changes in demand and/or supply, the probable future trend is the opposite of the past one.

STOCK MARKET SPECULATION

In most cases, markets are self-correcting—if the price of a product or service rises, this increase will dampen buying of the item and encourage higher production of it so that its price will stop rising and perhaps fall.

An interesting exception is the case of markets, such as stock markets, in which *speculation* is an important factor. If an increase in the price of a company's shares leads people to expect that this price is likely to *rise further,* the result can be the opposite of the usual situation as described above. The price increase can actually generate *increased buying* of the stock by buyers who are willing to pay higher prices for it because they believe that they will soon be able to sell the stock for an even higher price than they paid for it. The same expectation of rising prices can also make holders of the stock less willing to sell it, thus reducing the supply of it on the market and pushing its price even higher.

This combination of increased demand and reduced supply can sometimes cause the price of some shares to rise very rapidly. Often, the price of such shares may reach levels that are unrealistically high when compared to the company's past performance and future prospects, generating what is known as a speculative "bubble."

Questions

1. How long could such a speculative "bubble" last?
2. What would happen then?

Government Intervention: Price Supports and Price Ceilings

We have been describing markets in which prices are free to increase or decrease to their equilibrium level in response to changes in demand and supply. However, sometimes markets are not allowed to operate freely in this way—sometimes, governments will intervene in markets in order to keep prices either above or below their equilibrium levels.

For instance, if apartment rents (the price of using an apartment) are rising rapidly, tenants may put political pressure on the government to pass laws that hold rents below their market rate. In the case of some farm products, the opposite has happened—prices have been so low that the government has tried to keep them above their equilibrium level, so as to help the farmers. On the surface, this seems like a fairly simple solution to problems of prices that are seen as "too high" or "too low," but as we consider each of these policies in turn, we will see that they are not as simple as they appear.

Price Supports (Price Floors)

A good example of a government **price support** program designed to hold prices above their equilibrium level is one of the methods used to subsidize farmers. For many years, North American farmers have suffered from a tendency to oversupply the market. Improved technology and farming methods greatly increased the productivity of farmers, oversupplying the market and driving prices down. The problem was aggravated by the inelastic demand for food generally; as prices fell, people would not buy significantly more food, so the increased supply of food drove prices down more. In some cases farm prices and incomes were depressed to the point that they threatened the long-term survival of parts of Canada's agricultural sector.

price support (floor) An artificially high price, held above the equilibrium level by the government.

Unable to solve the problem on their own, some groups of farmers turned to the government, which provided assistance in a number of ways. One such program is *farm price supports*, under which the government would prevent the price of a farm product from falling below a certain level. The government could achieve this by *offering to buy the product* from the farmers at a certain price. Then no farmer would have to sell for a lower price, so all farmers would be guaranteed at least that price for their entire crop.

While such a program would support farm prices and incomes, it would have complicating side effects, which are illustrated in Figure 6-8. As the graph shows, the equilibrium point would have been E, making the

FIGURE 6-8 The Effects of Farm Price Supports

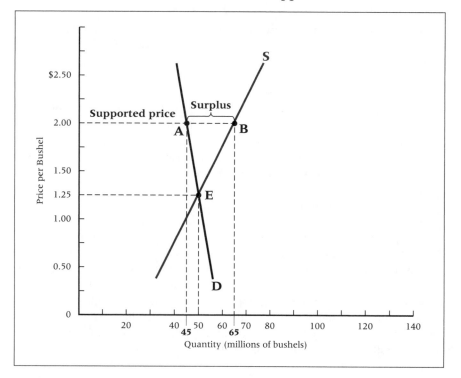

equilibrium price of wheat $1.25 per bushel and the equilibrium quantity 50 million bushels. However, if the government supported the price at $2, two adjustments would take place. First, at the higher price, somewhat less wheat would be demanded: on the graph, point A shows that at a price of $2, 45 million bushels would be bought, which represents a decline in sales of 5 million bushels.

This decline is a fairly small change, because the demand for wheat is quite inelastic. The second change, however, could be considerably greater: assured of a price of $2, farmers would increase their production. On the graph, point B shows that the quantity supplied would increase from 50 million to 65 million bushels as farmers responded to the incentive of a guaranteed higher price. The combined effect of these two adjustments to the new, higher price (a 15-million-bushel increase in quantity supplied and a reduction of 5 million in the quantity demanded) would be a *surplus* of 20 million bushels—20 million more bushels of wheat will be produced than people would be willing to buy at the $2 price.

Where would this surplus go? It would wind up in the possession of the government, which would act as a *reserve buyer* in the wheat market, supporting the price by buying whatever the farmers produced at a price of $2 per bushel. In some cases, such surpluses grew to sizes that they became costly and caused political embarrassment. This situation led governments to try other ways of supporting farm prices and incomes, such as paying farmers *not* to grow certain crops and setting up marketing boards empowered to set maximum production limits for farmers so as to reduce the supply of products. These policies are discussed further in Chapters 9 and 15.

Price Controls (Price Ceilings)

price control (ceiling)
A legal limit on a price or on increases in a price, which holds the price below its equilibrium level.

Sometimes, governments want to hold a price *below* its equilibrium level. Controls of this sort are known as **price controls** (or **price ceilings**). *Rent controls* (legal limits on the level of rents and/or on the rent increases charged by landlords) are probably the best illustration of such policies. In response to the complaints of tenants (who constitute a significant political pressure group in some areas), governments have imposed various sorts of rent controls to limit the rents charged by landlords to lower levels than could have been charged under prevailing market conditions. While rent controls benefit tenants who are already in apartments, they can have the unfortunate side effect of creating shortages of rental accommodation, as illustrated in Figure 6-9.

While the graph shows an equilibrium rent of $900 per month and a government-controlled rent of $700 per month, this information should not be interpreted as meaning that the government arbitrarily *reduced* rents by $200 per month. Rather, it should be interpreted as meaning that rent controls were imposed some time ago and have held rents to $700 per month, but since then demand has increased to the point where, without the controls, rents *would now be* $900 per month in a free market. Point E represents what would have happened if rents were not controlled—the equilibrium price (rent) would have been $900 and the equilibrium quantity would have been 55 000 rental units on the market.

FIGURE 6-9 The Effects of Rent Controls

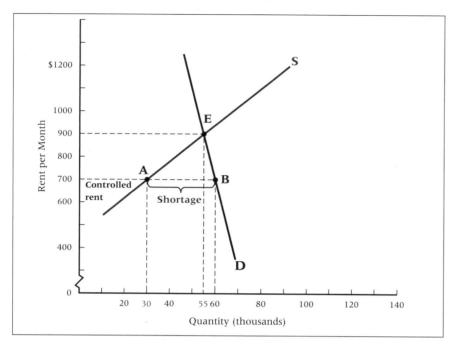

At the controlled rent of $700 per month, the situation is quite different. As point B shows, the lower rent has caused a small (5000-unit) increase in the quantity demanded, from 55 000 units to 60 000 units. There is a much more important adjustment on the supply side. Here, as point A shows, the quantity supplied at the controlled rent of $700 is only 30 000 units, whereas at the uncontrolled rent of $900 the quantity supplied would have been 55 000 units. In other words, there are 25 000 fewer rental units on the market at the $700 controlled rent than there would have been without the rent controls. When this 25 000-unit reduction in quantity supplied is added to the 5000-unit increase in quantity demanded due to the lower rents, the effect of the rent controls is to create a shortage of apartments to the extent of 30 000 units. The reason for the shortage is not that the landlords of existing buildings refuse to rent their apartments at the controlled rents; they have little choice but to accept the situation (although some landlords may convert their apartments to condominiums, which they can sell as private residences at prices not subject to government controls).

Rather, the shortage will occur mainly because the construction of new apartments will be depressed by the rent controls, which make apartments a less attractive investment. Developers will invest less capital into apartments and more into projects on which their returns are not controlled, such as single-family dwellings, townhouses, condominiums, shopping malls, and offices. Because of this problem, governments often use what are called "soft controls," which exempt new buildings from controls for several years and/or allow rents to rise when landlords' costs increase.

....

Prices: A Final Perspective

Prices are much more than tags on items telling buyers how much they must pay to get those items. Rather, prices play the role of *a key link in a market system* between the demand side and the supply side of markets. If the demand for an item rises, higher prices will create incentives to produce more of it. Conversely, declining demand will depress prices and discourage production of an item. Another perspective on this process is that, as demand and supply constantly change, changes in prices send *signals to buyers and sellers* that indicate how much of an item they should buy or produce and sell. And if government policies increase the price of an item or decrease it, those policies will interfere with these signals. Once a competitive market has established an equilibrium price, governments cannot change that price without affecting the amounts that buyers are willing to buy and sellers are willing to offer for sale. Programs to support prices above the equilibrium level will have the side effects of generating surpluses of that product, while controls that hold prices below their equilibrium level will create shortages of those products.

Chapter Summary

1. In competitive markets, supply and demand interact freely to determine the equilibrium price and quantity, which will change as supply or demand changes. (L.O. 1)
2. Generally, the more elastic the supply and the demand, the more rapid and complete will be the adjustments to changes in supply or demand. (L.O. 2, 3)
3. By using information concerning the sales volume and price of an item, together with other information on market developments, you can determine what has caused those changes in price and sales volume and often forecast future changes. (L.O. 4)
4. If the government intervenes in a market to hold the price of a product above its equilibrium level, the result will be a surplus of that product. (L.O. 5)
5. If the government intervenes in a market to hold the price of a product below its equilibrium level, the result will be a shortage of that product. (L.O. 6)

Questions

1. Using the graph shown here as a starting point,
    (a) draw a graph showing the new demand and/or supply curve(s) associated with each of the following events, and
    (b) explain the changes that occur in the market as a result of that event.

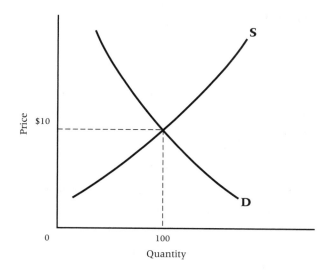

Events:

(i)   The prices of substitutes for the product increase.

(ii)   A technological advance enables producers to produce the product more efficiently, at a significantly lower production cost per unit.

(iii) New substitutes for this product come onto the market.

(iv)   The cost of producing this product increases considerably.

(v)   The government puts price controls on this product, making it illegal to charge more than $5 per unit for it.

(vi)   A severe recession occurs, reducing the consumer income available for purchasing this product.

(vii) The government imposes a $2 per item tax on this product.

(viii) A strike at several producers limits the production of this product (temporarily) to 80 units per week.

(ix)   The government supports the price of this product at $15 per unit by standing ready to purchase it at that price.

(x)   This item becomes much more popular with consumers *and* many new producers enter the industry.

2. What would be the most likely causes of each of the following?

(a) Compared to a year ago, sales of corn are up 8 percent and corn prices are 6 percent lower.

(b) Over the past three months, sales of natural gas (used for heating homes) have risen by 12 percent and the price of natural gas has risen by 6 percent.

(c) Compared to the same period last year, the number of boats being rented has decreased by 15 percent and boat rental rates have fallen by 10 percent.

(d) Compared to last year, strawberry sales are down 20 percent and prices are 25 percent higher.

3. Each winter, the price of fresh fruit in Canada rises, sometimes to very high levels.

   (a) Draw a graph that explains seasonal increases in fresh fruit prices.

   (b) Why does the government not attempt to protect consumers against such price increases by placing legal limits on fruit prices?

4. From 1997 to 2001, the price of coffee on world markets fell from US$1.60 per pound to US$0.56 per pound.

   (a) What is the most logical cause of such a decrease in price?

   (b) Why would the price decrease be so large?

   (c) Draw a graph representing the factors in parts (a) and (b).

5. By 2002, several golf courses in the Greater Toronto Area were charging as much as $130 to $235 for a round of 18 holes. Explain what contributed to such high prices, referring in your answer to factors

   (a) on the demand side of the market, and

   (b) on the supply side of the market.

6. One effect of the internet on markets is that, with more and more businesses using websites, consumers can contact a larger number of sellers from the convenience of their homes. What effect would you expect this factor to have on the average prices paid by buyers, and why?

7. Some people in large urban areas post notices of their garage sales on the internet. What effect would you expect this to have on the prices received by the people holding these garage sales, and why?

8. Draw a graph showing the market for houses with an equilibrium price of $200 000. Now suppose that housing prices are expected to increase considerably *next year*. Show on the graph how this expectation would affect the demand curve for housing, the supply curve for housing, and the price of housing *over the next two or three months*.

9. Suppose that on an average day, about 500 000 shares in Moose Pasture Gold Mines have been bought (and sold) at a price of about $2.00. On Tuesday, activity in the stock increases to 900 000 shares and the price rises to $3.00. On Wednesday and Thursday, the usual 500 000 shares are traded and the price stays around $3.00. On Friday, trading in the stock increases again, to the 900 000-share level experienced on Tuesday; *however, on Friday the price falls* to $1.50. What could explain this fall in price?

10. At the 1992 World Series in Toronto, scalpers were reportedly selling tickets for more than $1000 each in some cases.

    (a) Explain why scalpers could charge such high prices.

    (b) Should the law permit scalping of tickets in this manner? (At that time, the penalty for scalping was a small fine.)

(c) If the government wanted to prevent scalping, how could it do so?

11. Some people have suggested that, to make it possible for more Canadians to buy their own homes, a legal ceiling, or maximum, should be placed on mortgage interest rates. Do you agree that such a policy would be beneficial?

12. In the greater Metropolitan Toronto area in the early 1990s, there was a surplus of office space and commercial space such as shopping malls at the same time that apartments were in quite short supply. What could explain this apparently distorted pattern of construction?

13. In mid-1998, the Ontario government changed its rent control legislation so that rent controls no longer applied to apartments that had been vacated—for new tenants rents could be set at "market value." In the year that followed, the vacancy rate for apartments in Toronto was 0.9 percent, meaning that only 9 in 1000 apartments were available for rent. It is estimated that a 3-percent vacancy rate is needed in order to have reasonable competition among landlords.

    (a) What would you expect to happen to rents in the short term under these conditions?

    (b) If the rental housing market operated effectively, what developments should occur in the market over the longer term?

    (c) What has actually happened concerning rents and vacancy rates in Toronto since 1999? (Current statistics are available from Canada Mortgage and Housing Corporation's *Canadian Housing Statistics,* which is in most libraries.)

14. Many governments have passed minimum wage laws in order to protect the less-skilled members of the labour force against exploitation by unscrupulous employers. The following figure shows the market for such labour, with an equilibrium wage rate of $6 per hour. What effects would a minimum wage rate of $8 per hour have on this market and on the labour force in this market?

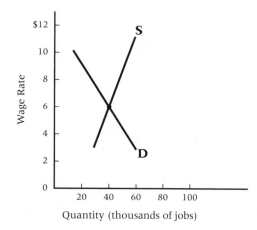

Chapter 7

Market Structures

Learning Objectives

After studying this chapter, you should be able to:

1. State the three characteristics of a perfectly competitive industry, sketch the demand curve for an individual firm in that industry, and explain the strategies that such firms will tend to pursue.

2. State the three characteristics of a monopolistically competitive industry, sketch the demand curve for an individual firm, and explain the strategies that such firms will tend to pursue.

3. Identify the three things that a group of firms must achieve in order to exercise market power.

4. Define *oligopoly*, and explain the types of competitive strategies that oligopolists tend to favour and those that they tend to avoid.

5. Identify five barriers to entry into industries, and explain the relationship of such barriers to oligopolistic market power.

6. List four factors that could prevent oligopolists from raising prices as much as they might like.

7. Define *monopoly*, and explain how a monopolist maximizes profits.

8. Explain why some industries are considered to be natural monopolies.

FIGURE 7-1 Market Structures

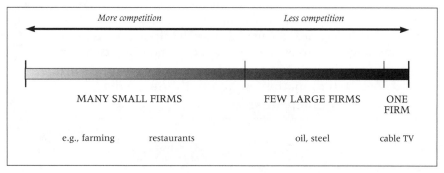

We have seen how prices are determined through the interaction of the demand side (buyers) and the supply side (sellers) of markets. In this chapter, we will examine in more detail the supply side of markets—that is, the industries that produce goods and services. The supply side of markets varies widely—in some industries such as farming, the supply side consists of large numbers of small producers, while in other industries such as cable television, there is only one seller (in any given market). Also in this chapter, we will organize industries according to how much competition there is between producers/sellers, as shown in Figure 7-1. The most competitive industries are at the left end of the spectrum in Figure 7-1, while the least competitive are at the right end.

The left side of Figure 7-1 represents industries in which there is strong competition among large numbers of producers/sellers. Such competitive industries comprise a large and important part of the Canadian economy—the small business sector as described in Chapter 3. To the right are industries that are dominated by a few large firms, and at the far right are monopolies, in which there is only one seller. Together, these last two types of industries comprise the big business sector of the economy, as was also discussed in Chapter 3.

In this chapter, we will see how these different supply side conditions ("market structures") can affect the decision making of producers/sellers about pricing, output levels, marketing, and product design. In addition, we will see how different market structures can result in quite different results for consumers. First, we will consider the "competitive" industries on the left side of Figure 7-1.

Part A: Competitive Industries

In Chapters 5 and 6, we saw how, in competitive markets, supply and demand interact to determine the prices of goods, services, and labour. In such markets, there are large numbers of both buyers and sellers, and neither buyers nor sellers are organized in such a way as to influence the price. As a result, the price will be determined impersonally and automatically by the *total supply* of all sellers and the *total demand* of all buyers in the marketplace, as illustrated in Figure 7-2. Once the market price for the product has been determined in the marketplace, all producers and sellers will have to keep their prices at or very near the market price. If a firm's price is too high, there are many competitors to whom the firm's customers can readily switch.

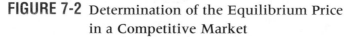

FIGURE 7-2 Determination of the Equilibrium Price
                  in a Competitive Market

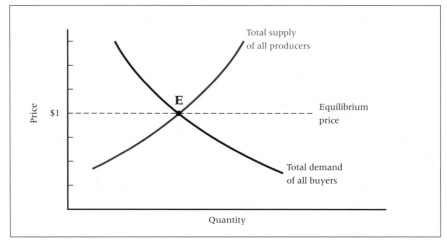

This, then, is the essence of what we have called *competitive* industries— industries in which there are so many small firms and it is so easy for new firms to enter the industry that producers have little or no influence over the price. The market determines the price, and each individual producer is a *price-taker*; that is, each producer has no choice but to charge a price equal to or very near the market price. Economists divide competitive industries into two types: *perfect competition* and *monopolistic competition*.

Perfect Competition

perfect competition A term describing industries that consist of a large number of small firms, where entry to the industry by new firms is easy, and where all firms in the industry sell identical products.

Perfect competition is the most competitive situation imaginable. It is considered to exist only if the following three conditions are met:

(a) there are *many small firms* in the industry,

(b) it is *easy for new firms to enter* (and exit) the industry, and

(c) all firms in the industry sell *identical products*.

It is the last condition that makes perfect competition so extremely competitive and quite rare. If each producer's product is *identical* to those sold by the other producers, each producer will be forced to charge *exactly the same price* as the others; in Figure 7-2, all producers will have to charge the market price of $1 per kilogram. If any producer charges more than $1, that producer's sales will *fall to zero*, as buyers will buy instead from the numerous competitors who would be charging less for an identical product.

FIGURE 7-3 Market Demand, Market Supply, and the Demand Curve for the Individual Producer's Product in a Perfectly Competitive Market

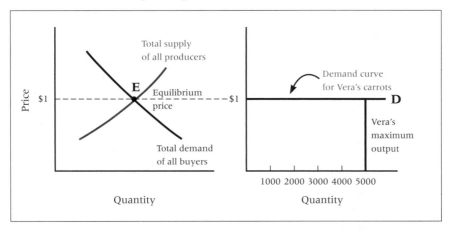

For example, suppose the product is carrots, the buyers are wholesalers, canners, and processors, and the sellers consist of a large number of very small farmers, each selling identical products—carrots. If the going price for carrots is $1 per kilogram, each farmer will be able to sell his or her entire output of carrots at $1 per kilogram, but only at $1.If one farmer were to try to charge more than $1 per kilogram, that farmer's sales would be zero. The buyers will be able to get plenty of carrots from the other farmers, and will simply not find it necessary to buy that farmer's output.

Figure 7-3 illustrates the position of one producer in this market—Vera's Vegetable Farm. Vera operates one of many small farms in the industry, with a maximum ("capacity") production of 5000 kg of carrots per year. If Vera produces 1000 kg, she will get a price of $1 for each kilogram; if she produces 2000 kg, the price would be the same; and if she produces all she can (5000 kg), the price she receives will still be the same. The price remains the same because Vera is such a small part of the overall supply that variations in her output will have no effect on the total market supply and therefore on the price.

As a result, the demand curve for Vera's carrots will consist of a *perfectly horizontal line* at a price of $1, as in Figure 7-3. This unusual demand curve illustrates an unusual situation. At the market price of $1, Vera can sell all the carrots that she can produce. However, if Vera tries to charge more than $1, her sales will fall to zero. This demand curve illustrates **perfectly elastic demand**, reflecting the fact that *any* increase in price will cause *all* sales to be lost. Obviously, the case of perfect competition is the most competitive situation imaginable, where the seller has *no control over the price* of the product, because there are so many sellers competing to sell identical products.

Because perfect competition is restricted to situations involving industries with many small firms, easy entry into the industry, and identical

A Canadian farm that produces 35 000 bushels of wheat might seem large. Total world wheat production would be about *600 000 times* that farm's output.

perfectly elastic demand A situation in which any price increase above the market price will cause a firm's sales to fall to zero; represented by a horizontal demand curve.

products, this type of competition is rare. It is, for the most part, restricted to markets for certain agricultural products and natural resource products, where buyers can be sure that the products are identical, and to markets in which the buyers are processors or wholesalers.

Incentives and Strategies for Producers

What types of business strategies can Vera utilize so as to make as much profit as possible? As we have seen, she cannot *increase her price* because her sales would collapse. And a *price reduction* would serve no purpose—she can already sell all that she can produce, so why reduce her price? A strategy of *product differentiation* (making her product different from her competitors') is out of the question—a carrot is, after all, a carrot. For the same reason *advertising* would be futile—Vera's carrots are identical to everyone else's carrots, and the buyers know this. All that Vera (and all of her many competitors) can do is:

(a) reduce production costs per unit of output to the lowest possible level; that is, produce as efficiently as possible;

(b) produce as much output as is profitable at these low unit-cost levels (which usually means as much output as possible); and

(c) sell the product for whatever price the market determines.

This is essentially what producers in such industries actually do—small vegetable farmers cultivate as large a crop as they can afford, as efficiently as possible (at the lowest possible cost per unit), harvest it, and, together with all the other farmers, sell it on the market for whatever price they can get for it. In seeking to maximize their own profits in this way, these competitive producers contribute to the welfare of consumers, not only by producing what consumers want to buy but also by maximizing their output of it, and minimizing production costs and prices.

While such behaviour is beneficial to the consumer, it makes matters quite difficult for the producers. Generally, the intensity of competition in such industries will force the profits of the average firm to very low levels, and there will be many marginal producers who are barely able to stay in business. Unable to develop a product that is different from its competitors' and unable to charge a higher price, the only way a producer in such industries can earn an above-average profit is to increase productive efficiency so as to reduce production costs per unit and thereby increase profits per unit of output. Those producers who are able to achieve these goals will be able to earn profits above the average for the industry, representing a reasonable rate of return on their capital. However, if the rest of the producers in the industry imitate these improvements in efficiency, production costs will fall across the industry, and competition will drive prices still lower and profits back down to minimal levels.

As noted above, perfect competition is a rare situation. Much more common (but still very competitive) is the case of monopolistic competition, which is discussed in the next section.

Monopolistic Competition

Typically, even in competitive industries, each producer is not selling an identical product or service. While there may be large numbers of sellers selling products that are very similar, each seller's product is usually at least a little different from the rest, particularly in industries that cater to the consumer. We will use the term **monopolistic competition**[1] to describe such industries. Monopolistic competition has three characteristics:

(a) there are many small firms in the industry,

(b) it is easy for new firms to enter the industry, and

(c) all firms' products are not identical—each firm's product or service is in some way different from those of its competitors.

monopolistic competition
A term describing industries that consist of many small firms, where entry to the industry by new firms is easy, and where the products or services of individual firms, while basically similar, are differentiated from each other to a degree.

The facts that there are many small firms and that it is easy to enter the industry ensure that there will be strong competition and that prices and profits will be held down to low levels. However, the fact that each firm sells a product that is in some way different from the other firms' products adds a new dimension to the situation: because the products of different firms are not identical, their prices do not need to be identical. Thus, a firm in a monopolistically competitive industry has some (small) opportunity to increase the price of its product—although not by much, because the large number of competitors selling similar products would cause many sales to be lost if one firm's price increased by much.

Product Differentiation

To the extent that a firm can make its product or service *more different* from those of its competitors—that is, practise **product differentiation**—it can increase its ability to raise prices (within limits) without losing too many sales.

product differentiation
Attempts by individual firms to distinguish their products or services from those of their competitors.

For instance, Harry's Hamburg Haven is a firm in a monopolistically competitive industry (fast foods) comprising a large number of small outlets, each with its own characteristics such as product, service, and location. Harry's Hamburg Haven is differentiated by its location (between the beer store and the drive-in theatre), its product (Harry's hamburgers are not prepackaged, but charbroiled and dressed to the customer's taste), its service (Harry's employees are carefully selected), and its ambiance (Harry's is somewhat of a sports bar/hamburger place, and Harry has a personal following in town because he was the highly popular penalty leader for the local intermediate hockey team for several years). At a price of $5 per meal (the

---

1. This is a very confusing name for describing this type of industry. The term *monopolistic competition* is meant to convey the impression that, while the industry is highly *competitive* (due to the large number of firms), each producer's position can be regarded (to a *slight* degree only) as similar in a small way to that of a monopoly, because its product is different from those of other firms. However, the basic nature of the industry is very competitive. It is essential to avoid confusing this with the position of a real monopoly, such as Canada Post, which is the *only* firm in a particular market.

average price in the area), Harry sells 2000 meals per week, as indicated by the dot on the diagram in Figure 7-4.

FIGURE 7-4 Demand Curve for Harry's Hamburg Haven

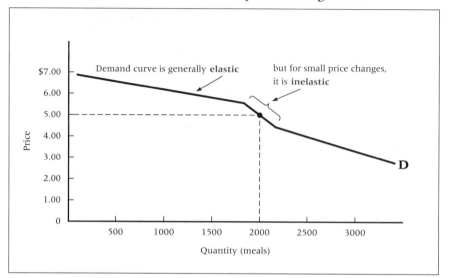

The demand curve in Figure 7-4 is generally quite elastic, due to the competitiveness of the industry. However, around the market price of $5, it is *less elastic*, due to the fact that Harry's product can be differentiated from his competitors'. For instance, Harry could raise his price *a little* (say, to $5.50) without losing many sales. While some of his customers would abandon him, the vast majority would stay with him. Although perhaps not delighted about paying the premium price, they would feel that the combination of location, product, service, and atmosphere made eating at Harry's worth a little more. Thus, for a small price increase, the demand for Harry's meals could be *inelastic*, making it profitable for Harry to raise his price a little. However, if Harry were to raise his price a lot (say, to $6.50), he would likely find that the demand for his burgers becomes elastic, as numerous customers decide that Harry's burgers are not worth the extra $1.50 each to them, and switch to other eating places, causing Harry's sales (and probably his profits) to fall. At prices above $7.00, not even his mother will eat at Harry's. So, in monopolistic competition, the fact that each firm's product is somewhat different from its competitors' can give it an opportunity to raise its price, but only by quite a limited amount.

A similar effect occurs with price reductions: a *small* price cut by Harry will not likely attract many more customers from his competitors—these customers are patronizing Harry's competitors because they prefer their product, location, or other features, and will not likely be lured away by the prospect of saving a few cents per burger at Harry's. A *large* price cut is out of the question in an industry as competitive as this—while it would increase Harry's sales greatly, he would lose money on every sale and go bankrupt.

In summary, then, the demand curve for the differentiated product of a firm in monopolistic competition is basically very elastic, but for small changes around the market price, it will probably be inelastic. As a result, the firm might have the opportunity to increase its price by a small amount. Whether or not it actually decides to do so is a matter of business strategy.

Incentives and Strategies for Producers

What business strategies are available to Harry for increasing his profits? Like Vera's situation of perfect competition, the highly competitive nature of Harry's industry limits his ability to raise prices. This restriction creates a strong incentive for producers in monopolistic competition to *increase productive efficiency*, or to produce at the lowest possible cost per unit.

However, Harry can adopt some strategies that Vera could not. A firm in monopolistic competition can practise *product differentiation* in order to widen the difference between its product and its competitors', and so gain an advantage in the marketplace.

If Harry's customers prefer his place, he may have an opportunity to *raise his prices*, at least a little. So Harry can choose between making a smaller profit per unit on a larger volume of units sold or making a higher profit per unit with a lower volume of sales. Vera did not have this choice.

Not surprisingly, many sellers in monopolistically competitive industries will try hard to differentiate themselves from their competitors. A key differentiating factor for many small businesses, especially in service industries, is their *location*. Restaurants stress their special menus, atmosphere, type of entertainment, and so on. Retailers strive to establish their own identity through the character of their shops, special product lines, and special services (parking, delivery, exchanges, returns, refunds, and so on). Some businesses providing services (such as dry cleaning) emphasize the speed of service, while other service businesses stress quality or extended hours. To the extent that a firm is successful in these efforts at product differentiation, it can alter its demand curve by making it more inelastic. For instance, Harry's competitive position would be enhanced strongly if his were the only hamburger stand in a prime location, or if he developed a unique and highly popular product line. On the other hand, a monopolistically competitive market is a very dynamic situation, and Harry must live with the risk that his competitors—or a brand-new firm starting up—may successfully imitate his advantages, reducing the degree to which Harry's firm is differentiated and making the demand for his hamburgers more elastic again. Worse yet (from Harry's viewpoint), some of them may come up with even better ideas to differentiate their products, placing Harry at a disadvantage. People who have operated small businesses successfully in this kind of environment for years tend to downplay flashy promotional stunts as short-term tactics, and stress instead the importance of establishing a reputation as an honest, reliable firm, if long-term success is to be achieved. They claim that this is the most valuable type of product differentiation that a firm can establish.

> Suppose that Harry earns $10 of profit on $100 of sales. If he increased his prices by 1 percent, his profits would grow by $1 (10 percent), *if* the price increase did not reduce the number of meals people will buy.

In conclusion, product differentiation, however achieved, can benefit the firm in two ways. First, it can build *consumer loyalty* to the firm and its products, and thus protect the firm against competition; and second, it can provide an opportunity for the firm to *charge higher prices* for its products, to the extent that consumers believe the product differentiation to be worth a higher price. All firms welcome the advantages of consumer loyalty; some will also charge a higher price.

Product differentiation can introduce a slight degree of monopoly power into a basically very competitive situation, in the sense that each firm's product or service is, in a small way, unique. Obviously, the degree to which this occurs will vary from situation to situation: it is one thing to be the only one of eight hamburger stands in town with a particular location, and quite another to be the only Chinese restaurant in town and the only restaurant in the town's indoor mall that has a liquor licence and entertainment. Nonetheless, new restaurants can easily open, emphasizing the fact that, while monopolistic competition is less competitive than perfect competition, it still represents a highly competitive situation. As a result, profits in monopolistically competitive industries generally tend to be relatively low, with many firms earning only marginal profits. However, firms that enjoy cost advantages, or that have succeeded in practising product differentiation to their advantage, will earn above-average profits, and some can be very profitable indeed.

Competitive Industries in Review

Let's review and compare the two types of competitive industries that we have discussed. While the large number of firms and ease of entry into the industry make both perfect competition and monopolistic competition highly competitive, product differentiation gives firms in monopolistic competition somewhat more room to manoeuvre. Harry can at least try to make his Hamburg Haven more different from his competitors and possibly charge a slightly higher price, whereas Vera has no such opportunity—the only "strategy" open to her is to produce as much as she can and sell it on the market for whatever she can get for it.

Economists' descriptions of competitive industries sometimes place such emphasis on *prices* that students get the impression that an industry cannot be classified as competitive unless producers practise aggressive price-cutting tactics against each other on a day-to-day basis, to the point of nearly driving each other out of business, as the "In the News" box on the next page describes. Since few industries fit this description, the concept of competitive industries can seem more theoretical than realistic.

However, the economics of competitive industries are more subtle. Because it is so easy for new producers to enter competitive industries, such industries tend to become "crowded" with large numbers of producers. And because producers as a group are unable to control supply (partly because there are so many of them and partly because it is easy to enter the industry), the incentive for each is to produce as much as possible. When all producers do so, the result is a *high supply*, which generates downward pressure on prices and profits.

IN THE **NEWS**	Now *That's* a Price War

Monday, August 27, 1983. That's the day of the Great Winnipeg Gasoline Price War. The hostilities began on Saturday the 25th when a new Domo gas station reduced prices as an opening promotion. Two neighbouring stations owned by Mohawk Oil and Petro-Canada matched the Domo price. But Domo had a big sign announcing that it would keep its price four-tenths of a cent per litre below the competition.

On Monday the war began in earnest, reduction matching reduction, all day long. At the peak of the battle a Domo worker used binoculars to spy on the prices on the Petro-Canada pumps, shouting numbers to a fellow worker sitting on the top of a stepladder while he changed prices on the Domo sign.

Regular leaded gas went from 47 cents per litre on Saturday to 1.6 cents per litre on Monday. In a last charge for victory Domo offered to pay customers 0.3 cents per litre to take gas away. (No one ever said that the demand curve cannot cross the axis.)

Customers were delighted to help out. But the lines for the stations were so long they produced a traffic jam 1.5 kilometres long and a police officer asked the stations to close in order to relieve the congestion. The interruption may have provided permanent relief: the next day prices were stable at the pre-war level of about 47 cents per litre.

Source: Adapted from *Common Sense Economics*, Issue 13, Vol. 7, No. 1, University of Waterloo.

Questions

1. Why do gasoline price wars like this one periodically break out?
2. What finally brings such price wars to an end?
3. If you owned one of the three gas stations in your town, how would you decide the price that you would charge for your gasoline?

The result—low prices and profits—is the same. However, the origin of this situation lies in the inability of producers to control supply rather than in any extraordinary tendency on their part to slash prices viciously.

The Extent of Competitive Industries

Determining the actual number and extent of competitive industries is not a simple matter, because of the difficulties in defining "small business" and deciding whether a particular firm is in a competitive industry or not. As we have said, perfect competition is a rare situation because of the requirement that products be identical; however, monopolistic competition is a very common form of market structure that includes most of the small business sector of the economy discussed in Chapter 3. Taken together, competitive industries probably account for more than half of the economy's output, concentrated for the most part in some sectors of agriculture and fishing, retail trade, small-scale manufacturing, and especially the large number of service industries (restaurants, fast-food outlets, retail shops, travel agencies, and so on) that have expanded rapidly in recent years.

Part B: Concentrated Industries

In Part A of this chapter, we examined "competitive" industries in which strong competition constantly pushes downward on prices and profits. In this section, we will examine industries of a different nature—industries where there is often less competition and where producers can influence the supply and the price of their product. These industries are described as *concentrated industries* because the supply side of such industries comprises, or is concentrated in, a small number of firms.

The Concept of Market Power

In Chapter 2, we introduced the concept of market power, which was described as the ability of producers or sellers to increase prices. In this chapter, we will examine more closely the concept of market power and how producers obtain it and exercise it. In order for the firms in an industry to exercise market power, the following conditions are necessary:

(a) the producers make an agreement concerning price and output;

(b) the producers maintain that agreement;

(c) newcomers and foreign competition are kept out of the industry; and

(d) the demand for the product is inelastic.

An Agreement Concerning Price and Output

The producers need to agree on the price to be charged, and not to undercut each other on price. Because less output could be sold at this higher price, the agreement must apply to *output* as well as to *price*. That is, each producer must agree to limit its production so as to avoid over-supplying the market. If output were not restricted, inventories of unsold product would accumulate, which could lead to an outbreak of price-cutting and the collapse of their agreement. (It should be noted that such agreements to restrict competition are illegal; however, at this point the focus is on the economics of this matter. The legalities will be considered in Chapter 9.)

Maintaining the Agreement

The producers must stick to their agreement. While this condition may sound obvious, there is considerable temptation for producers to enter into such an agreement and then break it, especially if it would be difficult for the other producers to know that this has been done. For instance, in the case of products sold by private contract to industrial buyers, one of the firms selling the product might be able to cut the price without its competitors knowing that it was breaking their price agreement.

Keeping Out Newcomers and Foreign Competition

An agreement among oligopolists could collapse if new competitors entered the market, either from new firms starting up or from foreign producers who were not party to the agreement. As we will see shortly, there are various obstacles that can prevent new domestic firms from starting up in many industries. Fending off foreign competition is more difficult and usually requires government assistance in the form of tariffs and other barriers to imports.

Because concentrated industries often have high prices and profits, they do tend to attract just these kinds of new competition from outside. For instance, many major North American industries that, in the past, had experienced relatively little competition have been more recently subject to considerable foreign competition, especially in the manufacturing sector.

Inelastic Demand

A final key to market power—and one over which the producers do not have much influence—is that the demand for the industry's product must be *inelastic.* With an inelastic demand, price increases will not reduce sales by too much, so that the industry's income will be increased if prices are raised. Generally, if demand is to be inelastic, there must be no close substitutes available.

As can be seen from the conditions outlined above, it is not an easy task for a group of firms to develop—and maintain—market power. What can be said, however, is that the fewer firms there are in an industry (or the more concentrated the industry is), the more likely they will be able to exercise market power. In this part of Chapter 7, we will consider two types of concentrated industries—**oligopoly**, in which an industry is dominated by a few large firms, and **monopoly**, in which there is only one firm. We will begin by examining the larger and more important of these—oligopoly.

oligopoly A situation in which four or fewer firms account for at least half of the sales of an industry.

Oligopoly

Oligopoly refers to a situation in which a few sellers (or producers) dominate a market (or industry). More specifically, an industry is called oligopolistic if four (or fewer) producers account for 50 percent or more of the industry's sales.

monopoly A situation in which there is only one seller of a particular good or service.

Behind this somewhat quantitative definition lie certain economic realities that are important to understand. When only a few firms dominate an industry, it's possible that they will band together to increase their prices and profits. For such oligopolistic power to exist, it is not necessary that the industry consist of *only* four or fewer firms. As long as the dominant four firms account for half the industry's sales, the rest of the sales could be split up among a considerable number of small firms. In these circumstances, the dominant firms would probably decide the price and the smaller firms would very likely follow along, making the industry oligopolistic, despite the presence of considerably more than four firms. Similarly, there could be hundreds of firms in an industry across Canada, but if they are fragmented into relatively small local markets with a few firms in each market, each of these markets will be oligopolistic. There are probably hundreds of road-paving firms in Canada, but all do not serve a national market: if a municipality offers a contract for road paving, bids may be received from only four or five local firms, a situation that certainly looks oligopolistic. In deciding whether an industry is oligopolistic, then, the total number of producers is less important than the number that buyers actually have to choose from.

This is the key about oligopoly: unlike the competitive situations we looked at earlier, in an oligopoly the market is dominated by a few firms that together have a strong grip on a large share of the market. This limitation on buyers' choices increases the potential market power of the producers.

The Extent of Oligopoly

Oligopolistic industries have historically comprised an important part of the Canadian economy. We can get an indication of their importance by listing some of them: steel, automobile manufacturing, banking, airlines, heavy machinery, farm implements, pulp and paper, tobacco, beer, liquor, soft drinks, electrical apparatus, aircraft, transportation equipment, explosives and ammunition, sugar, petroleum refining, cement, meat packing, and soap. As these examples show, a substantial proportion of the goods and services produced and consumed in the Canadian economy comes from industries that are quite different from the small businesses discussed in the first part of this chapter.

Barriers to Entry

Because they have more market power, oligopolistic industries will generally enjoy higher rates of profit than competitive industries. In competitive industries, such above-average rates of profit would attract new producers into the industry, causing output (supply) to rise and putting downward pressure on prices and profits, which does not happen so readily in oligopolistic industries because of the *barriers to entry* into these industries—factors that make it difficult for new competitors to start up.

A major barrier to entry into many oligopolistic industries, such as steel mills and automobile manufacturing, is the vast amount of *capital* required to start business on a large enough scale to be efficient and competitive. A related problem for newcomers is in winning a sufficient *volume of sales* to support an efficient level of production. A very high sales/production volume and *extensive advertising* are often required to compete with industry leaders in many manufacturing industries. Another problem facing a newcomer is *consumer acceptance*. Consumers have become familiar with the products of the established firms over the years, and this familiarity is strongly reinforced by the heavy advertising that oligopolists usually do. It can be quite difficult for a newcomer to break down these attitudes.

Another problem that prevents newcomers from imitating an established producer's product can be *patents*, through which a firm gains a legal monopoly over a product or process for a period of time. While patents are intended to provide incentives for the development of new products and processes, another effect is to give monopolies to those firms that hold patents. The drug industry is probably the most notable for using patents to protect firms against imitators.

Another obstacle facing new entrants to some industries is *government licensing*; for example, the need to obtain a taxi licence, a commercial airline licence, or a farm product quota poses major barriers to entry into these fields. While government licensing is intended to protect the consumer against unqualified businesses, it can also have the effect of reducing competition and supporting higher prices.

In the past, it was quite common for the established firms to engage in *predatory pricing*, or price wars, to drive newcomers out of business. Today, such tactics are illegal, and it is much more common for the established firms to buy out new competitors, through *mergers*. Some mergers are "friendly," in that the owners/managers of the firm are offered generous terms for surrendering control of their firm. Alternatively, there may be a "hostile takeover," in which one firm buys enough of another's shares to give it a controlling interest, after which it elects its own board of directors and replaces the management of the firm.

> Small regional airlines that attempt to start up in competition with Air Canada frequently complain that Air Canada cuts its fares in a deliberate attempt to drive them out of business.

The problem of foreign competition is more difficult, because foreign competition is beyond the direct control of oligopolists. Traditionally, industries hold off foreign competition by enlisting the assistance of their government in the form of *tariffs or other barriers to imports*. However, in recent years this tariff protection has been declining, exposing Canadian producers to considerably stronger foreign competition. This trend has been the result of a worldwide trend toward freer trade and increased international competition, and, of course, the North American Free Trade Agreement between Canada, the United States, and Mexico. This trend is extremely important as it means that some industries that formerly enjoyed powerful tariff-protected oligopolistic positions within the Canadian market are now being faced with strong import competition that can reduce or even eliminate their market power.

The barriers to entry described above provide formidable obstacles to the entry of new firms into some industries, and are less formidable in other cases. Generally, their effect is to limit competition and increase profits. Studies have shown that, as a general rule, the higher the barriers to entry into an industry are, the higher the profits (expressed in terms of rate of return on investment) of the firms in that industry tend to be.

Price-Fixing

When an industry is dominated by a few producers and is not subject to foreign competition, these producers will have an opportunity to reach an agreement among themselves for avoiding price competition, so that all of them can earn higher profits than otherwise would have been possible. As a result, the pricing policies of oligopolists sometimes reflect a "live-and-let-live" approach to competition, rather than the strong competition that often characterizes competitive industries.

The control of prices by producers is sometimes referred to as **price-fixing**, or administered prices. In order to control prices successfully,

> **price-fixing** Agreements among oligopolists to raise their prices above levels that would prevail in a competitive situation.

oligopolists must *control the supply* of their product. Therefore, price-fixing agreements must include an agreement concerning how much of the product should be produced by the oligopolists.

Typically, then, once the oligopolists have set the price of the product for a given period (say, one year, as with automobiles), they make every effort to maintain that price for the entire period. Such **administered prices** tend to be particularly resistant to downward movements. Should the demand for their product prove weaker than expected, the oligopolists will usually cut back their production rather than reduce their prices and risk an outbreak of price-cutting.

administered prices
A term used to describe prices that have been fixed by sellers. See *price-fixing.*

Price Stickiness

The reason why oligopolistic prices, once set by the industry, tend to remain unchanged for considerable periods is shown in Figure 7-5. The demand curve in Figure 7-5 represents the demand for the product of one firm in an oligopolistic industry in which it and three other companies are all pricing their product at $100.

FIGURE 7-5 Kinked Demand Curve of an Oligopolist

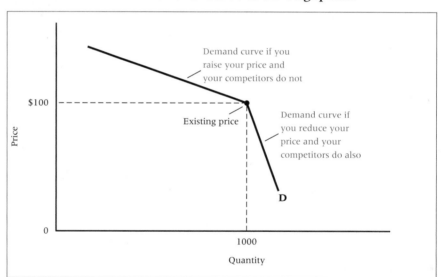

The unusual "kink" in the oligopolist's demand curve is the result of the following two situations.

First, if this one oligopolist *increases* its price, and the others do not, the oligopolist that raised its price will lose a considerable volume of sales. That is, for each firm, demand will be *elastic* for price increases, making a unilateral price increase an unattractive strategy.

Then what about a unilateral *price reduction* by one of the oligopolists? We must assume that any price cut by one oligopolist (in violation of their agreement, of course) would be matched by the other oligopolists, so that our oligopolist's strategy would not gain many sales. That is, for price reductions, demand will be *inelastic*. With the demand for a product elastic for price increases and inelastic for price reductions, the oligopolist finds that *neither* price increases *nor* price reductions are profitable.

Rather, the most profitable—and safest—strategy is to let the price remain at the present level of $100, until the producers *as a group* decide to change it. Thus, once set by the producers, oligopolistic prices tend to be quite *sticky*, or resistant to change. This price behaviour is quite different from the behaviour of prices in competitive markets, which fluctuate frequently as supply and demand change.

Oligopolistic Versus Competitive Price Behaviour

Generally, the prices of the products in highly competitive industries tend to fluctuate considerably more than oligopolistic prices. In competitive markets prices vary as supply and demand fluctuate; a good example is seasonal vegetable prices. By contrast, the administered prices of oligopolists tend to remain at the level set by the producers until the oligopolists decide to change them, which generally happens only periodically.

Also, competitive and oligopolistic industries respond quite differently to recessions during which demand decreases. In competitive industries, producers cannot control supply, so *prices* tend to decrease during a recession. In oligopolistic industries, on the other hand, producers often cut back on *output* (and lay off workers) in order to maintain prices during periods of weak demand.

Price-Fixing Techniques

There are various ways in which oligopolists can actually go about fixing prices, including the following:

(a) **Price leadership** is probably the most common technique for fixing prices. Under price leadership, the price leader in the industry (usually the largest firm) announces an increase in prices, and all the other firms follow suit in short order. The technique is especially well-suited to situations in which all firms are selling undifferentiated products, such as steel, aluminum, or gasoline, whose prices need to be identical because the products are so similar to each other.

price leadership
A technique of price-fixing in which one firm (the price leader) sets its price and the rest of the firms in the industry follow suit.

(b) *Formal agreements* are sometimes worked out by oligopolists to avoid competition. Such agreements generally cover matters such as prices, product quality, the division of the market into territories to be reserved for each firm, and techniques for fixing bids on government contracts. These agreements are sometimes quite complex, requiring meetings between executives of the firms and/or written communications and agreements. Because price-fixing is illegal, and such agreements increase the risk of detection, they tend to be used less frequently than price leadership. A group of oligopolists bound by a formal agreement is also known as a **cartel**.

cartel A formal agreement among producers to coordinate their price and output decisions for the purpose of earning monopoly profits.

(c) *Informal understandings* about prices are sometimes reached between oligopolists. In these situations, there is no apparent communication among the oligopolists and no clear indication of price leadership, yet the firms' prices come out remarkably close to each other. The automobile industry is believed to be an example of such a situation: knowing each other's costs reasonably well, knowing the general economic situation, knowing how each other calculates prices and each other's plans for model changes, each firm could work out its own prices in reasonable confidence that they would be quite close to the prices of the other firms. This process will not yield identical prices in the way that price leadership does, but automobiles themselves are a quite differentiated product, so identical prices are not necessary.

Non-Price Competition Among Oligopolists

As a means of competing, price-cutting has major disadvantages for the firms involved. First, price cuts are easily imitated—if one firm cuts its price, its competitors can quickly match its price cut, removing any competitive advantage that the firm might have gained. Second, price-cutting can escalate into costly price wars. And third, the costs of price-cutting fall on the producers through lower profit margins. With other forms of competition, known as **non-price competition**, these disadvantages are less of a problem.

> **non-price competition**
> Competition between sellers based not on price but rather on factors such as product differentiation and advertising.

While oligopolists may tend to avoid price competition, they certainly do not refrain from other types of competition. In fact, the marketing rivalry between firms in oligopolistic industries such as soft drinks, automobiles, soaps, detergents, beer, and so on is a well-known and highly visible feature of our economy. This rivalry, which uses a variety of methods other than price competition, is directed toward *increasing sales and market share*. One measure of the success of an oligopoly is its market share, which means its percentage of the total sales of the industry. Oligopolistic firms tend to be quite concerned with the size of their market share and whether it is growing or declining.

To increase their sales and market share, oligopolists extensively use non-price competition, such as *product differentiation, advertising,* and *sales promotion*. Product differentiation makes a product distinctive from the products of competitors, while advertising is used to persuade consumers that these differences are important. Sales promotion is a short-term tactic for boosting sales and market share.

Some efforts at product differentiation, such as more fuel-efficient cars, will serve real consumer needs; others, such as minor styling changes, will be trivial; and others, such as the "feeling" one supposedly gets from using a product, will be contrivances of advertising imagery. Many of them will be costly, as will the advertising and promotion campaigns associated with them. Generally, oligopolists are heavy spenders in the areas of market research, product design/differentiation, and advertising. Non-price competition is not cheap competition, but for oligopolists, it is preferable to price competition, for a few reasons.

First, an advantage gained through effective non-price competition, such as a new product or a unique advertising appeal, cannot be quickly offset by your competitors' simply imitating it, as they can with price reductions. Second, there is much less of a risk of non-price competition escalating in a costly manner, as can happen with price wars. The costs of non-price competition are more readily kept within limits; for instance, many oligopolists set their advertising budgets as a certain percentage of their sales. And third, assuming that the industry has a price-fixing arrangement, at least part of the cost of advertising and product differentiation can be passed on to the consumer through higher prices. As a result, oligopolists prefer, when possible, to practise non-price competition rather than price competition.

Predicting Behaviour

Earlier, we noted that once oligopolists have set the price of their product, the price tends to be "sticky," or resistant to change. However, we have not yet considered how oligopolists *actually decide* what price to charge and what output to produce in the first place. Considering the importance of oligopolistic industries in the economy, this is an important question.

Unfortunately, it is quite difficult to generalize about, or predict, the pricing behaviour of most oligopolistic industries. In competitive industries, we can predict that prices will be driven downward toward a minimum level. But oligopolists often have considerably more discretion over the prices of their products, which makes it much more difficult to analyze and predict their pricing decisions.

> Research has shown that the widely held belief that oil companies regularly raise prices as long weekends commence is untrue.

While the domination of an industry by a few firms creates the *potential* for price-fixing, several factors will influence the *actual* pricing decisions of these firms and industries. The possible range of oligopolists' power over prices is quite wide. At one extreme, a tightly organized group of oligopolists without any foreign competition and facing an inelastic demand for its product is in an excellent position to raise prices to very high levels. At the other extreme, oligopolists facing strong foreign competition may find themselves without any real power over prices at all. In the following section, we will consider some of the factors that limit the power of oligopolists to raise prices.

Limits on Prices

Foreign competition has in recent years become the most important factor limiting the market power of many oligopolists, especially in the manufacturing sector of the economy. As international trade agreements have reduced tariffs both in North America and globally, many Canadian manufacturers have found themselves facing increasingly strong competition from imports. In many major industries, such as automobiles, steel, electronic equipment, and textiles, the market power of Canadian (and American) industries has been sharply reduced or even eliminated by competition from imports.

Lack of cooperation among oligopolists can also limit their control over prices. If any of the firms in the industry has a tendency to use price competition, either openly or by cheating on the agreement, the other firms will have to respond in kind, or face a decline in their market share. Price-cutting is more likely during recessions, when sales are slow.

Elasticity of demand for the product is another factor that can limit the ability of oligopolists to raise prices. If substitutes for the product make the demand for it elastic, sales will fall by so much that it will be futile for the oligopolists to raise prices. Usually there are few if any substitutes, since the oligopolists control the entire market for a given product; however, this is not always the case. For instance, in some uses, steel has to contend with competition from aluminum, plastics, and even glass, and the airline industry is to some extent in competition with other vacation packages. And, as technology generates new materials, processes, and products, this kind of inter-product and inter-industry competition has been presenting some previously secure industries with competition from new and unexpected quarters. This trend has been particularly evident in the communications field recently.

Fear of prosecution for price-fixing may also act as a deterrent to oligopolists. As we will see in Chapter 9, price-fixing is illegal under Canadian law, so companies that fix prices face a risk of being prosecuted and fined. While the law has not stopped price-fixing, it seems likely that it has acted as a deterrent.

www.opec.org

IN THE **NEWS**   OPEC

The Organization of Petroleum Exporting Countries (OPEC) is an organization of 11 countries that produce and export oil. OPEC countries produce roughly 40 percent of the world's oil. Periodically, the media report that OPEC is considering reducing production by its member countries in order to increase world oil prices. These media reports often include two other interesting comments. The first is that a seemingly small reduction in OPEC production (for example, 4 percent, which would represent about 1.6 percent of total world output) is expected to lead to price increases of about 20 percent (say, from US$20 to US$24 per barrel). The second is that, in the opinion of oil industry experts, OPEC will have great difficulty in achieving its objectives.

Questions

1.   What does this information tell us about the elasticity of the demand for oil?
2.   Why might OPEC have great difficulty in achieving a 20 percent increase in the price of oil?

How Much Market Power?

There is no simple answer to the question of how much market power oligopolists possess—it varies widely from industry to industry and from time to time, making generalizations impossible. In some situations, in which the oligopolists are well-organized and face no foreign competition, they can have considerable market power. In other cases, one or more of the factors outlined in the previous section can take away most or even all of their ability to charge high prices.

Furthermore, the effectiveness of these limits on prices can vary from time to time as conditions change. For instance, the automobile industry was for many years considered a classic example of a powerful oligopoly as a few dominant firms kept competition within bounds and both workers' wages and companies' profits were well above average levels. However, over the past quarter-century, import competition has limited the market power of both the companies and their unions.

Regardless of the factors that may—or may not—restrain the market power of oligopolists, the fact remains that some large corporations do possess considerable power over prices, particularly when economic conditions are favourable. These large corporations, and the market power that some of them possess, are a long way from the competitive industries described in the first part of this chapter. This difference is reflected in the fact that, on average, the profits of larger corporations represent a significantly higher rate of return on the owners' investment than do the profits of smaller businesses.

Monopoly

Suppose that as the result of a patent,[2] Global Gadgets, Inc., is the only producer of a particular component used in snowmobiles. Since Global Gadgets is the only producer of this product, the total market demand for the product and the demand for Global Gadgets' product are the same thing. This demand is illustrated in Figure 7-6, in both schedule and graph form.

What price will the monopoly charge for its product? While our initial response may be that the monopoly will select the highest price, Figure 7-6 shows that the *highest* price may not be the *most profitable*. By charging a price of $5 and producing 700 units per week, the monopoly can make a higher total revenue than if, for instance, the price were raised to $6, and sales dropped to 500 units per week. (Note that we are only looking at the *revenue* side of the picture, and are ignoring the *costs*. In effect, we are assuming that if the monopoly maximizes total revenue, it is also maximizing profits.)

Under these assumptions, the monopoly will raise its price as long as the demand is inelastic. At prices above $5, the demand becomes elastic as buyer resistance to such high prices undercuts sales and revenues.

At a price of $5, only 700 products can be sold per week. If more were produced, they could not be sold without lowering the price. Thus, the key to the monopolist's ability to raise the price to $5 lies in the fact that the monopolist *controls the supply* of the product, and can restrict the supply to 700 per week.

Monopoly Compared to Competition

By making *prices higher* and *output lower* than they would otherwise be, monopoly imposes a twofold burden on society economically. In Figure 7-6,

2. A patent gives the inventor of a product a legal monopoly over the production of it for a certain period.

suppose that the minimum price for which the product could be sold profitably were $3. If there were strong competition in the industry, the price would fall to $3 (instead of $5) and production would be 1000 units (instead of 700). But with a monopoly in the industry, the public is burdened with *both* higher prices *and* lower output than would exist under competition (see the "You Decide" box below).

FIGURE 7-6 Demand for Global Gadgets' Product

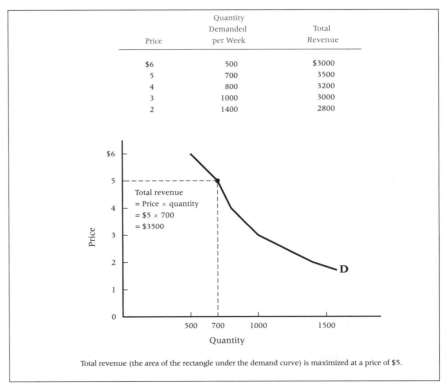

Price	Quantity Demanded per Week	Total Revenue
$6	500	$3000
5	700	3500
4	800	3200
3	1000	3000
2	1400	2800

Total revenue
= Price × quantity
= $5 × 700
= $3500

Total revenue (the area of the rectangle under the demand curve) is maximized at a price of $5.

YOU DECIDE

THE INTERNATIONAL DIAMOND MONOPOLY

One of the most famous and profitable monopolies of all time is the international diamond monopoly organized by De Beers Consolidated Mines, Ltd., of South Africa. For most of the twentieth century, De Beers has owned or controlled all the diamond mines in South Africa and owned diamond-trading companies in England, Portugal, Israel, Belgium, Holland, and Switzerland.

De Beers' success has stemmed not only from its control of the *supply* of diamonds but also from its ability to influence the demand for them. Starting in 1938 (at which time diamond prices had declined badly due to the Depression), the demand for diamonds in the United States was promoted by a sophisticated advertising campaign that virtually *created* a "tradition": the diamond engagement ring, and the association of diamonds with romance and permanence ("A Diamond Is Forever"). By the late 1950s a diamond was generally considered essential to an engagement in North America. In 1967 an advertising campaign was started in Japan, a potentially large market in which only 5 percent of brides wore a diamond engagement ring. By 1980, 60 percent of engaged Japanese women received diamonds, and diamond sales in Japan had reached $1 billion per year.

However, even a monopoly as powerful as De Beers is not without problems. As with most monopolies, its main concern involves losing control of the supply. In the 1960s, the diamond market was threatened by a large inflow of Russian diamonds, almost all of which were considerably smaller than De Beers' "traditional" South African gems. To avoid a depressed market due to this new source of supply, De Beers undertook to market these diamonds for the Soviets, in effect making Communist Russia a partner in the highly capitalistic diamond cartel. An advertising campaign was mounted to shift demand toward smaller diamonds, many of which were sold in new "eternity rings," which contained as many as 25 small Soviet diamonds and were targeted at older married women. This campaign was remarkably successful; however, it had the side effect of undercutting the market for De Beers' traditional larger diamonds. By the late 1970s these diamonds were being discounted by as much as 20 percent.

Meanwhile, other developments threatened De Beers' control of the diamond market. In the late 1970s, the discovery of vast diamond deposits in Western Australia made it even more difficult for De Beers to control the supply. In addition, political instability in South Africa made it uncertain whether De Beers would be able to hold together the key suppliers in that region.

When De Beers had tight control of the world supply of diamonds, it could control the price simply by cutting back on the volume of diamonds that it allotted each year to about 300 hand-picked dealers. However, as other suppliers came into play, De Beers found it increasingly necessary to keep its diamonds off the market by buying diamonds at the wholesale level. By the early 1980s De Beers had accumulated an inventory of diamonds worth over a billion dollars, and was finding itself short of cash to buy up additional diamonds in order to support the price.

And support of the price of diamonds is crucial to De Beers' strategy. According to conservative estimates, the public holds more than 500 million carats of gem diamonds—over 500 times the volume produced by the cartel in any one year. Since new demand each year is satisfied by new production from the world's diamond mines, it is essential that this half-billion carat stock of diamonds be retained by its owners, and not placed on the market. If only a small proportion were sold in any one year, the price could collapse. While it is unlikely that people would sell their engagement rings (a diamond is, after all, forever), there is an increasingly large stock of "investment diamonds" in the hands of both wealthy individuals and financial institutions. In the event of price declines, these "investment diamonds" might well be dumped onto the market, depressing prices further.

Ironically, only by maintaining the price of diamonds (described by some observers as the "diamond illusion") can De Beers prevent such a sell-off of diamonds, and the risk of a price collapse that this sell-off could bring. Yet, as additional suppliers come onto the diamond market, it becomes more difficult to preserve that price by controlling the supply.

Questions

1. Why might diamonds be considered a risky long-term investment?
2. According to some economists, monopoly can never be more than a temporary market condition. Explain the reasoning behind this theory, and why you agree or disagree with it.

The Extent of Monopoly

natural monopoly
An industry, such as public utilities, that by its nature lends itself to a monopolistic form of organization.

Monopoly is a relatively rare form of market structure. Most monopolies in the Canadian economy are in public utilities or public services such as electricity, water, postal service, natural gas, and cable television. The economic rationale for having a **natural monopoly** is that by having only one producer, the high costs of the capital equipment that is needed can be spread over the maximum number of users, reducing the cost of these services to each user. In order to protect the public against the market power of such monopolies, the government has usually either regulated the rates that they charge or taken over ownership and operation of them. In Chapter 9, we will examine in more detail the issues and the arguments concerning the question of government policy regarding these "natural monopolies."

In Conclusion

Figure 7-7 summarizes and compares the four basic types of market structures, ranging from perfect competition to monopoly.

It should be noted that these four market structures represent only *types* of market structures, and that any particular real-life industry may consist of some combination of these types. For instance, an industry with three major Canadian firms that have 50 percent of the market, several smaller Canadian firms, and imports from several large foreign firms would look something like Figure 7-8.

The industry in Figure 7-8 would fall very near the middle of the spectrum of industries shown in Figure 7-1 at the start of this chapter. While it might fall under the strict definition of *oligopoly (four firms or less having 50 percent of the market)*, there would be considerably more competition and less opportunity for price-fixing in it than in a "classic" oligopoly. Indeed, it might well be sufficiently competitive that firms in it would have to behave more like firms in a competitive industry than like oligopolists.

FIGURE 7-7 Summary of the Four Types of Markets

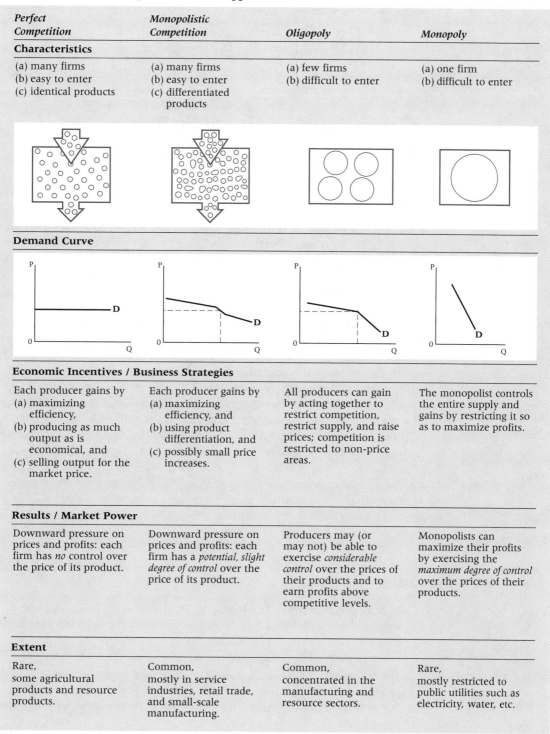

Perfect Competition	*Monopolistic Competition*	*Oligopoly*	*Monopoly*
Characteristics			
(a) many firms (b) easy to enter (c) identical products	(a) many firms (b) easy to enter (c) differentiated products	(a) few firms (b) difficult to enter	(a) one firm (b) difficult to enter
Demand Curve			
Economic Incentives / Business Strategies			
Each producer gains by (a) maximizing efficiency, (b) producing as much output as is economical, and (c) selling output for the market price.	Each producer gains by (a) maximizing efficiency, and (b) using product differentiation, and (c) possibly small price increases.	All producers can gain by acting together to restrict competition, restrict supply, and raise prices; competition is restricted to non-price areas.	The monopolist controls the entire supply and gains by restricting it so as to maximize profits.
Results / Market Power			
Downward pressure on prices and profits: each firm has *no* control over the price of its product.	Downward pressure on prices and profits: each firm has a *potential, slight degree of control* over the price of its product.	Producers may (or may not) be able to exercise *considerable control* over the prices of their products and to earn profits above competitive levels.	Monopolists can maximize their profits by exercising the *maximum degree of control* over the prices of their products.
Extent			
Rare, some agricultural products and resource products.	Common, mostly in service industries, retail trade, and small-scale manufacturing.	Common, concentrated in the manufacturing and resource sectors.	Rare, mostly restricted to public utilities such as electricity, water, etc.

FIGURE 7-8 Industry-Combining Market Structures

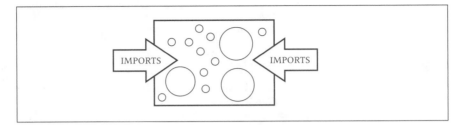

Competition in the Canadian Economy

Historically, there has been less competition in Canada's economy than in many other countries. In part, this has been the natural result of Canada's small market, since in some industries there was only room in the market for a few firms. However, government policies have also played a role in limiting competition. Many manufacturing industries were protected from foreign competition by tariffs, and government regulation of some sectors of the economy, such as communications and transportation, prevented competition.

In recent years, however, the situation has been changing as the intensity of competition in the Canadian economy has increased since the 1980s. In part, this change has been due to changing government policies. As tariffs on imports have come down under *trade agreements* such as the North American Free Trade Agreement and the World Trade Organization, some industries that were dominated by a few Canadian oligopolists have become much more like competitive industries. In addition, the *deregulation by governments* of some industries such as communications and transportation has allowed more competition in sectors previously dominated by monopolies. In part, the trend toward increasing competition has been the result of changes in the economy itself. The most important such trend has been the *growth of the service sector* of the economy. Service industries tend to consist of large numbers of smaller businesses, creating a highly competitive environment. As a result of these factors, there is more competition in the Canadian economy today than in the past.

Chapter Summary

1. In perfect competition, the most competitive situation possible, many small firms sell identical products, and no individual firm has any influence over the price of its product since it faces a perfectly elastic demand curve. Prices and profits tend to be low. (L.O. 1)

2. The incentives for a firm in perfect competition are to minimize production costs per unit (maximize efficiency), produce as much output as it can afford to, and sell its output for whatever price the market determines. (L.O. 1)

3. Monopolistically competitive industries are also very competitive but differ from perfect competition in that these firms have an opportunity to practise product differentiation, thereby making demand somewhat less elastic and (possibly) enabling the firms to increase prices a little. (L.O. 2)

4. To exercise market power, firms have to make and keep an agreement concerning both price and supply and have to keep out new competitors and foreign competition. Also, demand for their product must be inelastic. (L.O. 3)

5. Oligopolies consist of sufficiently few firms that they are often able to act together so as to fix prices, using various techniques. However, they often do compete strongly in non-price areas. (L.O. 4)

6. The high profits of some oligopolistic industries are protected by various barriers to entry that keep new entrants out of these industries. (L.O. 5)

7. Under some circumstances, oligopolists can possess considerable power over their prices. However, various factors, especially foreign competition, can restrict their market power. (L.O. 6)

8. A monopoly is able to restrict the supply and thus raise the price of its product so as to maximize its profits. (L.O. 7)

9. Monopolies are quite rare, being restricted mainly to public utilities, which tend to be "natural monopolies" that are regulated or owned by the government. (L.O. 8)

Questions

1. The text notes that service industries are generally very competitive. Why would this be the case?

2. Generally speaking, convenience stores carry the same merchandise as each other. Would you then consider the convenience stores in your neighbourhood to be in "perfect competition" with each other?

3. "Ebusinesses" provide an interesting example of a field made highly competitive by the ease of starting up a new business. By 2000, there were an estimated two million ebusinesses in North America, many of them start-up "dot-com" companies whose stocks excited investor interest as the internet grew explosively. However, it was also forecasted that the growth of the internet would slow sharply as it approached the "saturation point" of 70 percent of households early in the new century.

    What actually did happen to growth, profits, and stock prices in the dot-com sector, and why?

4. At one point in the 1920s, there were 241 automobile manufacturing companies in North America. Why did the market structure of the industry change so much over the next few decades?

5. Two of the most fundamental forces driving change in recent years have been *free trade agreements* (such as the North American Free Trade Agreement and the World Trade Organization) and *communications technology* (such as telecommunications and the internet). What are the implications of these changes for market structure and the degree of competitiveness in the Canadian economy?

6. At times, the world's major coffee producers have agreed to keep as much as 20 percent of their exports off the market.
   (a) What would be the objective of this agreement?
   (b) What would be required in order for this plan to achieve its objective?
   (c) What could go wrong with the plan?

7. When the price of gasoline increases considerably, some angry consumers sometimes try to organize a *boycott* of the products of one or more of the big oil companies.
   (a) What would be the objective of such a boycott?
   (b) How successful would you expect such a tactic to be?

8. What is the difference between the market position of a gas station in a large urban area and a gas station located on a limited-access super-highway? Is this difference reflected in the prices charged by each?

9. Over a period of several weeks, monitor the prices in your local super-market of *a popular breakfast cereal* and *fresh lettuce*. What differences do you observe in the behaviour of the price of each product? How do you explain these differences?

10. Of the 12 largest companies in the United States in 1900, 11 have not survived to the year 2000. What might be the significance of this fact?

Chapter 8

The Costs and Revenues of the Firm

Learning Objectives

After studying this chapter, you should be able to:

1. Explain the Law of Diminishing Returns.

2. Using sales revenue data for a firm, calculate and graph the average revenue per unit and marginal revenue per unit over a range of output and sales.

3. Using cost data for a firm, calculate and graph the average cost per unit and marginal cost per unit over a range of output and sales.

4. Using revenue and cost data for a firm, identify the level of output at which profits will be maximized, and calculate this maximum level of profits.

5. Using revenue and cost data, calculate the output/sales level above which a firm will make profits (its break-even point).

6. Using revenue and cost data, calculate the output/sales level below which a firm should shut down.

In Chapter 7, we examined the behaviour of the individual business firm under the four basic types of market structures—perfect competition, monopolistic competition, oligopoly, and monopoly. While we discussed various strategies whereby firms could increase their profits under various conditions, we focused our attention on the total (sales) *revenue* of the firm more than its *profits*; indeed, in some cases, we treated total revenue as if it were the same as profits, speaking in terms of the firm maximizing its total revenue rather than its profits. While this approach allowed us to discuss the limitations facing the business firm and its behaviour under various conditions, it is not really accurate to consider total revenue to be the same as profits. Total revenue is the result of the firm's sales, while profits are the net result of the firm's sales revenues *and* its production costs. In this chapter, we will examine the nature and behaviour of production costs and how they interact with sales revenues to determine not only the business firm's profits but also its decisions regarding prices and output.

As we saw in Chapter 1, the more effectively and efficiently a society's economic resources are used, the more economically prosperous its people will be. In a market economy, business firms make many of the key decisions about the use of economic resources. In seeking to increase their sales and sales income, business firms are trying to use economic resources *effectively*, by producing what buyers want. And in seeking to minimize their costs, business firms are trying to use economic resources *efficiently*, by getting the maximum output from the resources employed. So the more effectively and efficiently business firms use their resources, the higher their profits will be.

In this chapter, we will examine these decisions by business firms seeking to maximize their profits. First, we will consider production costs and then sales revenue, and how costs and revenue interact to determine profits.

Production Costs

To illustrate the nature and behaviour of the production costs of the firm, we will use the example of Barry's Bolts Ltd., one of many small manufacturing firms selling an undifferentiated product (bolts) to industrial buyers in a highly competitive market. Since competition limits Barry's price to $3 per 100 bolts, his success is mainly dependent upon his ability to keep his production cost per 100 bolts as low as possible, by producing bolts as efficiently as possible. From Barry's business, we can learn some of the basic facts related to the production costs of a firm.

Fixed Costs

fixed costs Production costs that remain constant, regardless of the level of output (for example, rent).

We will suppose that Barry has leased a building and equipment for his business, and that the cost of these, plus other overhead items such as light and heat, amounts to $120 per day. These are called Barry's **fixed costs**, meaning that they will remain at $120 per day regardless of how much he produces. Whether he produces only a few bolts per day or a large number of bolts per day, his fixed costs will be $120. This fact makes it essential that Barry produce and sell a certain number of bolts per day because if his production is too low, the fixed costs per unit (a unit is a box of 100 bolts) produced will be so high that he will be unable to make a profit. Barry's research into this matter is shown in Figure 8-1, which shows that fixed costs per 100 bolts are extremely high at low volumes of output. Considering that the market price of 100 bolts is $3, it is apparent that Barry can succeed only if he attains a sufficiently high volume of sales and production to spread his fixed costs over a large number of units. And in doing so, he will keep the fixed costs per 100 bolts low. Generally, then, fixed costs per unit of output are very high at low volumes of output, and decline as output is increased.

FIGURE 8-1 Fixed Costs per Unit

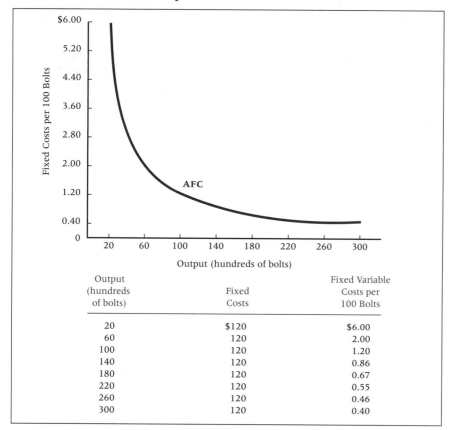

Output (hundreds of bolts)	Fixed Costs	Fixed Variable Costs per 100 Bolts
20	$120	$6.00
60	120	2.00
100	120	1.20
140	120	0.86
180	120	0.67
220	120	0.55
260	120	0.46
300	120	0.40

Variable Costs

In addition to his fixed costs, Barry will have **variable costs**: these are costs, such as direct labour and materials, that will increase as Barry's output of bolts increases.[1] To simplify our illustration, we will assume that there are no material costs, so that the only variable cost with which we will be concerned is direct labour.

variable costs
Production costs that vary with the level of output (for example, direct labour and direct materials).

----

1. "Direct" merely specifies that such labour and materials are directly used for producing the product, as distinct from office labour and materials, which are more like fixed or overhead costs.

The labour cost per unit (100 bolts) will depend on two factors: how much the average worker is *paid* per day, and how many bolts he or she *produces* per day. At first glance, we might expect both of these factors to be constant regardless of how many bolts the plant produces. That is, hiring additional workers should not affect either the daily wages or the average daily output of the workers. However, the average daily output of each worker will, in fact, change as additional workers are added to Barry's plant.

The reason for this change is that the plant is of a certain size, and is best suited to a certain level of production. If production is too far below or too far above this level, efficiency will suffer, and the average daily product of each worker will be below its peak. This relationship between average output per worker and the number of workers is illustrated in Figure 8-2. If only one or two people are working in the plant, the workers will not be able to specialize at particular tasks. Each worker will have to perform so many different tasks as to be unable to do any of them very efficiently. As a result, at low levels of production and with few workers employed, average output per worker will be very low (4 units per day if one person is employed and 14 units per day with two workers on the job).

FIGURE 8-2 Average Product per Worker

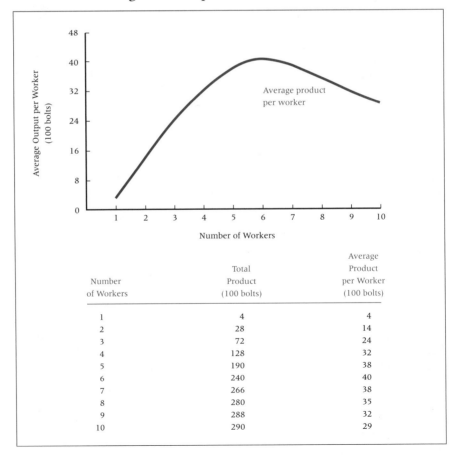

Number of Workers	Total Product (100 bolts)	Average Product per Worker (100 bolts)
1	4	4
2	28	14
3	72	24
4	128	32
5	190	38
6	240	40
7	266	38
8	280	35
9	288	32
10	290	29

Barry will find, however, that as he increases production and hires additional workers, average output per worker improves significantly. With more workers in the plant, each can become more specialized. Some can prepare materials for production, some can operate the bolt-making machinery, some can finish and paint the bolts, while others can package them for shipping. As each worker becomes more specialized, efficiency increases and average output per worker rises considerably, reaching 40 units per day when six workers are employed.

However, Barry will find that hiring additional workers improves output per worker only up to a certain point. As Figure 8-2 shows, once Barry hires additional workers beyond the sixth, average output per worker decreases because Barry's plant is only so large, and we have moved beyond the point at which it operates at *peak efficiency*. The addition of more workers does not increase the opportunities for specialization as it did earlier; in effect, the additional workers are crowding the fixed amount of equipment in the plant, and therefore are actually reducing the efficiency of the work force. By efficiency we mean average output per worker: as Figure 8-2 shows, the addition of the seventh through tenth workers causes the plant's *total* output to rise, but *average output per worker* declines once production is past the level of peak efficiency for that plant.

This phenomenon is known as the **Law of Diminishing Returns**, which can be stated in general terms as follows: "If additional units of one productive input (here, labour) are combined with a fixed quantity of another productive input (here, capital equipment), the average output per unit of the variable input (labour) will increase at first and then decrease."

The Law of Diminishing Returns places an important limitation on Barry's production decisions. While Barry *physically can* increase output to certain levels, doing so may reduce efficiency to such an extent that it becomes actually *uneconomical* to increase output.

Marginal Productivity

We can analyze the data in Figure 8-2 in another useful way: rather than looking at total output, or average output per worker, we can examine the increase in production resulting from the hiring of one additional worker, or the **marginal productivity** (marginal output) per worker. This information is presented in Figure 8-3, which shows that the hiring of the fifth worker increases production by 62 units, and the sixth worker adds 50 units to total output. After that, additional workers add much less. The seventh worker only increases production by 26 units, the eighth and ninth only add 14 units and 8 units, respectively, while the tenth worker barely adds to total output at all—his marginal output is only 2 units. It is important to remember that this does not mean that the quality of the workers is declining. The reason for the decline in marginal output per worker is the Law of Diminishing Returns: once production in Barry's plant moves past the point of peak efficiency, average output per worker will decrease because each additional worker will not add as much to output as previous workers did. This

Law of Diminishing Returns A physical law stating that, if additional units of one productive input (such as labour) are combined with a fixed quantity of another productive input (such as capital), the average product per unit of the variable input (labour) will increase at first and then decrease.

marginal productivity (per worker) The increase in production resulting from the hiring of one additional worker.

diminishing return will have an important impact on production costs, because the cost of the extra units (marginal output) produced by additional workers will rise very rapidly beyond a certain point, making it uneconomical to hire workers and increase output beyond that point. For instance, it is very doubtful that the marginal output of the ninth and tenth workers (8 units and 2 units, respectively) warrants hiring them. Or, viewed differently, the cost per unit of increasing output from 280 units to 290 units would be so high as to be uneconomical.

FIGURE 8-3 Average and Marginal Productivity per Worker

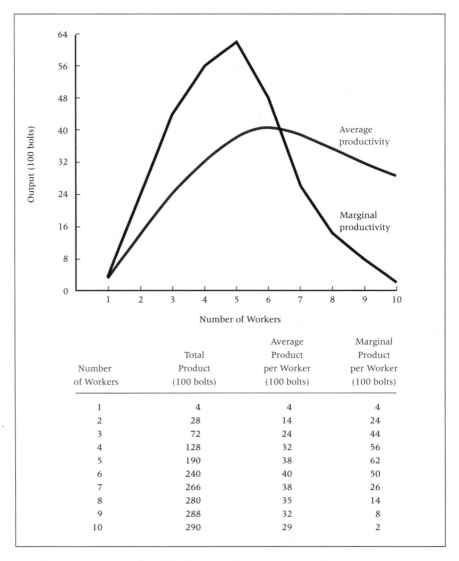

Number of Workers	Total Product (100 bolts)	Average Product per Worker (100 bolts)	Marginal Product per Worker (100 bolts)
1	4	4	4
2	28	14	24
3	72	24	44
4	128	32	56
5	190	38	62
6	240	40	50
7	266	38	26
8	280	35	14
9	288	32	8
10	290	29	2

The cost and productivity factors that we have been discussing restrict Barry's production decisions. Because fixed costs per unit are very high at low levels of output, he must achieve a certain level of production (and sales) in order to operate economically. However, due to the Law of Diminishing Returns, it will not prove economical to increase his output beyond a certain point, since the variable costs per unit (labour costs) will rise to higher levels, as Figure 8-4 shows.

FIGURE 8-4 Average Variable Costs per Unit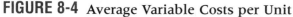

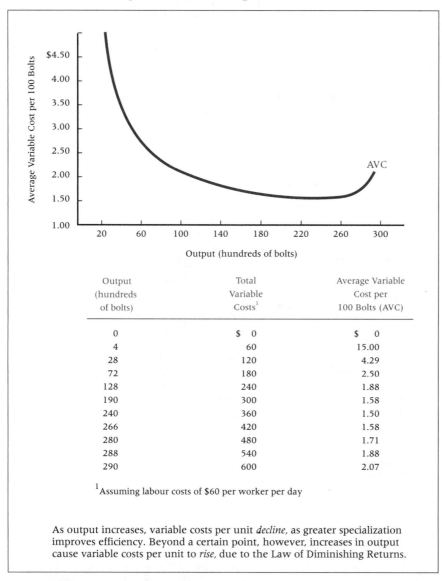

Output (hundreds of bolts)	Total Variable Costs[1]	Average Variable Cost per 100 Bolts (AVC)
0	$ 0	$ 0
4	60	15.00
28	120	4.29
72	180	2.50
128	240	1.88
190	300	1.58
240	360	1.50
266	420	1.58
280	480	1.71
288	540	1.88
290	600	2.07

[1]Assuming labour costs of $60 per worker per day

As output increases, variable costs per unit *decline*, as greater specialization improves efficiency. Beyond a certain point, however, increases in output cause variable costs per unit to *rise*, due to the Law of Diminishing Returns.

In general terms, then, we have outlined the situation Barry's firm faces with respect to production costs, and how this will affect its operations. On the basis of these two figures, Barry can make two more calculations that will help to decide exactly what volume of output to produce. These are the average cost per unit and the marginal cost per unit.

Average Cost per Unit

Table 8-1 summarizes the production costs of Barry's bolt plant. The information in the table is based on the production information discussed earlier: *fixed costs* of $120 per day regardless of the level of output, and *variable costs* consisting only of wages of $60 per day for each worker. *Total costs* are fixed costs plus variable costs, and *average cost per unit* is total costs divided by total output. As we saw earlier, at low levels of output, average cost per unit is high, because of high fixed costs per unit. As output increases, the plant operates more efficiently, reaching a minimum average cost per unit of $2 at a daily output level of 240 units. Further increases in output cause the plant to operate beyond its most efficient level, so that the Law of Diminishing Returns pushes variable costs per unit up again. As a result, average cost per unit increases still further, rising to $2.48 at an output level of 290 units per day.

TABLE 8-1 The Costs of the Firm

Number of Workers	Total Output	Fixed [a]Costs	Variable Costs	Total Costs	Average Cost per Unit[b]	Marginal Cost per Unit[c]
0	0	$ 120	$ 0	$ 120	—	—
1	4	120	60	180	$ 45.00	$ 15.00
2	28	120	120	240	8.57	2.50
3	72	120	180	300	4.17	1.36
4	128	120	240	360	2.81	1.07
5	190	120	300	420	2.21	0.97
6	240	120	360	480	2.00	1.20
7	266	120	420	540	2.03	2.31
8	280	120	480	600	2.14	4.29
9	288	120	540	660	2.29	7.50
10	290	120	600	720	2.48	30.00

[a] Output measured in units of 100 bolts

[b] $\dfrac{\text{Total costs}}{\text{Total output}}$ [c] $\dfrac{\text{Change in total costs}}{\text{Change in total output}}$

Marginal Cost per Unit

marginal cost per unit The addition to total costs resulting from the production of one more additional unit of output.

The last column in Table 8-1—marginal cost per unit—requires some explanation. **Marginal cost per unit** is the addition to total costs resulting from the production of one additional unit of output. For instance, when output is increased from 4 units to 28 units, total costs rise from $180 to $240. In other words, it costs $60 more to increase output by 24 units, making the cost of each additional unit (the marginal cost per unit) $2.50 ($60 ÷ 24). These calculations, together with other examples, are shown in Table 8-2. Marginal cost per unit can be an important tool for the firm in deciding its output. Obviously, if the firm is considering expanding its production, it would be valuable to know the cost per unit of the increased output.

TABLE 8-2 Calculation of Marginal Cost per Unit

Total Output	Total Costs	Marginal Cost per Unit of 100 Bolts	= Increase in Total Costs / Increase in Total Output
0	$120		
4	180	$15.00	$= \dfrac{\$180 - 120}{4 - 0}$
28	240	2.50	$= \dfrac{\$240 - 180}{28 - 4}$
72	300	1.36	$= \dfrac{\$300 - 240}{72 - 28}$

Figure 8-5 presents the average cost per unit and marginal cost per unit data graphically. This graph illustrates a fact concerning the relationship between the two curves: the marginal cost curve always intersects the average cost curve at the lowest point on the average cost curve. If average cost per unit is falling, additional units of output are pulling the average cost down, meaning that the marginal cost of the additional units must be lower

FIGURE 8-5 The Average Cost per Unit and Marginal Cost per Unit Curves of the Firm

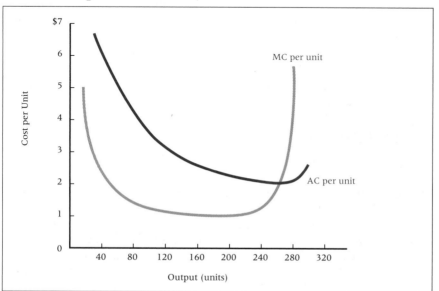

than the average cost per unit. Similarly, if average cost per unit is rising, additional units of output are pulling the average cost up, because the marginal cost of the additional units is higher than the average cost per unit. Thus, when average cost is falling, marginal cost is below the average, and when average cost is rising, marginal cost is above the average—it is only at that point where average cost is at its minimum (neither falling nor rising) that average cost per unit and marginal cost per unit are exactly the same, and the curves intersect. Beyond this output level, as Figure 8-5 shows, marginal cost per unit rises very quickly, as the Law of Diminishing Returns makes it increasingly difficult to increase output by simply adding more workers to the plant.

To summarize information about Barry's production costs, increasing output causes average cost per unit to decrease until it reaches a minimum at an output level between 240 units and 260 units per day. At output levels beyond these outputs, average cost per unit increases again, and rapidly rising marginal cost per unit makes increasing output beyond a certain point uneconomical. What this "certain point" is—and at what level of output Barry will actually decide to produce—will depend not only on how much additional units *cost* to produce but also on how much additional *revenue* they bring in. To complete our analysis of Barry's bolt firm, we must now consider the revenues, or *sales* of the business.

The Revenue Side

Average Revenue per Unit

We will assume that Barry's is one of many small firms in the highly competitive bolt industry, and that the market price of bolts is $3 per unit of 100 bolts. At this price, the firm can sell as many bolts as it can produce, up to its maximum possible output of 290 units per day. In other words, the demand for Barry's product is perfectly elastic, as shown by the demand schedule and demand curve in Figure 8-6. Figure 8-6 also shows that the *price* of the product can be viewed as the *average revenue per unit*; since the firm can sell as many as it produces for $3 per unit of 100 bolts, the *demand curve* can be viewed as the *average revenue per unit sold*.

Marginal Revenue per Unit

marginal revenue per unit The addition to total revenue resulting from the sale of one additional unit of output.

From the demand for Barry's bolts, we can develop a table of information concerning the firm's sales revenues, as shown in Table 8-3. Since the firm can only charge $3 per unit, the average revenue per unit is always $3. *Total revenue*, which is simply price (or average revenue) times quantity demanded, rises in proportion to sales. **Marginal revenue per unit** is the addition to total revenue gained from the sale of one more unit. It can be calculated in the same way as we calculate marginal cost per unit, by dividing the increase in total revenue by the increase in units sold; in each case, total

FIGURE 8-6 The Demand for Barry's Bolts

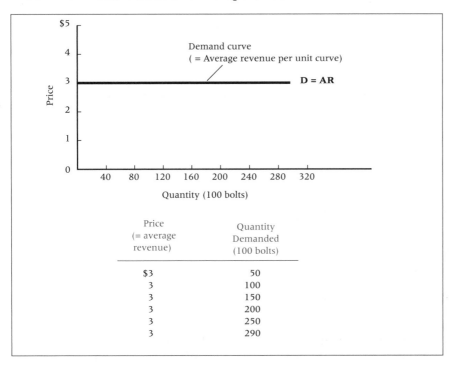

Price (= average revenue)	Quantity Demanded (100 bolts)
$3	50
3	100
3	150
3	200
3	250
3	290

revenue rises by $150 and the number of units sold rises by 50, making the marginal revenue per unit $3 at all levels of sales. With the price always $3 per unit, each additional unit sold must bring in marginal revenue of $3, making the marginal revenue curve identical to the demand curve and the average revenue curve, as Figure 8-7 shows.

TABLE 8-3 The Revenue Side of Barry's Bolts

Price (= Average Revenue)	×	Quantity Demanded	=	Total Revenue	Marginal Revenue per Unit[a]
$3		50		$150	
3		100		300	$3
3		150		450	3
3		200		600	3
3		250		750	3
3		290		870	3

[a] $\dfrac{\text{Increase in total revenue}}{\text{Increase in quantity demanded}}$

FIGURE 8-7 Marginal Revenue per Unit

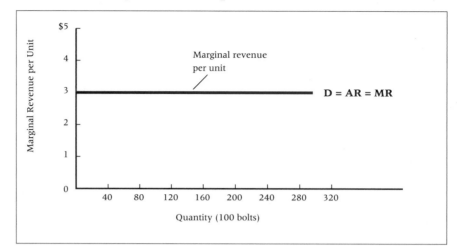

Quantity (100 bolts)

The Most Profitable Output

We now have all of the information about Barry's costs and revenues that the firm needs in order to decide what level of output to produce. Table 8-4 summarizes all of the information we have developed about Barry's costs and revenues and adds a column for total profits, which are total revenue minus total costs. The table shows that low levels of output are unprofitable due to fixed costs, and that profits are maximized at $258 per day by producing 266 units of 100 bolts per day, using 7 workers.

TABLE 8-4 The Costs and Revenues of Barry's Bolts

Number of Workers	Total Output	Fixed Costs	Variable Costs	Total Costs	Total Revenue	Total Profit (+) or Loss (−)	Average Cost per Unit	Marginal Cost per Unit	Marginal Revenue per Unit
0	0	$120	$ 0	$120	$ 0	−$120	—	—	—
1	4	120	60	180	12	− 168	$45.00	$15.00	$3.00
2	28	120	120	240	84	− 156	8.57	2.50	3.00
3	72	120	180	300	216	− 84	4.17	1.36	3.00
4	128	120	240	360	384	+ 24	2.81	1.07	3.00
5	190	120	300	420	570	+ 150	2.21	0.97	3.00
6	240	120	360	480	720	+ 240	2.00	1.20	3.00
7	266	120	420	540	798	+ 258	2.03	2.31	3.00
8	280	120	480	600	840	+ 240	2.14	4.29	3.00
9	288	120	540	660	864	+ 204	2.29	7.50	3.00
10	290	120	600	720	870	+ 150	2.48	30.00	3.00

Tools of Analysis

While it is easy to see why Barry would choose to produce 266 units per day, we can use this simple example to develop other, more sophisticated concepts. Why didn't Barry choose to produce 240 units per day? (This is the output at which the firm operates at peak efficiency and production costs per unit are minimized at $2.) The answer lies in the marginal cost per unit and marginal revenue per unit columns. For each of the extra 26 units (from 240 units to 266 units per day), the *marginal cost* was $2.31 and the *marginal revenue* was $3. So each of these additional units *added* $0.69 of profit to the firm. From this, we can conclude that, *whenever marginal revenue exceeds marginal cost, it is profitable for the firm to increase its output*.

Why, then, did Barry not increase output *beyond* 266 units per day? Again, the answer lies in the marginal revenue and marginal cost columns. While each additional unit of output beyond 266 units per day will still bring in *marginal revenue* of $3, the *marginal cost* of producing each unit will be $4.29. So it is unprofitable to produce these additional units. The Law of Diminishing Returns has made further output increases uneconomical by forcing marginal cost per unit to high levels.

To summarize, it will be profitable to increase output as long as marginal revenue per unit exceeds marginal cost per unit. However, as diminishing returns set in, marginal cost per unit will rise, and once marginal cost per unit

FIGURE 8-8 **Using Marginal Cost and Marginal Revenue to Determine a Firm's Output**

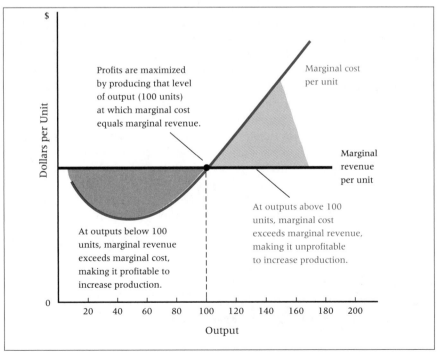

becomes greater than marginal revenue per unit, it will no longer be profitable to increase production. Thus, profits will be maximized at that level of output at which marginal cost equals marginal revenue—that is, where the marginal cost curve intersects the marginal revenue curve. This principle is illustrated in Figure 8-8, which shows that profits are maximized by producing 100 units of output. In the remainder of this chapter, we will use this approach to analyze the price and output decisions of business firms under different market structures, starting with perfect competition as discussed in Chapter 7.

Different Market Structures

Perfect Competition

As noted in Chapter 7, perfect competition is a rare situation in which there are many small firms in an industry, it is easy for new firms to enter the industry, and all firms are selling identical products. The result is the most competitive situation imaginable, in which producers have no control over the price of their products and there is constant downward pressure on profits. Using analysis based on costs and revenues as developed earlier in this chapter, we can now examine the case of perfect competition more closely.

The costs and revenues of the firm in perfect competition will be like those of Barry's Bolts Ltd., which we described as a small firm in a highly competitive industry. The cost curves will have the usual shapes as were described earlier in this chapter,[2] with average cost per unit declining as output increases up to a point, then increasing again. The marginal cost per unit curve rises quite sharply beyond a certain output level and intersects the average cost per unit curve at that curve's minimum point, as shown in Figure 8-9. In perfect competition, the existence of many small firms selling identical products ensures that the demand for any one firm's product will be perfectly elastic. Thus, if the market price of the product is $3 per unit, the demand curve of the individual firm will consist of a horizontal line at a price of $3, as in Figure 8-9. This line will also represent the *average revenue* from each sale (AR) and the *marginal revenue* (MR) for each additional sale, as indicated on the graph.

Figure 8-9 shows a profitable individual firm in a perfectly competitive industry. *Profits* are maximized by producing the output at which marginal cost equals marginal revenue (or price), which is 275 units per day, as point E indicates. Total revenue will be $825 per day ($3 × 275 units). Point F indicates that, at an output level of 275 units, average cost per unit is $2.05, and total costs are $564 ($2.05 × 275 units). So total daily profit will be

---

2. The shapes of the cost curves are determined by physical factors such as the Law of Diminishing Returns; as a result, cost curves have the same general shape regardless of whether the firm is small or large, or in an industry that is highly competitive, oligopolistic, or monopolistic.

FIGURE 8-9 The Firm in Perfect Competition with Profits

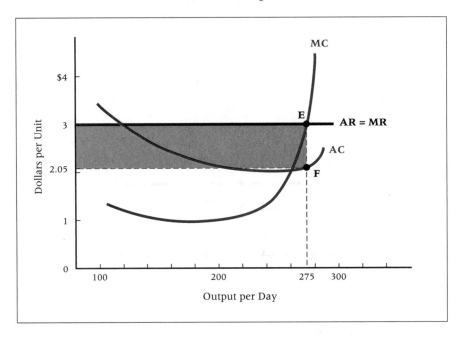

maximized at $261 ($825 − $564), at an output level of 275 units. The shaded area on the graph represents the total profit (275 × $0.95) earned by the firm in this situation.

Dynamics of Perfect Competition

If the firm we have been discussing is a typical firm in the industry, the situation cannot remain as it is shown in Figure 8-9. The profitability of firms in this industry will attract new competitors into the industry, increasing the supply of the product and *reducing its price*. When this happens, the demand curve (labelled AR = MR on Figure 8-9) will move downward as the price declines, reducing the profits of a typical firm. How far can the price fall? Figure 8-10 shows what would happen if the price fell to $1.50: at *every* level of output, average cost per unit exceeds average revenue per unit. As a result, it would be impossible to make a profit at a price of $1.50. By producing 250 units, where marginal cost equals marginal revenue, the firm could minimize its losses, but it would still be losing money.

If the typical firm in the industry were losing money, it is obvious that some firms would have to leave the industry—a polite way of saying that they would go bankrupt. As they left, the supply of the product would decrease, and the price would increase again. How high will the price rise, and at what level will it settle? Figure 8-11 provides the answer: the price will rise to (and settle at) just under $2 per unit, at which point output will be 260 units. At this price, two conditions exist:

FIGURE 8-10 The Firm in Perfect Competition with Losses

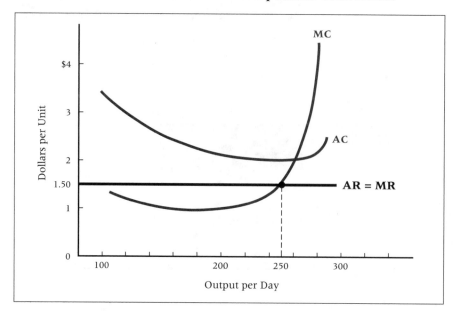

(a) marginal cost equals marginal revenue, so that the firm's profits are maximized, and the firm has no incentive to increase or decrease its output, and

(b) average cost equals average revenue, so that profits are zero, providing no incentive for anyone to enter or leave the industry.

Since one might wonder why anyone would even stay in a business with no profits, we should define profits more precisely. By "profits" we mean business income *over and above the owner–manager's salary,* which represents the opportunity cost of the owner's time and capital. Viewed differently, we assume that the owner–manager will only continue in business if a certain minimum income level is earned, and include that person's salary in the production costs of the business, as a fixed cost.

In conclusion, then, our marginal revenue/marginal cost analysis confirms what we said in Chapter 7 about the firm in perfect competition: the intense competition in such industries will exert constant downward pressure on prices and profits, tending to drive profits to minimal levels. In these circumstances, the only way an individual producer can earn above-average profits is to operate more efficiently than average, so as to enjoy lower-than-average costs per unit.

Monopoly

Monopoly represents the other extreme from perfect competition: a situation in which there is only one producer in the industry, who is able to select the level of output that maximizes profits. In Chapter 7, we discussed *total revenue*

FIGURE 8-11 The Firm in Perfect Competition with No Profits

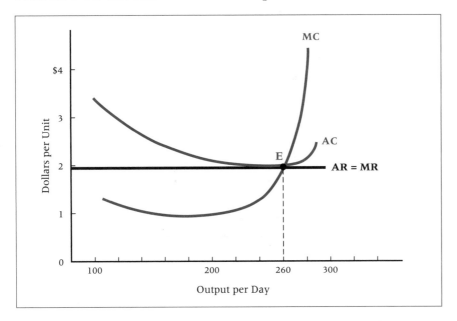

as if it were profit, but now that we have both cost and revenue information, we can analyze the monopolist's price and output decisions more precisely.

For our average and marginal cost curves, we will use the same curves as we used in the example of perfect competition so that we can readily compare the results of the two situations. Under monopoly, however, the *demand* for the product will be *less elastic* because there is only one seller. Since monopolists have more freedom to set prices, the average revenue per unit and marginal revenue per unit curves will be significantly different from those of the firm in perfect competition, as Figure 8-12 shows.

As output is increased, marginal revenue per unit falls more rapidly than average revenue per unit, or the demand curve. The reason why marginal revenue per unit falls so rapidly is that, in order to *sell more units*, the monopolist must *reduce the price*, not only on the additional units sold but also *on all units sold*. For instance, when sales are increased from 85 units to 145 units by reducing prices from $6 to $5, the additional 60 units sold bring in $300 ($5 × 60), but there is $85 less total revenue on the 85 units, because they are selling for $1 less per unit. Thus, the net marginal revenue on the 60 additional units is $215 ($300 − $85), or $3.85 per unit, as shown in Figure 8-12. As sales increase, the monopolist's marginal revenue curve will fall, and will fall more steeply than the demand curve does—a fact that will have an important bearing on the monopolist's price and output decisions.

Price and Output Decisions

To maximize profits, the monopolist will follow our rule of producing that output at which marginal revenue equals marginal costs. Figure 8-13 shows

FIGURE 8-12 Average and Marginal Revenue per Unit for a Monopolist

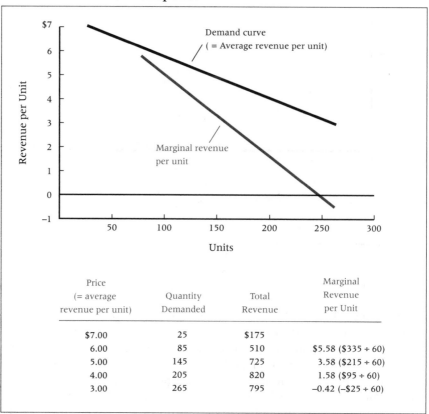

Price (= average revenue per unit)	Quantity Demanded	Total Revenue	Marginal Revenue per Unit
$7.00	25	$175	
6.00	85	510	$5.58 ($335 ÷ 60)
5.00	145	725	3.58 ($215 ÷ 60)
4.00	205	820	1.58 ($95 ÷ 60)
3.00	265	795	−0.42 (−$25 ÷ 60)

that doing this will result in a decision to produce 220 units of output per day. Point P on the demand curve shows that, to sell 220 units per day, a price of $3.75 per unit must be charged. Thus, the monopolist will maximize profits by charging a price of $3.75 and producing 220 units per day. At this level of output, the monopolist's average revenue per unit will be $3.75 (the price), and average cost per unit will be $2.10 (from point C on the average cost curve). The average profit per unit will then be $1.65 ($3.75 − $2.10), and the monopolist's total profits will be $363 per day ($1.65 × 220). The shaded area on the graph in Figure 8-13 represents these profits.

Monopoly and Competition Compared

In a perfectly competitive industry, we saw that the price of each firm's product would be $1.95, the output of a typical firm would be 260 units per day (Figure 8-11), and that competition would push profits downward toward the "normal" level, or the minimum required to keep firms in business. Under monopoly, and using the same cost curves, the price would be $3.75, output would be 220 units (Figure 8-13), and there would be substantial

FIGURE 8-13 The Monopolist's Price and Output Decisions

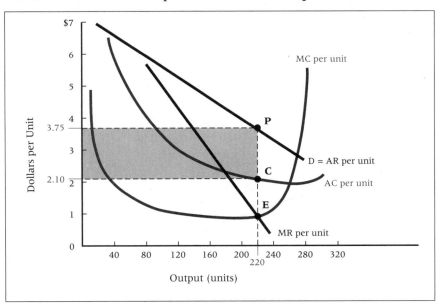

profits.[3] Furthermore, because new firms cannot enter the industry, these profits are secure from competition.

Oligopoly

In Chapter 7, we saw that, while the price and output decisions of oligopolistic industries were of great importance, we could not develop a theoretical basis for analyzing and predicting those decisions. In this chapter, we have developed considerably more sophisticated techniques for analyzing the costs, revenues, and price and output decisions of the firm. However, we are still unable to analyze and predict the decisions of oligopolists precisely, even using these techniques.

The problem lies in the nature of the oligopolist's demand curve. Figure 8-14 shows the demand curve for one firm in an oligopolistic industry in which the firms have agreed upon a price of $6. If this one firm increases its price and the other firms leave their prices at the agreed level of $6, the firm that increases its price will suffer a considerable loss of sales and profits. And if one firm reduces its price, it is reasonable to assume that the other firms will match its price reduction. In that case, the firm that reduces its price will not gain in terms of its market share, and will very likely lose financially. So the demand curve for an oligopolistic firm tends to be "kinked," as

---

3. For comparative purposes, we have used the same cost curves for the small firm in perfect competition and for the monopolist. This ignores the possibility that the monopolist's costs may in fact be *lower* than the small firm's, due to improved technology and mass-production techniques. We will consider this possibility further in Chapter 9.

Figure 8-14 shows. For price increases, demand is elastic, while for price reductions, it is inelastic. Therefore, a single firm cannot gain by either increasing or decreasing its price. So once the price has been established, there is an incentive for each firm to leave its price at that level, until all the firms agree to a new price.

FIGURE 8-14 The Kinked Oligopolistic Demand Curve

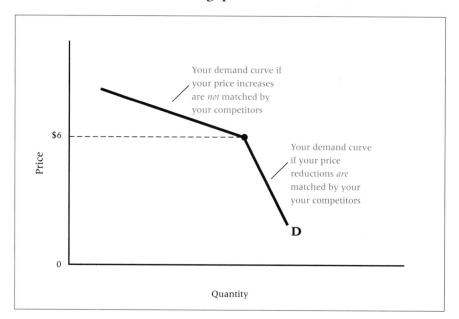

Marginal cost and marginal revenue analysis does not help us to analyze oligopolists' decisions further. As Figure 8-15 shows, even the most modest kink in the demand curve causes strange changes in the marginal revenue curve. At the level of output where the demand curve is kinked, the marginal revenue curve becomes *discontinuous* (see the dotted line in Figure 8-15), leaving us with no clear intersection point for the marginal cost and marginal revenue curves. As a result of this, marginal cost and marginal revenue analysis cannot help to pinpoint oligopolists' price and output decisions. All we can say is that the existence of a kinked demand curve provides a strong incentive for individual oligopolists to leave their price and output unchanged. As Figure 8-15 shows, it would take a major increase in production costs (upward shift of the marginal cost curve) to cause our oligopolist to reduce output and increase prices, while no reduction in costs would induce a price reduction. So all that we can conclude concerning oligopolistic prices through marginal cost and marginal revenue analysis is what we concluded in Chapter 7—that, once set by the industry, oligopolistic prices tend to be quite sticky, and especially resistant to downward movements.

FIGURE 8-15 Marginal Cost and Marginal Revenue Curves for the Oligopolist

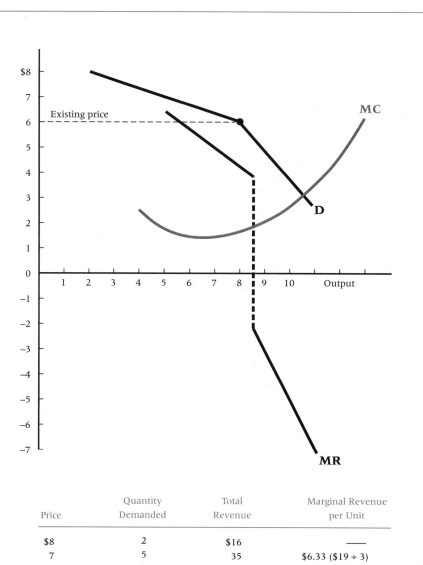

Price	Quantity Demanded	Total Revenue	Marginal Revenue per Unit
$8	2	$16	—
7	5	35	$6.33 ($19 ÷ 3)
6	8	48	4.33 ($13 ÷ 3)
5	9	45	−3.00 ($−3 ÷ 1)
4	10	40	−5.00 ($−5 ÷ 1)
3	11	33	−7.00 ($−7 ÷ 1)

How Realistic Is All This?

A student can reasonably ask the following question about marginal revenue/marginal cost analysis: "Does anybody actually *do* all this?" In the sense of making detailed calculations and drawing exact graphs, the answer to this question is certainly "not many people—mostly economics students."

However, this does not mean that marginal analysis is irrelevant in the real world. While few if any businesspeople make the kinds of calculations referred to in this chapter, it is certainly arguable that the *basic approach* of marginal analysis is used implicitly by businesses. A decision whether to hire additional workers, whether to add more machinery to a plant, or whether to increase output necessarily involves some *estimates* of the impact that decision would have on the costs and revenues (and thus the profits) of the business. Some large companies that have sophisticated cost accounting systems use marginal cost calculations and make pricing decisions based on marginal costs. Implicitly, *every* decision involves marginal considerations; that is, whether the additional costs of the decision are warranted by the additional benefits. While it is not always (or even often) possible to reduce these considerations to numbers as we have done here, the fact remains that marginal analysis is a useful tool for making all kinds of decisions.

Other Business Decisions

We have seen in this chapter how cost and revenue data (in particular, marginal cost and marginal revenue) can be used to determine the most profitable level of output for a firm. There are two other basic business decisions for which cost and revenue data are vitally important: whether to start a new business and whether to shut down an existing business. For example, the owner of Barry's Bolts can use the cost and revenue data in Table 8-1 to decide:

(a) what volume of sales he must achieve in order to justify *starting up* the business, and

(b) how low his sales could fall before he should *close* his business.

The Start-Up Decision

In deciding whether to start up his business, the owner of Barry's Bolts faces the key question of whether he can sell enough bolts to cover his costs. Because high fixed costs per unit cause the average cost per unit to be high at low levels of output, the firm must achieve a certain volume of sales in order to cover its costs, or break even. To make this decision, the owner will use average cost and average revenue data rather than the marginal cost and revenue data for determining the most profitable level of output.

Figure 8-16 shows the relationship between average cost and average revenue in this way: if the price per 100 bolts (average revenue per unit) is

$3, Barry must sell more than 118 units of 100 bolts per day in order to make a profit. At point A, with an output of 118 units, average cost and average revenue per unit are equal, making Barry's profit zero—the firm is breaking even.

FIGURE 8-16 The Start-Up Decision

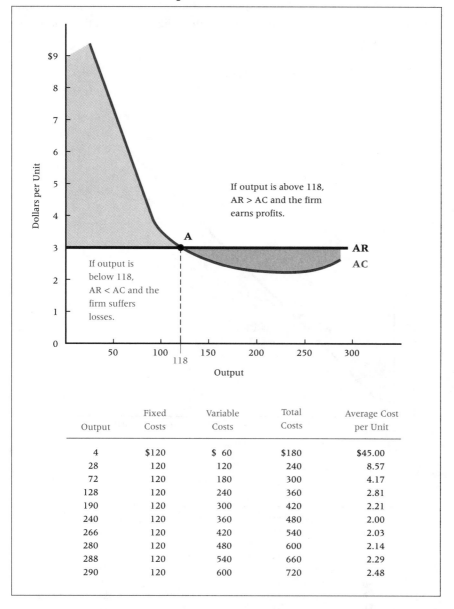

Output	Fixed Costs	Variable Costs	Total Costs	Average Cost per Unit
4	$120	$ 60	$180	$45.00
28	120	120	240	8.57
72	120	180	300	4.17
128	120	240	360	2.81
190	120	300	420	2.21
240	120	360	480	2.00
266	120	420	540	2.03
280	120	480	600	2.14
288	120	540	660	2.29
290	120	600	720	2.48

At output levels below 118 units, average cost exceeds average revenue per unit, and Barry loses money, while at output levels above 118 units, average revenue exceeds average cost per unit, and Barry earns a profit.

Unless the firm's owner can realistically plan on sales in excess of 118 units per day, he should not start up in business.

In business terminology, 118 units per day is said to be Barry's *break-even point*, because at this level of output the firm just barely covers its costs, or breaks even. Break-even analysis similar to that shown in Figure 8-16 is useful when considering whether to start a business; however, it is usually done with *total cost* and *total revenue* data, as shown in Figure 8-17, rather than with average cost and revenue data.

FIGURE 8-17 Break-Even Analysis

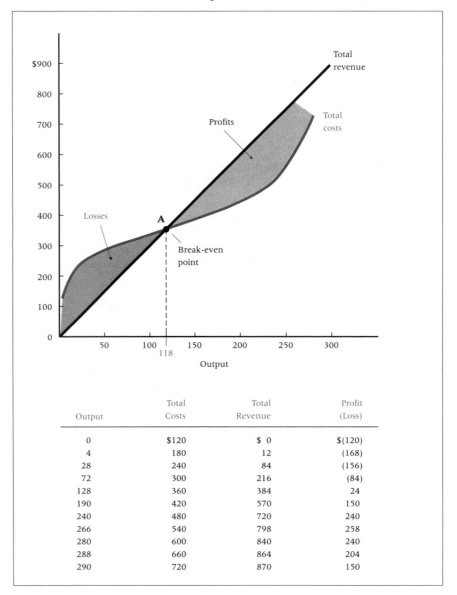

Output	Total Costs	Total Revenue	Profit (Loss)
0	$120	$ 0	$(120)
4	180	12	(168)
28	240	84	(156)
72	300	216	(84)
128	360	384	24
190	420	570	150
240	480	720	240
266	540	798	258
280	600	840	240
288	660	864	204
290	720	870	150

The total cost and total revenue data in Figure 8-17 led Barry to the same conclusion reached earlier: the firm must sell more than 118 units per day in order to make a profit. At sales of 118 per day (point A), it breaks even, with total revenue equal to total costs. At lower levels of output, total costs exceed total revenue, causing the firm to lose money. Only by selling more than 118 units per day can Barry earn a profit.

Figure 8-17 illustrates another point seen earlier in this chapter: the firm will not maximize profits by producing as much output as is physically possible. If output is increased beyond a certain point, the Law of Diminishing Returns causes costs to increase rapidly, making it unprofitable to increase output further. Rather, profits are maximized at an output level of 266 units per day, as we saw earlier.

The Shut-Down Decision

Suppose that, some time after Barry's Bolts was established, the firm's sales begin to decrease. How low can sales fall before the owner should decide to go out of business?

The key factor in this situation is that, even if he stops production, he must still pay his fixed costs, such as rent, interest on debt, and so on.[4] To stop production means incurring fixed costs (losses) of $120 per day. Consequently, it would be better for Barry's Bolts to remain in business (at least in the short run), as long as its losses are *less* than $120 per day. For instance, the table in Figure 8-18 shows that if sales fall to 72 units per day, the firm will lose $84 per day—$36 *less* than the $120 it would lose by stopping production altogether. Why is this so? Because while the firm *is* incurring losses, its total revenue of $216 exceeds its variable costs of $180 by $36. As a result, by continuing production, it can use this $36 to offset some of the fixed costs, so that it loses $84 rather than the $120 it would lose by stopping production completely. The firm is therefore $36 better off (or less badly off) to remain in business producing 72 units per day, than to stop altogether.

As a general rule, we can conclude that as long as total revenue exceeds variable costs, the firm should remain in business rather than close down, because its losses will be smaller. Put differently, only when variable costs exceed total revenue should the firm close. For Barry's Bolts, this occurs when sales fall below 55 units per day, as the graph in Figure 8-18 shows. If the firm cannot sell 55 units per day, it should close down.

---

4. These fixed costs must still be paid in the short run; for instance, rent must be paid until his lease expires. Over a longer period of time, all costs can be viewed as variable (particularly if he goes out of business).

FIGURE 8-18 The Shut-Down Decision

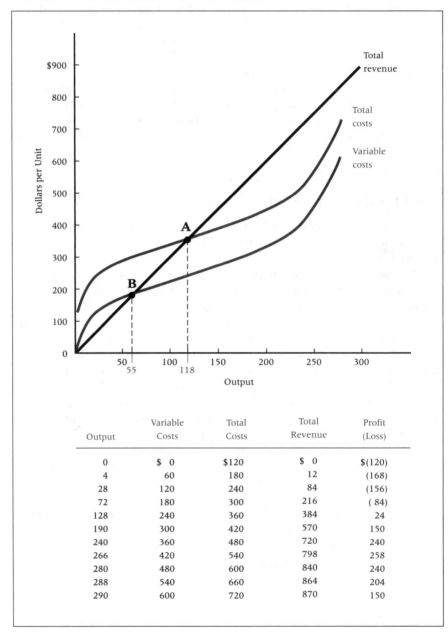

Output	Variable Costs	Total Costs	Total Revenue	Profit (Loss)
0	$ 0	$120	$ 0	$(120)
4	60	180	12	(168)
28	120	240	84	(156)
72	180	300	216	(84)
128	240	360	384	24
190	300	420	570	150
240	360	480	720	240
266	420	540	798	258
280	480	600	840	240
288	540	660	864	204
290	600	720	870	150

Thus, cost and revenue data can be used not only to determine the most profitable level of output for a firm but also to determine the minimum level of sales required to start up a business, and the level of sales at which a decision is made to shut down the business.

Chapter Summary

1. A firm's average costs per unit are high at low levels of output, due to high fixed costs; then, they decline as output increases. Beyond a certain output level, however, average costs per unit rise again, as variable costs per unit increase due to the Law of Diminishing Returns. (L.O. 1)

2. The marginal cost per unit curve will rise quite sharply beyond a certain output level, intersecting the average cost per unit curve at that curve's minimum point. (L.O. 1, 3)

3. A firm's profits will be maximized by producing the output level at which marginal cost equals marginal revenue. (L.O. 2, 3, 4)

4. Under perfect competition, there will be a horizontal demand (or average revenue or marginal revenue) curve, which will be forced downward by competition until the marginal revenue curve intersects the marginal cost curve at the minimum point on the average cost curve. (L.O. 2, 3, 4)

5. The result of this situation will be an equilibrium, in which profits are zero. There is no incentive for each firm to increase or reduce output, and no incentive for firms to enter or leave the industry. (L.O. 4)

6. Under monopoly, as output increases, marginal revenue per unit decreases, falling faster than the demand (average revenue) curve. (L.O. 2)

7. As a result, under monopoly, the marginal cost and marginal revenue curves intersect at a lower level of output than under competition, the result being lower output, higher prices, and higher profits under monopoly than under competition. (L.O. 2, 3, 4)

8. Because an oligopolist's demand curve is "kinked," the marginal revenue curve is not continuous at the existing price and output, providing no clear intersection point for the marginal cost and marginal revenue curves and thus creating an incentive for each oligopolist to leave the price at the existing level once it has been set. (L.O. 2, 3, 4)

9. A firm's revenue and cost data can be used in a similar manner to determine the output/sales level above which profits will be earned and below which the firm should be shut down. (L.O. 5, 6)

Questions

1. The following data show recent prices for "cool white" fluorescent lighting tubes of various sizes:

    *   15": $9.49

    *   48": $1.69

    Why do you suppose the larger tube has the lower price?

2. What explains the fact that the classic 939-page *Dr. Spock's Baby and Child Care* sells for the same price as a relatively unknown novel of less than half its length by a relatively unknown author?

3. Complete the last five columns of the following table:

Output	Fixed Costs	Variable Costs	Total Costs	Average Fixed Cost per Unit	Average Variable Cost per Unit	Average Total Cost per Unit	Marginal Cost per Unit
0	$600	$ 0	$___	$___	$___	$___	$___
5	600	150	___	___	___	___	___
10	600	200	___	___	___	___	___
15	600	225	___	___	___	___	___
20	600	340	___	___	___	___	___
25	600	600	___	___	___	___	___

(a) As output increases, why do the following change as they do:
    (i)   average fixed cost per unit,
    (ii) average variable cost per unit, and
    (iii) average total cost per unit?

(b) What does "marginal cost per unit" mean? Why does it change as it does as output increases?

4. Sally's Shirts Ltd. sells shirts at a price of $22 each. Sally's fixed and variable production costs are indicated in the following table:

Units of Output per Day	Fixed Costs	Variable Costs	Total Costs	Average Cost per Unit	Average Revenue per Unit	Marginal Cost per Unit	Marginal Revenue per Unit
0	$200	$ 0	$___	$___	$___	$___	$___
10	200	170	___	___	___	___	___
20	200	320	___	___	___	___	___
30	200	440	___	___	___	___	___
40	200	580	___	___	___	___	___
50	200	800	___	___	___	___	___
60	200	1100	___	___	___	___	___

(a) Complete the five remaining columns in the table.

(b) On graph paper, plot the average cost per unit, marginal cost per unit, average revenue per unit, and marginal revenue per unit curves.

(c) Use the graph that you drew for your answer to part (b) above to determine the following:

    (i) The level of output at which profits will be maximized is ___ units per day.

(ii) At this level of output, the level of profits will be $___ per day. (Show your calculations.)

(d) Is Sally's Shirts Ltd. operating in a perfectly competitive market? If this firm is in a perfectly competitive industry and is a typical, profitable firm, what adjustment will occur in the price of the product, and how will this affect the profits of this typical firm? What will be the final equilibrium price?

5.

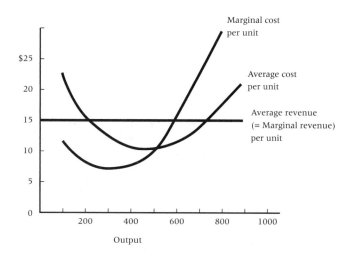

For the firm whose costs and revenues are shown in the graph above,

(a) profits will be maximized at a level of output of ___ units, and

(b) at this level of output, profits will be $___. (Show your calculations.)

(c) Is this firm operating in a perfectly competitive market? If this firm is in a perfectly competitive industry and is a typical, profitable firm, what adjustment will occur in the price of the product, and how will this affect the profits of this typical firm? What will be the final equilibrium price?

6. The following are the cost and revenue data for tables produced by Peter's Patios Ltd.:

If the company charges this price per table:	It will sell this many tables per week:
$38.00	0
33.50	20
29.00	40
24.50	60
20.00	80
15.50	100
11.00	120

The company's fixed costs and variable costs are shown in the following table.

Units of Output per Week	Fixed Costs	Variable Costs	Total Costs	Average Cost per Unit	Average Revenue per Unit	Marginal Cost per Unit	Marginal Revenue per Unit
0	$400	$ 0	$___	$___	$___	$___	$___
20	400	180	___	___	___	___	___
40	400	330	___	___	___	___	___
60	400	430	___	___	___	___	___
80	400	560	___	___	___	___	___
100	400	780	___	___	___	___	___
120	400	1080	___	___	___	___	___

(a) Complete the five remaining columns in the table.

(b) On graph paper, plot the average cost per unit, marginal cost per unit, average revenue per unit, and marginal revenue per unit curves.

(c) Use the graph that you drew for your answer to part (b) above to determine the following:

(i) The level of output at which profits will be maximized is ___ units per week.

(ii) At this level of output, the level of profits will be $___ per week. (Show your calculations.)

(d) Is Peter's Patios Ltd. operating in a perfectly competitive market? If this firm is operating in a perfectly competitive industry and is a typical, profitable firm, what adjustment will occur in the price of the product and the profits of this typical firm? What would be the final equilibrium price?

7.

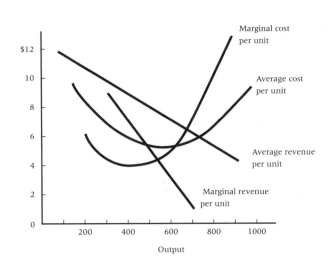

For the firm whose costs and revenues are shown in the previous graph,

(a) profits will be maximized at a level of output of ___ units, and

(b) at this level of output, profits will be $___. (Show your calculations.)

(c) Is this firm operating in a perfectly competitive market? If this firm is in a perfectly competitive industry and is a typical, profitable firm, what adjustment will occur in the price of the product, and how will this affect the profits of the typical firm? What will be the final equilibrium price?

8. Kermit's Kandles Ltd. sells candles at a price of $8 each. The following is a table showing Kermit's fixed and variable production costs.

Units of Output per Day	Fixed Costs	Variable Costs	Total Costs	Total Revenue
0	$400	$ 0	$____	$____
100	400	1000	____	____
200	400	1700	____	____
300	400	2200	____	____
400	400	2500	____	____
500	400	3200	____	____
600	400	4400	____	____

(a) Complete the remaining two columns in the table.

(b) On graph paper, draw the total revenue, total costs, and variable costs curves.

(c) The graph indicates that the minimum level of output (sales) required for this firm to reach the break-even point is ___ units per day.

(d) The graph indicates that, before this firm should go out of business, its sales should fall below a level of ___ units per day.

Explain the reasons for your answers to parts (c) and (d).

9. Peter's Pet Food sells bags of pet food to retail stores for a wholesale price of $8 each. The table on the next page shows Peter's weekly costs and revenues. Complete the remaining columns in the table.

Output (bags per week)	Fixed Costs	Variable Costs	Total Costs	Total Revenue	Profit
0	$800	$ 0			
100	800	400			
200	800	800			
300	800	1200			
400	800	1600			

10. Peter is considering a different business model in which, instead of selling to retailers at the wholesale price of $8 per bag, he establishes a website, becomes an ebusiness, and sells the pet food directly to consumers (who order over the internet) at a retail price of $16 per bag. However, this business model will also involve higher costs, as follows: due to the cost of the website and other assets he will need, his fixed costs will double from $800 per week to $1600 per week, and due to higher costs of delivery and customer service, his variable costs will double from $4 per bag to $8 per bag.

(a) Complete the following table showing Peter's costs, revenue, and profits.

Output (bags per week)	Fixed Costs	Variable Costs	Total Costs	Total Revenue	Profit
0					
100					
200					
300					
400					

Compare the profits of the "conventional" business model in Question 9 to this model at each level of output and sales shown:

(b) What is less attractive about the ebusiness model? Why does this risk exist?

(c) What is more attractive about the ebusiness model? Why does this opportunity exist?

(d) What will Peter have to achieve in order to avoid the risks and secure the opportunities of the ebusiness model so that it is more profitable than the "conventional" model?

(e) What obstacles will he have to overcome in order to achieve the goals outlined in part (d)?

11. Some ebusinesses produce and sell only electronic products, such as packages of information or entertainment. Unlike physical products, once the original product has been created, the production process consists of simply duplicating the original. As a result, the marginal cost per unit of producing more of these products is extremely low, and stays very low as output is increased.

What are the implications of this production process for the business strategies of producers of these products?

Chapter 9

Government Policy Toward Business

Learning Objectives

After studying this chapter, you should be able to:

1. Give examples of how government policy tends to be supportive of businesses in industries that are highly competitive, while being more restrictive toward businesses in industries that are less competitive.

2. State two ways in which government policies support the incomes of farmers.

3. State three ways in which government policies assist small businesses.

4. Describe two types of government actions that have negative effects upon small businesses.

5. Give four reasons for the high degree of industrial concentration in the Canadian economy.

6. Summarize the arguments in favour of and against governments restricting mergers of large Canadian corporations.

7. Explain how Canada's Competition Act attempts to address the arguments both for and against governments restricting mergers of large corporations.

8. Describe two traditional government methods for protecting consumers against the market power of natural monopolies.

9. Give two reasons why governments have recently opened up some natural monopolies to competition and have privatized some government enterprises.

The Ideal of Competition

Chapter 1 stressed the importance of producers being *effective* (by producing things that are useful and wanted) and *efficient* (by producing those items without wasting scarce economic resources). Generally, economists and government policy-makers have tended to prefer competitive industries to concentrated ones, on the grounds that competition serves the consumer best, by promoting both effectiveness and efficiency. In competitive industries, consumer demand pushes businesses to produce whatever consumers will buy, and competition pushes businesses to produce it efficiently. Strong competition among businesses also ensures that consumers will not pay excessively high prices and that producers' profits will be reasonable.

The Theory of Laissez-Faire ...

If the entire economy were competitive in this way, it would comprise a self-regulating system for determining the answers to basic economic questions such as what to produce and how to produce it. The marketplace would do such a good job of promoting effectiveness and efficiency that there would be no need for government intervention to improve the operation of the economy.

This theory of a competitive economy that serves the consumer so well that there is little or no need for government regulation or intervention is known as **laissez-faire**. The concept of laissez-faire originated in France at the time of Louis XIV, as a reaction to a web of government regulations of business that had grown so complex and restrictive that it stifled incentives and was actually causing the economy to stagnate. By comparison, a free competitive economy would be much more effective at promoting prosperity.

laissez-faire The doctrine or philosophy that from the viewpoint of the public interest, it is neither necessary nor beneficial for governments to intervene in the operation of the economy.

... Versus Economic Reality

But our modern economy is not as simple as that of the theory of laissez-faire. Vigorous competition in an industry is not a stable condition; rather, it can eliminate so many firms that only a few are left. And as we saw in Chapter 7, in some industries such as steel and petroleum, the competitive marketplace has evolved to the point where there are only a few corporations left, raising concerns that in those industries there is *too little* competition. At the other extreme, in parts of the agricultural sector, there are so many small producers with low incomes that there are concerns that *excessive* competition will force too many farmers out of business and undermine this important industry.

In pursuing the ideal of vigorous competition, then, governments have found themselves in some cases introducing policies that seek to *restrict and regulate* the market power of large firms with little competition, while in other cases government policies seek to *support and assist* small firms in highly competitive environments.

Government Policies Toward Business

In Chapter 7, we examined the four basic types of market structure:

*   perfect competition, the most competitive possible situation,
*   monopolistic competition, which characterizes most of the small business sector of the economy,
*   oligopoly, in which industries are dominated by a few large firms, and
*   monopoly, in which there is only one seller.

The market power of firms operating under these market structures ranges from none whatsoever (in the case of perfect competition) to very great (in the case of a monopoly). Accordingly, government policy toward businesses tends to differ from one type of market structure or industry to another. In general, we will find that the more competitive an industry is, the more *supportive* government policy will be, and the less competitive it is, the more *restrictive* government policy is likely to be. In this chapter, we will consider some of the highlights of government policies toward business in Canada, the reasons for the variations in these policies, and some of the problems concerning them. To organize the discussion, we will use the four types of market structure described above.

Government Policies Concerning Competitive Industries

Perfect Competition

The sector of the Canadian economy that most closely resembles perfect competition is *agriculture*. In agriculture, there are large numbers of producers, mainly family farms, selling products that are more or less identical to those of other farms. Technological advances have increased farm productivity to the point where there is a general tendency to oversupply markets, with the result being low farm prices and incomes. To make matters worse, fluctuations in weather and crop size cause farm prices and incomes to be unstable as well as generally low.

Because of the extreme competitiveness of agricultural markets and the problems that this creates for farmers, the general thrust of government policy has been to *support farm prices and/or incomes* through a variety of programs.

As we saw in Chapter 6, governments have sometimes employed *price supports* for some farm products. Under this method, the government establishes the price of the farm produce and undertakes to purchase from the farmers at that price any produce that is unsold. As we also saw in Chapter 6, the result of farm price supports will be surpluses of farm produce. To avoid the problem of crop surpluses, governments have sometimes employed *acreage restrictions*. Under such a program, farmers are paid *not* to grow crops on part of their land in order to reduce the supply of farm products and increase their prices.

Canadian governments have several programs under which *direct payments* are made to farmers if crop prices or yields fall below the long-term average. These programs are partly funded by farmers themselves, and partly financed by the government. These programs are very important to farmers—in bad years, as much as 75 percent of farmers' net income can come from such government programs.

In addition to this assistance, governments help to increase some farmers' incomes through **marketing boards**. These are government-sponsored organizations of farmers that are intended to restrict how much farmers produce, so as to keep prices higher. As such, a marketing board is a form of government-approved price-and-production agreement similar to the oligopolistic agreements discussed in Chapter 7. To protect the high prices charged by marketing boards, the government must provide further assistance by *restricting imports* of cheaper products to prevent these from competing with Canadian products. We cover government agricultural policy in much more detail in Chapter 15.

marketing boards
Government-sponsored organizations of farmers that support farm incomes by restricting the supply of produce, usually through a system of quotas on individual farmers.

Monopolistic Competition

In monopolistic competition, there are many small firms producing and selling differentiated products or services in a highly competitive environment. This is a reasonable description of the small business sector of the Canadian economy, which, as we saw in Chapter 3, has played a vital role in the creation of jobs.

Because small businesses operate in such a highly competitive environment and face many difficulties as described in Chapter 3, various government programs are available to assist them. Both the federal and provincial governments offer loan guarantees or lower-cost, longer-term financing for small businesses. At the federal level, the Business Development Bank of Canada makes term loans to new or existing businesses that are unable to obtain the required funds from other lenders on reasonable terms and conditions, and offers an extensive management training program. Most provincial governments offer financial help through similar agencies, with loan guarantees arranged through regular financial institutions and screening processes to minimize failure rates.

www.bdc.ca

The Canada Small Business Financing Act (1998) helps small businesses to obtain financing by providing government guarantees of 85 percent of losses to lenders (mostly banks) for certain types of loans to small businesses. Counselling programs are also available from the federal government and most provinces to assist small business owners with their management problems. Such programs help small businesses that are unable to afford expert counselling, utilizing various people, including Masters of Business Administration students, retired executives, and professional counsellors. Also, marketing programs are offered by all provincial governments. These programs are intended to assist small businesses in the opening up of new markets, both in Canada and abroad, and some are designed to complement programs offered through the federal Export Development Corporation.

www.edc.ca

Some provinces also offer personnel assistance programs to help small businesses find skilled employees, and in some cases, the wages of employees are subsidized by the government in order to aid small businesses in recruiting. Finally, government programs provide research and development assistance in the form of subsidies and by helping small businesses apply new technology in various ways.

In total, there is a bewildering array of well over 500 programs for small business offered by the federal, provincial, and municipal governments. According to some observers, a major problem facing many small business owners is finding the time to evaluate the wide variety of programs that could be of value, and to work through the extensive paperwork that many of them require. To aid in these matters, some governments have set up information centres to help small businesses determine where to look for aid, and have undertaken to reduce the amount of paperwork involved.

www.cfib.ca

However, not all government policies and programs are helpful to small business. According to the Canadian Federation of Independent Business (CFIB), *taxation* and *government regulation* are the two major impediments to the operations and growth of small and medium-sized businesses in Canada.

In January 2001, the federal corporate tax rate on business income (profits) between $200 000 and $300 000 was reduced from 28% to 21%. On profits over $300 000, the federal tax rate will be reduced to the same extent by 2004.

CFIB research has shown that labour-intensive small businesses actually pay a higher proportion of their profits to taxes than many larger businesses do. The main reason for this anomaly is that the burden of payroll taxes, such as Employment Insurance, workers' compensation premiums, and taxes for health care, falls most heavily on smaller, more labour-intensive businesses, whose labour costs are a higher proportion of their total costs. (See Question 4 at the end of Chapter 3.)

Government red tape and paper burden was the second most frequently identified problem by CFIB members. Small business owners cannot afford the considerable amount of time they are required to divert from managing their operation to filling out government forms relating to statistical information and tax collection—for many, this amounts to 5 to 10 hours per week.

Finally, there is the question of how much assistance should actually be given to small businesses. Sometimes, businesses should be allowed to fail because they are not viable, or the people involved do not have the abilities required to operate a successful business. But neither the government, nor anyone else, quite knows how to recognize the potential of a new, small business or how much assistance is appropriate. Nonetheless, the importance of small business to the Canadian economy has led to a variety of government programs intended to help small businesses, particularly in starting up.

Government Policies Regarding Concentrated Industries

Oligopoly

In Chapter 7 we saw that, when an industry is dominated by a few large firms, or oligopolists, it's possible that these firms will agree among themselves to fix prices. It was also mentioned in Chapter 7 that this practice is illegal in Canada, as it is in most countries. However, as we will see, the question of Canadian government policy toward large corporations is considerably more complex than such legalities suggest.

Industrial Concentration in the Canadian Economy

To the extent that a particular industry or market is dominated by a few firms, it is said to be *concentrated*. Studies have repeatedly shown that industrial concentration in the Canadian economy is not only high but also considerably higher than in the U.S. economy.

> **industrial concentration**
> The degree to which an industry is dominated by a few firms.

This domination of much of Canada's economy by large corporations is viewed with concern by some, especially consumer groups. In the corporate concentration in certain sectors of the economy, they see a dangerous extent of oligopolistic power. On the other hand, defenders of big business argue that large corporations increase the prosperity of Canadians by making their industry more efficient and better able to compete internationally, a consideration made more important by the trend toward freer trade in recent years.

The debate between critics and supporters of big business becomes more heated whenever there are *mergers* of major corporations, such as those that have occurred in recent years in key industries such as brewing, oil, airlines, steel, retailing, forest products, and bookstores. Critics oppose such mergers on the grounds that they only increase the domination of Canadian markets by fewer and larger corporations. But defenders of the mergers argue that Canadian firms can only succeed in highly competitive international markets if they merge in order to grow larger and more efficient.

In this section, we will consider the reasons for the high degree of industrial concentration in Canada, the debate over whether large corporations are a threat or an advantage to Canadians, and the important question of what government policy toward industrial concentration and mergers should be.

Reasons for Concentration

There are various reasons why some industries come to be dominated by a few large firms. One basic reason is the *elimination of firms by competition*: in a competitive market economy, successful firms will expand, and unsuccessful ones will not survive. A major contributing factor to this tendency is economies of scale—as successful firms expand, they use mass-production technology that gives them additional production-cost advantages over their competitors.

> **economies of scale**
> Lower production costs per unit made possible by higher volumes of production that permit the achievement of increased efficiencies.

The *small size of the Canadian market* is also a significant factor in Canada's high degree of industrial concentration. With a total market size about one-tenth that of the United States, there is often simply not enough room in Canada for more than a few plants that are large enough to capture the economies of scale that exist in modern manufacturing.

Finally, *mergers of corporations* also increase corporate concentration. During the 1990s, merger activity in Canada was spurred by another consideration—the need for Canadian firms to become more efficient and internationally competitive. Since the early 1980s, there has been a trend toward increased international competition, or the **globalization** of many markets. This trend, together with the Canada–U.S. Free Trade Agreement and the North American Free Trade Agreement, not only created more intense foreign competition for many Canadian industries in Canadian markets but also increased export opportunities for Canadian firms. To improve their ability to compete with their often larger foreign counterparts in the United States and Europe, some Canadian firms merged with others, so as to gain economies of scale, more complete product lines, stronger marketing networks, better access to financial resources, and so on. For instance, the Molson–Carling O'Keefe merger was intended to increase the efficiency and capacity of the company's Canadian brewing operations while giving it access to the worldwide distribution network of Elders IXL Ltd., Carling's Australian parent company. Similarly, Dofasco's merger with Algoma Steel made it the fourth-largest steel-maker in North America while giving it an expanded and balanced product line that was expected to position the company well for competing in the U.S. market. And the 1999 takeover of Canada's MacMillan Bloedel by U.S. giant Weyerhaeuser made the Canadian company a key part of the world's third-largest forest products company.

globalization The growing internationalization of business, trade, and finance that has characterized the period since the early 1980s.

During the 1990s, merger activity increased sharply in many countries, driven in large part by firms' desire to achieve the scale needed for global competition. This trend was assisted by rising stock prices in the 1990s, since in many mergers one firm uses its own shares as payment to shareholders of the firm being acquired. The lower interest rates of the 1990s also helped firms to finance their purchases of other companies. Another factor was conglomerates' sale of companies as part of the trend toward focusing on their core business. Examples of such sales included Imasco's sale of Canada Trust to Toronto-Dominion Bank and Molson's sale of Beaver Lumber to Home Hardware.

In Canada, it was not unusual to see as many as 1000 mergers per year during the 1990s as firms repositioned themselves to deal with international competition both in foreign markets and in Canada. This merger activity was unprecedented in terms of both the numbers of mergers and the size of many of the enterprises that resulted from these mergers.

The Debate Over Bigness in Business

Critics of big business argue that since the Canadian economy has a high degree of industrial concentration, Canadian consumers are exposed to a high risk of price-fixing by oligopolists. They point to the fact that Labatt and

Molson hold a combined market share of about 90 percent of the Canadian beer market as a prime example of unhealthy corporate concentration. In the retail sector, they see evidence of decreasing competition in Hudson's Bay Co.'s purchase of Kmart and its merger of Kmart with its Zellers division, Home Hardware's purchase of Beaver Lumber, and the bookstore merger of Indigo and Chapters. They also point to periodic convictions of corporations for price-fixing and note that the profits of many oligopolists represent a considerably higher rate of return on investment than that earned by an average business.

According to this view, if competition cannot be relied upon to keep prices and profits in check, the government must set down rules for oligopolists to follow and must "police" their behaviour. In particular, governments must not only prevent price-fixing and other measures that reduce competition but also prevent mergers of companies where these would reduce competition, and even break up excessively dominant corporations into smaller firms if necessary.

Defenders of large corporations argue that these big firms actually contribute to the economic prosperity of Canadians. They emphasize the reinvestment of the profits of big business into capital equipment and improved technology that improve productivity in the Canadian economy.

They argue that this higher productivity benefits Canadians in two ways. First, as we have seen, higher output per worker is the basis for *higher living standards*. By using mass-production technology, large producers can reduce production costs so much that even after their above-average profits are added, the price to the consumer is still lower. If productivity is high enough, it is possible for workers to have high wages, companies to have high profits, and consumer prices to be low. And, as supporters of big business point out, if you wanted to show someone a showpiece of Canadian technology, you would probably go to one of the country's vast automobile assembly plants that uses computerized industrial robots and turns out as many as 75 cars per hour.

Second, there is the question of the *international competitiveness* of Canadian producers. Much of Canada's manufacturing industry has historically been small-scale by world standards and, therefore, not very efficient or competitive internationally. So it can be argued that mergers of Canadian firms into fewer but larger and more efficient operations contribute to Canada's international competitiveness. This point is particularly important because so much of the output of the Canadian economy is exported, and so many jobs rely upon the success of Canadian firms in export markets.

The Policy Dilemma

The arguments for and against bigness in business present government authorities with a very real dilemma in deciding government policy toward industrial concentration. To leave the power of big business unchecked would risk exposing consumers to price-fixing. On the other hand, strong restrictions on big business could limit the growth and efficiency of Canadian firms and their ability to compete internationally.

> "People of the same trade seldom meet together, even for merriment and diversion, but the conversation ends in a conspiracy against the public, or in some contrivance to raise prices."
>
> Adam Smith, *The Wealth of Nations* (1776).

> "[Mergers] reduce Canadian competition, raise prices for consumers and cause job losses. I can't see how any of those things in any way benefit Canadians or the economy."
>
> David McKendry, Consumers Association of Canada.

This dilemma is especially troublesome in Canada, where the situation can be summarized as follows:

(a) industrial concentration in Canada is *substantially higher* than in comparable industries in the United States;

(b) however, the average size of Canada's 100 largest industrial corporations and Canada's 25 largest financial corporations is *very much smaller* than the average size of their counterparts in the United States and other developed countries.

This awkwardly contradictory state of affairs is illustrated in Figure 9-1. It shows that many corporations that are sufficiently large to dominate markets and raise concerns about threats to consumers *within Canada* may be relatively small and not competitive by *international standards*. And, in order to become internationally competitive, these firms would have to grow larger, and thus *more* dominant within the Canadian market. These facts make the policy dilemma referred to earlier particularly severe for Canadian policy-makers—while industrial concentration in Canada is presently high enough to support the argument for strong laws restricting further growth and concentration, policies that do so could prevent Canadian corporations from growing to the size needed to be internationally competitive.

FIGURE 9-1 The Competition Policy Dilemma

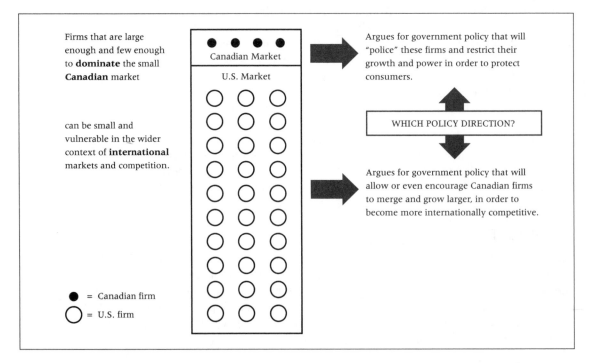

The Changing Economic Environment: Globalization

Historically, Canadian government *trade policy* and *competition policy* were geared to *national markets*. Through its *trade policy*, the government imposed tariffs on imported goods in order to foster the development of Canadian manufacturing industries by protecting them against foreign competition. On the other hand, the government's *competition policy* sought to protect Canadian consumers from price-fixing and other anticompetitive practices by oligopolistic industries (many of which were, themselves, protected by the same government's tariffs against foreign competition). So the government was in the position of trying to *promote competition* among Canadian producers within the Canadian market, while at the same time *restricting competition* from foreign firms in that same market.

The more recent trend toward freer trade has made the concept of gearing policies to national markets less relevant. As nations cut tariffs, international competition became more intense and markets became more international—the process known as *globalization.* As new trade agreements were signed (the Canada–U.S. Free Trade Agreement of 1989, NAFTA in 1994, and the 1995 World Trade Organization agreement), Canadian industry was faced with the prospect of growing competition. Also, the economic integration of Europe into a single market of 340 million made it likely that North American producers would soon face stronger competition from larger and more efficient European firms. These trends toward the globalization of markets pushed policy-makers toward thinking more about *international* concerns, especially the ability of their nation to compete in global markets. In this context, big business came to be seen in a less unfavourable light than in the past.

The trend toward freer trade had some major implications for the debate on industrial concentration in Canada. First, freer trade made it more important than ever that in framing its policy regarding big business, the Canadian government take into account the ability of Canadian corporations to compete internationally. Also, the increased competition from imports that would come with freer trade reduced concerns about the market power of large Canadian corporations. In the view of many observers, *freer trade* would do more to protect Canadian consumers against the market power of oligopolists than *Canadian laws* possibly could.

The Competition Act

Canada's competition legislation is the Competition Act, which was passed in 1986. The basic goal of the law is to promote and preserve competition in Canadian markets.

Under the Competition Act, the basic test is whether the effect of firms' actions would be (or had been) to *lessen competition substantially* in a given market. Obviously, a price-fixing agreement between competitors would have this effect and therefore be illegal. With respect to mergers, the situation is less clear-cut—the key is not simply the size of the companies or their share of the market, but rather the effect of the proposed merger on competition in the marketplace. The test of a merger under the Competition Act is

> "The core of the policy is the likely effect of a proposed merger on competition, whether domestic or foreign."
>
> Professor William Stanbury, UBC Faculty of Commerce and Business Administration.

whether competition would be substantially lessened by the merger.

In addition, the Competition Act explicitly allows for the approval of mergers that would likely result in *efficiency gains* that would offset any likely reduction in competition. This allows companies to defend mergers that would increase their *ability to compete internationally.*

The Competition Act is administered by the Competition Bureau, which is attached to the Department of Industry (Industry Canada). The Bureau must be notified of any plan to merge or acquire businesses in which the total assets or total annual revenues of the firms exceeds $400 million. After notifying the Bureau, the parties must wait for 7 days to 21 days before completing the merger.

The Bureau then reviews the proposed merger or acquisition, considering whether:

(a) it is likely to lessen competition substantially, and
(b) there are likely to be real gains in efficiency that will exceed, and offset, the lessening of competition.

Other factors to be considered include barriers to entry to the particular market (which would affect future competition), the extent of foreign competition, the effectiveness of the competition that would remain after the proposed merger, and the availability of alternatives (such as selling all or part of a firm involved in a merger to other firms).

If the Bureau has concerns about the effect of the proposal on competition, it will seek to negotiate amendments to the proposal with the companies involved. The result is usually a negotiated agreement. However, if the Bureau has doubts, it can also grant conditional approval for a merger and then monitor the competitive conditions in the market following the merger.

If the Bureau and the companies are unable to agree, the matter is taken to the Competition Tribunal for a decision. The Competition Tribunal is chaired by a judge of the Federal Court of Canada, and consists of 12 members, including business and consumer authorities as well as judges. The Tribunal operates under the same procedural rules as a civil court, and its decisions may be appealed to the Federal Court of Canada.

For instance, in 1996, the Competition Tribunal issued an order that required Interac Inc. and the nine banks and other financial institutions that comprised the charter members of Interac to open up its network to potential participants on a nondiscriminatory basis, and to cease levying new member entry fees that had deterred entry into Interac. The order was issued in response to an application from the Competition Bureau that alleged that the charter members of Interac substantially or completely controlled the market for the supply of shared electronic-network banking services in Canada.

Experience with the Competition Act

With respect to mergers, since the Competition Act was passed in 1986, the Competition Bureau has examined on average some 150 merger proposals each year. Most of these have been accepted without challenge; however, in

---

http://cb-bc.gc.ca

The Competition Bureau generally will review a merger if the market share of the merged firms would exceed 35 percent.

In 2003, Air Canada's market share was about 73 percent.

a few cases, the Bureau asked for changes to proposed mergers or challenged them. In several other cases, the merger plans were voluntarily abandoned by the parties following objections by the Bureau. While the names of the companies involved were not revealed, it is reported that several of these plans involved large and well-known firms. Almost all of the Bureau's concerns were resolved through negotiations; only a small number of cases were forwarded to the Tribunal for adjudication.

The most common type of negotiated settlement between the Bureau and the companies involved restructuring proposed mergers through the sale of some assets to competitors in order to maintain competition in particular markets. For instance, in the Imperial Oil–Texaco merger, Imperial agreed to sell various Texaco assets, including over 600 gas stations across the country, mostly in market areas where competition would be reduced by the merger. And in order to gain the approval of the Bureau for their merger, Indigo and Chapters agreed to sell 13 superstores and 10 of Chapters' smaller mall-based stores. In such cases, the Bureau's objective is to find a balance that would allow the companies to achieve the economies of scale that they were seeking without reducing the number of competitors in the market so far as to substantially lessen competition.

With respect to price-fixing, there was general agreement that the new law was more effective than the previous law in that convictions were easier to obtain and penalties were more severe, including a maximum fine of $10 million. Following the passage of the new law, there were several noteworthy cases involving heavy fines.

Probably the most notable of these occurred in 1998, when Archer Daniels Midland Co., a huge American food company, was fined U.S.$16 million for conspiring with seven other companies to fix the prices of a feed additive and a flavour enhancer. Similar offences had resulted in a U.S.$100-million fine in the United States in 1996. And in 1999, three European and two Japanese pharmaceutical companies were fined U.S.$88.5 million for fixing the prices of various vitamins. The international nature of the companies' actions raised the question of whether some sort of international competition legislation was required for the new era of globalized markets and multinational corporations.

www.admworld.com

Canada's Banks—To Merge or Not To Merge?

Canada's banks are big in the small Canadian market, comprising five of Canada's largest 15 corporations in 2001. But they are small compared to European, Japanese, and American banks—the assets of Canada's largest bank (Royal Bank of Canada) are less than one-third those of any of the largest banks in the world. And recently, banks and financial institutions in other countries have been growing even larger as they merged and formed business alliances as part of the process of globalization. In 1996, the Dominion Bond Rating Service observed that, "Ultimately, we believe consolidation within the Canadian banking sector is inevitable if Canadian banks are to remain globally competitive."

In January 1998, the Royal Bank of Canada and the Bank of Montreal announced their intention to merge, and in April, the Canadian Imperial Bank of Commerce and the Toronto-Dominion Bank announced similar plans. Both mergers would require the approval of both the Competition Bureau and the federal Minister of Finance.

A flurry of controversy greeted the announcements. Defenders of the mergers argued that unless Canadian banks merged, they would be unable to compete with larger foreign banks, and pointed to bank mergers in Europe, Japan, and the United States that were creating even larger global giants. They also cited studies showing that Canadian banks' profits were, contrary to public opinion, only about average when compared to their U.S. and European counterparts, and that service charges to customers were lower than in the United States. In addition, they noted that studies showed that Canadian banks were less cost-efficient than leading banks in the United States and the United Kingdom, presumably due to the smaller size of the Canadian banks. Finally, they argued that the federal law limiting any one shareholder to 10 percent of the shares of a bank was preventing Canadian banks from participating in international mergers and partnerships, and that Canada's banks risked being left behind in (or worse yet, left out of) the trend toward larger banks and international partnerships.

Critics of the mergers argued that there was already too little competition in the Canadian banking industry, and that the banks had been earning record-high profits. There was also fear of branch closings and job losses, as well as reduced competition, reduced service, and higher service charges. The banks' claim that mergers were required in order to remain competitive was questioned by a C.D. Howe Institute study that found that there was no relationship between banks' size and their profitability. It was also reported that the Competition Bureau had found that in nearly 40 percent of the geographical areas it examined, the merged bank would have more than a 35 percent market share, which is the "trigger" for Competition Bureau concern regarding concentration.

Regardless of these arguments, the overriding reality was a political one—Canada's banks were unpopular with the Canadian public, mainly because of their record-high profits. In December 1998, the federal government decided to turn down the two proposed mergers. However, few observers believed that this would be the end of the matter.

For their part, the banks intensified their lobbying for the removal of the 10-percent limit on the holdings of any one shareholder, which would allow them to pursue more business partnerships and alliances with foreign financial institutions that could buy into Canadian banks. Within a few months of the federal government's rejection of its merger with CIBC, Toronto-Dominion announced plans to purchase Canada Trust. The TD/Canada Trust merger would create Canada's largest bank in terms of retail customers, personal deposits, and personal loans. Within three weeks, three Japanese banks added a different perspective by merging to form the world's largest bank, with combined assets more than seven times as large as the merged TD/Canada Trust.

And for its part, the federal government moved ahead with plans to allow increased foreign competition in the Canadian banking sector, as required by a 1997 World Trade Organization agreement. In the context of the worldwide trend toward mergers into larger banks, many observers regarded the government's rejection of the mergers of Canadian banks as a decision that was politically useful at the time, but one that might well be reconsidered at a future time, when there was more foreign competition in the Canadian banking sector and when the political climate was less hostile to bank mergers.

IN THE **NEWS**   The Superior Propane Case

In 2000, the Competition Tribunal made quite an unusual decision involving a proposed merger between Superior Propane and ICG Propane. Despite the fact that the merger would substantially lessen competition in 66 of 74 local markets for propane and create a monopoly or near monopoly in 16 other local markets, and would increase the price of propane by an estimated 8 percent, the Competition Tribunal *upheld the merger*. The Tribunal gave as its reason the "efficiency exception," arguing that the increased efficiency of the merged firm overrode the interests of propane consumers. The Competition *Bureau* then took the unusual step of appealing the decision of the Competition *Tribunal* in the Federal Court of Appeal!

The court agreed with the Bureau and directed the Tribunal to reconsider its decision. The Tribunal refused to change its decision, stating that of the estimated $40.5-million negative impact of the merger on consumers, only the $2.6-million effect on *low-income* consumers should be counted against the efficiency gains. In April 2002, the Competition Bureau again appealed the Tribunal's decision to the Federal Court of Appeal.

This case strikes at the very purpose of the Competition Act. The Competition Bureau has been providing updates on the progress of this key case on its website. Visit this website to check for updates and to see if there is a final resolution of the case.

www.strategis.ic.gc.ca/ SSG/ct01250e.html.

Questions

1. What appears to be the reasoning of the Competition Tribunal in reaching its decision?

2. If the courts were to uphold the Competition Tribunal's position, what do you think would happen next?

Monopoly

As we saw in Chapter 7, monopoly is the market structure under which there is the strongest market power, because the monopolistic seller has complete control over the supply of the product, and hence its price.

Monopoly is therefore regarded as the least desirable of all of the market structures we have examined.

Natural Monopolies

Nonetheless, there are certain industries in which monopoly is the most logical form of organization. Generally, these industries are *public utilities and services,* such as water and public transit. The economic rationale for having monopolies in such industries starts with the fact that such utilities often require *very heavy capital investment* in facilities and equipment. This in turn results in *high fixed costs,* such as depreciation and interest on funds borrowed to finance these investments. The best way to keep these fixed costs as low as possible *to each customer* is to spread them over the maximum possible number of customers. By giving one producer a monopoly that guarantees it all of the available customers, the natural monopoly should be able to provide the service at a lower cost per customer than would otherwise be possible.

Creating a monopoly in this way will lower the production costs of the firm, but how can the government ensure that the benefits of this efficiency go to the consumer in the form of lower prices, and not to the monopoly itself? A way to protect consumers is for the government to *nationalize* the monopoly, by placing it under government ownership and having the government operate it on a nonprofit basis. Canada Post is an example of this approach. Another approach is to leave the monopoly under private owner- ship but subject its rates (prices) to *government regulation*—Bell Canada's local telephone service is an example of this approach. The government will regulate the monopoly's rates (prices) in such a way as to permit the company to earn a reasonable rate of return on its shareholders' investment, so as to be fair to shareholders of the utility as well as to consumers.

It may seem that if natural monopolies are owned or regulated by the government, the public will be protected against overcharging. However, the matter of regulating monopolies has not turned out to be quite as simple as that. In order to regulate the prices to be charged by a natural monopoly, the people responsible for determining the regulations must possess considerable knowledge about that industry, its operations, and its costs. The most likely source of people with such knowledge is the industry itself, in the form of retired senior officials of the enterprise being regulated. Even if the regula- tors come from outside the industry being regulated, they must depend heavily for their information on the management of the monopoly. So the process of regulation is sometimes not the simple, objective, and effective procedure that it is intended to be. It is neither possible nor fair to generalize concerning the effectiveness of regulatory boards, since some seem to be much more effective protectors of the consumer's interests than others.

More recently, some critics have called into question the basic premise that natural monopolies are economically beneficial to consumers. One crit- icism is that some natural monopolies have charged *excessively high prices,* not because they earn high profits (in fact, many actually lose money), but rather because they employ excessive numbers of people and pay above-market wages and salaries. As a result, critics say, they have developed into inefficient bureaucracies with excessively high labour costs that become the justification for forcing up the rates that they charge to their captive customers.

A second reason for questioning the benefits of natural monopolies is that technological progress has created the possibility of *new forms of competition* for established natural monopolies. For instance, new technology now permits competition in long-distance telephone service, and fax machines, email, electronic banking, and telecommunications technology are breaking down Canada Post's monopoly over some kinds of mail service. In a similar way, changes in communications technology are breaking into the field that once was thought to "belong" to cable television companies. These changes suggest that it may prove more beneficial to the public to open up some established natural monopolies to competition than to maintain those monopolies subject to the traditional consumer protections of government ownership or rate regulation.

Whether critics are concerned about the rates charged by natural monopolies or about making alternative technologies and services available to the public, their usual recommendations are to *open up the monopolies to competition* and possibly to *privatize* them (sell them to private investors), with the goal of making them more efficient and effective through some combination of competition and the profit motive.

In some jurisdictions, government-owned electricity generation monopolies are being replaced (or supplemented) by private firms that

---

YOU DECIDE

LAISSEZ-FAIRE VERSUS GOVERNMENT REGULATION IN CANADA

Historically, there has been considerable *government regulation* in Canada of various industries, such as transportation and communication, on the grounds that government regulation benefits and protects the public. More recently, we have seen a trend toward *deregulation* of some industries, most notably telephone service, cable television, and airlines, on the grounds that the public benefits more from free competition among producers. Such deregulation of industries represents a movement in the direction of laissez-faire, in the sense that the government is relying more upon competition and less upon government regulation to benefit and protect consumers.

Questions

1. Do you think that the public benefits more from government regulation or from free competition?

2. Do you agree with the theory of laissez-faire's premise that, if the economy were comprised entirely of competitive industries, there would be no need for government intervention or involvement in the economy?

generate electricity and sell it to the distribution network in competition with each other. This approach brings us back in the direction of "laissez-faire," as shown in the "You Decide" box on the previous page.

Chapter Summary

1. Government policy toward business in Canada tends to be more supportive of businesses in more competitive industries, and more restrictive toward businesses in less competitive situations. (L.O. 1)

2. In the case of agriculture, which is the sector of the economy that most closely approximates "perfect competition," government policy is quite supportive in a variety of ways intended to both increase and stabilize farmers' incomes. (L.O. 2)

3. With respect to the small business sector, which fits the description of "monopolistic competition," many government programs are available, mostly to help small businesses to get started. However, small businesses find that two of their main problems—taxation and government "red tape"—also arise from the actions of governments. (L.O. 3, 4)

4. The Canadian economy has a high degree of industrial concentration for various reasons, including competition, economies of scale, the small size of the Canadian market, and mergers of firms. (L.O. 5)

5. However, many Canadian industrial corporations are small by international standards. As a result, while it can be argued that government policy should restrict mergers that would increase industrial concentration even further, it can also be argued that it is in Canada's best interests for some firms to merge so as to become more efficient and more competitive internationally. (L.O. 6)

6. The Competition Act is intended to provide the public with protection against anticompetitive behaviour by firms enjoying a dominant position in the Canadian marketplace, while allowing Canadian firms to merge for the purpose of increasing efficiency and thus improving their ability to compete internationally. (L.O. 7)

7. Traditionally, it has been Canadian government policy to allow "natural monopolies" in many public utilities and services in order to gain cost advantages, and either to place these monopolies under government ownership or to have their rates regulated by government. (L.O. 8)

8. Recently, concerns regarding the efficiency of some natural monopolies and the rates they have been charging have led governments in the direction of opening them up to competition and/or "privatizing" them. (L.O. 9)

Questions

1. If you were on the Competition Bureau, which of the following two merger proposals would you be more likely to accept and why:
    (a) a merger of two furniture manufacturers that would give the new company 65 percent of the Canadian market for a particular type of furniture, or
    (b) a merger of two national supermarket chains that would give the new chain 50 percent of the market in many areas?

2. With Labatt and Molson holding a 90 percent share of the Canadian beer market, is there anything governments could do to increase competition in this market?

3. In 2001, it was reported that the Competition Bureau would issue an order prohibiting Air Canada from *reducing* its fares below a certain point on certain flights in eastern Canada that were also serviced by low-cost carriers WestJet and CanJet.

    Ordinarily, one thinks of the Competition Bureau as opposing the *increasing* of prices. What would explain its objection in this case to Air Canada's *lowering* of prices?

4. Have there been any new developments in the area of bank mergers? If so, keep a clippings file on these and compile a report. Also, visit the homepage of the Competition Bureau at www.strategis.ic.gc.ca/SSG/ ct01250e.html.

5. Visit the Competition Bureau's website (see Question 4) and report to the class on any significant recent developments or cases involving the Competition Act and the Competition Bureau.

Chapter 10

Labour Markets and Labour Unions

Learning Objectives

After studying this chapter, you should be able to:

1. Explain, with the aid of a graph, how wages are determined in the nonunion sector of the labour force.

2. Give two reasons for the large differences in incomes that exist, and explain why these differences persist.

3. Explain, with the aid of a graph, the effects of a minimum wage law on a low-wage labour market.

4. Describe the collective bargaining process for employers and unions as required by law, and explain the purpose of each of its four steps.

5. Explain the difference between compulsory conciliation and compulsory arbitration with respect to industries other than essential services.

6. Describe the collective bargaining process for unionized employees in essential public services, and give two reasons why the final step in this process is not regarded as ideal.

7. Identify the year in which union membership as a percentage of the labour force reached its peak, and give three reasons for its decline since then.

In the past few chapters, we have examined *markets for goods and services*, and how prices are determined in these markets by supply and demand, under conditions ranging from highly competitive to monopolistic. In these markets, the sellers are business firms and the buyers are mostly households, or consumers. Markets for goods and services are shown by the flows in the top half of Figure 10-1.

The flows in the bottom half of Figure 10-1 show *markets for labour*. In labour markets, the roles of households and businesses are reversed—the sellers are members of households (workers) seeking to sell their labour services, and the buyers are business firms who want to employ people with various skills. The items being "bought" and "sold" are the time and skills of the workers, and the "price" is the wage or salary the workers receive. In labour markets, the supply of various occupational skills interacts with employers' demand for those skills to determine the wages and salaries (or prices) of different types of labour.

FIGURE 10-1 The Operation of a Market Economy

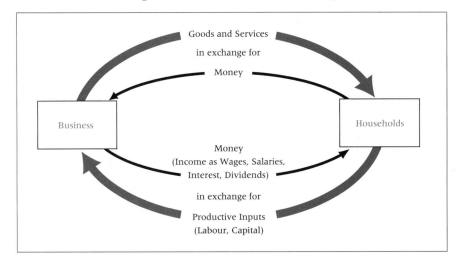

In Chapter 7, we saw that markets for products could be described as *competitive* or *concentrated*. In competitive markets, sellers are not organized for the purpose of controlling supply, so prices are determined by the free interplay of supply and demand. In concentrated markets, by contrast, producers can sometimes organize themselves to restrict the supply of the product and keep its price high. These two types of product markets are shown in Table 10-1.

Table 10-1 also shows that labour markets can be characterized in the same way that product markets can. *Nonunion* labour markets are similar to *competitive* industries in that there are large numbers of sellers (workers) who are *not organized* in order to increase their market power and thus gain economically. In contrast, *unionized* groups of workers are more comparable to *concentrated* industries in which business firms are *organized* and band together to gain market power and higher incomes.

TABLE 10-1 Markets for Products and Markets for Labour

Markets for Goods and Services	Markets for Labour
(a) Competitive Many sellers; *not organized* to restrict competition and control supply and price. Sellers deal as *individuals*.	*(a) Nonunionized* Numerous workers (sellers of labour); *not organized*; deal with buyers (employers) as *individuals*.
(b) Concentrated A few large sellers; sometimes *organized* to restrict competition and influence price by deal *as a group*.	*(b) Unionized* Workers are *organized* by unions to restrict competition among themselves; deal as a group with employers in pursuit of higher wages, etc.

In Chapter 1, we saw that one of the three fundamental economic questions is how to divide up the "economic pie" among Canadians. This allocation is decided by the incomes of Canadians, which are mostly determined in the labour markets that we will study in Chapter 10. First, we will consider the nonunion sector of the labour market, then the unionized sector.

The Nonunion Sector

The nonunion sector of the labour force embraces a wide variety of people, including the self-employed, managers, most office workers, most service-industry employees (ranging from banking and finance to small-scale service firms such as restaurants and retail shops), and many part-time workers in a variety of occupations. In total, the nonunion sector accounts for about two-thirds of Canada's labour force.

Tiger Woods and a gas-station attendant are both members of the nonunion sector of the labour force.

The incomes of these groups, and of individuals within each group, are determined by a variety of complex factors; however, certain generalizations can be made. Broadly speaking, in the nonunion sector, the forces determining wages and salaries are the *supply of* and *demand for* various types of labour, as shown in Figure 10-2.

The supply of a particular type of labour (for instance, window washers) depends on a number of factors, such as the number of people with the required abilities and training and their willingness to work in the field. Also, as the shape of the supply curve shows, higher wages will attract more of these potential workers to actually offer their services to employers. This is the same relationship that we saw in Chapter 5—higher prices (here, wages) result in a greater quantity of labour supplied.

derived demand The demand for a factor of production, which is generated by (derived from) the demand for the good or service that it is used to produce.

The demand for window washers is a **derived demand** because it is dependent on, or derived from, the demand for window washing. That is, the higher the demand for window washing is, the higher the demand for window washers will be. However, other factors, such as technological change, will also affect the demand for window washers, by altering the number of workers needed to wash a given number of windows.

FIGURE 10-2 The Market for Window Washers

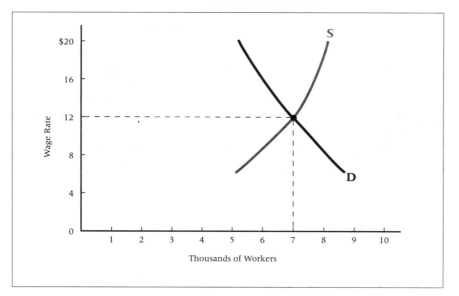

Finally, as the shape of the demand curve in Figure 10-2 shows, the number of workers actually demanded (employed) by employers will depend to a significant extent on the wages of those workers—at higher wages, it will not be economical to hire as many window washers as at lower wages. So a variety of factors underlie the demand and supply curves that determine the wage rate for nonunion workers. In the market for window washers depicted in Figure 10-2, the equilibrium wage rate is $12 per hour, and 7000 people will be employed.

Labour Markets

The Role of Labour Markets

Labour markets perform the important role of allocating labour to various occupations according to the demand of employers and, ultimately, the consumers who buy their products/services. In this role of allocating labour, wages—or, more precisely, *changes in wages*—play an important part. For instance, if the demand for window washing increased, the demand for window washers would increase, causing the demand curve to shift to the right, as shown in Figure 10-3. The result would be an increase in the wage rate of window washers from $12 to $16 per hour, which would attract an additional 2000 people to accept jobs in this field. So, in response to increased consumer demand, employment in this industry has risen from 7000 to 9000. And if the demand for window washing decreased, the market would operate in the opposite direction, as lower wage rates discouraged people from entering this occupation.

FIGURE 10-3 An Increase in the Demand for Window Washers

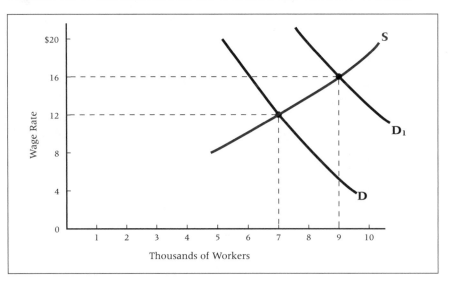

Labour Markets in the Short Run and the Long Run

Labour markets do not always adjust to changes rapidly and smoothly. In the **short run** (the period when some factors of production are fixed), an increase in wage rates may not call forth an increase in the number of workers, due to the time it takes to recruit and/or train workers. In the **long run** (the period in which the quantities of inputs *can* be changed), higher wage rates will attract more people into a field. But in occupations that require a great deal of training, such as medicine, this increase in the number of workers can take considerable time.

The more elastic the supply of labour is, the more smoothly a labour market will operate. Figure 10-4 illustrates this concept by comparing the response of the market for clerical workers and the market for computer programmers to an identical increase in demand. In the case of clerical workers, homemakers provide a pool of qualified workers who are not working but available for work. This makes the supply quite *elastic*—a relatively small increase in wages and employment opportunities will attract many additional workers into the market. As a result, the increase in demand from D to D_1 causes a large increase in employment (from 100 to 130) and only a small increase in wages (from $10 to $12).

In the market for computer programmers, the supply of labour is *inelastic*. Almost all qualified people are already working, and due to the training period required, the number of programmers cannot be increased very much, at least not in the short run. This inelasticity of supply is reflected in the steep slope of the supply curve in graph (b) of Figure 10-4, which shows that even a sharp increase in the wage rate will not bring forth a large increase in the number of computer programmers on the market. As a result, the same increase in demand as for clerical workers has a quite different effect, causing

FIGURE 10-4 Elasticity of Labour Supply and the Operation of Labour Markets

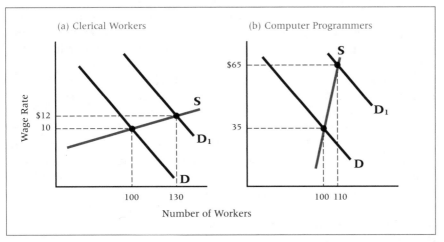

only a small increase in employment (from 100 to 110) and a very large increase in wages (from $35 to $65), at least in the short run. In the long run, the higher wages may attract additional people into computer programming; that is, the long-run supply curve may well become much more elastic.

The Dynamic Nature of Labour Markets

The days when a person would settle into one job or one employer indefinitely are long gone. Because of changes in underlying economic factors such as consumer demand, industrial technology, and international competition, as well as changes in general economic conditions such as periodic booms and recessions, labour markets tend to be very dynamic. In some sectors of the economy and some occupational areas, the number of jobs will be expanding, while in others it will be contracting. As a result, in any given year, there is a large flow of people into the labour market, out of the labour market, and between jobs within the labour market.

Because of these fluctuations, governments provide a variety of programs designed to help workers adjust to changing job markets. Such programs range from the temporary income support provided by Employment Insurance to programs that retrain workers and help them to relocate in order to take new jobs.

Statistics Canada has found that Canadians of working age are constantly in a state of labour market transition: going from job to job; from job to unemployment and back; from outside the labour force to a job; and from unemployment to out of the labour force (not seeking work). In a two-year study that tracked the labour market experience of a group of Canadians, Statistics Canada found that only 52 percent of the working-age population was without a transition in the two-year period studied, and just 38 percent remained in the same job throughout. The other 48 percent averaged more than three transitions. This flux amounted to 52 000 transitions per working day, or 7000 every working hour.

Income Differentials

The free interaction of supply and demand in the marketplace generates a tremendous range of incomes (income differentials), from those of star athletes and entertainers to those of part-time student workers. In competitive markets, one might wonder why such large income differentials persist over long periods of time. Computer programmers earn far higher incomes than clerical workers. So why wouldn't more people (including clerical workers dissatisfied with their low incomes) be attracted to become programmers, thus increasing the supply of programmers and reducing the income differential between them and clerical workers?

The answer, of course, lies mainly in the fact that there are often *obstacles* to entering certain occupations. Not everyone has the *abilities and skills* required to become a computer programmer, or the opportunity to pursue the education required, so the income differentials between the two groups tend to persist. Similarly, the scarcity of people with the talents to be top athletes or entertainers, or who will undertake unpleasant or dangerous jobs, causes their incomes to be very high compared to incomes for jobs that many people are able and willing to do.

Educational requirements are a major obstacle to entering certain occupations. Sometimes, educational requirements are based on specific knowledge that must be acquired in order to perform a job (such as accounting), while in other cases employers use educational requirements as a handy screening device for applicants (such as the requirement of a Bachelor of Arts degree for certain jobs).

Because of the cost of higher education, money is sometimes an obstacle to entering certain occupations. For instance, medical and law schools are more accessible to the children of well-off families than poor families. Because of this, many Canadians regard equality of educational opportunities as a key social policy objective, since education is the main way for the children of lower-income families to break out of the "poverty trap."

Obstacles to entering occupations are not the only reason for differences in incomes. Age and experience have a large influence on people's incomes, as most people's incomes are low in their early years of work and peak after age 50. Another factor is *market power*. We saw in Chapter 7 how business firms can obtain market power by acting together; in the second half of this chapter, we will see how some groups of workers do the same thing, by joining together into labour unions.

To summarize, differences in incomes are generated by various factors, including:

- abilities and skills,

- educational requirements,

- age and experience, and

- market power.

Minimum Wage Legislation

The fact that, in an open labour market, some groups earn very low wages has led governments to enact **minimum wage** laws that set legal minimums for the wage rates that employers can pay their employees. In Figure 10-5, the equilibrium or market wage rate is $4 per hour, but the government has set the legal minimum wage rate at $6 per hour.

The objective of minimum wage legislation is to increase the incomes of low-wage earners. However, as Figure 10-5 shows, minimum wage legislation also has the side effect of *increasing unemployment*. At the equilibrium wage rate of $4 per hour, 90 000 workers are employed, whereas at a legal minimum wage rate of $6 per hour, only 80 000 jobs exist (point A). There are fewer jobs because the higher wage rate reduces the number of workers that employers can and will employ. Furthermore, the higher wage rate attracts an additional 10 000 workers into the labour force who are looking for work, bringing the total number of people wanting to work to 100 000 (point B), and total unemployment of these workers to 20 000 (the distance AB).

FIGURE 10-5 The Effects of a Minimum Wage

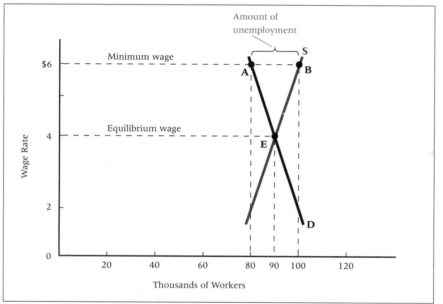

While there is little doubt that minimum wage laws do reduce the number of jobs, there is also considerable debate as to *how much* they increase unemployment. Generally, employers emphasize the job-destroying aspects of minimum wage laws, while labour unions and other groups that support minimum wages argue that the negative effects on employment are minimal. Supporters of higher minimum wage rates argue that past increases in the minimum wage rate have not been followed by layoffs of employees. However, the effect of higher minimum wages may be more subtle than this, as the "disemployment effect" may arise more from reduced hiring of new workers than from layoffs of existing ones. Then, as

About one million Canadians, or roughly 8 percent of the labour force, work for the minimum wage. The typical minimum wage earner is under 25, and many are females working in the food service industry.

It is estimated that slightly less than one-fifth of minimum wage earners are heads of households.

A study commissioned by the Ontario government estimated that a 10-percent increase in the minimum wage rate would increase unemployment in Ontario by about 25 000 and would raise the unemployment rate by about a quarter of a percentage point. A subsequent study indicated that a larger increase in the minimum wage rate, to about 60 percent of the average industrial wage rate, would cost about 50 000 jobs and would increase the unemployment rate for youths and women by about two percentage points.

workers who left were not all replaced with newly hired workers, the total number of jobs would be reduced. According to labour economists, minimum wage laws create a sort of "lottery," in which the winners are the workers who remain in (or get) jobs at the higher wage rates required by the law, while the losers are those who do not get jobs because of the minimum wage. In particular, researchers believe that minimum wages limit employment opportunities for women, many of whom work in service industries such as restaurants, and for younger workers, who are just entering the labour force and often must compete with more experienced workers for jobs.

While the extent of this *disemployment effect* is uncertain, the basic reality is that in order to lift low-wage earners out of poverty, the legal minimum wage would have to be increased substantially from the current levels. And most observers agree that such large increases in the minimum wage rate would have serious effects on the job opportunities of the very people the minimum wage was intended to help. So increases in the minimum wage rate would not be an effective way to combat poverty. In Chapters 11 and 12, we will consider the problem of poverty and other ways of assisting the poor.

To summarize, in the nonunion sector of the labour force, employees' wages and benefits are largely determined by **individual bargaining** between employees and employers. Each worker is free to seek the best deal he or she can get from an employer, and employers are free (subject to legislated rules such as minimum wage laws and employment standards legislation) to seek the best deal they can obtain from workers. The forces that determine how this bargaining process works out for the participants are the supply of and demand for various productive skills. If the demand for a particular type of skill is high and the supply is low, people with that skill will have the bargaining power to obtain high incomes. In the opposite situation, incomes will be low, because supply exceeds demand. Because there are great differences in the supply/demand balance for various skills, labour markets generate some extremely high incomes and some very low ones. Governments attempt to support low-wage earners with minimum wage laws; however, minimum wage rates cannot be made too high because they have the side effect of reducing employment opportunities for low-wage workers.

individual bargaining
The process through which workers deal as individuals with employers in negotiating their terms and conditions of employment.

The Unionized Sector

collective bargaining
The process through which employers and unions negotiate a new collective agreement.

In the unionized sector of the labour force, the situation is quite different. Individual bargaining is replaced by **collective bargaining**, in which a labour union negotiates with the employer on behalf of *all* the employees represented by the union. The bargaining relationship is thereby considerably altered, because while the last resort of an individual bargaining on his or her own behalf is to resign (and perhaps be easily replaced, depending on his or her skills), a union can call a *strike* of *all* the employees it represents. As a result, unionized employees are generally in a stronger position in negotiating with their employers.

Unions in Canada

As Figure 10-6 shows, the number of union members in Canada has grown substantially since 1950. However, when union membership is expressed as a percentage of the labour force, a more complex picture emerges, as shown in Figure 10-7. As unionization spread rapidly in Canadian industry in the 1940s and into the 1950s, union membership grew much more rapidly than the labour force, causing union membership as a percentage of the labour force to increase very rapidly, from about 5 percent to nearly 25 percent. From the mid-1960s until the second half of the 1970s, union membership as a percentage of the labour force continued to grow, although less rapidly, with most growth due to the spread of unionism among government employees.

FIGURE 10-6 Union Membership and the Civilian Labour Force, 1950–2002

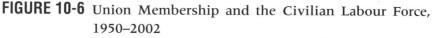
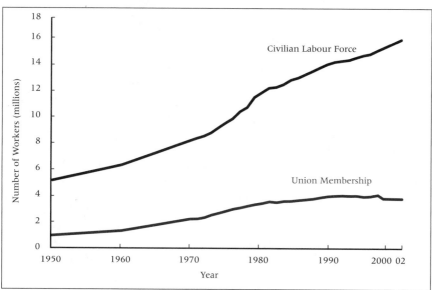

Source: Data for 1950–1998: Human Resources Development Canada, Labour Canada, *Directory of Labour Organizations in Canada*; data for 1999–2002: *Workplace Gazette*, Workplace Information Directorate, Labour Program, Human Resources Development Canada. Reproduced with the permission of the Minister of Public Works and Government Services Canada, 2003.

Union membership as a percentage of the labour force peaked at about 30 percent in 1976. Since then, union membership has not grown as rapidly as the labour force, causing union membership as a percentage of the labour force to decline to less than 26 percent by 2002. At the end of this chapter, we will examine the reasons for this slowing of the growth of unionism.

Like corporations, unions are quite concentrated—in 2001, the largest ten unions had 50 percent of total union membership in Canada.

FIGURE 10-7   Union Membership as a Percentage of the Civilian Labour Force, 1920–2002

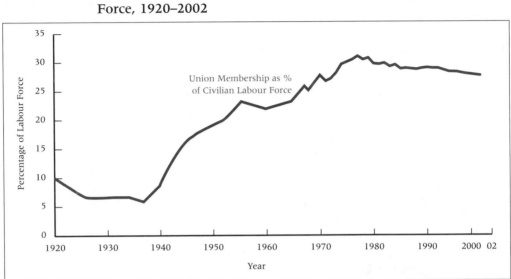

Source: Data for 1920–1998: Human Resources Development Canada, Labour Canada, *Directory of Labour Organizations in Canada*; data for 1999–2002: *Workplace Gazette*, Workplace Information Directorate, Labour Program, Human Resources Development Canada. Reproduced with the permission of the Minister of Public Works and Government Services Canada, 2003.

www.cupe.ca

The largest union in Canada is the Canadian Union of Public Employees (CUPE), whose president is Judy Darcy, with 505 000 members in 2002.

The percentage of employees represented by unions is much higher in plants than in offices. Heavily unionized sectors of the economy include government employees (nearly 90 percent of whom are covered by union contracts), construction, transportation, manufacturing, communications, utilities, logging, and mining. Generally, it is employees of larger businesses that tend to unionize. Broadly speaking, unions have made relatively little progress in the small business sector, nongovernment offices, service industries, retail and wholesale trade, and the financial sector, such as banks and insurance companies.

By international standards, Canada's level of union membership is neither large nor small, falling between the United States' low level (about 16 percent of the labour force) and European levels of about 40 percent to 80 percent.

Finally, the participation of women in Canada's labour unions has been increasing. In 1978, only about 28 percent of Canada's union members were women. By 2002, this figure had grown to more than 35 percent, mostly due to the more rapid growth of government unions, which include a larger proportion of women than the "traditional" union jobs in manufacturing and the skilled trades, where employment had been undercut by technological change and foreign competition.

Some Questions and Answers

How Do Workers Become Unionized?

A basic principle of Canadian labour law is that workers should decide democratically whether to form or join a labour union. Their views can be expressed in various ways, including the signing of a union card and the payment of a small deposit. However, if there is doubt as to the view of the majority, a vote of the employees—known as a *certification vote*—will be conducted by the Labour Relations Board, a government agency that oversees labour relations. If the majority of workers vote in favour of being represented by a particular union in a certification vote, that union becomes "certified" as the exclusive representative of those employees, meaning that management must deal with the employees *through the union*, rather than as individuals. (Conversely, if a group of workers no longer wishes to be represented by a particular union, they can vote to decertify it.)

> About one-third of Canada's labour force is *represented* by unions. Some workers are *represented* by a union, but have not *joined* that union.

Once it has been certified, a union must by law represent all of the employees in the group for which the union is certified (the "bargaining unit"). And, since all employees in the bargaining unit receive the economic and other benefits of union representation, the general rule is that they all must pay union dues, whether they have formally joined the union or not.

How Are Collective Agreements Negotiated?

A key service provided to members by their union is the negotiation of their **collective agreement**, or labour contract. The collective agreement sets out all of the terms and conditions of employment for its duration—from wage rates and hours of work to fringe benefits and pensions. The process through which employers and unions negotiate a new collective agreement is called *collective bargaining*. The bargaining process has been compared to buying a used car—both sides open negotiations by demanding more than they are prepared to settle for, as they attempt to get the best possible deal. Then, gradually, as they both become more concerned about the possibility of a strike, the positions of the union and management teams become more reasonable and compatible. Many contract negotiations are settled at this stage. However, it is quite common for the parties to require assistance from a neutral third party before reaching an agreement.

> **collective agreement**
> A contract agreed upon by an employer and labour union, specifying the terms and conditions of employment of the employees for a specified period of time.

This assistance generally takes the form of **compulsory conciliation**, through which a government-appointed conciliator enters the negotiations. The conciliator is a neutral person who has no authority to impose a settlement on the parties; rather, the conciliator's role is to *assist them to negotiate their own agreement*. Employers and unions must go through compulsory conciliation before a work stoppage (strike by the union or lockout by the employer) can occur.

> **compulsory conciliation**
> A procedure, required by law before a strike is legal, in which a government-appointed officer (conciliator) attempts to help a union and employer to reach an agreement on the terms of a new collective agreement.

Should conciliation prove unsuccessful, there is usually a further delay (a "cooling-off period," usually of two weeks' duration) before a strike or lockout can take place. This period gives both sides an opportunity to reconsider their positions, under growing pressure from the fact that they are facing a strike deadline that is growing closer each day. If the parties fail to reach a settlement under pressure of this strike deadline, a work stoppage can occur that will impose losses on *both* sides until an agreement is reached. In a work stoppage, the employees will lose wages, and the employer will lose sales and profits. The result is a test of the economic power of the two sides, with the side that has the greatest ability to withstand the economic pressures of the work stoppage more likely to prevail. The collective bargaining process is shown in Table 10-2.

TABLE 10-2 The Collective Bargaining Process

STAGE I:	STAGE II:	STAGE III:	STAGE IV:
Union and management negotiate on their own.	Negotiations continue with the assistance of a third party.	Waiting period before a strike or lockout is legal.	Work stoppage, with economic pressure on both sides.
Negotiations	*Compulsory Conciliation*	*Cooling-Off Period*	*Work Stoppage (Strike or Lockout)*
Management and union negotiate from opening positions toward compromises and an agreement.	A government-appointed neutral third party ("conciliator" or "mediator") tries to help the parties reach a negotiated agreement. No authority to impose a settlement (not an arbitrator).	Usually 2 weeks: time for both parties to reconsider, under the pressure of a strike/lockout deadline that is now (a) known and (b) close, and the knowledge that they alone can avert a work stoppage (conciliator is gone).	Economic losses suffered by both sides pressure them to compromise and settle.

Generally, somewhat less than half of contract negotiations are settled before conciliation, about the same number are settled through conciliation, and roughly five percent of negotiations end in a work stoppage (usually a strike by the union, but sometimes a lockout by the employer). At whatever stage a settlement is reached, however, a final requirement is that it be approved by the membership of the union through a *ratification* vote.

Why Permit Strikes?

Many people see strikes as a primitive way of settling labour disputes through a form of "trial by combat," and feel that the government should not permit strikes (or lockouts). They would prefer a way of settling labour disputes that is more civilized, reasonable, and fair.

However, it is important to appreciate that a basic premise of labour legislation is that industrial relations disputes are best worked out *by those directly involved*—the employer, through management, and the employees, through their union. As a result, the law does not provide for the government to intervene and impose a decision or a contract on employers and unions. Rather, the law establishes a framework within which unions and employers are expected to *negotiate their own solutions* to their problems, even if that involves a work stoppage.

The law also recognizes that work stoppages can be economically harmful not only to the employees and employer involved, but also to third parties such as customers and suppliers, and to the economy. That is why the law requires that the parties go through conciliation before a work stoppage occurs, in order to bring into the negotiations a knowledgeable and neutral third party whose expertise might help the parties to reach a settlement without a work stoppage. However, should the conciliator fail, the law leaves the parties on their own to settle—or face the consequences of failing to do so, which may include a strike or lockout.

It is also important to recognize that the threat of a work stoppage plays a very important *positive role* in the collective bargaining process. In a typical year, about 95 percent of all contract negotiations end in agreement without a work stoppage, mainly because *both* parties fear the consequences of a stoppage. So the right to strike or lock out (or, more precisely, the *threat* of a work stoppage) serves the important purpose of forcing *both* the employer *and* the union to negotiate seriously, with the usual result being an agreement *without* a work stoppage.

When Are Strikes Not Legal?

This can be a confusing matter because there are two very different types of disputes that arise between unions and employers. In the one type of dispute, it is quite legal for a strike or lockout to occur, but in the other, it is not (see Table 10-3).

The first type of dispute is the one covered in the previous section—the negotiation of a collective agreement. In such negotiations, it is generally legal to use a strike or lockout (as a last resort), although not until the previous collective agreement has expired and after the negotiations have passed through compulsory conciliation and a "cooling-off period," as required by law. The only exception is essential public services such as police and firefighters, in which work stoppages are generally not allowed by law. These are covered later in this chapter.

There is, however, a second and quite different type of union–management dispute. These are disputes not over the terms of a new contract that is *being negotiated* but rather over *alleged violations of an existing contract*. For instance, suppose that management fires a worker in a way that the worker and the union consider to be a violation of the collective agreement. How should they pursue this matter?

The law does not allow strikes (or lockouts) over such disputes. Instead, the worker must file a **grievance**, which is an appeal of management's

grievance An alleged violation of a collective agreement by an employer.

TABLE 10-3 Two Types of Industrial Relations Disputes

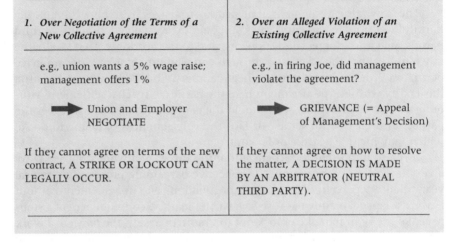

The collective agreement or "labour contract" between an employer and its union sets the terms and conditions of employment for its duration—i.e., constitutes "industrial law" for the parties.

There are two distinctly different types of disputes between employers and unions over the collective agreement:

1. *Over Negotiation of the Terms of a New Collective Agreement*	2. *Over an Alleged Violation of an Existing Collective Agreement*
e.g., union wants a 5% wage raise; management offers 1%	e.g., in firing Joe, did management violate the agreement?
➡ Union and Employer NEGOTIATE	➡ GRIEVANCE (= Appeal of Management's Decision)
If they cannot agree on terms of the new contract, A STRIKE OR LOCKOUT CAN LEGALLY OCCUR.	If they cannot agree on how to resolve the matter, A DECISION IS MADE BY AN ARBITRATOR (NEUTRAL THIRD PARTY).

arbitration

The resolution of union–management disputes by the decision of a third party; required by law for grievances that the union and employer cannot resolve by themselves; used to settle disputes over the terms of new collective agreements in cases where strikes of essential employees are prohibited.

decision on the grounds that it violates the collective agreement. This will lead to a series of discussions between management and the union to resolve the matter, starting at the lower levels of each organization and moving to higher levels if necessary. If these discussions fail to settle the grievance, the law requires that the dispute be taken to **arbitration**. Arbitration is a court-like process in which a neutral third party (an arbitrator) hears the evidence of both sides and decides whether the collective agreement has been violated. In the example in the previous paragraph of the grievance concerning the firing of the worker, the arbitrator might decide to uphold management's decision, or to reinstate the worker in his or her job with retroactive pay for the time missed from work during the grievance. The arbitrator's decision is binding on both the union and management, who cannot resort to a strike or lockout if they disagree with it.

Aren't Strikes Costly?

It is true that work stoppages can be costly to those directly involved—the employer loses profits and the employees lose wages. However, the effects of strikes on the nation's economy are greatly exaggerated by the general public. The working time lost due to work stoppages is an extremely small fraction of total time worked in the economy—during the 1980s, an average of less than 12 days per 10 000 days worked, or less than one-eighth of one percent of total time worked, as Figure 10-8 shows. In the 1990s, this figure fell to less than one-tenth of one percent.

This is a fraction of the working time that would be lost if all working Canadians were given one additional holiday per year. So, while industrial disputes do impose economic costs on society, it cannot be argued that strikes *in general* are ruining the nation's economy.

> According to the British government's statistical agency, Canada has the highest amount of working time lost due to labour disputes—12 times as high as the United States and nearly 7 times the average for all industrial nations in 1999.

FIGURE 10-8 Time Lost Due to Labour Disputes, 1976–2002

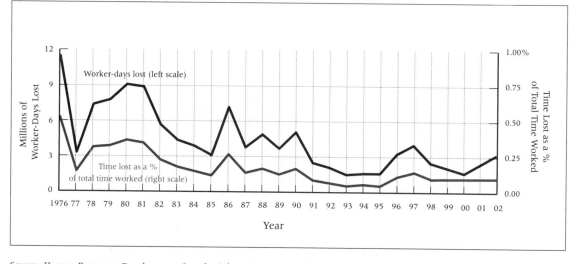

Source: Human Resources Development Canada, Labour Program, Workplace Information Directorate. Reproduced with the permission of the Minister of Public Works and Government Services Canada, 2003.

But What About Public Service Strikes?

While the percentage of total time worked in the economy that is lost due to work stoppages is small, the *impact* of work stoppages on the Canadian public is probably greater than these statistics would suggest, because compared to other countries, a higher proportion of Canada's work stoppages involve *government employees* and thus the interruption of *public services*.

http://labour-travail. hrdc-drhc.gc.ca. (click on Workplace Information)

Government employees in Canada enjoy considerably greater rights to unionize and to strike than do their counterparts in most other countries. Since the mid-1960s, it has been a general principle of Canadian labour law that government employees should have similar rights to unionize, bargain collectively, and strike as do employees in the private sector. As a result, governments for the most part have tended to withdraw the right to strike only from employees in *essential* public services, such as police, firefighters, and some hospital workers. As a result, Canada experiences more frequent work stoppages in public services than most other nations do.

In the case of a strike by, for instance, 1500 workers at a soft-drink company, the public can continue to consume the product until inventories run out, and then can switch to other brands of soft drinks until the strike is over. However, a strike by 1500 public transit workers or garbage collectors or teachers will prove much more disruptive, because there is no alternative supplier. Work stoppages in some public services (such as postal service, education, public transit, garbage collection, and health care) have represented a difficult problem in Canadian industrial relations, because they can have a considerable impact on the public and sometimes the economy.

Some say that the solution to this problem is simply to outlaw strikes by government employees. But the matter is not nearly as simple as this. It is not sufficient merely to remove the right of employees to strike—some alternative method must be used to settle their collective bargaining disputes promptly and fairly. Usually, when the right to strike is withheld from a group of employees, the law provides for negotiations and conciliation to take place as described earlier, but requires that if the dispute is not settled through these processes, it must be submitted to *compulsory arbitration*. In arbitration, a neutral third party considers arguments from both management and the union as to what the terms of the collective agreement (wages, benefits, etc.) should be, and then makes a final decision that is binding on both sides. The union cannot strike, nor can the employer lock out the employees.

While the general public tends to see arbitration as a simple solution to the problem, those actually involved in the process are much less satisfied with it. Compulsory arbitration requires that vital decisions be made by an outsider who lacks familiarity with the problems of the employees and management, many of which are often very complex. Another problem is the long delays in the negotiation/arbitration process—it is not uncommon for settlements (and employees' wage increases) to be held up for a year or more after the previous collective agreement has expired. Without the threat of a work stoppage, neither side (particularly the employer) may feel much pressure to negotiate quickly. Also, the arbitration process itself usually lasts several months, during which both sides make extensive submissions, both in writing and at hearings, backed up by large volumes of statistical data and arguments.

Management is not always pleased with arbitration either, because it takes very important matters away from management's control. Major decisions are placed in the hands of an outsider whose decisions cannot be appealed but which may impair management's ability to deliver effectively and efficiently the public service for which the organization is responsible. So arbitration is far from the ideal and simple solution to labour disputes that it may appear to be. For another perspective on the arbitration process, see the "You Decide" box.

Unionism at the Crossroads

Some observers believe that Canadian unionism is at a historic crossroads, in the sense that powerful economic forces are forcing fundamental changes upon it. In particular, unions face major challenges regarding the recruitment of members and their relationships with their employers.

Recruitment of new members has been a concern of unions since the late 1970s, when union membership, as a percentage of the labour force, peaked

LET'S PLAY ARBITRATOR

If you think compulsory arbitration of labour contract disputes is a simple matter, take the following opportunity to see the kinds of challenges involved.

A married couple whom you know only slightly are having severe marital problems and disputes, largely because their marriage is not living up to the expectations that each held for it. They agree that it would have been better if, before they were married, they had written up a marriage contract specifying the rights and responsibilities of each partner. However, given the present state of deterioration of their relationship, they are unable to agree on the terms of such a contract. They have asked you, as an impartial third party, to resolve the matter for them in the following way: you will listen to the views and arguments of each of the parties, their proposals for the terms to be included in the contract, and the exact wording of each clause; then you will, on your own, *write for them a complete, detailed marriage contract* that will provide a workable basis for a renewed marriage.

Good luck!

Questions

1. What is your major strength as the arbitrator of these people's differences?
2. What is your major weakness as the arbitrator?
3. After listening to the positions of each of the parties, will you have a clear picture of the facts of the situation?
4. If one of the parties disagrees with your decision or part of it, how committed will that person be to trying to make your decision work?

---

at about nearly 31 percent. From the 1940s well into the 1960s, the heart of Canadian unionism had been "blue-collar" workers in the manufacturing sector of the economy—workers in industries such as automobiles and steel. However, since the 1960s, the numbers of such workers—and of union members in these industries—have been undercut by a combination of technological change and international competition. These changes were very threatening to many unions. In the United States, similar trends reduced union membership in the private sector from 30 percent of employees to only 12 percent by 2000. In Canada, union membership in the private sector stagnated as it had in the United States; however, unlike the United States, unionism spread among government employees in Canada after the mid-1960s. But in the 1990s, union membership in the government sector stagnated as well, as budget problems undercut government employment. So, in the two most unionized sectors of the economy—manufacturing and government—employment growth was slow.

Where, then, were the new jobs? Since the mid-1970s, over 90 percent of all newly created jobs in the Canadian economy have been in the rapidly expanding *service sector*, in industries such as retail trade, restaurants, catering, hotels, entertainment, finance, travel and tourism, recreation, day care, lawn care, home repairs, and the like. This trend poses a challenge to union recruiters for various reasons. Many service-industry employers are small businesses with only a few employees, in which owner–managers and employees often work closely together without the "us-versus-them" relationship that makes unionization easier. In addition, many employees in the service industries do not have a long-term attachment to their jobs because they are part-time and because such jobs often have a high turnover rate. As a result of factors such as these, the service sector of the economy has tended to be only lightly unionized and quite resistant to attempts to unionize it.

Unions' relationships with employers have also been challenged by economic forces. In the past, Canadian unions in both the private and public sectors have won considerable gains for their members through the adversarial approach of hard bargaining and a willingness to resort to the strike weapon—confrontation was their style and it seemed to be effective. However, as we saw in Chapter 9, the economic environment changed. There were growing concerns about the ability of many Canadian producers to compete internationally, as well as about the financial position of Canadian governments. In short, it was no longer as easy as it once had been for many private employers to raise prices or for governments to raise taxes in order to make peace with their unions.

During the 1990s, it became apparent that neither unions nor employers could expect past trends to continue, as both private and public employers faced strong new pressures to increase efficiency and keep costs down. These problems raised fundamentally serious questions for many unions. Similarly serious questions were also raised for management in many enterprises. Faced with strong economic pressures to increase productivity and quality, some management teams were forced to reconsider whether they could expect to achieve these goals with a traditional authoritarian management style that fostered conflict with their employees rather than the cooperation they now needed.

Had the adversarial system in which Canadian unionism was so deeply and firmly rooted become outdated and counterproductive? Would their members' interests be better served by cooperative efforts between unions and management to improve productivity and competitiveness rather than on confrontation and strikes? And, if this were the case, how could unions adjust to such a new role? Could they act more like a partner with management with respect to productivity, but as its adversary in contract negotiations and grievances?

The 1990s saw some new trends in Canadian industrial relations, such as a significant decrease in work stoppages (see Figure 10-8) and various examples of union–management cooperation with respect to the training of workers and improvements to productivity and product quality. Some believed that the Canadian industrial relations system was evolving, as the difficult economic times of the 1990s pushed both unions and employers toward a more mature, even cooperative relationship. Others were more skeptical, and thought that unions and management would likely return to their old ways of confrontation if the pressures of the 1990s were to ease.

Chapter Summary

1. In the nonunion sector of the labour force, wages are determined by the supply of and demand for various skills. (L.O. 1)

2. Supply and demand in labour markets generate a very wide range of incomes; this is in large part due to obstacles to entering certain occupations. (L.O. 2)

3. Minimum wage laws can increase the wages of low-income groups; however, they also have the effect of increasing unemployment among those groups. (L.O. 3).

4. The terms and conditions of employment for unionized employees are negotiated by their union and employer through a collective bargaining process that generally includes requirements for conciliation and a cooling-off period before a work stoppage can take place as the final step in the process. (L.O. 4)

5. For disputes over alleged violations of an existing collective agreement, the grievance procedure is used; the final step in this process is a binding decision by an arbitrator. (L.O. 5)

6. For employees in essential public services, strikes are generally not legal; instead, the final step in the collective bargaining process is compulsory arbitration. (L.O. 6)

7. Union membership as a percentage of the labour force reached its peak in the late 1970s, and has declined slightly since then, largely because employment growth has been in the service sector rather than in the more heavily unionized manufacturing and government sectors. (L.O. 7)

Questions

1. Look at Figure 10-8. Why do you think the time lost due to work stoppages after 1990 decreased as it did? Has the time lost due to labour disputes continued to decrease? What do you think might be contributing to this trend? (Current statistics on work stoppages can be obtained from Human Resources Development Canada's website at http://labour-travail.hrdc-drhc.gc.ca/.)

2. Suppose that hairdressers employed by salons organized into a union in an attempt to increase their incomes. What obstacles would they face concerning:
   (a) the demand for labour?
   (b) the supply of labour?

3. A lockout is a work stoppage that is initiated by the employer rather than by the union representing the employees. Why would an employer lock out its employees rather than let them continue working until they decided to strike?

4. The text refers to the *attitudes* of labour and management as an obstacle to improving Canada's labour relations environment. What are some of these attitudes, and why have they developed?

5. "If employers had profit-sharing with their employees and employee stock ownership plans whereby employees could become shareholders, there would no longer be any need for unions." Do you agree or disagree? Why?

6. Why should Canadians be concerned that their record for time lost due to labour disputes is the worst in the world?

7. As the statistics in the table below show, for many years the population of the Atlantic provinces has grown considerably more slowly than the population of Canada as a whole. Despite this, the unemployment rate in Atlantic Canada has increased quite steadily, not only in absolute terms but also relative to the unemployment rate for Canada as a whole. In 1970, the unemployment rate in Atlantic Canada was the same as Canada's, while by the 1990s, it was 1.6 times as high as Canada's.

| | POPULATION | | UNEMPLOYMENT RATE | |
Year	(millions)	% of Canada's	% of Labour Force	Relative to Canada's
1970	2.0	9.6	5.7	1.0:1
1980	2.3	9.2	11.1	1.5:1
1990	2.4	8.5	12.7	1.6:1
1998	2.4	7.8	12.9	1.6:1

(a) What might be some *causes* of the trends shown?

(b) What are some of the social problems arising from these trends?

(c) What could governments do to try to improve the unemployment situation in Atlantic Canada?

Chapter 11

Employment and Incomes in the Canadian Economy

Learning Objectives

After studying this chapter, you should be able to:

1. Describe the trends in employment in the main sectors of the Canadian economy since 1950, and explain the basic causes of these trends.

2. Give four reasons for the increase in female participation rates and in the percentage of women in the Canadian workforce since 1950.

3. Describe the changing trends in average real family income since 1951, and explain the two basic causes of these changes.

4. Compare the size of the male–female pay gap both before and after economic factors are taken into account, and explain the main cause of that part of the gap that arises from gender factors.

5. Explain the definition of "poverty" used by Statistics Canada's Low-Income Cut-Offs (LICOs), and state the national poverty rate that is estimated by using the before-tax LICOs as poverty lines and by using the after-tax LICOs as poverty lines.

6. Explain the definition of "poverty" used by the market basket measure (MBM) approach, and how the poverty lines and poverty rates under this MBM approach differ from those under the LICO-based poverty lines.

7. Explain how problems in defining and measuring "poverty" result in estimates of the poverty rate that vary from as low as 3 percent to over 20 percent.

8. Identify four groups that have a strong tendency to be poor, and explain why each group tends to be poor.

In Chapter 10, we examined the operation of the labour markets in which Canadians obtain jobs and earn incomes. In this chapter, we will consider more closely two important aspects of those labour markets: (a) the current and future *trends in employment* in labour markets, and (b) two important *trends in Canadians' incomes*—the level of incomes and how those incomes are divided among various groups, or how the economic pie is divided up.

Employment Trends in Canada

Over the past half-century, major changes have taken place in the nature of the work performed by Canadians. In the broadest terms, as Figure 11-1 shows, the number of people working in the *goods-producing sector* of the economy (industries such as agriculture, forestry, mining, fishing, manufacturing, and construction) has increased quite slowly, while there has been a dramatic increase in employment in the *services-producing sector* (industries such as business and personal services, government and community services such as health care and education, retail and wholesale trade, finance, insurance and real estate, transportation, and communication.

FIGURE 11-1 Canadians Employed in Goods and Service Industries, 1950–2002

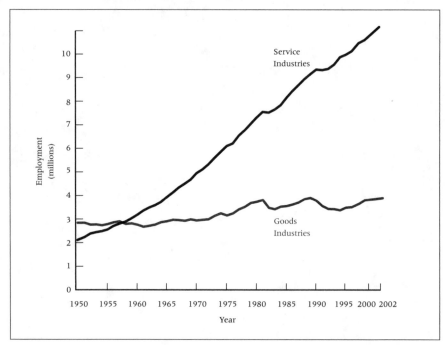

Source: Adapted from Statistics Canada, *Historical Labour Force Statistics*, Catalogue No. 71-201, 2001.

The result of these trends, as Figure 11-2 shows, has been that the proportion of Canadians working in the goods-producing sector of the economy has declined from over 56 percent in 1951 to less than 26 percent by 2002, while there has been a corresponding increase from 44 percent to over 74 percent of the work force employed in the service sector of the economy. Table 11-1 breaks this trend down into its component parts: a dramatic decline not only in the proportion but also the actual number of Canadians employed in agriculture; a steady decline in the proportion of employment accounted for by the manufacturing sector; a slight increase in the proportion of employment provided by trade, finance, insurance, and real estate; and a dramatic increase in employment in a variety of community, business, and personal service industries and public administration (or the government sector). From 1976 to 2002, 90 percent of the increase in employment in Canada occurred in the service sector of the economy. These trends have already caused major changes in the ways in which Canadians learn, live, and earn their living, and will continue to do so. In the following sections, we will examine the causes, the effects, and the future implications of these trends.

FIGURE 11-2 **Shares of Total Employment of the Goods-Producing and Services-Producing Sectors**

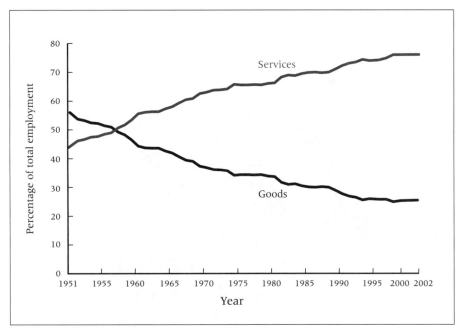

Source: Adapted from Statistics Canada, *Income Distribution by Size in Canada*, Catalogue No. 13-207, 1997 and the CANSIM II database, Table 202-0701.

TABLE 11-1 The Changing Nature of Employment in Canada

	Percent of Total Employment in Each Sector in:					
	1951	1961	1971	1981	1991	2001
Agriculture	18.4	11.2	6.3	4.4	3.5	2.2
Non-agricultural primary industries	4.4	3.0	2.7	2.9	2.3	1.9
Manufacturing	26.5	24.0	21.8	19.3	15.1	15.1
Construction	6.8	6.2	6.0	5.9	5.7	5.6
Total goods-producing sector	56.1	44.5	36.9	32.5	26.6	25.6
Transportation, storage, communication and utilities	8.8	9.3	8.7	8.3	7.4	5.9
Trade	15.1	16.9	16.5	17.1	17.6	15.8
Finance, insurance, real estate	3.0	3.9	4.9	5.4	6.1	5.8
Community, business and personal services and public administration	18.0	25.3	33.0	36.6	42.2	46.9
Total service-producing sector	43.9	55.5	63.1	67.5	73.4	74.4
Total all industries	100.0	100.0	100.0	100.0	100.0	100.0

Source: "The Changing Nature of Employment in Canada," adapted from Statistics Canada, *Historical Labour Force Statistics,* Catalogue No. 71-201, 2001.

www.statcan.ca/english/
Pgdb/labor10a.htm

Figure 11-3 shows the distribution of jobs among various industries in 2002, with more detail concerning the different types of jobs in the service sector.

FIGURE 11-3 Shares of Total Employment, 2002

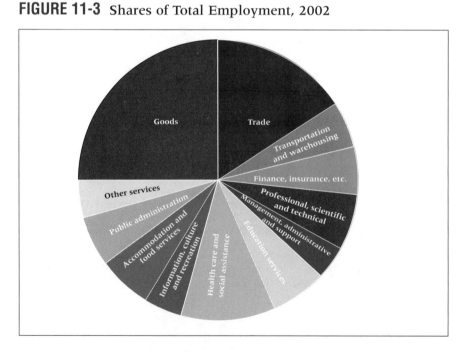

Source: Adapted from Statistics Canada, CANSIM II database, Table 282-0008.

Causes of Trends in Employment

To understand why the nature of employment has changed so greatly, we must consider some fundamental changes that have occurred on both the *demand side* and the *supply side* of labour markets in Canada.

The Demand Side

Technological Change

Technological change is the most basic force underlying the changing nature of employment because it has generated major shifts in employers' demand for labour. While technology affects all industrial production methods, it has generally proven easier to apply labour-saving technology to the production of goods, which lend themselves to mass-production techniques, than to the production of services. Many services (such as haircuts, medical services, education, and legal services) are "labour-intensive"; that is, they require more of a person-to-person delivery. By contrast, the production of many goods can be very "capital-intensive," as the worker-hours per unit of output can be reduced considerably through using capital equipment, including computer-controlled industrial robots.

At the start of the twentieth century, most Canadians worked in the *agricultural sector* of the economy. In Canada, as in other nations, the first impact of technological change was in the agricultural sector of the economy, which is well-suited to extensive use of capital equipment. The result was a dramatic increase in agricultural productivity over that century, and a corresponding decline in the number of workers required in the agricultural sector. Viewed differently, technological change "freed up" large numbers of workers from agriculture, making them available for work in the manufacturing and service sectors of the economy.

Many of the workers no longer needed in agriculture were able to find employment in the *manufacturing sector* of the economy, where employment increased strongly until the late 1970s. However, much of the manufacturing sector is also quite well-suited to mass-production technology. From 1981 to 2002, the output of the manufacturing sector of the Canadian economy increased by about 72 percent, while employment in manufacturing increased by only 9.5 percent. Over the same period, employment in the service sector grew by 52 percent. So the gradual decrease in the percentage of the labour force employed in the manufacturing sector, shown in Table 11-1, has been mainly the result of the introduction of labour-saving technology.

From 1987 to 2002, the number of jobs grew fastest in the managerial area (by 122 percent), followed closely by professionals (by 107 percent). In manufacturing, employment grew by 14 percent.

Changes in Consumer Demand

Obviously, the rapid growth in service-industry employment shown in Figure 11-1 could not occur without major increases in the *demand for services*. A key factor in the growth of the demand for services was the process of technological change described in the previous section. By increasing output per worker (productivity), technological change has *increased the standard of living of Canadians*. And, as their living standards rose, people spent an ever-increasing proportion of their incomes on services such as restaurants, entertainment, and travel. Since most service industries are labour-intensive, the rising demand for services generated a vast number of service-industry jobs, sufficient to allow the economy to provide work for the people freed up from the agricultural and manufacturing sectors by technological change. And so, for the most part, the shift of employment from the goods-producing sector of the economy to the service sector was achieved fairly smoothly, without undue increases in unemployment. As a result, employment has risen very rapidly in the service sector, in fields such as retail trade, food service, sales, accounting, finance, human resources, health care, education, law, computer services, and so on.

During the twentieth century, then, the nature of the work done by Canadians underwent major changes. Early in the century, most young people stayed and worked on the farm; later, most would go to work in manufacturing plants; now, in the early twenty-first century, the vast majority find jobs in offices or service industries. Similar trends have occurred in all industrialized economies, suggesting that economic progress and change is driven by the same basic technological and economic forces that generate similar results. These forces and their results are summarized in Figure 11-4.

FIGURE 11-4   Shifts in Employment, 1951–2002

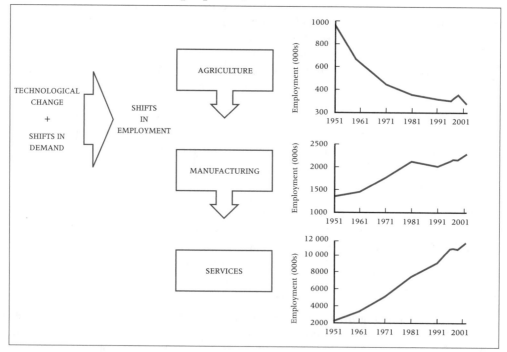

Source: Adapted from Statistics Canada, *Historical Labour Force Statistics*, Catalogue No. 71-201, 2001.

International Economic Forces

A third factor that has undercut employment in some manufacturing industries has been the growth of international trade and competition since the 1970s—the process known as "globalization." Competition from low-wage countries has been especially difficult for Canadian manufacturers in industries such as clothing, footwear, furniture, and assembly operations. Caught between low-productivity labour-intensive production methods, high Canadian wages, and low-wage import competition, many could not continue operating in Canada. Many of those that were able to survive did so through extensive "labour shedding" in order to reduce costs; the result in both cases was a reduction in manufacturing employment in some industries in Canada.

The Supply Side: Working Women

On the supply side of the labour market, there is no doubt that the most dramatic and important development has been the great increase in the number of working women. In 1950, the percentage of women of working age participating in the labour force—the *participation rate*—was 23.2 percent. By 2002, it was 60.7 percent. Participation rates increased most rapidly for married women, who accounted for only one-eighth of the labour force in 1961, but over one-quarter by 2000. Overall, women comprised more than 46 percent of the labour force in 2002, compared to less than 22 percent in 1950. These trends are reflected in Figure 11-5, which highlights the rising participation rate of women since the 1950s.

There are several reasons for this remarkable growth of the female work force. Probably the most frequently mentioned factor is the *squeeze on family incomes*. After the mid-1970s, wages and salaries in general barely kept up with inflation, making it more important for families to have a second income. However, as Figure 11-5 shows, the increase in female participation rates was underway long before this became a factor. This trend suggests that other factors were also at work.

> In 2000–01, women represented 59 percent of university undergraduate enrolment, and 51 percent of graduate enrolment.

One such factor was the *rising education levels and aspirations of women*. Many more women are completing high school and going on to college and university for higher education than in the past. And, as women's education levels have risen, so have their expectations concerning their jobs, incomes, and careers.

However, these factors only increased the numbers of women *wanting* to work. For this goal to be achieved, there would have to be more *job opportunities* for women.

These opportunities were provided by the rapid growth of the *service sector* of the economy, as described earlier in this chapter. Women have a high incidence of employment in the service sector for several reasons. Unlike many goods-industry jobs, most service jobs do not require physical strength so much as the ability to think and to deal with people. Also, many service industries, such as retail trade, provide part-time work, which appeals in particular to working mothers. The importance of the growth of the service sector to the increase in the number of working women can be measured by

FIGURE 11-5 Participation Rates of Men and Women, 1950–2002

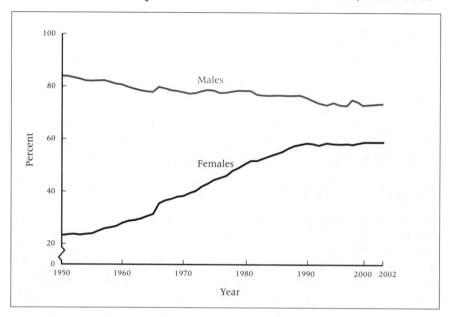

Source: Adapted from Statistics Canada, *Historical Labour Force Statistics,*
Catalogue No. 71-201, 2001.

the fact that, in recent years, nearly 87 percent of employed women have
been working in the service sector of the economy. And this trend appeared
likely to continue, as the fastest-growing areas of employment were accounting, human resource management, sales, and advertising—fields in which
the number of women was increasing more than three times as rapidly as the
number of men.

Finally, many more women are self-supporting than in the past. It is
estimated that six in ten women at some time in their life will be self-
supporting. More women are opting for careers, and more marriages break
down now than in the past.

Figure 11-6 shows the changes in the composition of the labour force
from 1967 to 2002. Due to the rising female participation rates already
discussed, the proportion of women in the labour force rose steadily over this
period. The 1970s saw a similarly rapid increase in the proportion of *young
Canadians* (age 15–24) in the labour force, as the postwar "baby boom" came
of working age. However, in the early 1980s, this surge of young entrants to
the work force subsided, while the proportion of women in the labour force
continued to rise.

FIGURE 11-6 Labour Force Composition by Demographic Groups, 1967–2002

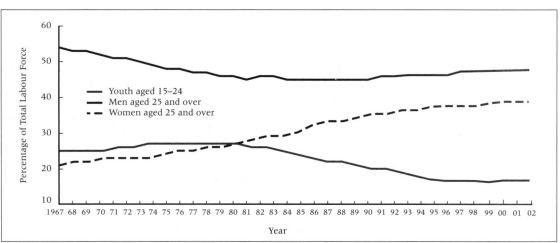

Source: Adapted from Statistics Canada, *Historical Labour Force Statistics*, Catalogue No. 71-201, 2001.

Adjusting to Change

The technological and economic forces discussed in this chapter—revolutionary changes in production technology, massive shifts in consumer spending toward services, and the addition of nearly 3.5 million women into the work force in 25 years—have generated and will continue to generate fundamental changes in the way that Canadians work and live. In the following sections, we will examine some of these changes in the past, the present, and the future.

The urbanization of society was one of the most dramatic effects of technological change in the first half of the twentieth century. As technology reduced the number of workers needed on the farm and drew workers into city-based manufacturing plants, Canada's population became increasingly concentrated into a few large urban areas, with all of the advantages—and disadvantages—of city dwelling. *Rising living standards* were another major result of technological progress, as the increases in output per worker generated by improved technology became the economic basis for a generally rising prosperity among Canadians.

Rising educational requirements were an inevitable aspect of this process because much work became more technical and because many of the new service-industry jobs required specialized knowledge. This trend led to the expansion of the nation's universities and to the establishment of new systems of colleges to provide the "middle-level" skills for which demand grew rapidly as the economy evolved. *Later marriages, working women,* and *higher-income but smaller families* were three other features of the modern society that emerged in the second half of the twentieth century. As noted, the rapid growth of the service industries provided women not only with greatly increased opportunities for employment but also with the prospect of fulfilling and rewarding careers. Longer periods of education and increased interest in women's careers pushed marriage back several years for many, and resulted in much higher family incomes and considerably smaller families than in the past. The *slower population growth* that resulted from these developments eventually led to a government policy of *increased immigration*. To keep the labour force growing at a pace that would provide enough working people to support the baby boomers in their retirement years after 2010, the government increased the inflow of immigration significantly in the 1990s.

Part-time work grew rapidly to over 18 percent of all jobs, in large part due to the rapid growth of service industries such as food service and retail trade, which employ part-time workers. Students and many homemakers welcomed the growth of these part-time job opportunities, but about 30 percent of part-time workers really wanted full-time jobs and were unable to find them. See the "In the News" box below for some facts about how the Canadian labour force has changed since 1976.

IN THE **NEWS**   Labour Force Facts

From 1976 to 2002 in the Canadian economy:

- the number of jobs increased by 5 636 000, or 58 percent;
- employment in the service sector grew by 5 056 000, or 79 percent;
- employment in the goods-producing sector grew by 580 000, or 17 percent;
- of the 5 636 000 growth in jobs, 29 percent were part-time; this brought part-time jobs up to 18.7 percent of total employment (as compared to 12.6 percent in 1976); and
- the number of part-time jobs increased by 135 percent, while full-time employment grew by 47 percent.

Questions

1. What do you think are the causes of part-time employment growing so much faster than full-time employment?

2. Has part-time employment's share of total jobs increased from its 2002 level of 18.7 percent? (You can find updated statistics in Statistics Canada's *The Labour Force* (71-001), with monthly data from Statistics Canada's *Canadian Economic Observer* (11-010-XPB), or visit www.statcan.ca/english/Pgdb/labor12.htm.

Technology and Employment

After the mid-1980s, the pace of technological change in Canadian industry increased considerably. Such rapid technological change naturally raises fears that new production technology would displace people from their jobs and condemn ever-higher numbers of people to unemployment, creating economic and social hardship.

Economists are generally skeptical about such doomsday scenarios. They point out that similar alarms were raised in the past when new agricultural, manufacturing, and computer technologies were introduced. In fact, no long-term increase in unemployment occurred because the effects of technological change on the economy are more complex than they seem. It's generally agreed that technological change can generate *short-term* increases in unemployment by displacing some workers from their jobs. However, this displacement has not created a growing problem of *long-term* unemployment, because there are other, less-noticed aspects of technological change that have positive effects upon employment.

First, by increasing output per worker, technological progress generates *higher living standards and higher consumption of services*. As employers are able to pay higher wages to more productive workers, and as the prices of more efficiently produced goods come down, consumers have more buying power, creating jobs in other sectors of the economy, most notably the *service sector*, which has received a large share of rising consumer spending over the past quarter-century and which is generally labour-intensive.

Second, by improving productivity, technological progress enhances the *ability of Canadian industry to compete internationally*. Many Canadian jobs depend on the ability of Canadian producers to export to foreign markets or compete with imports in Canadian markets. Because of this fact, it can be argued that, by improving the efficiency and competitiveness of Canadian producers, technological change could actually increase employment.

Figure 11-7 summarizes these factors—the loss of some jobs and displacement of some workers, and the creation of other jobs through increased demand for services and improved international competitiveness. The right side of Figure 11-7 also shows the *process of change* in the labour force, as labour "shifts" from the manufacturing sector to the expanding service sector. Some of the figures shown making this shift are workers who were displaced from jobs by technology, and others are new entrants to the work force who will find work in the service sector rather than in goods-producing industries.

In 2000–01, Canada's unemployment rate reached its lowest level in 25 years. So, over the long term, the evidence is that technological change has tended to *change the nature of work* rather than *reduce the number of jobs*. And, as we have seen, the basic change in the nature of work has been from jobs producing goods to jobs in the service sector. However, making this type of transition to new types of work has required that the labour force adapt to change to a greater extent than in the past.

FIGURE 11-7 The Effects of Technology on Employment

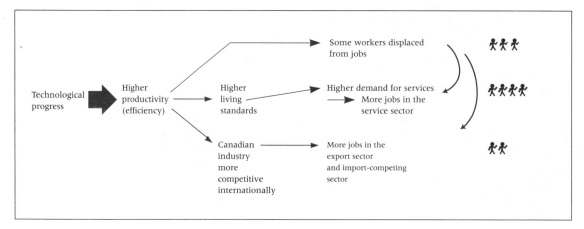

Adapting to Change

The key to adapting to change is education and training. It is projected that nearly half of the new jobs created in the future will require more than 16 years of training (a combination of schooling and on-the-job experience) as compared with only 23 percent in 1986.

From the viewpoint of *the individual*, the benefits of education and training are obvious, as these increase the probability of finding rewarding employment. Education and training also bring benefits to *business*, in the form of higher productivity. And for *society in general*, investment in education and training is beneficial not only because it improves productivity and prosperity but also because a high-quality labour force tends to attract job-creating business investment.

It is generally agreed that education and training are areas in which Canada needs to improve. Spending on education and training by the Canadian private sector has been low compared to other industrialized countries, and Canada lacks excellent apprenticeship programs such as those of Japan and Germany. While government spending on education in Canada is among the highest in the world, and the average level of educational attainment is high, employers complain that many graduates of Canadian high schools lack the basic literacy and numeracy skills needed to make them productively employable in a modern economy.

Even when there are over a million Canadians unemployed, employers are often unable to recruit qualified workers, and it has been necessary to "import" certain types of skilled workers. According to a report by the Organization for Economic Cooperation and Development, Canada's weaknesses with respect to education and training were undermining Canada's international competitiveness, and educational spending should be redirected so as to place greater emphasis on the basic literacy, numeracy, and technical skills needed by a modern workforce (see the "In the News" box on the next page).

> "If you think education is expensive, try ignorance."
>
> Derek Bok, former President of Harvard University

www.oecdwash.org

IN THE **NEWS**	Is Education in Canada a Good Value?

A report by the Organization for Economic Cooperation and Development (OECD) noted that Canada was the heaviest spender on education of the major industrialized nations, "... but does not appear to be getting good value for the money." The report went on to say the "[t]oo many students are graduating from high school functionally illiterate and/or innumerate. The dropout rate remains high. Few students at high school are involved in vocational courses and there are few apprentices, especially in the dynamic parts of the service sector."

Questions

1. Do you agree with the OECD that Canada's educational system is not preparing young people well for the demands of the workplace of the twenty-first century?
2. What changes would you like to see made to the educational system?

Income Trends in Canada

As Figure 11-8 shows, the average real[1] family income of Canadians has increased considerably since 1951. In fact, average family income in 2000 was more than 2.5 times as high as it was in 1951, after adjusting for inflation.

More detailed examination of the statistics in Figure 11-8 reveals some significant facts and trends. Average family income rose most rapidly during the 1960s, when it gained almost one-third. The 1950s saw the second-greatest gains with about 27 percent, with the 1970s following with 24 percent. However, most of the 1951–2000 growth in real income occurred between 1951 and 1976—the gain from 1951 to 1976 was 139 percent, while the increase from 1976 to 2000 was less than 18 percent.

The rapid growth of average real family income until the late 1970s was generated mainly by two factors. The first of these was a significant increase in the number of income-earners per family, mainly the result of *more wives working*. The second factor was *rapidly rising productivity*, which, as we have

---

1. "Real income" refers to income after adjusting for inflation. Because of inflation, increases in incomes *seem* larger than they *really are*. For instance, if your income rose by 4 percent but inflation caused the prices of the things you buy to rise by 3 percent, you would be only 1 percent better off, not 4 percent. The figures used in the text and Figure 11-8 show average family income *after allowing for inflation*. Using our earlier example, the graph would rise by 1 percent, not 4 percent. So whenever the line on the graph rises, it shows an increase in the real income (before taxes) of an average Canadian family of two or more people.

FIGURE 11-8 Average Family Income in Constant (1997) Dollars, 1951–2000

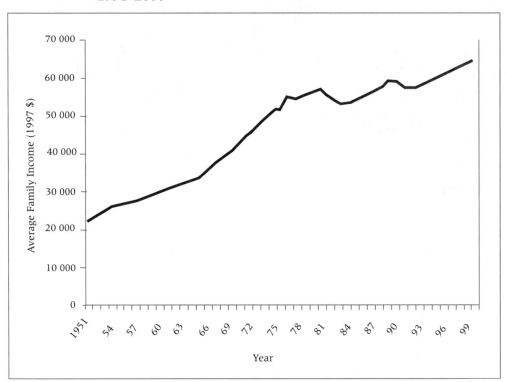

Sources: Adapted from Statistics Canada, *Income Distribution by Size in Canada*, Catalogue No. 13-207, 1997 and *Income in Canada*, Catalogue No. 75-202, 1999.

seen, is the most basic source of growing economic prosperity. After the late 1970s, however, the situation changed with respect to both of these factors—productivity growth slowed sharply, and the number of income-earners per family grew less rapidly (and even declined in some years) after peaking at around 1.75. And, when the growth of these two key factors slowed after the late 1970s, so did the growth of average real income per family. Average real income *per capita* rose more rapidly, however, owing to the fact that average family size continued to decrease.

Dividing Up the Economic Pie: How Incomes Are Distributed

The previous section deals with trends in the *level* of average incomes in Canada; however, another important consideration is how incomes are *distributed* among various occupational groups and between lower-income groups and higher-income groups. This concept of distribution concerns the third of the three basic economic questions from Chapter 1—how the economic pie is divided up among Canadians.

In Chapter 10, we saw how incomes are determined in labour markets, under conditions ranging from the almost free interplay of supply and demand in markets for part-time student labour to markets in which trade unions and professional bodies regulate the supply of labour by limiting how many people can enter some occupations.

On a broader scale, there is the question of how income is distributed among different *income groups*, that is, what share of the economic pie goes to the lowest-income 20 percent of families, to the highest-income 20 percent, and to the various groups in between?

As Table 11-2 shows, the distribution of before-tax total income (earned income plus transfer payments from governments) between various income groups has remained remarkably steady over the years, with roughly 40 percent of total family income going to the top 20 percent of families, 24 percent of income to the second-highest 20 percent, 18 percent to the middle 20 percent, and only 12 percent and 6 percent to the second-lowest and lowest 20 percent of families, respectively. These statistics show a degree of inequality in the distribution of income that is not only *considerable*, but also *remarkably consistent* from year to year. For nearly 50 years, the top fifth of Canadian families have had a share of before-tax income roughly seven times as large as the share going to the bottom fifth.

TABLE 11-2 Distribution of Total Family Income in Canada (before taxes)

	1951	1961	1971	1981	1991	2000	*Averge Family Income for Each Quintile, 2000*
	Percentage of Total Income Received by Each Fifth						
Lowest fifth of families	6.1	6.6	5.6	6.5	6.4	6.3	$21 413
Second fifth	12.9	13.4	12.7	12.9	12.2	11.8	40 156
Third fifth	17.4	18.2	18.0	18.3	17.6	17.0	58 206
Fourth fifth	22.5	23.4	23.7	24.1	23.9	23.5	80 090
Highest-income fifth	41.1	38.4	40.0	38.3	40.0	41.5	141 770
All families	100.0	100.0	100.0	100.0	100.0	100.0	68 327

Source: Adapted from Statistics Canada, *Income Distribution by Size in Canada,* Catalogue No. 13-207, 1997 and CANSIM II database, Table 202-0701.

The division of the economic pie is among the most controversial issues in the field of economics, because it raises serious issues of equity. Is the distribution of income reflected in Table 11-2 *fair*? To some, higher incomes represent a *reward* for effort and education; to them, such high incomes not only reflect those people's greater *contribution* to society but also provide *incentives* for Canadians to improve themselves and work harder. To others, these differences in income are much greater than can be explained by differing contributions or by the need to provide incentives. These people view the income-distribution process as one in which a small number of

Canadians use their *economic power* to extract an excessive share of the economic pie from the system for themselves, leaving only the crumbs for the poor, who lack the market power to command high incomes.

Which view is correct? How much of this inequality is necessary in order to provide incentives? Is this distribution of income fair or not? The tools of the economist can help to explain *why* such a distribution of income exists, but are of little help in making what are, in essence, subjective value judgments as to whether it is a *fair* or an *appropriate* distribution of income.

However, the controversial nature of this matter does make it important that statistics such as those in Table 11-2 be interpreted carefully and accurately. In particular, the persistent inequality shown by the statistics—40 percent of income going to the top 20 percent of families and only 6 percent of income going to the bottom 20 percent of families, decade after decade—creates the impression that these high- and low-income groups comprise the same families, year after year. In particular, the image is generated of the same families stuck with low incomes decade after decade, without hope. While this is certainly the case with many such families, the situation is more complex than this image would suggest. The lowest-income group also includes families whose income is *temporarily* low: for instance, students at school who work only seasonally or part-time, or recent graduates whose low income reflects the fact that they have worked half the year or less. And, as we will see, the low-income group also includes some families of retired persons whose income is low, but who possess considerable assets, such as a paid-for home. So the low-income group is not simply a fixed group of families year after year, but rather comprises to a significant extent a changing group of households, who flow into and out of the low-income group as their circumstances change.

Finally, the inequalities in the Canadian distribution of income shown in Table 11-2 are not significantly different from those in other industrialized nations. International statistical comparisons are imprecise; however, it seems that income in Canada is distributed a little more unequally than in most European countries and a little less unequally than in the United States.

The Male–Female Pay Gap

The income differentials that have attracted the most attention in the past 30 years have been the pay differences between men and women. Different studies have estimated this pay gap differently, with most concluding that, on average, women earn roughly 72 percent of what men earn for full-time work. The existence of such a large income differential raises questions of gender discrimination in Canadian labour markets.

However, most of this difference between the incomes of men and women can be explained by economic factors. One such factor is the number of *hours worked*—on average, men work roughly 40 hours per week compared to about 35 hours for women, a difference of 15 percent. Most studies estimate that if differences in hours worked are considered, the male–female wage gap shrinks by nearly half. Somewhat less than another one-fifth of the gap can be attributed to "productivity factors," such as *training, education,* and

Statistics on incomes are collected each year by Statistics Canada through a survey of about 30 000 households that is known as the *Survey of Labour and Income Dynamics (SLID)*.

In 2001, women comprised 46 percent of Canada's labour force, but only 10 percent of the members of the boards of directors of Canada's largest 500 companies were women.

experience. The fact that many women interrupt their career for child-raising holds back their advancement and incomes. In addition, women have shown a tendency to leave the work force earlier than men—the participation rate for women drops rapidly after age 55, depressing the average income of women by reducing the number of them working during these higher-income years.

Both *marital status* and *age* are also significant factors making women's incomes lower than men's: single women's incomes are about 91 percent of those of single men, while married women earn only 65 percent of what married men earn. And incomes of women in the 15–24 age group are 86 percent of men's, while women over 55 earn only 64 percent of what men earn.

After allowance has been made for the hours worked and "productivity" factors, there remains a male–female wage gap of about 10 percent that can best be explained by "gender factors." The main such gender factor seems to have been *occupational segregation*: approximately three-quarters of female employees work in five occupational groups—clerical, service, sales, medicine/health care, and education. Since so many women are concentrated into these occupational groups that contain many relatively low-paying jobs, the average income of women in general tends to be below average.

There seem to be at least two basic origins of this occupational segregation. One is *society's stereotypes* concerning the role of women, which probably condition many young women to think in terms of working as secretaries, waitresses, and the like. The other is *selection procedures,* for both hiring and promotion. The people in a given occupational field or workplace tend to hire and promote people with whom they are comfortable and who they believe will "fit in." If the field is dominated by males, this makes it much more difficult for females to enter it. These two factors are illustrated in Figure 11-9.

FIGURE 11-9 Sources and Results of Occupational Segregation

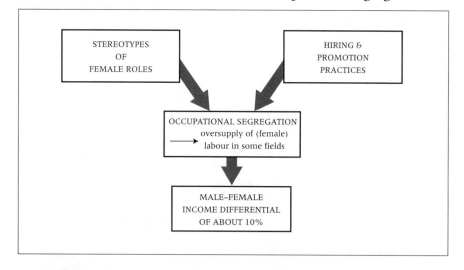

Figure 11-9 also shows the economic effects of these forces. If large numbers of women are steered by stereotyping and deflected by selection procedures into a few occupational areas, the result will be an oversupply of (female) labour in those occupations, with low wages the result.

Such male–female wage gaps raise important issues of government policy. In a sense, one of the most basic steps that must be taken is to break down the traditional female stereotypes. The educational system attempts to do this by showing both women and men in nontraditional occupational roles in schoolbooks from the earliest grades. Another basic step would be to change selection procedures by promoting "employment equity," either through persuasion or by legislation. And to deal with the income inequities, there is pay equity legislation. The first step toward dealing with this matter was legislation ruling that people who do the same work must receive the same pay—"equal pay for equal work" legislation. Such legislation has existed for many years in many provinces and is widely accepted. However, its effect is limited to situations where men and women are performing the same jobs. It does not address the main source of male–female wage differences—the fact that women tend to be concentrated in certain types of jobs with below-average pay.

equal pay for work of equal value The concept that the values of different jobs may be measured against each other using a point system that incorporates a variety of criteria, including skill levels, effort, degree of responsibility, and working conditions.

More recent and more controversial is the concept of **equal pay for work of equal value**. Under this approach, the "value" of a job is measured by a point system that takes into account factors such as skill, effort, responsibility, and working conditions. Such a system allows the pay of quite different jobs to be compared, by adding up their points—the more points a job has, the more it is "worth."

"Equal pay for work of equal value" legislation applies to government employees in several jurisdictions. However, the application of the same legislation to private employers is much more controversial, due to concerns regarding employers' ability to compete with other firms that are not subject to such requirements.

For various reasons, the male–female pay gap has been narrowing over time. However, another gap—the gap between the incomes of the skilled and the unskilled—has been *widening*, as discussed in the "In the News" box below.

IN THE **NEWS**   The Skills Gap

"... there is evidence that technological change is biased in favour of skilled workers, and wage differentials between skilled and unskilled workers are widening in many industries."

(From a 1997 study by the C.D. Howe Institute.)

With the passage of time, the male–female pay gap has been narrowing, making this less of an issue than it was in the past. However, as the male–female pay gap has been narrowing, another has quietly been widening—the pay gap between skilled and unskilled workers. In the market for skilled workers, there are literally "too many jobs

⇨

chasing too few people," causing the incomes of skilled workers to rise at an above-average pace. In the market for unskilled and semi-skilled workers, the combined effects of technological change and competition from imports have reduced job opportunities. In these job markets, there are too many people chasing too few jobs, causing incomes to increase slowly or even decrease. The result of these effects has been a growing gap between the incomes of skilled workers and those of unskilled and semi-skilled workers.

Questions

1. From your own observations, does the pay gap between skilled workers and the semi-skilled and unskilled seem to be widening?

2. If the pay gap between skilled and unskilled workers were to continue to grow to the point that it was considered inequitable and socially undesirable, what could the government do about this?

Poverty in Canada

On average, Canadians enjoy one of the highest standards of living in the world, but we have seen that this prosperity is distributed far from evenly among Canadians.

How many Canadians have such low incomes that they are living in poverty? According to some estimates, from 5 000 000 to over 7 000 000 Canadians (over 20 percent of the population) are "poor," while others place the number as low as 2 000 000, or even 1 000 000 (3 to 6 percent of Canadians). These widely varying estimates of the extent of poverty arise from the fact that there are very different ways to *define* what "poverty" actually means.

This is an important debate—by some definitions, poverty is a national crisis that demands massive government action, while according to others, it seems to be a much less widespread problem. First, we will consider the challenges in defining what "poverty" is and measuring how many people are living in poverty.

What Is Poverty?

Defining "poverty" and determining how low someone's income must be in order to be considered "poor" is far from being simple. There are two fundamentally different philosophical approaches to this question. One approach might be called a *physical* definition of poverty—by this standard, people or families would be considered poor *if they could not afford the necessities of life*. By this standard, the number of poor people in Canada has been estimated to be as low as 1 000 000 to 1 500 000. The other basic approach is based on *social and psychological considerations*; that is, a person or family would be considered to be poor if their income were *too far below the average income*. By some such measures, nearly 7 000 000 Canadians—over one in five—can be considered to be poor.

Canada's "Poverty Lines"

poverty lines Income levels below which families or individuals are considered to be poor.

Poverty lines are income levels below which families or individuals are considered to be poor. The statistics that have most commonly been used for this purpose are Statistics Canada's **Low-Income Cut-Offs** (LICOs). However, in late 1998, governments adopted a quite different set of poverty lines based on a **"market basket measure"** (MBM). This little-noticed change in the definition of the poverty line reduced the official estimate of poverty in Canada by nearly one-third. We will start by comparing these two very different ideas of what "poverty" means.

Low-Income Cut-Offs Income levels (as determined by Statistics Canada) below which families or individuals spend 56.2 percent or more of their income on food, clothing, and shelter. The 56.2 percent is 20 percentage points higher than the national average of 36.2 percent.

Using Statistics Canada's Low-Income Cut-Offs (LICOs) as poverty lines reflects the view that people are poor if their income is too far below the average income. An average family spends 36.2 percent of its gross income on the necessities of life—food, shelter, and clothing. The lower a family's income is, the higher will be the percentage that is spent on these necessities. If a family's income is so low that 56.2 percent is spent on necessities (20 percentage points above the average), Statistics Canada defines this family as a "low-income" family, relative to the average family income.

Statistics Canada's purpose in developing the LICOs was not to define "poverty" but rather to identify low-income Canadians so as to gather statistics on this group. Nonetheless, many groups, including the **National Council of Welfare** (NCW), consider the LICOs to represent poverty lines and use them as such to estimate the extent of poverty in Canada.

"market basket measure" Poverty lines based on the cost of a "basket" of goods and services that a family requires in order to live above the poverty line.

There are two sets of LICOs—one that uses before-tax income and one that uses after-tax income. They lead to quite different conclusions. According to the before-tax LICOs, 4 886 000 Canadians (16.2 percent of the population) were living in poverty in 1999. (The actual before-tax incomes that these LICO-based poverty lines represent are shown in Table 11-3.) But according to the after-tax LICOs, 3 569 000 Canadians, or 11.8 percent of the population, were poor.

National Council of Welfare A citizens' advisory body to the Minister of Human Resources Development Canada on matters of concern to low-income Canadians.

The use of the LICOs as poverty lines has been criticized for exaggerating the extent of poverty. The main criticism has been that the LICOs *measure inequality rather than poverty*. Critics argue that if the incomes and living standards of all Canadians, including the poor, were to double, it would seem logical that the number of poor people would decrease considerably. However, according to the LICOs, the percentage of people who are poor would not decrease, because there would still be as many people whose incomes were *far enough below the average* to be classed as "poor." This is one reason why, despite generally rising living standards, the percentage of Canadians who are poor has not decreased by much, and has even increased in some years. It also helps to explain why in Canada, with an average income of over $30 000 per person, 16 percent of its people can be considered poor, not that

www.ncwcnbes.net

TABLE 11-3 National Council of Welfare Estimates of Statistics Canada's Pre-Tax Low-Income Cut-Offs for 2001*

Family Size	Cities of 500 000+	Community Size 100 000– 499 999	30 000– 99 999	Less than 30 000	Rural Areas
1	18 849	16 167	16 055	14 940	13 026
2	23 561	20 209	20 070	18 674	16 283
3	29 303	25 134	24 958	23 224	20 251
4	35 471	30 424	30 214	28 113	24 513
5	39 651	34 010	33 773	31 425	27 402
6	43 830	37 595	37 333	34 737	30 292
7+	48 010	41 181	40 893	38 049	33 181

* Based on estimate of 2.6 percent inflation in 2001.

Source: National Council of Welfare, *Poverty Profile 1999* (Summer 2002). Reproduced with the permission of the Minister of Public Works and Government Services Canada, 2003.

far below the 25 percent official estimate of poverty in Bangladesh, where the average annual income is around $450.

Market basket measure (MBM) poverty lines reflect the view that poverty means the inability to afford the necessities of life. MBM poverty lines are based on the cost of a "basket" of goods and services that a family requires in order to live above the poverty line.

Many people regard MBM-based poverty lines as more realistic and more understandable than the LICOs. But using MBMs as poverty lines is not as simple as it might seem. The most basic problem is deciding just what should go into the "basket" in order to keep people above the poverty line. Deciding this takes us back to the problem of defining "poverty" discussed at the beginning of this topic—in a wealthy society, what should be considered a "necessity of life"? Establishing MBM poverty lines is further complicated by the fact that the cost of the same "basket" of items (especially shelter) varies widely from place to place across Canada.

> "Statistics Canada has clearly and consistently emphasized... that the LICOs are quite different from measures of poverty."
>
> From Statistics Canada, *Income Distribution by Size in Canada*, 1997.

New Poverty Lines for Canada

In late 1998, Canadian governments adopted a new definition of poverty and new poverty lines based on the MBM approach. As an example of the meaning of this change, a family of four would be considered to be "poor" if it did not have:

- enough income to eat nutritious meals as defined by Health Canada,
- enough income to buy clothing for work and social occasions,
- enough income to rent a median-cost three-bedroom apartment, and
- additional income equal to 60 percent of the combined cost of the food and clothing budgets, for the purchase of other necessary items such as personal care, household needs, furniture, telephone service, public transit, reading, recreation and school supplies.

The poverty lines were to be adjusted for family size and for variations in living costs in different regions.

The adoption of these new poverty lines had significant effects. Since the MBM poverty lines were roughly 20 percent lower than the LICOs, the number of Canadians classed as "poor" would fall by about 1.5 million and the **poverty rate** (the percentage of the population considered to be poor) would be reduced by nearly one-third. The cost of the government's undertaking to eliminate child poverty would be cut in half, and welfare costs in some provinces could be reduced.

poverty rate The percentage of any given group that has an income below the poverty line.

Other Measurement Problems

Critics argue that both the LICOs and the MBM poverty lines exaggerate the extent of poverty, due to problems in actually estimating the number of poor people.

One problem is that the income statistics on which estimates of poverty are made come from surveys, and some people will *underreport their income*, usually to evade income taxes. One example would be people in the food service industry who earn minimum-wage incomes that are supplemented significantly by cash tips, much of which is not reported. Studies have also found that people tend to underreport their Employment Insurance benefits by about 40 percent and their welfare benefits by about 20 percent.

Another measurement problem arises from the fact that the poverty lines consider *money income only*. For instance, there are retired people who have low money incomes, but a reasonably comfortable lifestyle because they possess assets bought earlier in their lives, especially a *paid-for house*. Not having to pay rent or mortgage payments represents a major economic benefit for such people, often the equivalent of several thousand dollars per year of additional income that does not get counted when money income is the only factor considered in defining "poverty."

Additional measurement problems arise from the fact that poverty statistics include people in transition, whose incomes are *only temporarily low*. This group would include some new entrants to the work force who only worked part of the year, some immigrants (only income earned in Canada is counted), some people following marital breakups, and others whose low-income situation is only temporary, but who are counted as living in poverty. Also included are college and university students, whose low earned income may not be reflective of their lifestyle if they share rent or live rent-free at home when not at school.

When all is said and done, defining "poverty" and developing accurate estimates of the number of Canadians who are poor is a task that is complex, difficult, and controversial. As a result, estimates of the number of poor Canadians continue to vary widely, from as low as 3 percent of the population to over 20 percent.

Who Are the Poor?

These difficulties in measuring the number of poor people do not mean that there is no "poverty problem" in Canada, only that we are uncertain as to its extent. There certainly are many Canadians who are poor, and it is important to know who they are. This will help us to understand the nature and causes of poverty, and to develop effective policies for addressing this problem.

In the following sections, statistics from the National Council of Welfare (NCW) are used. Because the NCW uses the LICOs as poverty lines, the poverty rates will be higher than those using the new MBM poverty lines; however, these statistics will provide the best available estimates of the characteristics of those Canadians who are poor.

According to the National Council of Welfare, probably the most important overall factor influencing the risk of poverty is *family type*. This factor refers to the subcategories of families and unattached individuals shown in Figure 11-10. These groups are arranged according to the poverty rate (the percentage of each group that is below the LICOs) for each group. Figure 11-10 uses the poverty lines established by the *after-tax* LICOs.

Figure 11-10 shows that single-parent mothers are the group with the highest poverty rate, with 41.3 percent of this group having low after-tax incomes in 1999. The second-highest poverty rate was for unattached women under 65 (most of whom were very young women), 37.8 percent of whom had low after-tax incomes. Unattached men under 65 (again, mostly the very young) had a poverty rate of 29.6 percent. They were followed by unattached women 65 and over with a poverty rate of 23.6 percent and unattached men 65 and over at 16.6 percent. By far, the lowest poverty rates were among couples, with couples over 65 and childless couples the least prone to low incomes.

Statistics on poverty can also be analyzed according to *age* and *sex*, as shown in Figure 11-11 on page 239. These statistics show that poverty rates are highest among young people in general, and among older unattached individuals. The high poverty rates among young people reflect factors such as the lower pay earned by newer entrants to the work force due to lack of experience and seniority, as well as the intermittent work and high unemployment rates experienced by many in this group. Causes of low incomes among older unattached individuals include the fact that this group includes a large number of widows, as well as the low pensions received by some older people and problems finding work. However, it should also be noted that the poverty rate among seniors has declined sharply, from 33.6 percent in 1980 to less than 18 percent in 1999.

Figure 11-11 also shows that across all age groupings, *women* have a higher poverty rate than men, but that the difference between women and men is particularly great among seniors. Most of the high poverty rate for women under 65 can be attributed to the high poverty rates of two subgroups within this group: unattached women and single-parent mothers.

Poverty rates can also be analyzed according to the *education* of those with low incomes. As would be expected, poverty rates are generally higher for those with less education—for people with less than a high-school diploma, the poverty rate is roughly two or three times as high as for people with a post-secondary diploma or degree. The poverty rates for *family heads* are only one-third to one-half of those of unattached individuals, presumably because most families have more than one income-earner.

FIGURE 11-10 Poverty Rates (After-Tax Basis) by
Family Type, 1999

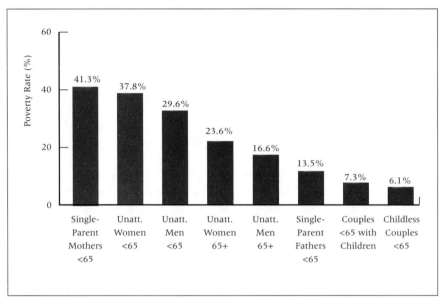

Source: National Council of Welfare, *Poverty Profile 1999*, Summer 2002. Reproduced with
the permission of the Minister of Public Works and Government Services Canada, 2003.

The Working Poor

While many poor people do not work, a larger low-income group that
deserves attention is the "working poor." For this group, low wages and/or
intermittent employment means low incomes despite the fact that they do
work considerably.

In 1999, 25 percent of poor family heads worked full-time and another
33 percent worked part-time. Also, 16 percent of poor unattached individuals worked full-time in 1999, and another 38 percent worked part-time.
These figures show that many—indeed, most—of the poor had considerable
attachment to the labour force.

Many of these "working poor" live on incomes that are actually lower
than they would receive if they were on welfare. Nonetheless, the social welfare system has provided little help for these people, because their work
activity often makes them ineligible for assistance. People working for the
minimum wage rate generally fall below the poverty line, but as we saw in
Chapter 10, if the minimum wage rate were increased to above-poverty-line
levels, job opportunities for the low-income group could be reduced.

FIGURE 11-11 Poverty Rates (After-Tax Basis) for Persons by Age Group and Sex, 1999

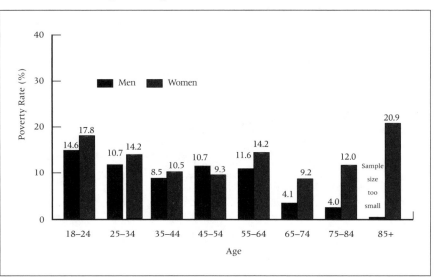

Source: National Council of Welfare, *Poverty Profile 1999*, Summer 2002. Reproduced with the permission of the Minister of Public Works and Government Services Canada, 2003.

Sources of Income for the Poor

Low-income Canadians, particularly those over 65, receive a high proportion of their income in the form of *transfer payments* from governments. These transfer payments include Employment Insurance, welfare, Canada and Quebec Pension Plan benefits, the federal Old Age Security pension and Guaranteed Income Supplement, the federal Child Tax Benefit and the federal GST credit.

Trends in Poverty Rates

As Figure 11-12 shows, the poverty rate has generally followed quite closely the general condition of Canada's economy. When the economy grows and the unemployment rate falls, the poverty rate falls as well; however, when recessions such as occurred in the early 1980s and early 1990s cause the unemployment rate to rise, the poverty rate also increases.

However, Figure 11-12 also shows that during the 1990s a different trend emerged, with the poverty rate *rising* over a period during which the unemployment rate *declined*. One possible explanation of this trend is the growing gap between the incomes of highly skilled workers and the less skilled that was described earlier in this chapter. It is too early to determine whether this is a longer-term trend or a temporary aberration.

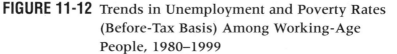

FIGURE 11-12 Trends in Unemployment and Poverty Rates (Before-Tax Basis) Among Working-Age People, 1980–1999

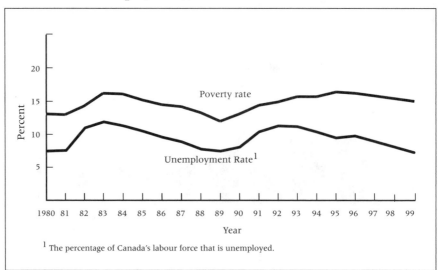

Source: National Council of Welfare, *Poverty Profile 1999*, Summer 2002. Reproduced with the permission of the Minister of Public Works and Government Services Canada, 2003.

In Conclusion

While there are different views as to how "poverty" should be defined and how many poor people there really are, there are some matters upon which there is fairly broad agreement. The risk of having a low income is greatest among single-parent mothers and unattached young people, and lower levels of education increases the risk of poverty considerably.

Women have a higher risk of poverty than men, especially single mothers, younger unattached women with low levels of education, and elderly women living on their own. In the past, seniors have had a high incidence of poverty due to the inadequacy of many pension plans. However, as pensions and government assistance to seniors have improved, and many retirees have benefited from selling their homes at high prices, poverty has become much less of a "seniors' problem" and more of a "youth problem" and "women's problem." Also, child poverty has become more of an issue in Canada in recent years, in large part due to the persistently high poverty rates of younger parents, especially single mothers. Finally, poverty rates vary quite widely across the country, ranging in 1999 (on a before-tax basis) from a low of 13.5 percent in Ontario to 20.7 percent in Newfoundland and 19.5 percent in Quebec.

Chapter Summary

1. Due to changes in technology and demand, the composition of Canada's labour force has changed greatly since 1950. Employment in the goods-producing sector has increased only slightly, whereas employment in the services sector has increased greatly. (L.O.1)

2. There is some evidence that the gap between the incomes of skilled and less skilled workers has been growing wider, probably as a result of the effects of technological change on the demand for labour. (L.O. 1)

3. The increased participation of women in the labour market has been the outstanding trend in the labour force since 1950. This trend is due to various factors, including higher education levels and aspirations among women, the need to add to family incomes, the need of more women to be self-supporting, and the growth of job opportunities in the service sector. (L.O. 2)

4. The average real family income of Canadians in 1999 was more than 2.5 times as high as in 1951, with most of the increase occurring by 1976. Since then, slower growth of both productivity and the number of income-earners per family have generated slower growth of family income. (L.O. 3)

5. There exists a pay differential between men and women of about 10 percent that is attributed to gender factors. In particular, women have tended to be concentrated in certain occupational groupings within which many jobs have below-average incomes. (L.O. 4)

6. Statistics Canada's Low-Income Cut-Offs (LICOs) estimate how many Canadians have an income that is below the average income by more than a certain amount. Using the before-tax LICOs as poverty lines, 16.2 percent of Canadians would be classed as "poor" in 1999, and using the after-tax LICOs as poverty lines, 11.8 percent would be classed as "poor." (L.O. 5)

7. In 1998, Canada's governments adopted a Market Basket Measure (MBM) definition of poverty, under which poverty lines are based on the cost of the necessities of life. Using MBM poverty lines, which are roughly 20 percent lower than the LICOs, reduced the number of Canadians classed as "poor" by about one-third. (L.O. 6)

8. Estimates of the poverty rate vary widely, from as low as 3 percent to as high as 20 percent, largely due to differences over whether the poverty line should be an income needed to buy the necessities of life or an income that is below the average income by more than a certain amount. In addition, there are differences over the accuracy of the income statistics used and over how non-income benefits such as ownership of a paid-for home should be treated. (L.O. 7)

9. The risk of having a low income is highest among single-parent mothers, unattached young people, and the poorly educated. (L.O. 8)

Questions

1. "Only a society with no sense of real values would pay an uneducated lout of a hockey player ten times the salary of its prime minister or a doctor." Discuss this statement from the perspectives of *why* such income differentials exist, and whether you agree with the statement.

2. Why has the labour force participation rate of women, especially married women, increased so greatly? Why would it be expected to rise more slowly in the future?

3. The labour force participation rate of women falls off sharply after age 55. Why do you think this is the case? Would you expect this to change in the future?

4. Look at the poverty lines in Table 11-3. To you, do these incomes seem to be reasonable approximations of what individuals and families need in order to barely escape poverty?

5. If we use the *before-tax* LICO incomes as poverty lines, 16.2 percent of Canadians would be classed as poor in 1999. If we use the *after-tax* LICOs as poverty lines, only 11.8 percent of Canadians would be classed as poor. But the poor do not pay much if any income tax. So why are so many fewer Canadians classed as poor if we use after-tax incomes as the measuring stick?

6. In the two decades after about 2010, the baby boomers will retire. What are the implications of this for Canadian society and the living standards of Canadians?

7. In 1999, poor women over 65 outnumbered poor men over 65 by about 4 to 1 (204 000 women to 53 000 men, based on after-tax incomes). What might explain this large difference?

8. Unattached men and women under 65, most of them young people, account for about 29 percent of all poverty in Canada. For such individuals living in cities of over 500 000, the National Council of Welfare's poverty line in 2001 was a before-tax income of $18 371 per year. Would you favour a government policy that would guarantee these people an annual income of at least $18 371? (This would be the equivalent of working 37 hours per week for 50 weeks at a wage rate of $9.93 per hour.)

9. Some of the "working poor" earn less than they would receive if they went onto welfare and did not work at all. Why, then, do you think they decide to work?

10. Under many social assistance (welfare) programs, the benefits that people receive are *below* the Low-Income Cut-Offs that many regard as the "poverty line." What might explain this seeming inconsistency?

Chapter 12

The Government Sector

Learning Objectives

After studying this chapter, you should be able to:

1. Summarize the development of the three main aspects of Canada's social welfare system.

2. List the four main sources of government tax revenue, and explain the main limitations on increasing each of these.

3. Summarize how Canadian governments' transfer payments and income taxes redistribute income among Canadians.

4. Describe the purposes of federal government transfer payments to the provincial governments.

5. Summarize the situation that developed regarding federal government budget deficits and debt in the years following 1975, and how this situation reached a crisis point in 1993.

6. Explain the two main factors that contributed to the elimination of federal government budget deficits over the 1994–98 period.

7. Explain how reforms such as targeting of social welfare benefits and increasing work incentives for recipients of social welfare benefits help to reduce government budget deficits.

8. Summarize the types of reforms made to health care and education in response to reductions in government funding.

9. Identify the three basic alternative uses for the federal government budget surpluses that developed after 1997, and state the arguments in favour of each of these.

As discussed in Chapter 2, the Canadian economy is characterized as a *mixed free-enterprise* economic system. With about 80 percent of economic activity being carried out by private businesses in response to the demand of buyers, the economy is basically "market" in nature. However, there is also a substantial amount of *government involvement* in the economy. As we saw in Chapter 2, governments provide extensive *public services*, such as health care and education, and they own and operate various enterprises, such as the Canadian Broadcasting Corporation and Canada Post. In addition, government taxation and transfer payment programs *redistribute income* from those with higher incomes to those with less, and *government regulations* establish in countless ways the economic "rules of play" for Canadian businesses, workers, and consumers, from advertising practices to employment standards.

Furthermore, the role of government in the Canadian economy has grown considerably over the years. While the federal government attracts the most public attention, spending by *provincial* and *local (municipal)* governments has exceeded federal government spending since the mid-1960s. The reason is that the provinces have the primary responsibility for education and health care, both of which have expanded greatly since the 1960s.

Figure 12-1 shows the growth of the grand total of spending by all three levels of government—federal, provincial, and local—on all government programs, such as health care, education, Employment Insurance, welfare, pensions, national defence, police, firefighters, subsidies to businesses,

FIGURE 12-1 Government Spending[a] as a Percentage of Gross Domestic Product, 1950–2001

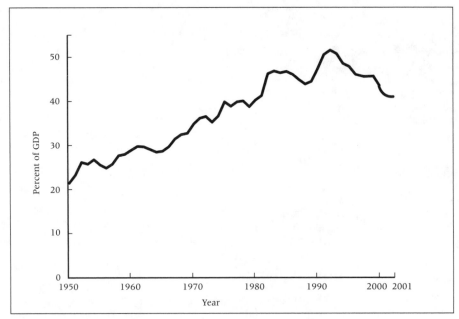

Source: Adapted from Statistics Canada, *National Income and Expenditure Accounts, Quarterly Estimates*, Catalogue No. 13-001, 2002.

interest on government debt, and so on. After many years of growth, total government spending reached a peak in 1992 of almost 52 percent of Canada's Gross Domestic Product. Figure 12-1 shows another important aspect of government spending—its decline as a percentage of GDP since 1992, a development that we will examine later in this chapter.

Impressive though they may be, these spending statistics understate the role of government in the economy by a considerable amount. They do not include the activities of government-owned *Crown corporations* such as Canada Post and the Canadian Broadcasting Corporation, nor do they include the myriad of *government regulations* of economic activity that have been enacted over the years.

So the role of government in the Canadian economy has expanded greatly over the past half-century. In this chapter, we will examine the reasons for this growth, and look at recent developments and possible future trends with respect to the role of government in the Canadian economy.

The Growth of Canada's Social Welfare Programs

As we have seen, Canadian governments spend substantial amounts of money on social welfare programs, with most of it going to the three key areas of *income security* (such as Employment Insurance, welfare, and pensions), *health care*, and *education*. Government spending on these programs has risen dramatically during the twentieth century. Why has this happened?

In the most basic sense, the growth of the social welfare system was brought about by the transition from a rural, agrarian society of small communities to a modern, urban society with a large industrial work force. In the earlier society of small, closely knit, and stable communities, traditional institutions such as the family, the church, the local community, and private charity were able to provide for the needs of those who required assistance. However, as Canada evolved into an urban society with a large, mobile work force largely comprising industrial employees, the situation changed significantly. People and families were exposed to increased risks of loss of income due to unemployment (or layoff), illness, disability, and old age. And as the traditional social institutions became less able to provide for Canadians' social needs, it became increasingly necessary for governments to provide assistance to those who needed it.

The growth of the government's role acquired considerable momentum from the Great Depression of the 1930s. The Depression destroyed faith in the *laissez-faire* philosophy that the economy could be counted upon to automatically provide employment for all who wanted it and that people could therefore be expected to take care of themselves economically. By doing so, the Depression made much more acceptable the idea that the government should provide assistance to the victims of economic forces beyond their control in the form of benefits for those without jobs and incomes of their own.

> "Income security, health, and education represent central supports of the welfare state."
>
> *Royal Commission on the Economic Union and Development Prospects for Canada* (Ottawa, Minister of Supply and Services, 1985).

Income Security Programs

In the decades that followed the Great Depression, Canada's social welfare programs expanded greatly. In the field of *income security programs*, Unemployment Insurance was introduced in 1942, Family Allowances in 1945, Old Age Security in 1952, various social assistance programs in the 1950s, the Canada and Quebec Pension Plans in 1965, the Canada Assistance Plan for social welfare and the Guaranteed Income Supplement in 1966, the Spouses' Allowance in 1975, and the Child Tax Credit in 1978. Also, in the 1970s, benefits under the Unemployment Insurance and Family Allowance programs were increased significantly.

tax credits Credits that reduce the income taxes payable by Canadians in order to offset a variety of factors that adversely affect their living standards, including dependants, property taxes, and sales taxes.

Another important, although less visible, way in which governments support people's incomes is through **tax credits** in the income tax system. These tax credits reduce the income taxes payable by Canadians in order to offset a variety of factors that adversely affect their living standards, from children and other dependants to sales taxes and property taxes. Some of these tax credits are structured so that they benefit only lower-income individuals and families, partly by reducing the taxes that they pay and in some cases entitling them to tax refunds.

Health Care

Health care represents the second key element of Canada's social welfare system. Health care can be extremely expensive, exposing individuals and families to the risk of heavy costs and even financial ruin. As a result, it was decided as a matter of social policy that all Canadians should have access to health care without having to pay the costs themselves, giving Canadians one of the most liberal health-care systems in the world. Following the introduction of hospital-insurance and medicare programs, government expenditures on health care grew to one of the largest government-spending programs. The Canadian Institute for Health Information (CIHI) estimates total government spending on health care in 2002 to be almost $80 billion.

www.cihi.ca

Education

Education, which represents the third pillar of Canada's social welfare system, is completely financed by tax revenues in the case of primary and secondary education. Post-secondary education is subsidized by governments through grants to colleges and universities that allow them to charge tuition fees that represent a relatively small proportion of the cost of students' education. These government expenditures are justified in part on economic grounds, as an investment in the "human capital" needed by a modern economy. Also, government support of education is seen as a key aspect of social policy, as a means of providing equality of opportunity for all Canadians to obtain the education needed for their lives and careers. Canadian governments spend about 6 percent of GDP on education ($64 billion in 2002), which is fairly high by international standards.

Taken together, these programs involve a great deal of government spending. In 2002, program spending (spending on all items other than interest on government debt) by all levels of government in Canada amounted to almost $388 billion, or more than $12 000 for every Canadian man, woman, and child. This brings us to the question of how governments raise all the revenues to pay for these expenditures.

Paying For It: Sources of Government Revenues

In 2002, Canadians paid about $391 billion in taxes of various sorts. There are four basic types of taxes that pay for government spending:

- taxes on *incomes* (personal and business income taxes),
- taxes on *spending* (sales taxes, or **consumption taxes**),
- taxes on *assets* (mainly, property taxes), and
- taxes on *employers' payrolls* (such as Canada Pension Plan and Employment Insurance premiums).

consumption taxes Taxes levied when consumers buy goods and services; for example, sales taxes.

These taxes raise the funds that provide us with government services and benefits. But each type of tax also brings its own type of costs to the economy, as we will see in the following sections.

Taxes on Incomes

Taxes on incomes such as personal income taxes and business profits taxes are the largest tax source in Canada, mainly because they can be applied to millions of people and businesses. The personal income tax alone raises nearly 40 percent of all tax revenues collected by governments in Canada.

A key feature of the personal income tax is that the rate of taxation (the percentage of income taken by taxes) can be tailored to people's ability to pay. People with low incomes can pay a low percentage of their income to taxes or none at all, while people with high incomes can be taxed at much higher rates. Taxes that take a higher percentage of the incomes of the "rich" than of the "poor" are known as **progressive taxes**. The most prominent of these is the personal income tax, and in the view of many, this makes the personal income tax a particularly fair tax.

progressive taxes Taxes that take a higher percentage of high incomes than of low incomes.

The major limitation regarding income taxes is that if the rate of taxation becomes *too* high, it can have a negative effect on incentives to work, save, and invest. The key here is what economists call the **marginal tax rate**, which is the tax rate payable on any *additional* income that is earned over and above one's present income.

marginal tax rate The percentage of any additional income that is earned that goes to taxes.

The Marginal Tax Rate

Let's illustrate with an example. If Fred earns $40 000 per year working in a library and pays income taxes of $8000, he is paying a 20-percent tax rate on his income—on average, he pays 20 cents in taxes on every dollar he earns.

This, however, is not Fred's marginal tax rate—his *marginal* tax rate is the percentage of any *additional* income that he earns that goes to taxes. For instance, suppose that Fred works nights as a professional wrestler and earns *an additional* $10 000. If he has to pay $3500 in income taxes *on this $10 000 of extra income*, his marginal tax rate is 35 percent.

It is the marginal tax rate that affects Fred's incentive to work, because it applies to extra income that Fred can decide to earn or not earn. Even if the tax rate on Fred's main income as a librarian is increased sharply, he has little choice but to continue working—he needs this main source of his income. But a sharp increase in the marginal tax rate on his extra income as a wrestler might cause him to decide to retire from the ring, or wrestle less often.

> In 2001, the federal government began a 5-year series of cuts to personal and corporate income taxes that, by 2005, would amount to over $30 billion per year. From 2001 to 2005, the total tax cuts would be about $100 billion.

High marginal tax rates can generate disincentives in various ways. As the example of Fred shows, high marginal tax rates can discourage people from working overtime or at a second job, or from saving and investing money in order to earn investment income. High marginal tax rates on business profits can discourage capital investment to improve efficiency, or even discourage businesses from investing in the country or province with those high tax rates. So marginal tax rates that are high enough to create disincentives to work, save, and invest will have negative effects on productivity and on the economic prosperity of society.

Taxes on Consumption

regressive tax A tax that takes a higher percentage of low incomes than of high incomes.

Another basic type of tax is *taxes on spending* by consumers. The most visible such taxes are of course provincial sales taxes (PST) and the Goods and Services Tax (GST); however, the very high taxes on tobacco, alcohol, and gasoline are also consumption taxes. By taxing a broad base of consumer spending, sales taxes can be a significant source of revenue for governments—for instance, revenues from the GST amount to roughly $25 billion per year.

> Patricia earns $40 000 and owns a house on which she pays property taxes of $2000 per year. Her property taxes amount to 5 percent ($2000 ÷ $40 000) of her income. Pat earns $24 000 and lives in an apartment for which he pays rent of $600 per month, or $7200 per year. Of this, approximately 20 percent, or $1440, goes to cover the property taxes paid by the landlord. His property taxes amount to 6 percent ($1440 ÷ $24 000) of his income. In this case, the property tax is regressive—the person with the lower income pays a higher percentage of that income to property taxes than the higher-income person pays.

The main disadvantage of sales taxes is that they are **regressive**—that is, they take a higher percentage of the incomes of low-income earners than from those with high incomes. Certainly, the rich pay *more dollars* in sales taxes than the poor do, because they buy much more. But the poor pay *a higher percentage* of their income to sales taxes, because their incomes are so low. This is why sales taxes are more burdensome to lower-income people than to those with higher incomes.

Taxes on Assets

The third major source of tax revenue is *taxes on assets*. The largest of these is *property taxes*, which are a major source of revenue for local governments—about $32 billion in 2001.

Because they apply to fewer people (those who own particular types of assets, mainly real estate), these taxes raise less revenue than either income or sales taxes. In addition, property taxes often are regressive, in that they take a larger percentage of the incomes of low-income people than of those with high incomes. As with sales taxes, the rich pay more dollars in property taxes, but people with low incomes pay a higher percentage of their income to these taxes, as illustrated by the case of Pat and Patricia.

Taxes on Payrolls

Payroll taxes are levied on employers, based on the *size of their payroll*. These taxes include Employment Insurance premiums, Canada Pension Plan premiums, workers' compensation premiums, and, in some provinces, a tax to help pay for the costs of health care and post-secondary education. These taxes must be paid whether the employers make a profit or not.

The problem with payroll taxes is that they amount to taxes on employing people, in the sense that the more people a firm employs, the higher the taxes it must pay. A 1993 study estimated that, on average, payroll taxes added 7.8 percent to Canadian employers' payroll costs; that is, to the cost of employing people. Furthermore, the burden of these taxes falls especially heavily on small businesses, many of which are much more labour-intensive than most larger businesses. As a result, payroll taxes are criticized for discouraging hiring by the small business sector, which has created a high proportion of new jobs in Canada in recent years.

> **payroll taxes** Taxes paid by employers based on the number of their employees or the amount of their payroll.

> In 2001–02, the federal government collected $18.0 billion in Employment Insurance premiums (taxes) and paid out $13.7 billion in Employment Insurance benefits.

How Much Do Government Programs Redistribute Income?

One major aspect of Canada's social welfare system is *public services* such as health care and education, as described earlier in this chapter. The other major component of the social welfare system is *redistribution of income* from people with higher incomes to those with low incomes. Income is redistributed by both the tax system and government transfer payments. Those with higher incomes pay a larger percentage of their incomes to taxes, mainly due to the progressive nature of the personal income tax. And those with lower incomes receive various types of transfer payments, such as welfare, pensions, and Employment Insurance benefits. The overall result of these programs is the redistribution of income that is reflected in Table 12-1.

There are three definitions of "income" used in Table 12-1:

- *Market income*, which is income earned in the marketplace (wages, salaries, investment income, etc.),
- *Total income*, which is market income plus government transfer payments, such as welfare or Employment Insurance benefits, and
- *Income after transfers and taxes*, which is total income less income taxes paid.

Table 12-1 shows that in 2000 an average family in the lowest 20 percent of income-earners earned $8562 in market income and received $12 851 in transfer payments, for a total income of $21 413. This average family paid income taxes of $1569, leaving it with an income after transfers and taxes of $19 844. On balance, transfer payments and income tax added $11 282 to its income. At the other extreme, an average family in the highest 20 percent group paid $35 687 in income taxes and received $2868 of transfer payments, so it contributed $32 819 to these redistribution programs.

TABLE 12-1 Redistribution of Income by Transfer Payments and Income Taxes, 2000 (for economic families with two or more people)

	Lowest 20% of Incomes	Second 20% of Incomes	Middle 20% of Incomes	Fourth 20% of Incomes	Highest 20% of Incomes
Average market income	$ 8 562	$31 874	$52 767	$76 095	$138 902
Average transfer payments received	12 851	8 282	5 439	3 995	2 868
Average total income	21 413	40 156	58 206	80 090	141 770
Average income tax paid	1 569	4 997	9 995	15 736	35 687
Average income after transfers and taxes	19 844	35 159	48 211	64 354	106 083
Net effect of transfers and taxes	+11 282	+3 285	−4 556	−11 741	−32 819

Source: Adapted from the Statistics Canada CANSIM II database, Table 202-0701.

Problems Financing Government Programs

As noted earlier, government social service programs (such as health care and education) and income redistribution programs (such as welfare and Employment Insurance) are costly to operate. And much of the burden of financing these programs is the responsibility of the provincial governments.

Under the Constitution Act, 1982, health care, education, and welfare are the responsibility of the provincial governments, not the federal government. After the mid-1960s, the rapid growth of spending on health care, education, and welfare put severe strains on the finances of provincial governments. By contrast, the federal government possesses greater taxation powers than the provinces, mainly because it levies the personal income tax, the largest single source of government revenue in Canada.

Federal Transfer Payments to the Provinces

One way that was developed to deal with this imbalance in taxation powers and spending responsibilities was for the federal government to transfer some of its revenues to the provinces to help to finance their programs in health care, post-secondary education, and welfare. These federal–provincial transfer payments grew rapidly, from about $1 billion in 1967 to nearly $27 billion in 1993, when they comprised almost 23 percent of total provincial government revenues. In the first half of the 1990s, the provinces were receiving transfer payments from the federal government amounting to almost $1000 per citizen per year, which the provincial governments were spending on health care, post-secondary education, and welfare.

Federal Budget Deficits Following 1974

During the 1970s, the federal government made a series of policy decisions that increased benefits under various social programs, such as unemployment insurance and pensions, and made commitments to transfer large amounts of federal funds to the provincial governments to help finance provincial government spending on health care, welfare, and post-secondary education.

At the same time, the federal government introduced various tax reductions on both personal and business income, which had the effect of depressing its tax revenues. These spending and taxation decisions by the government caused an imbalance to develop between government spending and revenues, so that federal government spending regularly exceeded the government's revenues, usually by a large amount.

Financing Deficits

When the government's spending is larger than its revenues, there is said to be a government **budget deficit**. For instance, in 1978 the federal government's spending was about $49 billion and its revenues were about $38 billion, giving it a budget deficit of $11 billion. To raise this $11 billion, the government would *borrow*, mostly by *selling government bonds*. Most of these bonds are long-term in nature; that is, repayable in 10 years or more. Such bonds are mostly bought as long-term investments by large institutional investors, such as pension funds, mutual funds, banks, and so on, although individuals buy them as well. Mostly, they are sold to Canadian investors, although foreign lenders also buy them.

budget deficit An excess of government spending over government revenues.

Figure 12-2 shows the federal government's budget deficits both before and after 1974. Note how the deficits were infrequent and small through 1975, but after that they became not only *much larger*, but also a *regular annual event* until the late 1990s. The deficits—and the government debt in the next section—are expressed as a percentage of the size of the economy, so that inflation will not exaggerate the size of the figures.

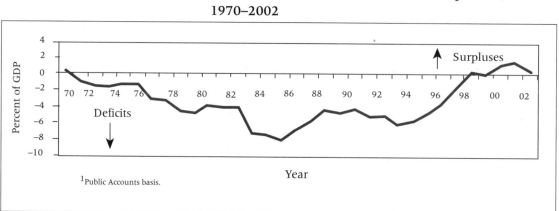

FIGURE 12-2 Federal Government Deficits and Surpluses[1], 1970–2002

[1]Public Accounts basis.

Sources: Adapted from Statistics Canada, *National Income and Expenditure Accounts, Quarterly Estimates,* Catalogue No. 13-001, 2001 and Department of Finance, *Fiscal Reference Tables October 2002.* Reproduced with the permission of the Minister of Public Works and Government Services Canada, 2003.

Deficits and Debt

With annual budget deficits of more than $10–20 billion after 1975, the federal government sold large volumes of government bonds each year. In the process, the federal government accumulated a very large debt. By 1985, the federal government's debt was over $200 billion, eight times its 1974 level of $26 billion and the second-highest government debt (as a percentage of GDP) of all major nations in the world. Furthermore, government budget deficits in excess of $30 billion per year were pushing the debt higher and higher at a rapid pace. Both the size and the rate of growth of the federal government's debt were becoming serious concerns.

In the second half of the 1980s, the government restrained its spending and increased various taxes in an attempt to reduce its budget deficits. But by this point another factor was driving the federal budget deficit upward—*interest payments on the government's massive and growing debt.* From 1984 to 1990, the federal government's interest payments grew from $21 billion to $42 billion, becoming the second-largest item of current government expenditure. Despite the government's spending restraints and tax increases, this growth of interest payments kept the government's deficits high, forcing the government to borrow further. The government was borrowing more in order to pay the interest on its debt, and that borrowing was driving the debt even higher. Figure 12-3 shows the growth of the federal government's debt during this period.

Provincial Budget Deficits

One way in which the federal government tried to reduce its budget deficits after 1985 was by limiting the transfer payments to the provincial

FIGURE 12-3   Net Federal Government Debt as a Percent of GDP, 1970–2002

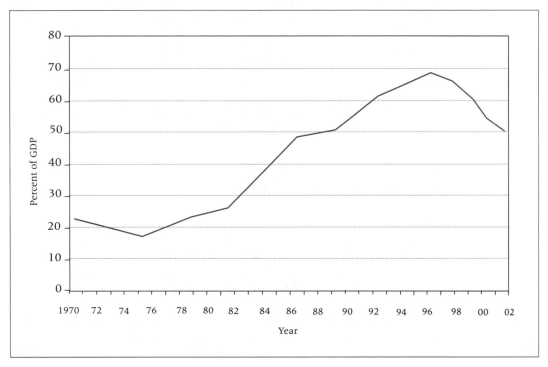

Sources: Adapted from Statistics Canada, *National Income and Expenditure Accounts Quarterly Estimates*, Catalogue No. 13-001, 2002 and Department of Finance, adapted from *Fiscal Reference Tables October 2002.*

governments, which helped the provinces pay for programs such as health care, welfare, and post-secondary education. The reduction in these transfer payments left the provinces with growing budget deficits of their own. When the recession of the early 1990s undercut provincial tax revenues and increased provincial spending on welfare, the combined budget deficits of the provincial governments soared to about $20 billion.

The Critical Point

By 1993, the situation had become critical. The combined budget deficits of the federal and provincial governments amounted to over $50 billion per year. The total net debt of all Canadian governments was over 90 percent of GDP, and interest payments on the debt were driving it higher, in an upward spiral. In addition, as the interest payments on their debt grew, governments were continually being forced to cut spending in other areas, especially social programs.

To finance their massive budget deficits, Canadian governments (mostly the provinces) had for several years been borrowing increasingly heavily *from foreign lenders*. Canada's debt to foreign lenders, about half of which was owed by Canadian governments, was by far the largest in the world and was rising rapidly. Canadian governments, especially the provinces, were increasingly dependent upon foreign lenders to finance their deficits by buying their bonds.

But, by the early 1990s, the heavy and growing indebtedness of Canadian governments was seen as a threat to the economic prosperity of Canadians. Foreign lenders were becoming concerned about the creditworthiness of Canadian governments. The credit ratings of some provinces deteriorated, forcing the provinces to pay higher interest rates on their bonds in order to attract lenders. These developments forced both the provincial and federal governments to finally confront their budget problems and to make some difficult choices.

Eliminating the Deficits

The only two ways for governments to reduce their budget deficits are to *increase taxes* or *reduce spending*. Taxes had already been increased substantially during the 1980s, and were so high that further tax increases were not possible. The only alternative left was to reduce government spending. The key point is considered to be the federal budgets of 1994 and 1995, which announced reductions in federal spending over a period of several years.

> "For years, governments have been promising more than they can deliver, and delivering more than they can afford. That has to end. We are ending it."
>
> Finance Minister Paul Martin, 1994.

The most publicized aspect of the deficit elimination program was the *reductions in federal program spending*, which is all spending except interest on the government's debt. From 1994 to 1997, annual federal program spending was cut by over $15 billion. The largest cuts were to the federal transfer payments to the provinces for health care, post-secondary education, and welfare that were described earlier in this chapter. From 1994 to 1998, these transfer payments to the provinces were cut by $6.4 billion, or 24 percent. This reduction in provincial revenues led to a series of major spending cuts by the provincial governments on their own programs. Hospital services were reduced, grants to colleges and universities were cut (which led to substantial increases in tuition costs for students), and welfare benefits were reduced, in some cases by more than 20 percent.

Even as the federal government's spending was being cut, its tax revenues increased considerably in the second half of the 1990s. This was mainly the result of economic growth, which increased employment and total personal income during this period. In addition, government revenues from taxes on corporate profits rose considerably, also due to the economic growth of the second half of the 1990s.

Mainly due to this strong growth of government revenues, the federal deficit was eliminated by 1998, when the government posted its first budget surplus since 1970, followed by substantial surpluses of $13 billion in 2000, $18 billion in 2001, and $9 billion in 2002, which led to an unexpected turn—the next public debate would be over how to use government budget *surpluses*! But before considering these more pleasant choices, we will briefly review some of the effects of the cuts in government spending.

Coping with Spending Cuts: Reform of the Social Welfare System

As noted at the start of this chapter, Canada's social welfare system is built around the three keystones of *income security programs* (Employment Insurance, welfare, pensions, and so on), *health care,* and *education.* The financial problems of governments were so great that they forced governments to consider the most fundamental changes to these programs in many years. In the following sections, we will consider some actual and proposed reforms of each of these types of government program.

Income Security Programs

Two major aspects of Canada's income security programs that underwent reform were the *targeting of benefits* and *improvement of incentives to work.*

Targeting of Benefits

Until governments encountered the financial crisis of the 1990s, several large transfer payment programs (such as Unemployment Insurance and Old Age Security) paid benefits to all Canadians who qualified for them, regardless of the total income of their families. As a result, billions of dollars in transfer payments were paid to people who did not need them.

The concept of *targeting* social welfare benefits is to pay these benefits only to those who need them. This goal can be achieved by either withholding benefits from some people or by paying benefits as in the past, but then *taxing back* part or even all of the benefits if the family's income is above a certain level. For instance, a *clawback tax* was introduced that took back 100 percent of Old Age Security benefits from recipients with incomes above a specified level.

Incentives to Work

While many people feel that welfare recipients are simply lazy and prefer welfare to working, the situation is usually more complex than this. In fact, welfare programs often have a negative effect upon the *incentive to work.*

A welfare system will discourage welfare recipients from working if, for every dollar a welfare recipient earns by working, his or her welfare benefits are reduced by so much that there is little or no incentive to work. The intention of the welfare system is not to kill incentives, but rather to focus benefits on those who need them—and the more a recipient earns, the less welfare he or she needs. So, as earned income rises, welfare benefits will be reduced. But, to welfare recipients, this can mean that if they earn some income by working, their welfare benefits will be reduced by so much that it is not worth working. This has the same effect as a *very high marginal tax rate* on their income (see the cases of Joan and Sandy in the "You Decide" box on p. 256), which reduces the incentive to earn income and to get off the welfare system.

YOU DECIDE

THE MARGINAL TAX RATE AND THE ECONOMIC INCENTIVE TO WORK

The *marginal tax rate* is the percentage of any extra income that is earned which goes to taxes. Because it determines how much of any additional income a person gets to keep, the marginal tax rate is very important to the incentive to work; specifically, the higher the marginal tax rate, the lower the economic incentive to do additional work.

We will consider the marginal tax rates of two people. Joan, a teacher, is wondering whether to teach a night course. The course would pay her $1000, but after taxes, Joan would receive only $600, because her marginal tax rate is 40 percent. Joan complains that there is little incentive for her to teach the night course because of these high taxes, which go to support people who she describes as "lazy welfare bums."

Sandy is on welfare, receiving $800 per month. If she earns $100 per month working part-time, her welfare will be reduced to $720 per month, leaving her $20 better off for having earned $100. In other words, Sandy's marginal tax rate is 80 percent. Sandy declines the job on the grounds that it's not worth the trouble.

Questions

1. Is Sandy just being "lazy"?
2. If we want to get Sandy off welfare and working, what kinds of changes do we need to make to the welfare system?

Studies of this problem have estimated that many recipients of social welfare gain so little by working that if they do work, they are in a similar position to someone who is paying a marginal tax rate of *from 70 to 100 percent*. In some cases, this can work as a "trap" in which welfare recipients become caught indefinitely. To escape from this trap, a person usually has to find a reasonably steady full-time job, so as to break completely clear of the welfare system. But unless one has skills and experience, it is unlikely that this can be achieved, so the welfare cycle tends to go on and on, from year to year, and even from generation to generation.

In an attempt to improve work incentives, some social assistance plans have been modified so as to allow recipients to earn at least some income without suffering a reduction in their welfare benefits. Such changes do help to improve the incentive for welfare recipients to earn some income by working at part-time jobs. But beyond a certain level of earned income, their welfare benefits are reduced, and if this reduction occurs too rapidly, the same disincentive effect will occur, although at a higher level of earned income.

Advocates of reform to the social welfare system argue that there are real benefits in improving the work incentives in the system. This would help to keep welfare recipients in the work force (even if only combining part-time work with their welfare) and earning both income and self-esteem, rather than passively relying on welfare. Also, by encouraging welfare recipients to earn more, it could actually reduce their reliance on welfare and thus reduce the total amount of welfare benefits that governments pay out, thus helping to reduce the cost to society.

The Employment Insurance program has often been criticized as having negative effects upon incentives. In particular, the EI program has been criticized on the grounds that it actually *increases unemployment*. For instance, the availability of EI benefits for about 10 months can prolong the job searches of some recipients, causing them to remain unemployed longer. Most labour-market experts agree that the Employment Insurance program should be reformed in order to place less emphasis on merely passively providing income to claimants for as long as they are eligible, to encourage retraining so as to reduce the probability that claimants will fall back on EI in the future, and to increase incentives for them to find and take jobs that are available. See the "In the News" box below for a look at the incentive to work while receiving EI benefits.

IN THE **NEWS** Working While on Employment Insurance

You are allowed to earn up to $50 a week or 25% of your regular benefits (whichever is higher) without facing any loss of benefits. All earnings above that limit will be deducted *dollar for dollar* from your weekly benefits.

From a pamphlet issued by Human Resources Development Canada (emphasis added).

Question

1. In effect, what is the marginal tax rate faced by recipients of EI benefits on earnings above the stated limits?

Health Care

Of all of Canada's social welfare programs, reform of the health care system probably confronted governments with the most politically difficult challenge. Canadians have an understandably strong attachment to their system of universal free health care, which they regard as both a major protection and a fundamental right. On the other hand, the costs of this system had been escalating, and governments are concerned that health care costs will skyrocket when the baby boomers move into their senior years. By some estimates, as much as 90 percent of a person's lifetime medical costs are incurred after retirement, and the baby boomers are getting older every year.

To help control its own budget deficit, the federal government began around 1990 to restrict its transfer payments to the provinces for health care. These funding limitations led provincial governments to cut back on health care services in various ways, such as restricting health care coverage for Canadians outside the country, closing hospital beds, and eliminating coverage for certain procedures. As the resources of the health care system were unable to keep up with the demand for services, Canadians faced longer waits for many types of operations. A variety of other measures were proposed to control health care costs, including reduced use of hospitals (the most costly method of health care delivery), increased emphasis on prevention of health problems, and encouragement to doctors to help to curb excessive use of the health care system. In spite of these efforts, however, continuing growth of health care costs remains a major concern of governments.

As the problem of health care costs continued to grow, there was increasing discussion of the controversial question of **user fees**. Advocates of user fees argue that charging modest fees each time that people use the health care system, such as for visits to the doctor, would have a significant impact on the cost of the system, in two ways. In their view, not only would user fees raise funds to help finance the health care system, but also—and more importantly—they would curb excessive use of the system, by ending people's perception that health services are "free." However, there has been strong opposition to the introduction of user fees for health care. Opponents of user fees argue that health care is a basic right of Canadians, and that user fees would violate this right. In particular, they fear that poorer people's access to the health care system could be restricted. For example, a fee of, say, $5 for a visit to the doctor would be insignificant to people with high incomes, but might deter low-income Canadians from obtaining necessary medical attention. Because of considerations such as these, governments have remained reluctant to introduce user fees for health care.

user fees Charges to the users of government services.

Education

Chapter 11 stressed the importance of education not only to the individual, in terms of access to better jobs and a rewarding career, but also to the economy, in terms of the higher productivity of a trained and educated work force. In addition, the matter of access to post-secondary education is a significant social issue—with post-secondary education so often the gateway to better jobs and careers, it is considered important as a matter of social policy that the cost of post-secondary education not present an unfair barrier to members of lower-income families. As a result, governments undertook to subsidize post-secondary education quite heavily so as to keep its cost within reach of people of modest means. This subsidization was done mainly through grants to colleges and universities that enabled them to keep tuition fees low; in addition, student loan programs were available to those who needed them.

The economic problem with education is that it is by nature a labour-intensive service—that is, it is difficult to increase the number of products (that is, students; no offence intended) per teacher in the same way that technology can increase manufacturing output per worker. Because of this difficulty, education has become quite costly. For governments with less money to spend on post-secondary education, this situation forced very difficult choices between such strategies as limiting enrolments in colleges and universities, increasing class sizes, or increasing students' tuition fees. During the 1990s, Canadian colleges and universities grappled with these problems with a combination of enrolment restrictions, larger classes, and tuition-fee increases that seemed to satisfy no one.

After the Deficits: How to Use the Surpluses?

By the late 1990s, the combination of reductions in government spending and increases in tax revenues had turned the federal government's budget deficits into *surpluses* from 1998 to 2002 that totaled nearly $47 billion over five years. The deficits of the past and the battle to eliminate them had left various scars on Canadians: heavy government debt, reduced public services, and high taxes. Around 1999, public attention turned to the question of how the government should use these surpluses. There were three basic ways to use the government surpluses: *reduce government debt, increase government spending,* or *reduce taxes.*

www.pwgsc.gc.ca/recgen/
text/pub-acc-e.html

Reduce Government Debt?

Federal and provincial government deficits had left Canada with a massive government debt that was costing taxpayers nearly $70 billion per year (about $2300 per person) in interest in the late 1990s. This burden made it attractive for the government to use part of its budget surpluses to reduce its debt. On the other hand, government debt was so high that reducing it would necessarily be a long-term undertaking—the combined federal budget surpluses from 1998 to 2002 amounted to only about 8 percent of the federal government's debt in 1997.

From 1996 to 2000, 29 cents of every tax dollar collected by the federal government went to pay interest on the government's debt.

Increase Government Spending?

Reductions in federal transfers to the provinces had undercut the nation's social welfare system in ways that concerned many Canadians. The cuts to health care spending had left hospitals with inadequate staffing and many Canadians waiting for medical care that they required. There was concern whether the nation's health care system would be able to deal with Canadians' needs as the baby boomers aged. Public opinion polls showed that Canadians placed the highest priority on health care, and were very concerned about the effects of spending cutbacks. In the field of education, cuts in grants to colleges and universities had led to large increases in tuition that left graduates with heavy debt loads from student loans. And cuts to the social welfare system had left many worse off than before, and had turned onto the streets people who had previously been cared for in public institutions.

Reduce Taxes?

Finally, the tax increases that had been a major aspect of the deficit reduction program since the mid-1980s had made the total tax burden on Canadian citizens and businesses significantly higher than in the United States. In 1996, Canadian taxes amounted to 36.8 percent of GDP, as compared to 28.5 percent in the United States. Canada's personal income taxes were the highest of all major nations, and taxes on Canadian businesses were also high by international standards. Canada's high taxes raised concerns that businesses would be discouraged from investing in Canada and skilled people would choose to work elsewhere, making it difficult for industries that required highly skilled people to operate and grow in Canada.

After years of facing problems associated with its budget deficits, the federal government in the late 1990s found itself presented with an opportunity—how to use its budget surpluses. A strong argument could be made for each of the three alternatives. Canada's government debt was among the highest in the world, its social welfare system had been eroded by spending cuts, and its taxes on people and businesses were high by international standards. By 2002, the government had taken steps in all three areas—federal debt had been reduced by nearly $47 billion, significant reductions in personal and corporate income taxes had been introduced, and some health care funding had been restored. But the debate about how to use any future surpluses continued.

Government Benefits and Services in Perspective

Underlying the debate over government benefits and services is the basic economic reality of *scarcity,* as discussed all the way back in Chapter 1. In that chapter, the people in the island mini-society had to deal with the reality that they did not have the economic resources to produce all of the food, fuel, and security that they needed and wanted. If they decided to produce more of any one item, the *opportunity cost* would be that they would have less of the others.

Concerning government social welfare programs, the situation is essentially the same—the more that resources are employed in the government sector of the economy, the less that are available for private consumption by households and investment by businesses. Thus, the opportunity cost of having improved health care or educational services might be that Canadians have to make do with fewer restaurant dinners and video rentals. Viewed from the opposite perspective, if Canadians want lower taxes so that they can have more restaurant dinners and video rentals, the opportunity cost will be reduced government services and benefits.

For nearly two decades after the early 1970s, Canadians seemed to have avoided these realities, as they enjoyed higher levels of *both* private consumption *and* government benefits and services. However, much of this was made possible by borrowing that could not go on forever. By the mid-1990s, economic reality had asserted itself, and Canadians were being forced to decide what balance between their private consumption and the level of government benefits and services they wanted for their society. The choice was not an easy one, and ensured difficult decisions and controversy for years to come.

Chapter Summary

1. The three main aspects of Canada's social welfare system are income security programs, health care, and education. (L.O. 1)

2. The four main sources of tax revenues for governments are taxes on incomes (personal and business), consumption taxes, property taxes, and payroll taxes. (L.O. 2)

3. The effect of Canadian governments' transfer payments and income taxes in 2000 was to increase the annual income of the lowest and second-lowest 20 percent of Canadian families by about $11 300 and $3300, respectively, to reduce the income of the middle 20-percent group by about $4500, and to reduce the income of the second-highest and highest 20-percent groups of families by about $11 700 and $33 000, respectively. (L.O. 3)

4. The federal government transfers large amounts of revenues to the provincial governments to help pay for the health care, post-secondary education, and welfare programs for which the provinces are constitutionally responsible. (L.O. 4)

5. From the early 1970s to 1997, the federal government's spending exceeded its revenues in every year, the result being the accumulation of a very large government debt. (L.O. 5)

6. After 1985, the federal government tried to reduce its deficits through various tax increases and spending restraints. However, the government's large deficits persisted, mainly due to high and rising interest payments on the government's massive and growing debt. (L.O. 5)

7. By 1993, the combined deficit/debt problems of the federal and provincial governments, which included a large and growing debt to foreign lenders who were growing concerned, forced Canadian governments to take steps to reduce their deficits. (L.O. 5)

8. To reduce its deficits, the federal government cut its program spending, especially its transfer payments to the provinces. The other key contributor to the elimination of the federal deficits was a major increase in tax revenues, largely as a result of the economic growth of the second half of the 1990s. (L.O. 6)

9. To deal with spending reductions, a number of reforms to the social welfare system were introduced. These included targeting of benefits to those who needed them, improving work incentives for recipients of welfare and Employment Insurance, and a variety of changes to delivery systems for health care and education. (L.O. 7, 8)

10. The three basic alternative uses for the federal budget surpluses that developed after 1997 were to reduce government debt, to increase program spending, or to reduce taxes. (L.O. 9)

Questions

1. John works in a manufacturing plant. If he works 5 hours of overtime, he will earn an additional $150. If his income taxes increase by $60 as a result of the overtime earnings, what is his marginal tax rate?

2. Yvette is on welfare, receiving $900 per month. If she works part-time and earns $200, her welfare benefits will be reduced to $750. In effect, what is the marginal tax rate on Yvette's earnings?

3. What do you think would have happened after 1993 if Canadian governments had not reduced their spending and deficits?

4. The alternative to cutting government spending was to increase taxes. List the economic and political advantages and disadvantages of increasing each of the following taxes:

    (a) personal income taxes

    (b) corporate income taxes

    (c) gasoline taxes

    (d) consumption taxes (such as the GST)

    (e) payroll taxes

    (f) taxes on tobacco and alcohol

5. Do you agree or disagree with user fees for health care? Have any user fees for health care been introduced? If so, what are the details concerning them and their effects?

6. Would tariffs (import duties) on imported goods be a regressive or progressive tax?

7. Since 2001, what has been the situation concerning the federal government's budget? Has the government used its surplus revenues to increase program spending, to cut taxes, or to pay down its debt? (Regular updates can be obtained from Statistics Canada's Canadian Economic Observer [11-010-XPB]).

8. (a) Fill in the columns in the following table for budget deficit/surplus and government debt for each year through 20X4. (Assume that the government's debt at the start of 20X1 was $300 billion.)

| | | *(Billions of dollars)* | | |
Year	Government Revenues	Government Spending	Budget Deficit (−) or Surplus (+)	Government Debt
20X1	$100	$110	$ _____	$_____
20X2	105	117	_____	_____
20X3	110	125	_____	_____
20X4	114	132	_____	_____
20X5	___	___	_____	_____
20X6	___	___	_____	_____

(b) Develop a combination of spending reductions and/or tax increases for 20X5 and 20X6 that eliminates the deficits (balances the budget) by 20X6.

(c) If the budget were to remain balanced in each year after 20X6, what would happen to the level of government debt?

9. In 1999, 12 percent of Canada's population was over the age of 65. By 2030, this percentage will increase to an estimated 22 percent, and by 2050, to 42 percent.

(a) Why are such large increases in the senior population forecasted?

(b) What are the implications of this trend for the living standards of Canadians?

(c) What can be done to reduce the negative economic effects of an aging population?

10. The text refers to cuts to federal income taxes on persons and corporations over the 2001–05 period that would amount to about $100 billion in total. What would be the federal government's goal in implementing these tax reductions?

11. In late 2002, the federal government suggested that the Goods and Services Tax might be increased from 7 percent to 10 percent in order to raise an additional $10 billion per year for health care. Why could it be viewed as economically logical for the government to increase consumption taxes (sales tax) at the same time as it was reducing income taxes, as noted in Question 10?

Chapter 13

The Politics of Economics

Learning Objectives

After studying this chapter, you should be able to:

1. Summarize the major economic goals of right-wingers, and explain how they believe these can best be achieved.

2. Summarize the major economic goals of left-wingers, and explain how they believe these can best be achieved.

3. Explain why it is generally believed that the most effective approach to economic issues involves government policies that contain a balance of the left and right approaches.

As Chapter 12 suggests, the fields of economics and politics are closely inter-twined. Because they affect people in so many important ways, economic issues often become major political issues, and there are sharply divided views regarding the appropriate role of government in the economy. Often, profoundly different philosophies concerning economic and social matters and values underlie such disagreements. This chapter provides a rudimentary guide to these different philosophies, which are usually described as *right-wing* (or simply "right") and *left-wing* (or "left"), and how they apply to economic issues.

How Right-Wingers See the World

The right-wing view is characterized by a strong belief in *free enterprise*, the *market system*, and *individual responsibility* for one's own economic fate or fortune. Right-wingers tend to believe that, generally, the best solution to economic problems lies in the operation of free markets, along the lines of the ideal of *"laissez-faire"* as described in Chapter 9. Through these markets, they see society's prosperity enhanced by free enterprise, competition, and the profit motive. As they see it, *consumer sovereignty* directs businesses to produce what consumers want, the *profit motive* induces private producers to operate as efficiently as possible, and *competition* ensures that the consumer is well-served regarding price, quality, and service. And according to right-wingers, the differences in incomes that develop in free markets for labour provide incentives for people—and rewards for being effective and efficient.

www.fraserinstitute.ca

    The value system of right-wingers emphasizes factors such as *incentives*, *efficiency*, and the *creation of wealth*. They view free enterprise and private ownership of business as the most effective way of achieving this, largely through the profit motive. Right-wingers are less concerned about how equally the benefits of prosperity are divided—their individualistic philoso-phy tends to make them believe that one is responsible for one's own share of the economic pie, and that people generally get what they earn in the marketplace. To them, personal responsibility is an important aspect of the incentive system associated with the marketplace.

    In summary, right-wingers are believers in individualism, economic freedom, the marketplace, and private enterprise. They believe that through the incentives for efficiency provided by these values, a society can best achieve the creation of wealth and economic prosperity.

How Left-Wingers See the Same World

While left-wingers also value economic prosperity as an objective, they do not agree that the right-wing approach is the best way to achieve it. In particular, left-wingers *lack faith in free markets* as a means of achieving prosperity. They believe that in a free market the economically powerful can and do take advantage of the economically weak—that big business can

www.canadians.org

exploit consumers and employers can exploit workers, so that the *distribution of income* in a free market will inevitably be unfair.

Another aspect of free markets that disturbs left-wingers is the *insecurity* that accompanies the marketplace—the exposure of people to the risk of lay-off due to factors such as recession and competition. Again, left-wingers point out, the victims of layoffs are usually the economically weak—those with limited experience and skills. Thus, they argue, the free-market system is so biased in favour of the powerful and wealthy that it cannot provide an equitable share of its wealth for the large numbers of people who lack the economic power to wrest it from the marketplace. In the view of the left-winger, the rich and powerful devour most of the economic pie, leaving only crumbs for the weak.

To remedy these weaknesses of the market system, left-wingers advocate an *active role for government* in the economy. In particular, they favour government policies that *redistribute income* from the rich to the poor, and laws that *regulate and restrict* the behaviour of the economically powerful, so as to protect both workers and consumers from big business. Such a role for government, they believe, will improve the overall prosperity of society, by ensuring a fairer distribution of economic welfare.

To summarize, the value system of left-wingers stresses the collective (as opposed to individualistic) aspects of society, and so emphasizes *fairness, security*, and *an equitable distribution of income*. If it can be said of right-wingers that they focus on incentives for the *creation* of wealth and more or less take the distribution of wealth for granted, it could also be said of left-wingers that they stress a *fair distribution* of wealth and tend to take the continuing creation of wealth for granted. Because they see the free market as a threat to their objectives of security and fairness, left-wingers advocate a more collective approach to economic questions, with the government using its powers to tax, spend, and regulate in order to overcome the free market's natural tendency toward inequality.

As you might imagine, situations in which either extremely right-wing or extremely left-wing views dominate do not work out very well. The "In the News" box on the next page takes a look at the extremes of right-wing and left-wing ideologies.

Right Versus Left on Various Issues

In this section, we will illustrate the left and right philosophies by comparing their views on a variety of economic issues.

Business Enterprise

Right-wingers believe in *private ownership* of business, with competition and the profit motive as vital incentives for the productive efficiency that generates prosperity. They agree that monopolies are undesirable, but argue that, in a free market, monopolies do not tend to last for long, because monopoly profits will attract competition from other businesses or new products. Most long-lasting monopolies, they argue, are not private enterprises, but rather government-owned (or -regulated) enterprises, which the government itself protects against competition. Right-wingers are generally opposed to government ownership of business enterprises, which they criticize as inefficient because of the absence of competition and the profit motive.

IN THE **NEWS**   The Extremes

There are varying degrees of both right-wing and left-wing philosophies. In the extreme, the right-wing view would leave almost all economic activity to the free market, in which economic decisions would be made almost entirely by individual consumers and businesses. The role of government would be restricted to providing physical security (through the army and police) and a court system for the enforcement of contracts. There would be no government programs to redistribute income or provide economic security, as these would interfere with incentives. Those who wanted to help the needy could do so voluntarily, through private charity, but no one would be forced to do so through taxes.

At the opposite extreme, the left-wing approach would replace private enterprise with government ownership of business, or at least of all large enterprises. Through democratic socialism, elected governments would engage in thorough economic planning, which would decide (or strongly influence) the key economic decisions regarding what to produce, the production methods to be used, and the distribution of the economic pie. The distribution of income would be much more equal, or possibly even completely equal. In effect, economic decisions would be made collectively, through the government, rather than by individuals in the marketplace.

Questions

1. What problems would likely exist in an extremely right-wing society?
2. What problems would likely exist in an extremely left-wing society?

Left-wingers tend to question the social value of private ownership of business and the profit motive. In private enterprise, they see incentives leading not so much toward efficiency and service to the consumer as toward abuse of businesses' market power and exploitation of both consumers and employees. In the view of left-wingers, free markets and private business are basic sources of the problem of the inequitable distribution of income, because people are free to exploit other people. As a result, they believe that there should be considerable *government regulation* of business activities as well as considerable *taxation of business profits* in order to redistribute income in favour of the poor. Some left-wingers would place government regulations (such as price controls) on larger businesses, or have the government take over ownership of them (nationalization). This is not, however, a simple antibusiness bias; rather, its concerns focus on *big* business and its market power. Generally, left-wingers are considerably more sympathetic toward small businesses, which are usually subject to such strong competition that they lack the market power that concerns left-wingers. This is consistent with the left wing's tendency to sympathize with the underdog.

Profits

Right-wingers regard profits in the most positive terms: as an *incentive for efficiency*, as a *reward* for good management, and as a major *source of funds for capital investment*, which provides employment and productivity gains. In short, right-wingers view profits as a key to economic prosperity for society as a whole, and oppose heavy taxation of profits as damaging to prosperity.

Left-wingers tend to view profits (at least above a certain level) as evidence of market power that has been used to *exploit consumers and employees*. To left-wingers, profits are a prime cause of the *inequitable distribution of income* that concerns them, because the money that profits take from consumers and employees goes to the wealthy shareholders of businesses. So left-wingers would favour relatively heavy taxation of profits as part of a policy of redistributing income from the rich to the poor.

Investment Income

To right-wingers, investment income (interest, dividends, and capital gains) provides an incentive to people to save and to invest their capital in business enterprises, which provide employment and prosperity for society at large. They regard such investment income as earned and well-deserved, not only because of the risks undertaken by the investors (especially shareholders) but also because of the contribution their capital makes to the general economic prosperity of society.

> "Capitalism is the unequal sharing of plenty; socialism is the equal sharing of misery."
>
> A favourite old saying of right-wingers.

Left-wingers tend to see the labour of workers as the basic source of economic wealth, and regard investment income as not being as productive or as earned as wages. Also, because investment income mostly goes to higher-income people who have money to invest, left-wingers tend to see investment income as adding to the problem of an inequitable distribution of income.

The Distribution of Income

Right-wingers accept inequalities in the distribution of income quite readily. They regard high incomes as a way of encouraging people to become educated or trained, and to work, save, and invest. To right-wingers, higher incomes are *earned* by those who receive them, and reflect their contribution to society, as measured by the marketplace—that is, by the willingness of others to pay them for their services. Right-wingers are generally not very sympathetic to the poor who are able to work, believing that they should do more to help themselves.

> "Rugged individualism makes ragged individuals."
>
> A favourite old saying of left-wingers.

Left-wingers view the income-distribution process and its results quite differently. They see the issue mainly in terms of *market power*—the ability of some groups and individuals to extract from society, through the marketplace, an excessively large share of the pie, leaving only a small share for the less powerful. To left-wingers, incomes do not measure people's *contribution to* the economy and to society so much as their *ability to take from* the economy and society, through their strong bargaining power in the marketplace. As a result, left-wingers generally regard the poor as the victims of an economic system that allows some people to take advantage of others.

Social Welfare

Right-wingers tend to see social welfare and income-redistribution programs in terms of their effect upon incentives. They are concerned that excessive redistribution of income will have negative effects upon the incentives of all concerned—that the rich will be taxed so heavily that they will lose their incentive to work, save, and invest, and that the poor will receive such generous social welfare benefits that they will learn to rely on welfare rather than help themselves. Right-wingers are skeptical regarding the propriety and the value of government programs to redistribute income.

By contrast, left-wingers see redistribution of income as one of the most essential functions of government. Because the marketplace results in an unjust division of the pie, they believe it is the responsibility of government to promote *social justice* by redistributing income from the rich to the poor, through both taxation and transfer payments such as welfare.

Labour Unions

Right-wingers generally view labour unions with great mistrust. To them, unions tend to *reduce productive efficiency and prosperity* in various ways: by interfering with management's right to make decisions, by opposing efforts to increase labour productivity (because unions tend to regard efficiency as a threat to workers' job security), and by reducing the amount of business profits available for capital investment in improved facilities and equipment. Right-wingers tend to be concerned by Canada's historically bad strike record and its possible effect upon the willingness of business (both Canadian and foreign) to invest and create jobs in Canada. On the issue of public-service strikes, such as postal strikes, right-wingers can become quite agitated; many would remove the right to strike from all government employees.

Left-wingers are generally supportive of unions, which they see as organizations of workers trying to protect themselves against *exploitation by employers*, who enjoy more market power than individual employees. One value that unionists and left-wingers share strongly is *economic security*—the

The following is an excerpt from a famous speech by an American preacher named Conwell in the 1880s. The speech was given 6000 times and earned a total of $8 000 000. Its popularity derived from the fact that it reflected attitudes that were widely held at the time.

To secure wealth is an honourable ambition and is one test of a person's usefulness to others. I say get rich, get rich... Ninety-eight out of a hundred of the rich men of America are honest. That is why they are rich. I won't give in but what I sympathize with the poor, but the number of poor who are to be sympathized with is very small. To sympathize with a man whom God has punished for his sins, thus to help him when God would still continue a just punishment, is to go wrong, no doubt about it.

desire to be secure against both the marketplace and arbitrary decisions of management.

Philosophically, left-wingers are sympathetic to labour unions, and organized labour has traditionally supported Canada's left-wing political party, the New Democratic Party (NDP). However, when the NDP has been *in government,* it has not always automatically supported labour unions. Left-wingers believe that government should protect the public from the economically powerful. Usually, the "economically powerful" means big business; however, some labour unions also have considerable economic power. If the interests of powerful unionized groups are seen to be in conflict with the broader public interest (such as strikes that are having serious effects on the public), left-wing governments will intervene on the side of the public interest rather than the unions.

The Role of Government in the Economy

Not surprisingly, right-wingers believe in a smaller role for government in the economy. They believe in the market system as the best way to handle most economic decisions, and are skeptical about the value of government intervention in the economy. They regard "big government" as the main threat to economic prosperity because it preempts economic resources (through taxation and borrowing) that would be better used for private consumption and especially private investment. Also, they believe that government damages incentives to work, save, and invest, through its tax and welfare policies and through over-regulation of the business sector. Also, right-wingers tend to be very concerned about government budget deficits and debt, which they would deal with by cutting government spending rather than by increasing taxes. Generally, right-wingers see less government (taxation, spending, borrowing, and regulation) as a key to solving many economic problems.

Left-wingers have exactly the opposite view. Because they are not confident that free markets promote prosperity for all groups in society, they believe in a large and activist role for government in the economy. In particular, left-wingers favour government policies to protect workers and consumers against business, and to redistribute income from the rich to the poor, through a combination of higher taxes on the rich and transfer payments to the poor. Unless government actively plays these roles, they believe, the economically powerful will increasingly enrich themselves at the expense of the less powerful. Left-wingers tend to be less concerned about government budget deficits and debt, placing a higher priority on maintaining government programs to help those in need than on balancing the budget. Should it become necessary to reduce the government's deficits, most left-wingers would prefer to do this through higher taxes on business and on people with higher incomes rather than through cuts in government spending.

Politics

The views of left-wingers and right-wingers regarding politics are interesting, because *each* seems to think (or at least fear) that *the other* is in control of the political process. Right-wingers fear that democratically elected governments tend toward left-wing policies, because there are more lower-income voters than higher-income ones. As a result, right-wingers fear a continual growth of government and policies to redistribute income and regulate business (socialism), together with ever-higher government spending, taxes, borrowing, and debt, with very damaging effects on the economy in the long run.

Left-wingers are often equally cynical about politics, but for a different reason. They tend to see big business and the wealthy and powerful as exercising undue influence on governments and their policies. The result, according to left-wingers, is that government policies (especially tax exemptions and deductions) tend to favour big business and the rich, and government programs, on balance, do far less for the poor than they could or should.

The Need for Balance

Most people intuitively feel that the most effective approach to economic issues generally lies in a reasonable balance, or blend, of the left and right approaches, rather than an extreme of either one. Indeed, both extremes hold real dangers.

A society that goes too far toward the right-wing approach, or *laissez-faire*, would rely very heavily upon free markets to make its economic decisions and resolve its economic problems. In such circumstances, some powerful private-interest groups (both businesses and labour unions) would be free to use their market power to enrich themselves at the expense of others. There would be no protection for groups that lacked the economic clout to take care of themselves, such as consumers or unskilled nonunion workers, nor would there be social welfare programs for those who lacked an income due to unemployment, accident, illness, disability, or old age. The result would be a very *unequal distribution of income*; the rich might tend to stay rich over generations, inheriting both wealth and access to educational and career opportunities, while the poor would have difficulty getting out of the poverty trap, having no access to either money or education. In the extreme, the poorer classes could even strike back at the establishment, causing *social instability*.

Another possible problem could be *economic instability*. With income so heavily concentrated in the hands of the wealthy few, the economy would lack the consumer-spending support of a broadly based middle-income class, such as exists today, and would therefore be more vulnerable to economic downturn, or recessions. Without social welfare programs, *economic insecurity* would be a much greater problem—even a disaster—for many people.

Probably the left's favourite horror story about such matters is the United States' economy before and during the Great Depression of the 1930s. During the 1920s, passive governments watched benignly as the top 5 percent of income-earners received 33 percent of total personal income, and a largely unregulated business and financial sector erected very unstable financial structures that contributed to the collapse of the stock market in late 1929. Once the Depression had started, even with the unemployment rate in the

20-percent range, the government took years to come to grips with the problem and attempt to alleviate it. The American economy of that era graphically demonstrated the major flaws of the laissez-faire approach: extreme wealth for a few, but poverty and insecurity for many, together with general economic instability.

On the other hand, societies that go too far toward the left tend to wind up with problems that, though different, are no less severe. Socialist governments can become so big, so costly, and so interventionist in the economy that they erode incentives to work, save, and invest. Very high taxes on business and higher-income individuals can have this effect, as can excessive government regulation of business. Excessive government borrowing (or even, in extreme cases, printing) of money to finance its heavy expenditures tends to generate high interest rates that depress capital investment spending and slow economic growth. As incentives and capital investment are undermined, productivity and living standards stagnate. The government's preoccupation with *redistribution* of wealth and income can thus interfere with the *creation* of wealth, to the disadvantage of society generally.

Right-wingers revel in discussing their own favourite horror story, that of Great Britain after the Second World War. In Britain, left-wing governments built a massive welfare state centred on income redistribution and "free" government services to the public. However, the financing of all this extensive government spending required such heavy taxation of business and higher-income earners that incentives were seriously affected. Business investment languished, productivity performance was weak, British producers lost competitive ground to imports, and unemployment rose as a result. Capital—in the form of business investment, personal investment funds, and the "human capital" consisting of its younger, more skilled, aggressive and able people—left the country and went to nations that offered greater opportunities. Many observers believe that Britain's leftist economic policies were primarily responsible for the nation's economic decline in the post-war period.

....

Trends

The foregoing section reinforces the argument made earlier—that the most effective approach to economic policy-making should involve a balanced blend of the left and right approaches. However, it is much easier to agree on this concept *in principle* than it is to agree what the most appropriate blend actually should be *in practice*. As a result, there will always be an ongoing debate on whether getting to this ideal balance requires moving toward the left or toward the right regarding any particular issue.

Over the long term, the trend has been toward a larger role for government, as illustrated by Chapter 12's account of the growth of Canada's social welfare system. This trend gained momentum after the Great Depression of the 1930s dramatized the flaws of the market system and the need for government to assume a larger role in the economy. Similar trends occurred in most other industrialized countries, at different paces and with different timing.

According to some observers, Canada's situation was complicated by its perception of being positioned "between" Europe and the United States. Many European countries had extensive "cradle to the grave" social welfare systems, with heavy tax burdens to pay for them. The United States, on the other hand, had lower taxes and a correspondingly lower level of social welfare spending. Many Canadians admired Europe's social welfare programs, and wanted to emulate these with Canadian programs that would involve heavy government spending. However, when it came to paying the taxes required to finance such programs, many Canadians preferred to follow the American example. According to this view, the situation allowed Canadians seemingly to enjoy "free" benefits for a while; however, it also led to Canadian governments borrowing increasingly heavily in order to finance the benefits that they had granted to their citizens, accumulating the serious debt burden described in Chapter 12.

As noted earlier, most industrialized nations expanded their social welfare programs considerably in the three decades or so following the Second World War. This trend continued for so long that many observers came to regard it as permanent in nature. However, by the late 1970s, second thoughts were beginning to develop. As the performance of most industrialized economies stagnated, disillusionment with big government and the welfare state began to grow. These ideals did not seem to have achieved the great economic promises that had been held out for them—growth was slow, unemployment was high, taxes were high, and productivity and living standards had practically stopped rising. Rightly or wrongly, increasing numbers of people came to blame the size and the policies of government for many of these problems, and the pendulum began to swing back toward the right. In Britain and the United States during the 1980s, governments placed renewed emphasis on the "old virtues" of incentives, work, investment, profits, and productivity. Attempts were made to rein in the growth of government, to reduce or at least control spending on social welfare programs, and to ease the regulatory and tax burden on business, in order to promote business investment and improve the productivity and international competitiveness of their economies.

After 1985, Canadian governments gradually joined in this trend, as the federal government attempted to get its budget deficits under control while improving incentives, especially for private business investment, which was hailed as the engine of growth and provider of jobs for Canadians. However, only minor changes were made to the social welfare system, and spending and borrowing continued to grow. By 1993, a serious debt crisis forced Canadian governments into major reductions in program spending, suddenly and sharply reversing the long-term leftward trend toward more government spending. More fundamentally, it forced Canadians for the first time to consider very seriously the extent of social programs that they wanted for their society, and were prepared to pay for. In making these decisions, Canadians would decide the balance of "left" and "right" that they wanted for their society. As the new millennium began, Canadians continued to grapple with these most basic and difficult questions.

Chapter Summary

1. Right-wingers believe that economic prosperity is best promoted by free markets, with minimal government interference. This view emphasizes private enterprise, incentives, efficiency, and the creation of wealth. (L.O. 1)

2. Left-wingers emphasize the importance of economic security and a fair distribution of income. They believe that to provide real prosperity and equality, the government must actively intervene in the economy, particularly in order to redistribute income from higher-income earners to lower-income ones. (L.O. 2)

3. Theory and evidence both suggest that neither the left nor the right approach in itself will ensure good economic performance. Rather, some blend of the two, intended to retain the advantages of the free market while remedying its disadvantages, seems to be the most effective approach. (L.O. 3)

4. The long-term trend has been toward the left, but in recent years there has been a shift in policy back toward the right in the United States, Great Britain, and, more recently, in Canada. (L.O. 3)

Questions

1. What would a strong right-winger and a strong left-winger say about:

   (a) the Ontario government's 22-percent reduction in welfare benefits in 1995?

   (b) the federal government's 1994–95 plan for deficit reduction, which involved $7 of spending reductions for every $1 of tax increases?

   (c) deregulation of university and college tuition fees; that is, fees to be set by colleges and universities rather than by the government?

   (d) user fees for medicare (that is, the charging of a small fee for each visit to the doctor)?

   (e) a tightening of the Employment Insurance program, including more restrictive eligibility rules and a general reduction of benefits?

   (f) a surtax on investment income (interest, dividends, and capital gains) in order to finance subsidized day-care centres for the poor?

   (g) tax reductions on corporate profits?

   (h) the bailout by government of a near-bankrupt corporation that employs many people in the Atlantic provinces?

   (i) the removal of rent controls?

   (j) the replacement of the progressive income tax with a "flat tax" of 15 percent of all income earned by everyone, regardless of income?

   (k) the removal of the postal workers' right to strike?

(l) the sale of Crown corporations such as Canadian National to private buyers?

2. The text refers to the fact that in the United States in the 1920s, 5 percent of the people earned 33 percent of personal income. To get an idea of what this means concerning the division of the economic pie, work through the following exercise:

   You have $100 to divide among 100 people. If 5 percent of the people receive 33 percent of the dollars, what is the average amount received by each of them? What is the average amount received by each of the rest of the people?

3. In recent years, considerable media attention has been given to the large increases in the amount of food distributed by food banks. How might this be viewed by a strong left-winger and a strong right-winger?

4. As they grow older, do most people become more left-wing or more right-wing? Why?

Chapter 14

Environmental Economics

Learning Objectives

After studying this chapter, you should be able to:

1. Explain in terms of *private costs* and *social costs* why there are economic incentives to pollute the environment.

2. Show why a cleaner environment can be regarded as similar to any other good or economic benefit.

3. Summarize the implications of the Law of Diminishing Returns for decision making regarding environmental protection.

4. Explain how economic analysis of the costs and benefits of a pollution control program can help in designing the program and deciding who should pay its costs.

5. Describe the operation, advantages, and disadvantages of each of the following pollution control strategies: direct regulation, taxes on pollution, tradable pollution credits, lawsuits for damages, and government subsidies.

6. Explain the operation, advantages, and disadvantages of each of the following waste management strategies: landfills, incineration, recycling, and "pay to throw" plans for garbage collection.

For over 35 years, the environment has been a public issue in Canada and other nations. More recently, however, the growing seriousness and the scale of environmental problems such as global warming and the depletion of the ozone layer have made earlier concerns over air and water pollution seem minor by comparison. According to some projections, the environmental side effects of our economic growth and prosperity might even threaten our very existence.

Environmental concerns are not a new phenomenon. During the late 1960s and early 1970s, concerns over air and water pollution led to the first legislation governing automobile emissions and air pollution. From the mid-1970s to the mid-1980s, however, environmental issues took second place to "bread and butter" economic issues, such as unusually severe inflation and unemployment. During the second half of the 1980s, a combination of better economic times and serious pollution problems brought these environmental issues back to the forefront. And while other concerns, most notably unemployment, dominated much of the 1990s, environmental issues remained a high priority.

But much public discussion of environmental issues is not productive. Rather than focusing on the *causes* of environmental problems and setting realistic *objectives* and effective *strategies* for dealing with it, discussion of environmental issues too often focuses on predictions of catastrophe and on *fixing blame*, usually on someone else. Often, the problem is simply blamed on "industry," with the implication that if "industry" (that is, someone else) were more responsible, there would be no environmental problems.

A more productive approach is to analyze the *causes* of environmental problems. By doing so, we can not only gain a better understanding of them, but also formulate government policies that are most likely to be effective in dealing with them.

Economic analysis of this sort shows that environmental problems are much more than the result of industrialists' negligence. Environmental problems are deeply rooted in the very nature of our society and our economy, in at least two fundamental ways. The first of these is our desire for material benefits. To a significant extent, pollution is a by-product of the high levels of consumption and production that we have come to enjoy. One of the most telling illustrations of this reality is the fact that the largest single source of air pollution in North America is not industry, but rather our own automobiles. And the fact that, by 2001, half the new vehicles sold in North America were "light trucks" (SUVs, pickups, and minivans) provides an indication of consumers' true concern about the environment. The second reality is that there are strong *economic incentives to pollute* the environment. Whether you are a corporation dumping waste into the water and air, or a driver disconnecting the emission controls on your car to save on gas, it is to your short-run economic advantage to pollute the environment. From the viewpoint of the *individual* person or business, pollution pays. However, the *collective* effect of millions of individuals behaving in this way can be serious—even catastrophic—environmental damage in the longer run.

The Economic Incentive to Pollute

As noted in Chapter 2, in a market system, the profit motive provides important economic incentives for businesses to produce what consumers want and to produce it as efficiently as possible. These incentives contribute greatly to the economic prosperity of consumers.

But the profit motive also generates socially undesirable incentives. One of these is for producers to join together in price-fixing agreements, as discussed in Chapter 7. Another is the economic incentive to pollute the environment.

In discussing this problem of incentives, economists distinguish between two types of costs of producing a product:

(a) private (internal) costs, and

(b) social (external) costs.

private (internal) costs Production costs, such as labour and materials, that are paid by producers and ultimately included in the price paid by the consumer.

Private costs are ordinary production costs such as labour and materials. These costs are paid by producers, and are ultimately included in the price paid by the consumer. Because these costs are contained *within* the production/consumption system, they are called "internal costs."

social (external) costs Costs that are not paid by producers, but rather passed on to society at large.

Social costs are the costs to the environment, and thus to society at large, of actions such as the dumping of industrial wastes into the air and water. These costs may or may not be measurable in dollar terms, but they are real and often high, including health problems and costs for those affected. Because they are not paid for by the business that *produces* the product and not included in the price of the product paid by the consumer who *uses* the product, but rather are *passed on* to the environment and to society at large, they are called "external costs."

The economic incentive is for producers to *minimize* their internal costs by being as efficient as possible. This encourages them to use economic resources such as labour and materials as efficiently as possible. It also encourages them to *maximize* their external costs by dumping as much of their waste as possible into the environment rather than paying to prevent or clean up the resultant pollution. It is important to note that such behaviour is economically beneficial (in the short run) not only to the *producer* (who gets higher profits), but also the *consumer* (who gets the product at a lower price). But the result can be serious effects upon the environment.

Externalities

externality An incidental cost, or side effect, inflicted on others by the production or consumption of a product. Also known as a *spillover effect*.

When the production or the consumption of a product inflicts incidental costs such as pollution on others, and these costs are not paid by those who inflict them, economists say that an "**externality**" exists. This is also known as a "spillover effect," because the effects of some people's actions spill over onto others. Pollution is among the most serious of these effects. In our pursuit of material prosperity, we—consumers as well as producers—are choosing to avoid paying some important costs of our prosperity, and choosing to pass these on instead to our environment, with potentially serious results.

As we have seen, the marketplace can solve many important economic problems. However, pollution is not a problem that the marketplace will solve on its own—the incentives within the market system tend to generate pollution, not reduce it. As a result, government action will be required to deal with this problem.

The Cost of a Cleaner Environment

Another fundamental reality of environmental economics is that pollution is mostly the by-product of the production and consumption of goods that most people are fond of having and reluctant to do without. You may be upset about the quality of air in your community, but are you willing to reduce your driving by one-third and do without your air conditioning in order to reduce air pollution from cars and electrical generating plants? Alternatively, would you be willing to pay significantly more for these and other consumer products in order to pay for the costs of making the producers' plants and the products themselves less damaging to the environment? (See the "You Decide" box below for an example of a dilemma involving cost versus environmental responsibility.)

YOU DECIDE   **A TRADE-OFF**

You need to buy a great deal of paper and are on a limited budget. You can buy this paper from the Purewater Paper Company, which has invested heavily in pollution-control equipment, and charges $10/kg for its paper, $3 of which covers the cost of the company's pollution control program. Alternatively, you can buy the same paper for $7/kg from Consolidated Killfish Inc., which is infamous for having annihilated virtually all life in the rivers below its pulp mills.

Questions

1. Which company's paper do you buy?
2. What could the government do to get you to buy Purewater's paper?

Many people have been reluctant both to accept these realities and to pay the cost, preferring instead to view the situation with alarm while blaming others. Such attitudes could explain the reluctance of many politicians to mount an effective attack on environmental problems. If government leaders believe that voters are unwilling to pay the cost of a cleaner environment, their efforts will tend to consist of strong words but weak action. For instance, they will tend to pass impressive-sounding legislation but enforce it ineffectively (see the "In the News" box below).

IN THE **NEWS**   Government Versus the Environment

In addition to the marketplace's incentives to pollute the environment, governments have at times provided incentives of their own.

Despite the known serious environmental effects of burning fossil fuels, governments have chosen to subsidize oil and gas developments (and thus encourage their consumption) rather than to tax and discourage the use of these fuels.

Governments have also chosen to subsidize the use of agricultural fertilizers and pesticides that pollute the environment.

And, by underpricing trees (through low "stumpage fees" charged to forestry companies for cutting timber), governments have encouraged forestry practices that are harmful to the environment.

Questions

1. Why do you think governments have ignored the environment in these cases?
2. What would it take to change this situation?

At the most basic economic level, a cleaner environment is like any other good or economic benefit: we can have more of it if we are prepared to accept less of other things. As we saw in Chapter 1, the fact that society has limited economic resources means that using more of these resources to produce one thing necessarily means having less available to produce other things. The people of the island mini-society of Chapter 1 could have used one of their workers to clean up the island, but that would have meant they would have to do without the food, fuel, or security that this person could have provided. A cleaner environment does have opportunity costs.

Similarly, if in our modern economy we choose to devote more of our economic resources, such as capital and labour, to producing pollution control equipment and thus a cleaner environment, we will have less of other products, or a lower standard of living. Viewed from a different perspective, if producers have to install costly pollution-control equipment, their production costs and the price consumers pay for their products will be higher. For instance, the cost of capping greenhouse gas emissions at 1990 levels has been estimated to be an additional 8 cents per litre on the price of gasoline—$300 to $400 per year for an average driver. This is a trade-off, like other economic choices, that we somehow have to make.

FIGURE 14-1 Trade-Offs Between Consumer Goods Production and the Environment

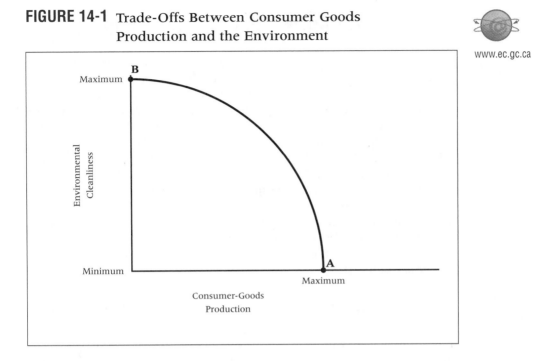

The trade-off between consumer goods and a cleaner environment can be shown with a production-possibilities curve of the sort discussed in Chapter 1 and illustrated in Figure 14-1. We could choose point A, at which we would have the maximum possible amount of consumer goods but devote no resources to pollution control and therefore have the dirtiest possible environment—perhaps one in which we would have to wear gas masks to work. At the other extreme, we could choose point B, at which we would have the cleanest possible environment, but a very low standard of living due to extremely strict environmental controls that highly restricted the production of consumer goods and made them more costly.

Points A and B represent the two extremes of environmental decision making. In reality, it would be reasonable to expect a choice somewhere between A and B that represents an *acceptable balance* between our material wants and the quality of our environment.

The trade-off between a cleaner environment and fewer consumer goods is the way that *the economist* sees the issue. *The consumer* sees it in terms of having to *pay higher prices* for products in order to cover the costs of pollution control measures and equipment used in their production, leaving the consumer with less money to spend on other things. The result is the same: a trade-off in which the outcome is a cleaner environment and a lower standard of living (consumption per person). The money that consumers must pay for emission controls on their automobiles cannot be spent on other consumer goods and services.

Diminishing Returns and the Environment

As with other economic benefits, the cleanup of the environment is subject to the Law of Diminishing Returns described in Chapter 8. That is, it may prove quite easy to reduce the level of pollution by, say, 20 percent, through relatively simple and inexpensive measures. However, to achieve a further 20-percent reduction of pollution may well involve higher costs, while improvements beyond this are likely to prove even more costly. To reduce pollution to very low levels could prove so costly that it might well be considered not worth doing.

This reality makes it all the more important that we have reasonable estimates of the costs of pollution (and thus of the benefits to be gained by reducing pollution) and of the costs of pollution-control measures, so that we can make rational decisions concerning pollution control. This would enable us to use our antipollution resources so as to achieve the maximum possible beneficial results.

Environmental Decision-Making and Cost–Benefit Analysis

Economists cannot tell society *which one* of the various possible combinations of environmental cleanliness and consumption is best, or *whether we should* improve our environment by *x* percent at the cost of a *y*-percent reduction in the volume of our consumption. These are decisions for the people of a society to make, mainly through their governments.

However, economic analysis can assist in the decision-making process by providing estimates of the *costs* and *benefits* of any given level of pollution; that is, who loses due to the pollution, and how much, and who gains economically due to the pollution, and how much?

For instance, suppose a pulp-and-paper company is polluting a river. Those who benefit from this situation would include the company itself, its shareholders, and employees. Less obvious beneficiaries would include consumers of paper, who get cheaper paper, and the local community, which benefits from the employment created by the paper mill, the taxes paid by the mill, and the spending of money by mill employees. Some of the social costs of the pollution could be estimated, such as damage to commercial fishing and tourism, water purification costs, and health costs. Other costs, such as damage to wildlife and the quality of the environment, would be more difficult to determine. However, it would be possible at least to estimate the costs and benefits of the situation as it is now, and estimate the benefits and costs of reducing the volume of pollution.

Such estimates can help in making decisions concerning the following matters:

(a) *The objective of the pollution control program:* Is the target the total elimination of the pollution, or would the Law of Diminishing Returns make this target too costly? What would be the benefits and the cost of reducing the pollution by 90 percent? 80 percent? 70 percent? Having estimates of the costs and benefits of these decisions can be quite helpful in setting targets for pollution control programs.

(b) *How to attack the problem:* As we will see shortly, there is a variety of possible approaches to protecting the environment. If we know who benefits and who loses from the situation, and the economic incentives involved, we should be better able to devise the most effective approach.

(c) *Who should pay the costs of attacking the problem:* Depending on the costs and benefits involved, it may be appropriate for the cost to be paid by the producer and/or the consumer and/or the government. Economic analysis can help to determine who should pay these costs.

The Current Environmental Situation

Until the late 1960s, the environment *seemed* capable of handling most industrial by-products—those that were not recycled by natural processes seemed to be spread sufficiently thinly so as not to constitute a serious concern. During this era, the prevailing attitude was summed up in the catchphrase "the solution to pollution is dilution." By the early 1970s, however, growing problems of air and water pollution made it clear that dilution was *not* the solution. Growing public concern led to legislation providing some protection for the environment, but this movement lost momentum in the second half of the 1970s and the first half of the 1980s, when public concern over severe inflation and high unemployment pushed economic concerns ahead of the environment.

After the mid-1980s, environmental concerns again came to the fore. Not only was the volume of waste larger than ever, but also much of it was more toxic than before, and included a variety of new chemicals. Most seriously, however, environmental concerns moved to a global scale. Problems such as *acid rain*, the *greenhouse effect*, and the *depletion of the ozone layer* were said to threaten worldwide disaster.

While the marketplace will solve many economic problems, environmental pollution is not one of these. So environmental problems call for action by governments, not only on a national level but also internationally.

What Can Governments Do?

We have seen that the basic reason for pollution is that there is an incentive for producers and consumers to pass on the external costs of their activities to the environment and to society at large. From the economic viewpoint, then, the objective of antipollution policy should be to *internalize* the external costs of pollution, so that those who benefit from pollution are forced to *pay all of the costs* arising from their activities. Then polluters will have an incentive to take steps to reduce or eliminate their pollution. The following sections describe four ways of doing this: *direct regulation and fines, taxes, tradable pollution credits,* and *legal liability.* In addition, we will consider the possibility that, in some cases, governments should pay for, or *subsidize,* pollution control. Finally, we will examine the question of *waste management.*

Direct Regulation

By far the most common form of government antipollution action is *direct controls.* Under this approach, the polluter is required by law, or by a government agency empowered by law to set pollution standards, to reduce the pollution to a certain level. The emission controls set by governments for automobiles are probably the best-known form of pollution control by direct regulation. The most common penalty for violating the law is fines.

While regulations appear to be simple ("pollution is bad, so make it illegal"), in practice, matters are more complex. The main problem is the setting of the limit, or standard, for the pollution. From the environmental viewpoint, it would seem desirable to set a standard of zero pollution, or ban pollution outright. However, as we have seen, it would prove extremely costly (and in some cases technically impossible) to achieve zero pollution. So outright bans are used only for substances that have such extremely severe environmental effects that they must be banned at virtually any cost. Generally, direct controls allow some pollution, but specify the acceptable limits. Setting such standards is a difficult and controversial matter, especially when the environmental costs and the costs of pollution control are not completely known. Almost always, polluters complain that the costs of meeting the standards are excessive and will result in lost jobs, while environmentalists believe the standards to be so lax that serious pollution will continue.

Once the standards have been set, there remains the problem of enforcing them. Enforcement of complex regulations requires considerable resources, mainly in the form of qualified inspectors. Environmentalists argue (often with justification) that governments tend to pass environmental legislation but fail to provide the resources to enforce it effectively.

On the other hand, very strict enforcement of some environmental laws can generate problems of a different sort. An example is provided by California, where the city of Los Angeles and farmers in the state's central valley depend upon water pumped from the San Joaquin River in Northern California. Because of this pumping of water, the delta smelt, a small fish that inhabits the San Joaquin River, became a candidate for the endangered species list. To save the delta smelt would require very costly changes to the complex systems that deliver water from Northern California to the south. When a proposal was made to build a reservoir that would hold winter rain runoff and reduce the amount of water that had to be pumped from the delta smelt's habitat, environmentalists discovered on the site of the proposed reservoir the home of a single family of rare kit foxes—another endangered species. This was not a unique case—residential and commercial/industrial developers found that governments frequently stopped their projects when antigrowth activists discovered some rare animal or plant on the site. While California had led the way in the environmental movement of the 1980s, there was by the 1990s a political backlash against excessive regulation, which was perceived as preventing socially and economically desirable projects. In economic terms, the regulations were considering only the *benefits* of measures to protect the environment, and not taking into account their *costs*.

Finally, it is essential that the penalties for violating environmental protection laws be sufficiently high to discourage polluters. Often, both the risk of prosecution for violating pollution control legislation and the fines levied on violators have been so low that the economic incentive is to take one's chances by ignoring the law, and pay the fines if caught.

Notwithstanding these difficulties, direct controls are the most common form of pollution control. When properly set and enforced, and with adequate penalties, direct controls can force polluters to pay the costs of pollution prevention or cleanup. By forcing producers—and consumers of the products, if their prices rise—to pay these costs, direct controls have the effect of internalizing the previously external costs that had been passed on to the environment and society at large, thus providing incentives to stop or reduce the pollution.

Taxes on Pollution

Another approach to pollution control is to levy a *tax on polluters* (a "pollution tax") equal to the external costs caused by their pollution. Such a tax would force polluters to pay the full external costs of their activities. More importantly, it would provide an incentive for polluters to invest in pollution control equipment. For instance, suppose that a firm is paying pollution taxes of $150 000 per year. If by investing $1 million in pollution-control equipment, it can cut its pollution so as to pay no pollution tax, it would save itself $150 000 per year—a rate of return of 15 percent (after tax) on the investment of $1 million. Such a rate of return would warrant investing the $1 million in pollution control equipment.

While attractive in theory, this approach also has certain disadvantages. In many cases, it may be difficult if not impossible to measure the external costs imposed by a polluter, making it very difficult to establish the amount of pollution tax to be paid. In addition, the pollution control authorities would have to monitor each polluter's performance so as to levy the appropriate taxes. Finally, there are political obstacles to this approach. While economists see pollution taxes as an incentive to invest in pollution-control equipment, the public tends to see them as a "licence to pollute" that wealthy firms will cheerfully pay while continuing to destroy the environment. As a result of these problems, governments have seldom employed this approach, and have relied mostly on direct controls.

Tradable Pollution Credits

The objective of a system of *tradable pollution credits* is for an industry to achieve an acceptable level of pollution at the lowest possible cost. Under this system, the government establishes an overall acceptable level of pollution

The Canadian Council of Ministers of the Environment (CCME) has established the objective of reducing smog in the Windsor–Quebec City corridor, which would require reductions in emissions of nitrogen oxides. According to a report commissioned by a group of Ontario industry associations and government ministries, the annual cost of complying with the CCME's recommendations by 2005 would be $316 million without trading of emissions credits between sources, as compared to $187 million with trading.

www.ccme.ca

for an industry—say, 100 000 tonnes of sulfur dioxide (SO_2) emissions per year into the air. Each producer in the industry is then allocated a share of the total credits, which gives each producer the legal right to emit a certain amount of SO_2. Older plants, which are the most difficult and costly to upgrade environmentally, will tend to pollute in excess of the amount permitted by their credits, while newer plants with better equipment will pollute less than allowed by their credits, giving them surplus credits. Rather than invest in very costly pollution-control equipment, owners of the older plants can buy pollution credits from newer, cleaner plants. Over a period of time, the government will reduce the total allowable pollution limit for the industry, which will increase the value (price) of the tradable pollution credits. This will give producers increased incentives to develop pollution-cutting innovations, so as to provide themselves with more surplus pollution credits that they can sell at higher prices to firms with higher pollution levels. In effect, *overall* emissions targets for the industry are met, while *within* the industry emissions are shifted from plants where the unit cost of pollution control is low to plants where it is high.

Advocates of tradable pollution credits argue that this system is not only a more efficient way of controlling pollution, but it also provides the best *incentives for firms to develop continual improvements in pollution-reducing technology*, by literally creating a profitable market for pollution-control technology. By contrast, they say, direct regulation tends to freeze pollution-control technology, by dictating that firms use certain equipment to control pollution, without providing incentives to do better. This system is used in the United States to reduce emissions from 107 coal-burning electrical utilities in the Midwest, and in 1993 the U.S. Environmental Protection Agency auctioned 150 000 one-tonne pollution permits to electrical utilities for about US$21 million.

Environmentalists and much of the public tend to dislike tradable pollution credits, on the grounds that this policy seems to make pollution socially acceptable, through the government selling licences to do it and promoting a market for those licences. The main limitation on this approach in Canada is that much of Canadian pollution comes from relatively few sources, making it more difficult to establish an effective market such as could exist among over 100 U.S. electrical-generating utilities. On a smaller scale, Ontario Hydro practised something like this by shifting sulfur dioxide emissions between its power stations in order to minimize the cost of meeting increasingly lower emission limits set by the government.

Lawsuits for Damages

Another way to force polluters to pay for the external or social costs of their activities is to allow the victims of their pollution to *sue them* for damages. If damages could be proven and the amount established, such lawsuits—

whether by groups of citizens, other businesses, or governments—could provide an incentive for polluters to invest in pollution-control equipment, in the same way as pollution taxes can. This approach is seen as a useful part of antipollution policy, but the complexities, cost, and time involved in taking a lawsuit to court have tended to restrict it to a minor role.

Subsidies

Much of Canadian industry operates in highly competitive world markets, which require that the industries manage costs very effectively. Canadian businesses often argue that if Canada forces them to invest in costly pollution-control equipment, they will be placed at a competitive disadvantage vis-à-vis foreign competitors who are not subject to such requirements. In the extreme, these costs might become so high that Canadian producers are unable to compete and must close. A variation of this argument is that corporations—both Canadian and foreign—will tend to establish new plants outside of Canada, where pollution controls are less strict and costly. This argument can be quite telling, because it places protection of the environment in direct conflict with another very high policy priority—jobs for Canadians. Such concerns are particularly high in communities that rely on one industry for employment, such as pulp-and-paper towns.

> "If you want this town to grow, it's got to stink."
>
> Mayor of a Northern Ontario town, in the 1970s.

If pollution control regulations would really seriously impair a firm's competitive position, government policy-makers are faced with a difficult choice—should they allow the firm to continue to pollute at an unacceptable rate, or impose regulations that might cost the firm's employees their jobs? In either case, an undesirable social effect will result. In such circumstances, it may be justifiable for society at large, through the government, to use public funds to subsidize the cost of pollution control equipment, so as to permit businesses to reduce their pollution without causing severe economic hardship.

Waste Management

The average Canadian household throws out more than 3500 kg of garbage each year. Each year, Canadians discard about 23 million tonnes of waste, 64 percent of which consists of paper and food wastes. Where should all this garbage *go*?

There are three basic alternatives for dealing with the vast amounts of waste generated by a modern industrial society: *landfills, incineration,* and *recycling.* Each of these has its own advantages and disadvantages, from the perspective of economics and the environment.

Landfills

Landfills (less elegantly known as garbage dumps) occupy a somewhat paradoxical position because while they are the *least costly* way of dealing with waste, they are very *unpopular politically.* Few issues will generate hostility in a community more quickly and strongly than the prospect of becoming host to a garbage dump. Consequently, there are few tasks for a government as politically awkward as finding a location for a new landfill site.

Notwithstanding its unpopularity, landfilling is clearly by far the lowest-cost means of disposing of waste. In most countries, even with rising government standards required for landfill sites, the cost of dealing with waste through landfilling is between 40 and 75 percent of the cost of incineration, the next-cheapest method. At least, then, the cost savings associated with landfilling raises the possibility of governments offering remuneration to communities that agree to provide landfill sites.

> The problem of landfill space is more a matter of politics than geology. It is estimated that if Canada continued to produce municipal waste at the present rates of use for 1000 years, the total waste could all fit into a space less than 50 km square and 10 m deep.

Incineration

As noted, incineration is the second-cheapest method of disposing of waste. Even if incineration produces energy that can be sold, it is still one-third to one-half more costly than landfilling. This is partly because government standards for incineration have also been rising, to protect against air pollution from incinerators. Rules governing air emissions from incinerators can require that as much as half the capital cost of a new incineration plant consist of air-pollution control equipment.

Recycling

In a sense, recycling is the opposite of landfilling, in that it is the most politically popular but least economical means of dealing with waste. Despite the popular appeal of recycling, the economics of recycling have often not worked out very well. Many recycling schemes have (at least so far) been costly money-losers, largely due to a lack of planning on the part of governments.

> "Many people love recycling. It seems to meet some deep need to atone for modern materialism, by saving some of the materials from the rubbish bin."
>
> *The Economist*, May 29, 1993 (Survey, page 8).

Seizing upon recycling as a popular way to reduce the volume of garbage to be sent for landfilling or incineration, governments have established very ambitious recycling targets. The result has been mountains of recyclable materials—more than can be sold to recyclers. This oversupply of recyclables—collected at considerable cost to the government—drives the market price of recyclable materials to very low levels. As a result, the governments lose money when they sell the materials to recyclers. In the case of household waste, which requires extensive collection and sorting, the price that can be gotten for the recyclables rarely covers even a fraction of the cost of collecting and sorting them. In the case of some waste plastic, the price has been negative; that is, the governments have had to pay companies to take the waste for recycling.

In part, the costs of the recycling process itself are a problem. The collection and sorting of recyclable materials is a labour-intensive and therefore quite costly process. Then there are the costs of recycling the waste into usable materials. Even when the waste "raw materials" are very cheap, the cost of processing them into finished products is often quite high, making it more economical to produce products from new materials. For recyclers, the "bottom line" is that they must compete with companies that produce materials from virgin raw materials. This is a particularly serious problem if new raw materials are available at a low price, as many have been in recent years. For instance, when the price of oil was high, companies would pay to collect and clean used engine oil; however, after the price of new oil fell, this business collapsed.

As a result of factors such as these, while recycling has certainly grown, it has not yet been able to play the role in waste management that was hoped for or expected. There is nothing inherently faulty with recycling; indeed, it is conceptually the most attractive way of dealing with waste. However, only once the right combination of technology, labour costs, and materials costs occurs can recycling become economical enough to play its potential role in waste management.

Recycling: The Government at Work

One area in which recycling can be helpful is with respect to household garbage. The recycling of some types of garbage, including paper, tin cans, and bottles, not only provides reusable materials but also reduces the volume of garbage and the strain on disposal facilities.

A major obstacle to recycling household garbage is sorting it into different categories, such as paper, glass, cans, and other materials. This task is most easily and economically done at the household level, but there is no direct economic incentive to do so. In fact, such sorting involves a cost to householders: the opportunity cost of the time spent to sort the garbage.

Some municipalities encourage households to recycle by providing free containers for recyclable garbage (a form of government subsidy) and by providing considerable publicity stressing the advantages to their community of using these containers. So, by spending a relatively small amount of public money, governments have been able to promote environmentally beneficial recycling.

Recycling: The Market at Work

A major environmental concern is the exhaustion of certain types of nonrenewable natural resources, such as minerals. Some futurists have painted economically disastrous scenarios in which the world runs out of many such resources.

However, market forces appear to be capable of dealing, at least in part, with this concern. As the most attractive low-cost sources of some minerals have run down, their prices have risen. These rising prices have provided incentives for both consumers and producers of these minerals to do some useful things. Faced with higher prices, users of these minerals have found ways to economize on their use and/or find substitutes. Meanwhile, rising prices have not only encouraged the development of new sources of such materi-

> A Japanese scientist projects that more than half of the world's consumption of paper could be produced from the waste of banana plantations, rather than by cutting down trees.

als, but also have made it more economical to *recycle* them. In effect, higher metal prices can change scrap metal into an economically viable alternative to mining.

In such circumstances, the market provides the necessary economic incentives for recycling, as recycled metals become cheaper than newly mined minerals. Even 20 years ago, the western world was obtaining 48 percent of its lead, 38 percent of its copper, 25 percent of its aluminum, 24 percent of its zinc, and 21 percent of its tin from recycling.

The Environment Industry

While many people see private industry and the environment as being in direct conflict with each other, the fact is that Canada is developing a significant "environment industry." One rapidly growing part of this industry is waste collection. In part, this is due to the lower costs of private waste-management firms as compared to government operations.

Other aspects of the environment industry involve consulting and equipment installation and maintenance. Statistics on the waste management industry are not easy to come by, but by some estimates there are more than 3500 environmental equipment and service firms operating across Canada, employing more than 110 000 people and generating sales of about $7 billion annually. Furthermore, the environmental sector is regarded as a growth industry, with projected growth rates of 20–40 percent per year. Nonetheless, compared to European nations, Canada's environment industry has been described by knowledgeable observers as "less developed."

Making Polluters Pay

In the previous sections, much has been made of the costs of waste disposal. This has led to proposals that would require polluters themselves to pay for the amount of garbage that they generate. In theory, such schemes would not only force polluters to pay, but would also provide incentives for them to reduce the amount of their pollution.

At the household level, this approach takes the form of "pay to throw" schemes for garbage collection of the type run in over 200 U.S. cities. Most such plans charge a fixed fee for a basic garbage collection service (say, two cans per week) and extra fees for additional garbage (say, $1.00 per can).

On the face of it, such schemes appear rather successful. One study for the World Resources Institute estimated that a fee of $1.50 on each 32-gallon (145-L) garbage container would cut the volume of waste by 18 percent.

But where does this 18 percent of volume of garbage *go*? A good deal of it still went out in people's garbage containers, but in a more compressed form. This compression was achieved by a manoeuvre known as the "Seattle stomp," after the largest American city with a pay-to-throw scheme. In one city, the average weight of a container filled with garbage rose by 42 percent. Worse, however, was an increase in illegal dumping, as people threw their garbage onto public (and private) property and into rivers in order to avoid extra charges. And when Seattle's pay-to-throw plan was introduced, local charities found their drop-offs and doorsteps swamped with unwanted "donations" that often resembled garbage.

Ultimately, then, a policy that seeks to force polluters to pay high costs through what amounts to a "garbage tax" will encounter the problem that it gives them a strong incentive to dump their garbage illegally. A more logical policy would be to tax not garbage, but rather consumption. The tax revenues could then be used to subsidize recycling and proper garbage disposal, giving people an incentive to use these socially beneficial methods rather than an incentive to dump illegally.

Energy and the Greenhouse Effect

Our lifestyle is tied to high energy consumption. We use energy to transport ourselves, to heat us in winter and cool us in summer, to fuel our industrial activity, and to operate the myriad of electrical appliances that we use daily. Even much of our leisure time is spent consuming energy through travel, the use of recreational vehicles, and so on.

> Because they are classed as "trucks," SUVs are exempt from government fuel-efficiency standards that apply to cars. This allows SUVs to burn much more gasoline than cars, adding greatly to greenhouse gas emissions.

The simple fact is that current large-scale energy sources generate significant amounts of pollution. The main problem is the burning of fossil fuels, mainly gasoline. The automobile is the largest single source of air pollution, accounting for about 40 percent of greenhouse gas emissions. It is followed by the coal and oil burned to generate much of the electricity that our lifestyle requires.

Some of the pollutants from the burning of fossil fuels can be controlled, but not all. The most intractable pollutant is *carbon dioxide*, which, unlike other pollutants from automobiles, cannot be controlled with pollution-control equipment. The resultant ongoing large-scale emission of carbon dioxide into the air has contributed to the "greenhouse effect"—the global warming trend that environmentalists fear will cause disastrous climatic changes around the world, including the raising of ocean levels and widespread flooding of coastal areas.

Unless technology can solve the carbon dioxide problem, the fundamental conflict will remain between our high-energy-consumption lifestyle and the environment in which we live. At present, the only way to control carbon dioxide emissions is through conservation: that is, by controlling and reducing our energy consumption (see the "In the News" box on the next page). This approach would require changing from a value system based on economic growth and high and rising living standards to one that embraced conservation and quality of life, and accepted limits on our lifestyles and energy consumption. The problem is that this would mean such a drastic change in people's attitudes and lifestyle that political leaders are reluctant to confront the problem.

The Outlook for the Environment

What is the outlook for improving our environment? Certainly, public concern has increased the pressure on both governments and business to pay increased attention to protecting the environment. However, there remains the reality of the trade-off discussed earlier in this chapter—that there are real costs to be paid in order to achieve a cleaner environment. The key to an effective attack on pollution, then, is not whether the public is *concerned* about the environment, but whether people are *willing to pay* to protect and improve the environment.

The evidence and the performance on this key matter has been somewhat mixed. During boom periods when economic concerns are distant, the public seems more concerned about the environment and more willing to pay the costs of environmental protection. However, when recessions increase unemployment and concerns about making ends meet, public concerns about the environment diminish. The track record of governments is also somewhat mixed; for instance, for years Ontario claimed to have exemplary environmental legislation, but a 1999 report found Ontario's actual pollution record to be the second-worst of all Canadian provinces and American states (Texas was the worst; Louisiana third). Similarly, the performance of industry has

---

IN THE **NEWS**   A Carbon Tax?

According to various well-researched studies, the most simplest and most efficient way to reduce greenhouse gas emissions would be through a steep "carbon tax" of perhaps $0.15/L to $0.25/L on gasoline. The studies conclude that such a tax (which would represent a price increase of about 25 to 35 percent for gasoline) would not only discourage excessive consumption of gasoline and the associated pollution, but also raise billions of dollars per year in tax revenues for financially pressed and debt-ridden governments. These funds could be used to pay down government debt or to finance increased spending on health care, or cuts to personal and business income taxes.

Questions

1. For such a tax to have the intended positive effects on the environment, what would have to be true about the elasticity of demand for gasoline?

2. Do you believe that, in reality, the elasticity of demand for gasoline is such that this plan would significantly reduce greenhouse gas emissions?

3. If a gasoline tax would improve both the environment and the financial position of governments, why have governments not enacted such a tax?

4. What is the logic of governments *reducing* taxes on the incomes of people and businesses at the same time as they are *increasing* taxes on gasoline?

been mixed. While some industries remained serious polluters, there were also examples of real concern and progress on the part of the private sector.

As of late 2002, attention focused on the Kyoto Accord, under which nations were to reduce their greenhouse gas emissions significantly. In Canada's case, emissions of carbon dioxide and other ozone-depleting pollutants was to be cut to 6 percent below their 1990 levels, over a period of ten years.

The prospect of Canada's ratifying the Kyoto Accord generated much controversy. Opponents of Kyoto argued that there was a lack of clear scientific evidence that such large cuts in emissions were necessary in order to prevent global environmental disasters. The Canadian Manufacturers and Exporters Association projected that Kyoto would cost Canada 450 000 jobs by 2010 and would increase gasoline prices by 80 percent, electricity prices by 100 percent, and natural gas prices by 60 percent. The automobile industry feared that Canadian plants would become uncompetitive with plants in the United States and other countries, and would be forced to close, with serious effects on the Ontario economy. The oil industry foresaw the closing of several multibillion dollar oil-development projects in the Alberta tar sands that were important to the Alberta economy. Most projections were that Kyoto would reduce Canada's Gross Domestic Product by about 2.5 percent, which would translate into something like $250 per Canadian family per month by 2010.

Supporters of Kyoto replied that these figures were exaggerated, and that in any event, they represented a small price to pay for the environmental benefits of Kyoto. (Furthermore, they argued, in the environmental disaster that would occur if Kyoto were *not* enacted, none of these economic statistics would matter much anyway.) Greenpeace projected that, under Kyoto, greenhouse emissions would be reduced by 70 percent, and the savings in health costs would be hundreds of millions of dollars per year.

Skeptics pointed out that what Canada did was unimportant anyway, since Canada only accounts for some 2 percent of the world's greenhouse gas emissions. They also noted that the federal government apparently had no plan for actually achieving the large reductions in emissions required by Kyoto by 2012. For its part, the federal government stated that it planned to take *until 2012* to *develop* a plan. Despite the absence of a plan, however, the government's own studies forecasted a loss of 200 000 jobs.

The situation was complicated by the fact that the U.S. federal government had indicated that it would not ratify the Kyoto agreement, which could leave Canadian producers at a competitive disadvantage if they had to bear the higher costs of Canada's acceptance of Kyoto. But the situation was not that simple. In the U.S., at the level of state governments, progress was being made in reducing emissions. And Canada's commitment to Kyoto was less complete than it seemed—Canada actually planned to cut its emissions by only 70 percent of its obligation under Kyoto, and to claim that the rest of its contribution to the environment was made up of its exports of clean natural gas to the United States. This outraged European nations, who charged that Canada was cheating on the agreement before it had even signed it. As 2002 drew to a close, the situation remained unclear.

Chapter Summary

1. There are economic incentives for both producers and consumers to pollute, by passing the external costs of their production or consumption on to the environment. (L.O. 1)

2. There is an economic trade-off in which society can have a cleaner environment if it is willing to accept a lower level of production and consumption of goods and services. (L.O. 2)

3. As with other economic benefits, the cleanup of the environment is subject to the Law of Diminishing Returns: as the level of pollution is lowered, it becomes increasingly costly to reduce it further. (L.O. 3)

4. Economic analysis of the costs and benefits of pollution control can help in making decisions concerning the objectives of a pollution-control program, how to attack the problem, and who should pay the costs of the program. (L.O. 4)

5. Some types of action that can be taken to protect the environment are direct regulation, taxes on pollution, tradable pollution credits, lawsuits for damages due to pollution, and government subsidies to help pay the cost of pollution controls. (L.O. 5)

6. With respect to waste management, landfilling is the lowest-cost disposal method, incineration is second-lowest, and recycling the highest-cost way of dealing with waste. Taxes on consumption and subsidies for proper garbage disposal and recycling are considered more environmentally effective than taxes on garbage itself, which tends to generate environmentally damaging illegal dumping. (L.O. 6)

Questions

1. One source of pollution is throwaway drink containers.
    (a) Identify some of the costs and the benefits of using such containers.
    (b) Identify the advantages and disadvantages of each of the following approaches to the problem of throwaway drink containers:
        (i)   prohibition of throwaway containers
        (ii) taxes on throwaway containers

2. "Setting pollution-control standards is simple—the standards should require that pollution be reduced to the maximum extent possible using modern technology."

    Do you agree with the above statement or not? If not, how should pollution-control standards be determined?

3. "The real problem with pollution is that people do not understand the side effects of their actions. What is needed to combat pollution, therefore, is a comprehensive educational program pointing out how pollution is caused and the dangers of it."

    Do you agree or disagree? Why?

4. Do you believe that the values of your generation concerning the environment and material goods and services are different from those of your parents' generation? Would you be prepared to reduce your living standard by 10 percent in order to create a much cleaner environment?

5. The text notes that the Law of Diminishing Returns leads to the logical conclusion that beyond a certain point, rising costs of additional pollution reduction tend to make it not worthwhile. Under what circumstances would this generalization not be appropriate?

6. Under the Kyoto agreement on greenhouse emissions, Canada would have to reduce its per-person energy use by as much as 27 percent by 2012. However, some experts questioned whether the "greenhouse effect" actually existed, and whether global warming was caused by human economic activity or was part of a natural temperature cycle lasting some 100 to 200 years. Given the costs of reducing these emissions, this is a critically important debate. Has research shed any additional light on this matter?

7. Did Canada ratify the Kyoto agreement? If so, is Canada actually making progress in reducing emissions? Has Kyoto led to any changes in government policies? Have gasoline taxes increased? Have electricity prices risen? Have you changed the temperature settings on the thermostat in your home? Are SUVs selling as strongly as they did in 2002? Explain your answers.

Chapter 15

The Agricultural Sector

Learning Objectives

After studying this chapter, you should be able to:

1. Describe the effects of technology in the twentieth century on agricultural productivity, output, and employment.

2. Explain why farm incomes have tended to be both low and unstable.

3. Using a graph to illustrate, explain the effects of an *offer-to-purchase* support program (for farms).

4. Using a graph to illustrate, explain the operation of an *acreage restriction* program.

5. Using a graph to illustrate, explain the operation of a *deficiency payments* program.

6. Describe the approach taken by marketing boards to try to increase and stabilize farm prices and incomes.

7. Identify three groups that are critical of Canada's marketing boards, and give the reason for each group's stance.

The agricultural sector of the Canadian economy stands in sharp contrast to the large corporations and labour unions of earlier chapters. In those sectors, the spotlight was often on the market power of corporations and unions, but in the agricultural sector the situation has generally been very different. In agriculture, there are large numbers of producers, mainly family farms, many of which have no real market power. Farmers have suffered so much from strong competition, overproduction, and low returns that governments have felt compelled to *support* them in order to maintain long-term stability in this industry. To understand the nature of the Canadian agricultural problems, we must first consider the nature of the industry, as well as the changes that have swept through it over the past few decades.

Profile of Agriculture

Agriculture is an extremely varied sector of the Canadian economy. Canadian farms range from highly mechanized prairie wheat farms of over 1000 hectares (ha) to small vegetable farms of less than 40 ha. The one feature that is common across all of Canadian agriculture is that most operations are *family farms*. According to the 2001 census, 98 percent of Canada's 246 923 farms were operated by families, the vast majority being sole proprietorships.

In 2001, there were over 90 000 female farm operators in Canada—26 percent of all farm operators in Canada.

Looking at a map may suggest that Canada has vast amounts of land available for agriculture, but this is not the case. Eighty-nine percent of Canada's land is not suitable for agriculture of any kind, and less than 0.5 percent is rated as class one—suitable for all types of crops. And not all suitable land is being used for agriculture—37 percent of all class-one land can be seen from the top of Toronto's CN tower, and is within commuting distance of Canada's largest and fastest-growing city.

While the agricultural sector's production amounts to less than 4 percent of the total output of the Canadian economy, and employment in primary agriculture is only 2.2 percent of total employment in Canada, the performance of the agricultural sector is of great importance to Canadians. Agricultural exports such as wheat make an important contribution to Canadians' economic prosperity, and the typical Canadian family spends about 18 percent of its budget on food.

The Agricultural Revolution

The changes that occurred in the agricultural sector during the twentieth century were so sweeping that they have been called "the agricultural revolution." The driving force behind the agricultural revolution has been *technological change*, such as improved equipment and fertilizers, improved strains of crops, better farming techniques, and so on. All of these have generated tremendous increases in *farm productivity*, as measured by output per hectare and output per farm worker. One result of these changes, as

Figure 15-1 shows, has been a long-term trend toward fewer but larger and more mechanized farms, producing food much more efficiently.

Another result of the agricultural revolution has been a sharp decline in the number of Canadians living and working on farms. In 1950, there were 1 018 000 Canadians working on farms. By 2002, there were only 330 000 Canadians working on farms, a decrease of 68 percent from 1950.

FIGURE 15-1 Number of Census Farms and Average Farm Size, Canada, 1871–2001

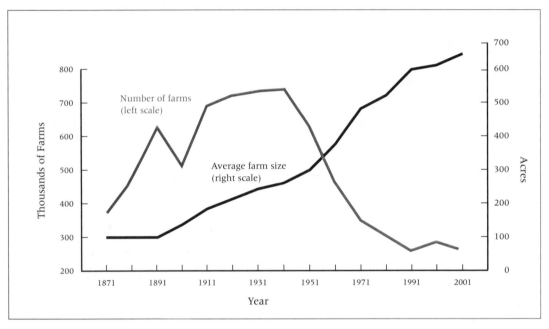

Sources: Adapted from Statistics Canada, *Farming Facts*, Catalogue No. 21-522, 2001, and the Statistics Canada 1996 Census of Agriculture.

Figure 15-2 shows the decline in the number of workers and in the percentage of the labour force employed in agriculture from 1950 to 2002.

The agricultural revolution has provided the economic basis for Canadians' high standard of living. As we saw in Chapter 11, technology has "freed up" large numbers of workers from employment in agriculture and has thus made them available for employment in the manufacturing and service sectors of the economy, where they can produce the goods and services that make Canadians' present lifestyle possible. Without these improvements in agriculture, nearly three million Canadian workers—nearly eight times as many as now work on farms—would have to be working in the agricultural sector producing food rather than other goods and services that add to our prosperity. Our economic progress would have been much slower and our standard of living much lower.

FIGURE 15-2 Employment in Agriculture, 1950–2002

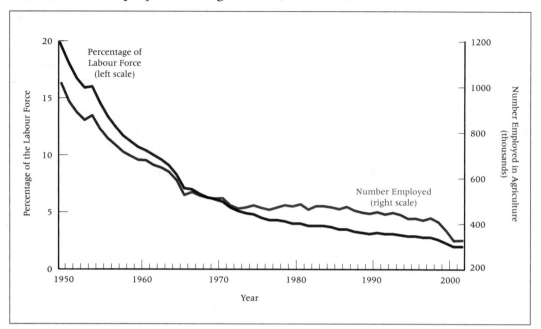

Source: Adapted from Statistics Canada, *Historical Labour Force Statistics*, Catalogue No. 71-201.

Economic and social changes on such a large scale naturally lead to concerns that they will create hardship, particularly unemployment. However, the agricultural revolution proceeded remarkably smoothly. With the economy usually growing reasonably well, the workers freed up from the agricultural sector generally found employment in the expanding manufacturing and service sectors. This very large-scale transition from the farm to other types of employment was made easier by the fact that it was mostly the *children* of farmers who made the transition, rather than their parents who had farmed for all of their lives.

But while these changes did not create an unemployment problem, they *did* contribute to certain other problems that the agricultural sector experienced. These are discussed in the following section.

The "Farm Problem"

Despite the impressive improvements in technology and productivity described in the previous sections, the agricultural sector of the Canadian economy, as in other nations, has had more than its share of economic difficulties. In particular, many farmers have suffered from problems of *low incomes* and *unstable incomes* that together are often characterized as "the farm problem." In the following sections, we will examine each of these problems.

Low Farm Incomes

Over the past 50 years, the prices that farmers have received for their crops and livestock have increased less than half as rapidly as prices in general. The main reason for low farm prices and incomes lies in the technological progress of the agricultural revolution. The great productivity improvements in agriculture have made possible large increases in the supply of agricultural products. But farmers have not gained from this improvement in their efficiency, because the demand for food is *inelastic*—increases in supply have driven prices down, but have not increased the amount of food demanded by consumers very much. The farmers' problem is illustrated in Figure 15-3.

FIGURE 15-3 With an Inelastic Demand, Rising Supply Means Lower Farm Incomes

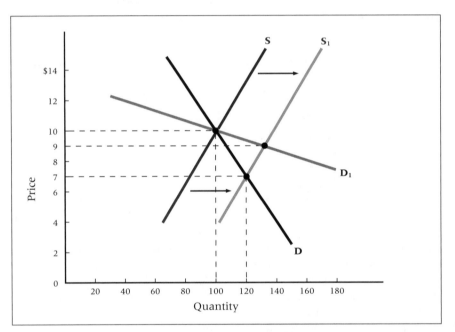

Suppose that S and D represent the original demand and supply curves, with an equilibrium price of $10 and sales of 100 units for a total revenue (farm income) of $1000. If technological improvements increase the supply to S_1, the price will fall to $7—a decline of 30 percent. Unfortunately for the farmers, the amount of food sold does not increase by as much as its price has fallen. As a result, the farmers wind up selling 120 units of food for $7, for total revenues of $840—a decline of 16 percent from their original $1000.

Clearly, the problem is that the demand for food is *inelastic*: people do not buy much more food simply because its price is lower. So when there is an increase in supply, prices must fall considerably in order to sell the higher supply. Demand curve D_1 shows what would have happened if the demand had been *elastic*—with consumers eager to buy more at lower prices, the price would have only had to fall to $9, rather than $7, in order to sell off the increased supply. Unfortunately for farmers, the demand for food generally is inelastic. So farmers' efforts to increase productivity tend to be self-defeating, in that the increased supply drives farm prices—and incomes—downward.

To make matters worse for farmers, the *income elasticity of demand* for farm products is also quite low. This means that, as consumers' incomes have risen, the amount of food that they buy has not increased as rapidly; rather, they have spent most of their increased income on other things, such as services and durable goods. As a result, farmers have not benefited as much as other Canadians from the economic progress of their nation. This slow growth of demand has combined with rising supply to generate surpluses of many farm products, together with low prices and low farm incomes. Figure 15-4 shows farm net cash income from 1971 to 2001.

FIGURE 15-4 Farm Net Cash Income, 1971–2001

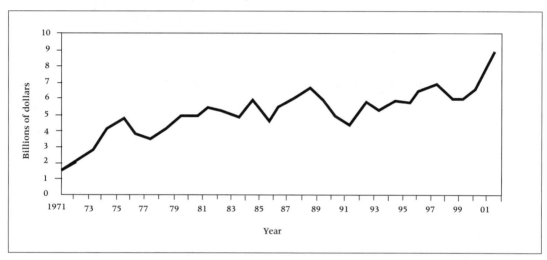

Source: Adapted from Statistics Canada, *Agriculture Economic Statistics*, Catalogue No. 21-603, 2001.

Unstable Farm Incomes

Low incomes are only part of farmers' economic difficulties. Farm prices (and thus farm incomes) are also notoriously *unstable;* that is, they fluctuate sharply from year to year. As Figure 15-4 also shows, it is not unusual for the incomes of Canadian farmers to vary greatly from year to year. Also, Figure 15-4 shows *total* farm income; for *individual* crops and *individual* farmers, the fluctuations are often much more severe.

Why are farm incomes so unstable? It is a well-known fact that variations in the weather cause fluctuations in crop sizes (the supply of particular agricultural products) and thus in farm incomes. But varying weather conditions are only part of the problem with unstable farm incomes, the other parts being the inelasticity of both the supply of and the demand for food. We have already seen that, on the demand side of the market, consumers' demand for food tends to be quite inelastic, that is, changes in prices will not change the amount of food that they buy by much. The supply side of the market is also inelastic—once a crop is harvested, the supply cannot readily be increased or reduced. Figure 15-5 shows how this inelasticity of both demand and supply results in instability in farm prices and incomes.

Graph (a) of Figure 15-5 portrays the market for agricultural products. Both demand and supply are inelastic—in fact, the supply curve (S) is perfectly inelastic. This means that 70 000 units have been harvested and must be sold, regardless of how high or how low the price goes. With demand as shown by the demand curve D, the price will be $6. However, if good weather conditions result in a much larger crop next year, so that supply increases by 20 000 units as shown by S_1, the price of this product will plunge to $2. The reason for such a large decrease in price is not merely the increase in supply—the inelasticity of both the demand and the supply play a big part in the price decline as well. This is shown by graph (b), in which the price starts out at the same $6 and the supply increases by exactly the same 20 000 units as in graph (a), *but* both the demand and the supply are elastic. The result, as graph (b) shows, is very different—the price declines by only about $1.

FIGURE 15-5 Supply Fluctuations Affect Prices Much More When Supply and Demand Are Inelastic

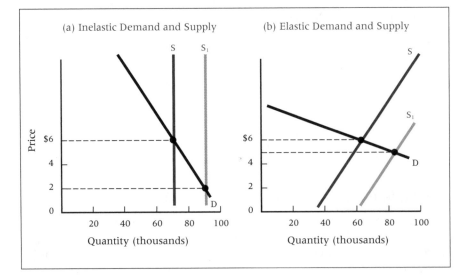

In summary, due to a combination of high and fluctuating supply, and inelastic demand and inelastic supply, farm prices and incomes tend to be both *low* and *unstable*. And because it is rooted in the very nature of agricultural markets, this "farm problem" exists not only in Canada but also in other countries.

Dealing with the Farm Problem

Since there is nothing farmers can do about the inelastic nature of the demand for farm products, the key to supporting and stabilizing farm prices and incomes lies in *controlling the supply* of farm products. In other words, farmers would benefit greatly from an oligopolistic price-and-production agreement among themselves, as described in Chapter 7.

The major obstacle to such action has, of course, been the very nature of farming (and, some would add, farmers). Farming is an excellent illustration of a highly competitive industry such as we saw in Chapter 7—it consists of many small, independent producers selling substantially similar products in a highly competitive marketplace.

Given these realities, it has proven very difficult to achieve any kind of agreement or coordinated action on the part of farmers, even when it would be in their best interests to do so. Attempts have been made to use *farm co-operatives* (co-ops) to restrict production and support and stabilize prices, but these efforts have seldom been successful. Such agreements are voluntary and lack any means of enforcement; as a result, too many farmers tended not to participate or to break the agreements. Consequently, co-ops have tended to be of more benefit to farmers in areas such as research, advertising, and securing volume discounts on purchases of supplies and equipment, rather than in restriction of supply.

When such efforts at self-help proved largely unsuccessful, farmers turned to *government assistance* with their problem of low and unstable incomes. Such government assistance can take various forms, the main ones of which are presented in the following sections.

Government Programs to Support and Stabilize Farm Incomes

Offers to Purchase

Under the **offer-to-purchase** method, the government establishes the price of the farm produce and undertakes to purchase from the farmers any produce that is unsold at that price. As we saw in Chapter 6, and as Figure 15-6 shows, the result of farm price supports will be *surpluses* of farm produce.

At the government-supported price of $2 per bushel, farmers will produce 65 million bushels but only 45 million will be purchased. The result is a surplus of 20 million bushels that the government will have to buy from the farmers and store. Unless market conditions turn favourable, the government will likely accumulate quite large crop surpluses that are costly to store and difficult to dispose of, which explains why the offer-to-purchase approach is no longer widely used.

offer-to-purchase A farm-income support program under which the government establishes the price of the farm produce and undertakes to purchase any unsold produce at that price.

FIGURE 15-6 The Effects of Farm Price Supports

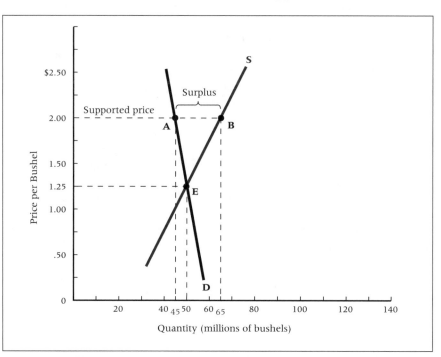

Acreage Restrictions

acreage restrictions A crop supply management program that either forces farmers to reduce their acreage under cultivation, or gives them financial incentives to do so.

To avoid the problem of crop surpluses, governments have sometimes employed **acreage restrictions**. Under such a program, farmers are either required to reduce their acreage under cultivation or are given financial incentives to do so; that is, they are *paid to not grow crops* on part of their land.

The result, as shown in Figure 15-7, is that the supply is reduced, shifting the supply curve left to S_1 and increasing the price from $1.25 to $2.00. Acreage restrictions have not always proven a reliable method of restricting supply, however, because farmers often take their least productive land out of cultivation and cultivate the remainder more intensively.

Deficiency Payments

deficiency payments A program for supporting farm incomes under which the government guarantees farmers a target price for a crop by subsidizing all sales of that crop that fall short of the target price.

Under the previous two programs we have examined, crop prices are increased by reducing the amount of food available to consumers—either by the government buying surplus produce and holding it off the market, or by causing less produce to be grown. A completely different approach, which does *not* reduce the amount of food available to consumers, is known as **deficiency payments**. Under this approach, the government sets a *target price* for the produce. If the actual market price is lower than the target price, the government will pay the farmers the difference between the target price and the market price.

Figure 15-8 shows how a deficiency payments plan works. In a free market, supply and demand would establish an equilibrium price of $3. Since

FIGURE 15-7 The Effects of Acreage Restrictions

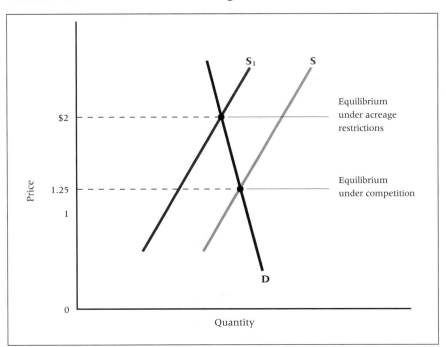

this price would be too low to allow many farmers to operate, the government establishes a target price of $5—high enough to provide what is considered a fair return to the producers. Knowing that they are guaranteed a price of $5, farmers undertake to produce 50 million units, as shown by point A on the supply curve. To sell this much output, point B on the demand curve shows that the price must be $2. So the government must pay each farmer a deficiency payment (or subsidy) of $3 for each unit sold at $2, to bring the farmers' return up to $5 per unit.

The deficiency-payments approach does not generate crop surpluses, and is the best approach from the *consumer's* point of view, because it does not restrict supply, and results in lower prices. On the other hand, by encouraging high production and low market prices, it can require considerable amounts of direct payments from the government to farmers, and therefore tends to be more costly to the *taxpayer.* Whereas offers to purchase and acreage restrictions assist farmers through *high prices*, deficiency payments assist them through direct *payments from the government* to farmers.

Canadian Direct Payments Programs

Canadian governments have several programs under which direct payments are made to farmers. One large program is crop insurance, to which both farmers and governments contribute and from which farmers can receive payments when market conditions reduce farm prices and incomes. There

FIGURE 15-8 The Effects of Deficiency Payments

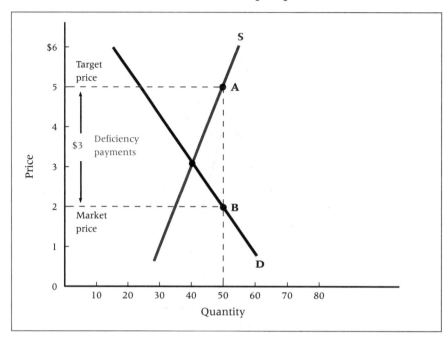

are various other plans that support farmers' revenues, such as the subsidy paid to dairy farmers. In addition, governments make payments to farmers to help to reduce their operating expenses, particularly interest on loans and property taxes.

In 2001, governments made direct payments of $3.8 billion to farmers. These direct payments amounted to about 10 percent of farmers' *cash receipts*, but represented about 43 percent of their *net cash income*. From 1985 to 1993, government direct payments accounted for about 51 percent of farmers' net cash income. As we will see later, however, these proportions declined considerably after 1993.

Direct payments such as these do not comprise nearly all of the assistance given Canadian farmers by governments. Another major type of government assistance takes the form of the higher prices for farm products sold through government-sponsored *marketing boards*.

marketing boards
Government-sponsored organizations of farmers that support farm incomes by restricting the supply of produce, usually through a system of quotas on individual farmers.

Marketing Boards: From Competition to Monopoly

In certain sectors of Canadian agriculture, a quite different approach to agricultural policy was initiated in 1972—the concept of *supply management* through marketing boards. **Marketing boards** are government-sponsored organizations of farmers that are intended to regulate the production and price of various farm products, such as poultry and dairy products.

The objective of marketing boards is to ensure that farmers receive a fair profit, by both *raising* and *stabilizing* the price of farm products. To do this, the marketing board establishes a price for a particular product (say, eggs), using a formula based on the costs of production of an average farm. The marketing board estimates the size of the market for a particular farm product at the price it has established, then *restricts the supply* of that product so as to keep the price at the level established by the board. The marketing board does this by assigning production quotas (limits) to individual farmers so that they will not produce more than the market can absorb. Individual farmers sell their production to the marketing board, which acts as a monopoly sales agent on their behalf, selling at the price established by the marketing board. For marketing boards to be able to control markets in this way, it is essential that the government *control imports* of those items so as to keep lower-price foreign produce out of the Canadian market. Originally, this was done through *import quotas* that strictly limited the amount of foreign products that could enter Canada.

Because they have the legal power to set production quotas for individual producers and so control supply and prices, marketing boards are in effect *monopolies*. Unlike other monopolies, however, marketing boards have been encouraged by the government, and exempted from anti-monopoly legislation. After 1972, when federal legislation paved the way for marketing boards, several sectors of Canadian agriculture (including eggs, chickens, turkeys, and dairy products) went through a dramatic transformation from highly competitive industries to virtual monopolies. By the mid-1990s, marketing boards covered nearly 80 000 Canadian farmers, and accounted for about 20 percent of total farm cash receipts.

Marketing boards seem quite simple in theory, but in practice they have become controversial. The main criticism of marketing boards is that they cause excessively high prices, because their formulas for calculating prices are often heavily weighted toward the higher production costs of smaller, less efficient producers. According to critics, the result of such calculations is not only high prices for consumers but also windfall profits for more efficient producers with lower-than-average production costs.

Related to the question of high costs and prices is the complaint that marketing boards *foster inefficiency* in farming. Because of the high prices established by marketing boards, many small, inefficient producers are kept in business. Furthermore, marketing boards' production quotas discourage farmers from expanding and consolidating into larger, more efficient units. In order to expand, farmers must *buy production quotas* from other farmers. Since the production quotas issued by marketing boards are in effect a piece of a monopoly, they can be quite expensive to buy. For instance, Ontario dairy farmers have had to pay as much as $9500 for the fluid milk quotas required in order to add just one additional cow to their herds. Not only does the cost of quotas discourage growth, but also the quotas themselves can prevent farms from growing to efficient sizes. For instance, while production costs per dozen eggs decrease substantially for operations with 50 000 or more hens, marketing boards in some provinces would not allow flocks that large. Finally, by forcing farmers to operate below their capacity levels, marketing boards reduce efficiency and add to costs and prices.

The result of these factors was that the prices of farm products produced under Canadian marketing boards were often 50 to 100 percent higher than U.S. prices for the same products. So, while marketing boards proved effective in raising farm prices and incomes, they became quite controversial, mainly because of their effect on agricultural efficiency and prices.

Farm Family Income

Rose Acre Farms Inc. is one of the three largest egg producers in the United States. In its high-tech farms in Indiana, Missouri, and Iowa, Rose Acre Farms has 12 million hens. Canada's 1435 egg farmers have a total of 17.2 million hens. Speaking of Canada, Marcus Rust of Rose Acre Farms observed that "big (U.S.) producers could do very well up there."

Since the surge in farm prices of the early 1970s, average farm family income has been quite close to the average income of husband–wife families in Canada. In recent years, farm family income has been about 90 percent of nonfarm family income.

However, a growing proportion of farm family income has been coming *from nonfarm sources*, as farm families have increasingly supplemented their farm income with nonfarm earnings. As Figure 15-9 shows, the share of farm income derived from nonfarm sources has increased from about 50 percent in the mid-1960s to over 70 percent today. In part, this reflects the economic problems of farmers, as they increasingly rely on sources of income other than their farm incomes.

FIGURE 15-9 Off-Farm Income as a Percentage of Total Income of Farmers

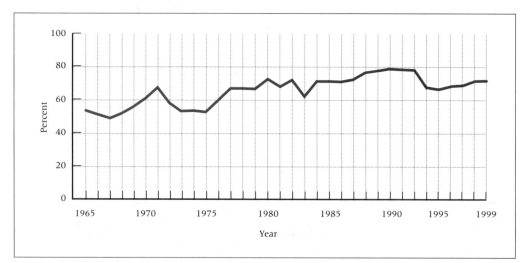

Source: Adapted from Statistics Canada, *Farming Facts*, Catalogue No. 21-522, 2001.

Pressures for Change to Canadian Farm Policy

In recent years, there has been growing pressure on Canadian governments to make changes to their farm income-support programs, especially marketing boards. This pressure has been coming from consumer groups, food processors, and Canada's trading partners.

Consumer groups have argued for many years that government farm programs were excessively costly to consumers. It was estimated that, by 1992, farm support programs were costing Canadians an estimated $440 per year per capita. For lower-income families, who spend a higher proportion of their budget on food, the burden was greater. And the benefits of government programs were also questioned – for each farm job saved by government assistance, the cost to consumers was estimated to be over $140 000.

Canadian food processors were another source of complaints. Their concern was that, under Canada's marketing boards, much government assistance to farmers took the form of higher prices, which translated into higher production costs for Canadian food processors. For example, prices of chicken, turkey, eggs, cheese, and industrial milk in Canada were higher than U.S. prices by 50 percent or more. For Canadian food processors that must compete with American processors who use low-priced American food inputs, this was a serious problem. (Because the United States was using deficiency payments more than Canada, U.S. farmers got their government support more through payments from governments than through the higher prices that occur under Canadian marketing boards.)

However, the most serious pressures on Canada's farm policies were generated by *Canada's trading partners*, through international trade negotiations. As noted earlier, the key to protecting the high prices charged by marketing boards is to keep imports of cheaper products out of the Canadian market, and Canada had used import quotas to do this. However, this policy conflicted with the 1995 agreement under the **World Trade Organization (WTO)**, which made the first serious attempt to reduce trade barriers between countries for agricultural commodities.

Under the WTO agreement, Canada could no longer use import quotas to bar imports; instead, the quotas had to be converted to the equivalent level of protection in tariff form ("tariffied"). Initially, these tariffs were to be extremely high, as Table 15-1 shows.

Such high tariffs would keep imports out of Canada as effectively as the quotas that had preceded them; however, under the WTO agreement, the tariffs were to be reduced by 15 percent over six years. This new approach would gradually reduce prices, bringing benefits to Canadian consumers; however, many farmers who had been operating under the protection of marketing boards and import quotas found it threatening. The government reassured them that it intended to preserve marketing boards; however, whether this would be possible was uncertain as the tariffs on agricultural imports decreased.

www.wto.org

World Trade Organization (WTO) An international organization through which over 100 member nations negotiate and enforce rules for international trade.

The financial problems of Canadian governments in the 1990s added to the pressure to change agricultural policy. As we saw in Chapter 12, the budget deficits and debt of both the federal and provincial governments forced them to cut back on spending in many areas, including assistance to farmers.

TABLE 15-1 Canada's Marketing Board Import Quotas Converted to Tariffs[a], 1995

Product	Tariff Equivalent to Previous Import Quota Protection
Butter	354%
Milk	277%
Chicken	273%
Eggs	192%

[a]Tariffs imposed when imports reach 3 percent of Canadian consumption.

Recent Trends

As Figure 15-10 shows, the amount of government assistance to farmers decreased during much of the 1990s, both in dollars and as a percentage of farm income. In part, this decline is due to reductions in government subsidy programs that have been forced by the financial problems of governments, as discussed in Chapter 12. Another reason for the decline in government support, however, has been that the prices of many farm products, especially wheat, strengthened during the 1990s, improving farm incomes. When farmers encountered difficult times again after 1998, government payments increased again, but not to the levels of a decade earlier.

Free trade has influenced Canadian agriculture considerably in recent years, by increasing both exports and imports of agricultural products sharply since 1990. For some farmers, especially those protected by marketing boards, freer trade meant increased competition. But free trade also brought export opportunities, not only for Canada's traditional exporters of wheat, oilseeds, beef, and pork, but also for niche producers selling value-added products in smaller segments of large export markets. Over the 1990–2001 period, Canada's trade surplus (of exports over imports) in agricultural and fish products grew from $4.6 billion to $10.5 billion. With world food demand forecasted to grow considerably in the new millennium, many observers saw a favourable outlook for many Canadian farmers.

FIGURE 15-10 Government Direct Payments to Farmers as a Percent of Net Cash Income, 1985–2001

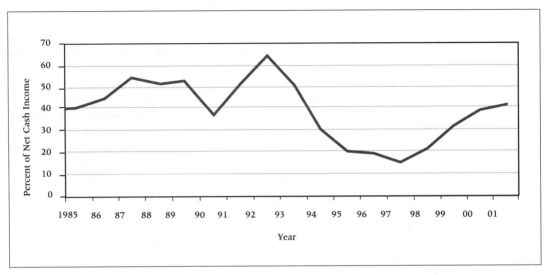

Source: Adapted from Statistics Canada, *Agriculture Economic Statistics*, Catalogue No. 21-603, 2001.

Agricultural Policy in Perspective

As we have seen, Canada has a variety of programs to support and stabilize farm prices and incomes, including price supports, acreage restrictions, deficiency payments, and supply management through marketing boards. As with all government programs, there are benefits and costs associated with agricultural programs.

Ultimately, of course, the cost of agricultural programs falls upon the public, through *higher food prices* and/or *taxes* to finance subsidies to farmers. On the other hand, there are various economic and social benefits associated with programs to support and stabilize farm incomes. Support of farmers ensures a more *healthy agricultural sector*, not only today, but well into the future, because producers are protected against adverse economic conditions beyond their control, and there are sufficient economic incentives to attract young, capable people into farming. Another argument on behalf of farm support programs is that they help to *preserve farmland*. By making farming a more economically attractive use of land, they reduce the incentive for farmers to sell their land for industrial or residential use, and thus help to preserve the amount of good agricultural land available to Canadians in the future. In these ways, it can be argued that agricultural support programs represent a trade-off, in which consumers pay higher food prices today in exchange for a more stable and healthy agricultural sector in the future.

> The 11 percent decrease in the number of farms between 1996 and 2001 was the fastest decrease since 1971.

Finally, assistance to farmers can be defended on grounds of *equity,* or fairness. Because farming is one of the most competitive sectors of the economy, farm incomes have tended to be lower than the incomes of other Canadians, many of whom belong to labour unions or professional associations, or are employed by large corporations or governments that have the means to pay higher incomes. Consequently, it can be argued that it is only fair that farmers have some protection against the harshness of a marketplace that is not only extremely competitive, but also quite unstable.

While support of farmers is widely accepted as a policy *objective,* there has been criticism of some of the support *methods* used in Canada. In particular, there are concerns about supply management and the operation of marketing boards, which restrict output and tend to foster inefficiency and high prices. With the trend toward freer international trade generating stronger international competition, Canada has been pushed in the direction of agricultural policies that do not restrict efficiency, supply, and imports, but rather promote efficiency.

According to many agricultural economists, the approach that is likely to achieve increased efficiency and output while still protecting farmers against periodic price and income declines would be some form of deficiency payments or crop insurance, as described earlier. While this approach stabilizes farm incomes to a significant degree (subsidized by the government if necessary), it does not reduce production or discourage the development of improved efficiency, as marketing boards do.

Chapter Summary

1. During the twentieth century, technological progress has greatly increased agricultural productivity, generating plentiful supplies of farm products despite agricultural employment declining to about 2 percent of the labour force. (L.O. 1)

2. Farm incomes have tended to be low, due to growing supply interacting with an inelastic demand, and unstable, due to fluctuating supply interacting with an inelastic demand. (L.O. 2)

3. One type of government program to support and stabilize farm incomes is the offer to purchase, under which the government establishes the price of the farm produce and purchases any unsold produce at that price; however, this program tends to result in crop surpluses. (L.O. 3)

4. Under acreage restrictions, the government either requires or pays farmers to reduce the amount of land under cultivation, so as to reduce the supply of produce and increase its price. (L.O. 4)

5. With a system of deficiency payments, supply is not restricted; rather, the price of the produce is directly subsidized by the government up to the target price level. (L.O. 5)

6. Marketing boards are government-sponsored organizations of farmers that increase farm incomes by restricting the supply of produce through production quotas for individual farmers and restrictions on imports. (L.O. 6)

7. Pressures for changes to Canada's marketing board system have come from consumer groups and Canadian food processors due to high prices, and from Canada's trading partners due to marketing boards' restrictions on imports. (L.O. 7)

Questions

1. For decades, the agricultural revolution has provided large amounts of labour to the manufacturing and service sectors of the economy, making large increases in their output possible. Now, however, with only about 2 percent of Canada's labour force employed on the farm, there is little scope for continuing this process. In the future, what will the manufacturing and service sectors have to do in order to keep their output increasing?

2. From the viewpoint of low-income families, which would be the more desirable approach to supporting and stabilizing farm incomes: marketing boards or deficiency payments?

3. As noted in this chapter, the production quotas assigned by marketing boards acquire market values, so that new or expanding producers must buy them. Why would quotas acquire prices in this way, and what would determine their price? How would freer imports of agricultural commodities affect the value of quotas?

4. Most industrialized nations tend to experience agricultural surpluses. Why don't they simply give their surplus food to Third World countries as part of their foreign-aid programs?

5. Have government support payments to farmers as a percent of net cash income (see Figure 15-10) increased or decreased in recent years? Why?

6. What have been the trends since 1998 in exports and imports of agricultural products? (Statistics can be found in Statistics Canada's *Canadian Economic Observer* [11-010-XPB] and at www.statcan.ca/english/Pgdb/gblec04.htm and www.statcan.ca/english/Pgdb/gblec05.htm.

7. In 1999–2001, there was considerable concern regarding low farm prices and incomes in Canada. Check Statistics Canada's *National Income and Expenditure Accounts* (Gross Domestic Product, Income Basis) to determine what changes occurred in "accrued net farm income" from 1998 to 1999 and since 1999. These statistics are available on Statistics Canada's website at www.statcan.ca or in Statistics Canada's monthly *Canadian Economic Observer* (11-010-XPB).

Chapter 16

Into the Future

Learning Objectives

After studying this chapter, you should be able to:

1. Define the term *resource wealth mentality* and explain how this term could be applied to Canada and to its government policies in the past.

2. Explain why the phenomenon known as "globalization" has presented Canada with major economic challenges and opportunities.

3. State three characteristics that help to make a nation's economy attractive to investment in high-technology industries in the globalized world economy.

4. Describe changes that Canada made to its policies regarding trade, government finances, and other matters in response to globalization, and explain how these changes were intended to help Canada to prosper in the globalized world economy.

For many years, Canada was an economically comfortable country, with high living standards and extensive government social programs for its people. In fact, Canada was consistently rated as one of the best countries in the world in which to live.

However, in the period from the late 1980s through the much of the 1990s, Canadians experienced considerable economic change and discomfort as Canada grappled with some major economic challenges. The most fundamental of these challenges was the changing international economic environment known as *globalization*. In addition, there were the problems of *government deficits* and *debt,* and the related problem of *high taxes*. Another basic problem was the very *slow growth of productivity* in the Canadian economy, which threatened both the standard of living of Canadians and the ability of Canadian industries to compete in the globalized world economy. How Canada addressed these issues would largely determine the economic prosperity of Canadians in the future.

Dealing with these challenges would involve fundamental changes in both government policies and in the Canadian economy itself. Before we consider these changes, however, we will review the background to this situation—the basic nature of the Canadian economy and government policy orientation that existed prior to the mid-1980s.

The Way We Were

Economically, Canada is a relatively small country, with an economy about one-tenth the size of the United States' economy and a population similar to that of the state of California. From Canada's very beginning as a nation, its economic prosperity was largely due to exports of natural resources and resource products, mainly to the United States. These exports, together with substantial inflows of foreign business investment (also mainly from the United States), provided Canadians not only with industry and jobs but also with the U.S. dollars with which they could purchase the imports that enriched their standard of living.

Canada used its prosperity to develop quite an extensive social welfare system, as was described in Chapter 12. Canadian governments established a broad range of social welfare programs for individuals and families (such as education and health care), an extensive support system for weaker and less efficient producers (including tariff protection for manufacturers, subsidies for farmers, and assistance of various sorts for many corporations in difficulty), and various forms of aid to economically weaker regions (including equalization payments, regional development grants, and subsidies to people and businesses in those regions).

"Traditionally, Canadians have lived in a relatively insulated environment brought about by paternalistic government policies, a history of market protection and the accumulated attitudes and experiences of both individuals and businesses.

This old economic order, as we call it, was a system where many prospered. However, because the old order generally provided insulation from external pressures and fostered limited internal pressures, many of the critical requirements for upgrading to more sophisticated and sustainable competitive advantages in Canadian industry have been missing or are only weakly present."

Professor Michael E. Porter, *Canada at the Crossroads: The Reality of a New Competitive Environment* (October 1991; a study prepared for the Business Council on National Issues and the Government of Canada).

resource wealth mentality The view that society's economic wealth is derived mainly from the sale of natural resources, as opposed to efficiency in the production of goods and services.

According to some critical observers, Canada had developed a **resource wealth mentality**—the view that wealth is not something that you *create* so much as something that *happens to you* through processing and selling resources that you are fortunate enough to own. With economic wealth so readily provided by resource exports and foreign investment, government policy in Canada tended to be less concerned with *creating wealth* than with promoting a *fair distribution of wealth*, by providing assistance to individuals, businesses, and regions that needed it.

In short, with high living standards supported by their exports of natural resources and by foreign investment, with tariffs to protect much of their manufacturing sector from import competition, and with government social welfare programs that sheltered them from competition and economic hardship, Canadians were able to enjoy a comfortable and secure economic prosperity.

Pressures for Change: Globalization and Competition

During the 1980s, a variety of factors combined to generate such a large increase in international trade, investment, and competition that this phenomenon would come to be known as *globalization*. The main source of globalization was freer trade, as nations lowered tariff barriers and markets were opened to international competition. Other important factors were improved computer, communications, and transportation technology that lowered the costs of doing business internationally and facilitated trade and investment on a global scale. With new technology, markets for many more goods and services became worldwide as designers, manufacturers, and retailers became able to communicate with each other more quickly and more effectively all around the world than was possible in the past within one country. And, with increased international competition came higher productivity and lower costs and prices.

Challenges and Opportunities

The new global economy with its increased competitiveness presented Canada with some major challenges. The most basic of these was the problem of Canada's lagging productivity growth, which was noted earlier. Much of Canada's manufacturing sector was not very efficient, having produced only for the small Canadian market and with tariff protection against foreign competition. Such industries were ill-prepared for the stronger international competition associated with globalization. And, despite the importance of trade to the Canadian economy, Canadian producers and governments were slow to adapt to this new, more competitive international environment. Rather than look outward to the opportunities presented by the global economy, Canada sought to maintain the "old order" described above, by protecting its less efficient producers against competition, with tariffs and government subsidies. Partly as a result of this protectionism, the efficiency, or productivity, of much of the Canadian economy failed to keep pace with improvements in other nations. As the 1980s progressed, Canada became less and less internationally competitive, especially in manufacturing.

But globalization brought tremendous opportunities as well as threats. For Canadian producers that *could* compete, there was the opportunity to break out of the small Canadian market and into much larger foreign markets. The Canada–U.S. Free Trade Agreement of 1989 alone gave Canadian firms secure access to a market *ten times* the size of the small Canadian market.

Coping with Change

In the new, globalized world economy, it was more important than ever for a nation to be efficient and competitive and to be an attractive location for business investment. Multinational corporations, including Canadian firms, search the world for the most economical locations for their activities. If a country can attract business investment and the jobs and production that this investment brings, that country will prosper economically. If it fails to attract investment, it will fall behind economically.

What makes a country an attractive location for business investment? Many people think that the answer is "cheap labour," but this is not usually the case. Low-wage labour is only important for labour-intensive manufacturing industries such as clothing and footwear. But in many industries, such low-wage, semiskilled labour has already been replaced to a great extent by technology.

To modern, high-technology industries, the key attraction is not cheap labour, but rather *skilled people* with *specialized knowledge*. In addition, a nation needs to have excellent *transportation and communication links* to the rest of the world, in order to function effectively as part of the new world economy.

From this perspective, a nation's key strategic assets economically are no longer its cheap labour or its natural resources, but rather the *quality of its labour force* and its transportation/communications *infrastructure*—the knowledge and skills of its people, and the support systems for linking the productive use of those skills into the global economy so that they can access markets and partners around the world. In addition, a nation's taxation system must be attractive to employers, investors, and skilled workers.

If a country has these qualities, it will tend to attract business investment and prosper economically. Its productivity will be high, the standard of living of its people will be high, and its industries will be internationally competitive. Its skilled work force will earn high incomes and its government will have a strong tax base, which can be used to invest further in better schools, research, and transportation and communications systems. These features will attract more investment, and the cycle of prosperity can be continued. For an economically small nation such as Canada, globalization offers the additional opportunity of increasing its exports into larger foreign markets, if its producers are able to compete.

For nations that lack a skilled work force and communications and transportation infrastructure, the opposite kind of cycle can take place. Unable to attract capital with their labour forces' skills and their infrastructure, such nations would be forced to resort to low wages and low taxes as inducements for businesses to invest there, and would be able to compete only in labour-intensive, low-wage industries.

Into the Future

Since the mid-1980s, there has been a gradual but persistent and significant shift in the emphasis of government policy in Canada, a key purpose of which has been to adapt to the globalized world economy. Less emphasis was placed on government support for individuals and industries, and increased emphasis was being placed on market forces, private enterprise, entrepreneurship and incentives for work, investment, productivity, and the creation of wealth. In short, the policy emphasis shifted from the *redistribution* of wealth toward the *creation* of wealth.

In this context, the 1989 Free Trade Agreement with the United States represented a landmark decision for Canada, by signalling Canada's intention to participate more fully in the increasingly globalized markets of the world. As such, it was the most visible part of a basic shift in Canadian policy toward an emphasis on productivity, competitiveness, and an outward-looking internationalism rather than on more inward-looking nationalistic policies that sheltered Canadian industries from international competition. The Free Trade Agreement was regarded not as an end in itself, but rather as the first step toward Canada's becoming productive and competitive on a global scale. In 1994, another step was taken as the North American Free Trade Agreement added Mexico to the North American free trade market.

Another major policy change occurred after 1993, when Canadian governments began to seriously address the problem of their budget deficits through reductions in government spending. And as government deficits came down, the confidence of lenders in Canada recovered. This allowed interest rates to fall to their lowest levels in many years, and business confidence in the future improved, laying the groundwork for better economic performance. The other side of these deficit-reduction policies was, of course, that cuts in government spending forced some basic and painful changes to Canada's social welfare programs, as discussed in Chapter 12.

And after the federal government's budget deficits were turned into surpluses, the government introduced a series of cuts to personal and business income taxes that totalled about $100 billion over the 2001–05 period.

In addition to these major initiatives of the Free Trade Agreement, deficit reduction, and tax cuts, a variety of smaller policy changes occurred. These policy changes had the same objective: to improve the efficiency—and with it the competitiveness—of the Canadian economy.

One such policy thrust was to *increase competition* in the Canadian economy, so as to increase efficiency. The first step in this direction had been taken in 1986 with the new Competition Act. As we saw in Chapter 9, the new law made it more difficult for businesses to reduce competition through tactics such as mergers with competitors and agreements to avoid price competition, or price-fixing. However, the new law specifically *allowed* mergers that would increase the efficiency and international competitiveness of the firms involved. The free trade agreements also exposed Canadian industries to increased foreign competition, forcing them to become more efficient.

Another policy change aimed at increasing competition was the **deregulation** of some industries. Over the years, Canada had accumulated a large body of government regulations of industries, many of which controlled prices and production and/or restricted the entry of new competitors into industries. Many of these regulations had the unintended effect of reducing competition and efficiency in the regulated industries. To improve productivity performance, the government deregulated some industries, such as airlines, financial services, and communications (most notably, long-distance telephone service).

deregulation Policies to reduce the extent of regulation of business by government, with the intention of promoting efficiency through increased competition.

Another change was *reductions in government subsidies* to business, which forced businesses to improve efficiency rather than rely on government subsidies. In addition, there was the *privatization*, or sale to private interests, of several Crown corporations (including Air Canada and Canadian National), forcing them to operate more efficiently and without the subsidies that they had received when owned by the government. Changes were made to the *social welfare system*, especially Employment Insurance; these included reductions in benefits, restrictions on frequent claimants, and a shift in the nature of EI toward retraining of the unemployed rather than simply supporting their incomes.

Government policy-makers also increasingly emphasized the *small business* sector of the economy, which had provided a high proportion of the new jobs created in the recent past and was expected to play a large role in the future. Unlike resource and heavy manufacturing industries, the emerging high-tech and service industries are not dominated by giant corporations; in fact, small size, innovation, and flexibility are often seen as advantages in these fields.

Taken together, these new policies represented a significant shift in Canadian economic policy. As noted earlier, government policies had traditionally been directed largely toward *redistributing economic wealth*, through an extensive social welfare system. But to improve productivity and competitiveness, the new Canadian policies emphasized the *creation of wealth*. This required incentives for enterprise, entrepreneurship, and investment, as well as increased emphasis on competition and efficiency.

In a broad strategic sense, the new direction of government policy was to shift the emphasis in the Canadian economy from *security and consumption* towards *efficiency and investment*—or from benefits that exist mainly in the present to longer-term gains.

Canadians want a great deal from their economic system. They want prosperity for themselves in the form of high levels of private personal consumption, high levels of government services (including a strong social welfare system, health care, and education), economic security, and protection of the environment. To provide of all these, the Canadian economy must be prosperous and productive. Only by becoming more productive, more efficient, and more competitive will Canadians find it possible to achieve all their economic and social goals.

Chapter Summary

1. Traditionally, Canada relied heavily upon natural resource exports to create much of its economic wealth, while government policies aimed more at redistributing income and providing social welfare programs than at promoting productivity, the creation of wealth, and competitiveness. (L.O. 1)

2. The increasing globalization of the world economy presented Canada with major economic challenges, the main one being the need to become more efficient and internationally competitive than in the past. Globalization also offered opportunities, as large markets outside of Canada opened up. (L.O. 2)

3. In the globalized world economy, a knowledgeable and skilled labour force and excellent transportation and communication links to the rest of the world are important in attracting business investment and the jobs and economic wealth such investment brings. (L.O. 3)

4. After the mid-1980s, in an attempt to improve the nation's productivity and competitiveness, Canadian government policy shifted away from redistribution of wealth and protection of industries from foreign competition, and more toward wealth creation and economic internationalism. (L.O. 4)

5. Specific government policies in pursuit of these objectives included:

    (a) the free trade agreements with the United States and Mexico,

    (b) reductions in government budget deficits, mainly through reductions in spending,

    (c) reductions in personal and business income taxes, and

    (d) various other policies to improve productivity and economic performance, including new competition legislation, deregulation of some industries, reduction of government subsidies to business, privatization of some Crown corporations, changes to the Employment Insurance system, encouragement of small business, and increased emphasis on investment in human resources. (L.O. 4)

Questions

1. As 2000 commenced, many forecasters were predicting that over the next few years, Canada would turn in one of the strongest economic performances of any major industrialized nation. In what ways have these expectations been met? In what ways have they not been met, and what might explain any failures to meet them?

2. Suppose that Canada had *not* made the policy changes described in this chapter. What do you think would have been the economic consequences for Canada?

3. Looking back at the major changes that were made, and looking ahead to the future, do you see these changes as bringing to Canadians the economic gains that they were intended to bring?

4. In the view of economists, the game (industry) of professional hockey provides a good example of how globalization, or the internationalization of markets, presents Canadians with both challenges and opportunities. Explain why this is the case, taking into account the perspectives of both players and teams.

5. How does the impending retirement of the baby boomers present another major economic challenge to the standard of living of Canadians? Explain how stronger productivity growth would help Canada to deal with this challenge.

APPENDIX
Answers to Boxed Questions

Chapter 1: What Is Economics?

YOU DECIDE: The Scarcity Problem on a Personal Level

1. As the situation is described, most people would say "no" to this question, because the opportunity cost is too high. Because you have borrowed a total of $400 at the high interest rates that are charged on credit cards, the repayments will cut into your future spending on consumer goods and services by considerably more than $400. These high interest rates add so much to the cost of buying things on credit cards that they should make people more careful when "paying with plastic." But for many people, the opposite happens—buying on credit is so easy that they do so without considering how costly it is. Buying on credit is simply paying for things out of your future income, and paying the lender for the use of the money in the meantime. This does not mean that one should never buy on a credit card, just that, before doing so, one should consider whether getting the item sooner is worth paying so much extra for it. Finally, if you conclude that getting the item right away is important to you, are there other ways to borrow the money and at a lower rate of interest?

2. Most personal finance advisers suggest paying the outstanding balance on credit cards on time each month, to avoid interest charges. Then the credit card becomes a convenience rather than a burden. But this requires that you restrain your credit-card spending each month to the amount that you can afford to repay. If this sort of self-discipline is not your style, the safest type of card to carry is a debit card that allows a vendor to take the money directly from your account.

YOU DECIDE: "There's No Such Thing as a Free Lunch"

1. While *you* do not have to pay for the sample, *someone, somewhere*, is paying the cost of that good or service. Maybe the cost falls upon the company that provides the sample (and its profits and therefore its shareholders), or maybe the company passes the cost on to buyers of the item through higher prices. The "bottom line" here is that economic resources were used to produce the item, and those resources cost someone, if not you.

2. Not really—the supply of air is so great that your use of the air does not prevent anyone else from using it. By contrast, your eating of a hamburger *does* prevent someone else from eating it. The only exceptions would be situations in which air was scarce, such as for divers or astronauts. In those cases, air would have a cost and a market value.

3. Not quite—in order for air to be "breathable," it must be relatively *clean*. As a society, we all pay for the air-pollution control equipment and processes that help keep our air clean, mostly through higher prices for the products we buy, which include the cost of the pollution controls. What we do *not* pay is a "user fee" for the air we use, which, like the "free" sample, obscures the fact that there *are* costs for what we are enjoying.

Chapter 2: Canada's Economic System

YOU DECIDE: The Economic Organization of a Prisoner of War Camp

1. Individual people had more of some commodities than they wanted and less of others that they wanted; this situation made them ready to trade, or to buy and sell.

2. (a) For a market to function, buyers and sellers must be able to communicate with each other. The bulletin boards in each bungalow helped greatly by allowing people not only to post offers to buy and sell various commodities but also to see the most recent market prices for those commodities.

    (b) If people were unable to move from one bungalow to another, prices of commodities would vary from place to place, as they do in localized markets. Conversely, if people could go to other bungalows, they could often obtain better prices as buyers or sellers. The result would be that the price of each commodity would tend to level out across the camp—the market would function better.

3. Barter was too inconvenient. A barter transaction requires that someone who has surplus sugar and wants chocolate has to find someone else who has extra chocolate and wants sugar. Cigarettes were suitable as a currency because they were standard in size/value (more or less), of convenient size, and reasonably durable. All of these qualities helped to make them acceptable as "money."

4. An influx of cigarette "money" from the Red Cross every three months would sharply increase the volume of money in circulation, driving prices up (or, if you will, the value of the more plentiful cigarette money down). As the camp's stock of cigarettes was used up, the amount of "money" in circulation fell and prices would decrease.

5. The main factor affecting the prices of individual goods relative to the prices of other goods was changes in the supply of each good; for instance, the arrival of larger shipments of oatmeal drove its price downward. Changes in demand also affected relative prices: in hot weather, the price of soap rose relative to the price of cocoa.

Chapter 3: Business Organization in Canada

YOU DECIDE: Update to the Saga of Dan's Doughnut Dens

1. *Sole proprietorship:* This is easy to start, and provides the owner–manager with strong incentives as well as independence. On the other hand,

sole proprietorships tend to suffer from a lack of management expertise since few individuals are strong in all aspects of management; partly for this reason, the workload of the owner–manager is often very heavy. If the business earns a high income, taxes on this income will be high since it will be taxed as the personal income of the owner. If, on the other hand, the business is unsuccessful, the personal liability of the owner can place his or her personal assets at risk.

Partnership: The partnership has advantages and disadvantages similar to the sole proprietorship's, except that a partnership can add management talent and capital. However, there is the disadvantage of potential conflict between the partners. In the event that the business fails, general partners have unlimited liability.

Corporation: Limited liability is a major advantage in two ways. First, the owners' (shareholders') personal assets are not at risk, but more importantly, this makes it much easier for a corporation to raise capital by selling shares to the public. Beyond a certain level of profits, tax rates on corporations are lower than on the personal income(s) of the owner(s). However, the process of incorporating a business is costly, and a possible risk (that Dan experienced) of selling shares is that control of the corporation may be lost.

2. 45.0% + 5.1% = 50.1% = control of the corporation by Dan and Ermyntrude.

3. First, Dan should determine his *objective(s)*—what does he want to accomplish through this business? For instance, does he want to become the biggest doughnut-shop operator in the city or the country (or in the world), or would he be happy to be a small independent player in this market? From this starting point, logical *strategies* can be developed for achieving his objective(s). Throughout the story, Dan seemed to let himself be carried along by events or be reacting to situations, rather than proactively pursuing strategies in order to reach objectives.

4. Mainly because larger businesses generally need to raise considerable amounts of capital, and the corporate form of organization is best-suited to this task due to its ability to issue shares to the public.

IN THE NEWS: Self-Employment in Canada

1. A key factor in the growth of self-employment (and small business generally) has been the growth in the *service sector* of the economy. A modern economy is capable of producing large volumes of *goods* with relatively few workers by using high-technology production methods. The high output per worker generated by this technology also increases people's standard of living, and consumers with higher living standards tend to buy more services, such as travel, entertainment, restaurants, and so on. And while the production of *goods* is often best-suited to large mass-production facilities (big business), *services* are generally

most effectively delivered by smaller enterprises that are convenient to the consumer. For instance, your car may have been built in a mass-production plant in Kansas City, but you get it repaired and washed by small business operators near your home.

Much of the growth of self-employment has been associated with the growth of the service sector as described above. In addition, the downsizing of many Canadian corporations and government agencies during the mid-1990s forced many people into self-employment. Also, some employers laid off employees and then reengaged them as self-employed "contractors," which saved the employers from having to pay payroll taxes and allowed the employees-turned-contractors to deduct work-related expenses from their incomes for tax purposes.

2. The rapid growth of employment opportunities in the service sector coincided with greater social and economic self-sufficiency among women, a result of their increased levels of education and career expectations. Growing numbers of women entrepreneurs have success-fully established themselves in the expanding service sector, because it is so well-suited to small businesses and self-employment.

3. There is a general expectation that these trends will continue. The driving forces behind these trends—technological advances and rising demand for services—seem likely to continue.

YOU DECIDE: A Competitive Market for Education?

1. The pressure of competition could push schools to improve the quality of the education they offer in order to attract students and "sales income," much as many private schools do.

2. There might be a "quality control" problem. Some schools might offer education that *looks* attractive but is in fact inferior in order to attract business.

3. The main thing would be *consumer knowledge*—the better-informed parents are about the educational "product" being offered, the more likely they are to make good choices, thus placing more pressure on schools to provide high-quality education.

Chapter 5: The Supply Side of Markets

IN THE NEWS: Price and Supply

1. In both cases, price changes are leading producers to increase or decrease production in desirable ways. Whether the low price is due to excess supply or low demand, the message from the market to produc-ers (through lower prices) is that more of that product is not needed or wanted at this time. And whether the higher price is due to increased demand or low supply, the market is telling producers (through higher prices) to produce more of it.

Chapter 6: The Dynamics of Competitive Markets

IN THE NEWS: The Market for World Series Tickets

1. The most basic reason is the *increase in demand* for playoff tickets. But a major contributing factor is that the supply of tickets is both *limited* (a stadium has only so many seats) and *inelastic* (even if the price skyrockets, there will still only be relatively few seats available for sale). The following graph illustrates such a market, and the effect that an increase in demand has on it.

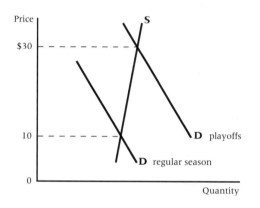

2. If the clubs did not raise prices, those who bought the tickets from the clubs at low prices would be in a position to take advantage of the high demand by reselling them at very high prices. The average price of a ticket would still be high, but the revenues from this would flow to the people who resold the tickets, rather than to the clubs and the players.

3. Practically nothing. As the answer to the previous question indicates, the increase in demand ensures that the price will rise; the only question is who will receive the economic gains from this price increase.

IN THE NEWS: Commercials During the Super Bowl

1. Advertisers buy *exposure to an audience* who will see their commercials. The Super Bowl draws a massive audience of over 130 million people, which makes advertisers willing to pay extremely high rates to advertise on the show; that is, it increases the demand for advertising time greatly.

2. On the supply side, the supply of commercial time is obviously both *low* (there are only so many minutes of commercial time during a football game) and extremely *inelastic* (the amount of commercial time cannot be increased even if the price rises to very high levels).

IN THE NEWS: The Monday Effect

1. The best theory concerning the "Monday (morning) effect" is that over a weekend, shareholders *have more time to worry* about their investments and make decisions to sell as soon as they can—on Monday morning.

2. This theory is supported by the fact that market declines on Fridays often triggered further declines on Monday mornings. Most of the selling on Monday mornings was done by small shareholders, who had grown more worried about Friday declines over the weekend.

3. By Monday afternoon, more sophisticated traders were probably picking up the bargains created by this selling. Their buying of shares would cause prices to edge upward again.

YOU DECIDE: Stock Market Speculation

1. The "bubble" will last as long as the buying of the stock is strong enough to keep pushing the price up. This, in turn, depends on whether prospective buyers believe that the stock will *continue* to rise in value. When the price becomes so high that people view the stock as overpriced and begin to doubt that it will continue to rise, two things are likely to happen. First, fewer people buy the stock, and second, more holders of the stock decide that this is the time to sell it. At this point, the price of the stock will "lose momentum"—it will rise less rapidly, or maybe not at all.

2. This loss of momentum will probably be interpreted by many people as a sign that the stock is about to fall in value. At this point, many people will sell it and few, if any, will be willing to buy it. It is possible in these circumstances for a stock to go into a "free fall" and plunge in value. This would continue until its price was so low that it was perceived by at least some people as more likely to go back up than to continue falling. These "bargain hunters" will then buy the stock, which will support its price and end its decline.

Chapter 7: Market Structures

IN THE NEWS: Now *That's* a Price War

1. The basic factor in this situation is that the gas station industry is very competitive—there are many dealers selling products that are essentially the same, in a marketplace in which sellers post their prices on huge signs everywhere. If, for some reason, one station starts cutting prices, others will have to respond in kind. In this case, a new station was using price reductions as a promotional tactic and the established stations refused to let it succeed. In other cases, oil companies may be trying to move surplus inventory of unsold gasoline by discounting it, often to independent dealers who cut prices, starting a price war with the branded stations.

2. As dealers' losses mount, the pressure on them to declare a truce increases. Also, when the oil companies end the shipments of discounted gasoline, the price war can end abruptly.

3. You would have to reach some sort of understanding with the owners of the other two stations; otherwise, the three of you would engage in price wars that would eventually drive two of you out of business. Many industries go through such a "maturing" process, with vigorous competition among many competitors in the earlier stages of their development giving way to a more "orderly" approach to pricing later when there are fewer competitors.

IN THE NEWS: OPEC

1. For such a small reduction in supply to cause such a large increase in price, demand must be very *inelastic*. This behaviour is what one would expect of the demand for oil, at least in the short run. Buyers of gasoline and fuel oil are not in a position to quickly change the equipment (vehicles and furnaces) in which they use petroleum products, so demand would be inelastic.

2. The key to achieving higher prices is to restrict the production of oil. But OPEC only controls 40 percent of world crude-oil production. If the higher prices that OPEC was seeking were to lead non-OPEC producers to increase their production, OPEC's price objective would not be achieved. In addition, the objective of a higher price would necessarily involve lower production quotas for each member of OPEC. But members of OPEC have often been known to cheat on their production quotas. If some OPEC members were to pump oil in excess of their quotas, the world supply of oil would be higher than OPEC had planned—and the price would be below OPEC's target.

YOU DECIDE: The International Diamond Monopoly

1. There is a real possibility that more diamonds will be found than can be absorbed by the market at current prices. Furthermore, the high prices of diamonds create an incentive to find more of them. If De Beers were to be unable to buy all such newly found diamonds, they might be sold on the open market, driving prices downward.

2. If the monopoly is charging high prices, its high profits will attract competitors. These could take the form of new firms producing the same product or substitutes.

Chapter 9: Government Policy Toward Business

IN THE NEWS: The Superior Propane Case

1. The general objective of the competition legislation is to protect consumers against the market power of producers/sellers. However, the "efficiency exception" introduced a need to estimate the cost of a merger to consumers and to weigh this cost against an estimate of the

cost savings (efficiency gains) due to the merger. The Tribunal decided that while this merger would increase the cost of propane to consumers by $40.5 million, only $2.6 million of it would fall on *low-income* consumers and should be considered socially undesirable. And since the efficiency gains of the merger exceeded $2.6 million, the Tribunal decided that the merger should be allowed.

2. The Tribunal's decision could make it much easier for mergers to proceed, since even if a merger would result in sharply higher prices for all consumers, only the cost to low-income consumers would be considered. Then the federal government would have to decide whether or not to amend the Competition Act in order to provide clearer direction as to whether only the costs to low-income consumers should be taken into account.

YOU DECIDE: Laissez-Faire Versus Government Regulation in Canada

1. Both regulation and competition can be beneficial in different ways. Regulation can protect the public against substandard or even dangerous products or services. However, if regulation becomes a *barrier to entry* into the industry, it can also raise prices. At this point, it can be argued that the public would benefit from more competition and less regulation, or some "deregulation" of the industry.

2. The government would not have to intervene in order to protect the public against the market power of producers; however, in such a competitive economy, there would still be other problems that would require some government intervention. For instance, producers in such a competitive environment might be inclined to treat employees unfairly, or to reduce product quality in order to cut costs.

Chapter 10: Labour Markets and Labour Unions

YOU DECIDE: Let's Play Arbitrator

1. You are neutral, and because of this neutrality, both sides accept you as arbitrator.

2. You are still an "outsider"—you have not actually *lived with* the problems that you are trying to resolve.

3. No. You will only know *what you have been told* by two people who are probably not interested in the facts so much as in getting a decision from you that suits them.

4. There is a real risk that this person will feel no commitment to making your decision work. It is too easy for this person to rationalize that the decision was made by someone else.

Chapter 11: Employment and Incomes in the Canadian Economy

IN THE NEWS: Labour Force Facts

1. In large part, the growth of part-time employment is the result of the growth of the *service sector* of the economy. While the production of goods lends itself to full-time work such as in manufacturing plants, services such as retail trade, restaurants, and entertainment often tend to be delivered at peak periods, making part-time employment particularly well-suited to these industries.

    However, financial pressures on employers also seem to be a factor in decisions between hiring full-time and part-time employees. During the economic boom of the second half of the 1980s, part-time employment *decreased* from 17.0 percent of all jobs to 16.6 percent. During the recession of the early 1990s, part-time employment increased to 19.1 percent by 1993, but in the boom of the late 1990s, it *fell again*, to 18.1 percent. So at least in some cases, employers seem to prefer full-time workers, but will hire more part-timers when pressed financially.

2. The Statistics Canada's web page also contains some interesting breakdowns of part-time employment by age and sex.

IN THE NEWS: Is Education in Canada a Good Value?

These questions are meant to be used for class discussion. To organize your thoughts concerning the answers to these questions, ask yourself if you are concerned about your own future, and what the school system could do to ease your concerns.

IN THE NEWS: The Skills Gap

1. While lacking conclusive data, most observers believe that the skills gap is in fact widening. The data in Table 11-2 are consistent with this view, in that the income share of the lowest three groups has decreased, while the share of the top two groups has increased. However, the incomes of the top two groups could have been pushed up by factors unrelated to employment income—for instance, the top two groups might have enjoyed unusual gains in the stock market.

2. Education and training could be improved; however, this would mainly serve to increase competition for highly skilled jobs. In such a competition, there would still be winners and losers. Beyond that, there are two basic approaches that governments could take to deal with the "skills gap." One would be to try to increase the incomes of the less skilled, through higher minimum wage laws. As we saw in Chapter 10, this would benefit some less-skilled workers, but at the expense of reduced employment for such workers as a group. The other approach would be to reduce income taxes on lower-income workers and provide them with more tax credits, shifting more of the tax burden onto the higher-income people.

Chapter 12: The Government Sector

YOU DECIDE: **The Marginal Tax Rate and the Economic Incentive to Work**

1.   No. She is merely responding logically to the incentives presented to her by the system. If Joan faced a marginal tax rate of 80 percent and decided not to teach night school because of it, her middle-class friends would say that she was behaving rationally and that the tax system was wrong.

2.   Sandy needs to be allowed to keep a higher proportion of any income that she manages to earn. In other words, her welfare benefits should not be reduced so rapidly when she earns money that her incentive to work is destroyed.

IN THE NEWS: **Working While on Employment Insurance**

1.   100 percent.

Chapter 13: The Politics of Economics

IN THE NEWS: **The Extremes**

1.   This would be a "survival of the fittest" society, in which there would be more wealthy people, but private charity would be the main source of assistance for the needy. There would be a real risk of serious social problems.

2.   In such a society, government would provide extensive benefits for people, and would tax higher-income people and businesses so heavily to pay for these benefits that many would leave the country, eventually creating a serious financial crisis.

Chapter 14: Environmental Economics

YOU DECIDE: **A Trade-Off**

1.   The economic pressure on you to buy the cheaper paper would probably be irresistible. If you didn't buy it, your replacement would.

2.   The government would either have to make Killfish's paper more costly or Purewater's cheaper. The most likely way in which this would happen is that pollution-control regulations could force Killfish to spend money on the environment in order to "internalize" the costs of its pollution, thus adding to its product costs and prices.

IN THE NEWS: **Government Versus the Environment**

1.   Politics. Such measures secure the political support of people associated with these industries. As long as the environmental side effects go unnoticed or affect relatively few voters, the practices will continue.

2. A change in politics. If public concern over the environment raises the possibility that more votes will be lost than gained by such practices, the government will probably change the laws.

IN THE NEWS: A Carbon Tax?

1. The demand for gasoline would have to be reasonably *elastic*, so that the higher prices caused by the taxes would lead to significantly lower consumption of gasoline.

2. In the short run, the demand for gasoline would be inelastic—people would not suddenly sell their SUVs and buy more fuel-efficient vehicles. In the longer run, more adjustments are possible—in the 1970s and 1980s, people did in fact switch to more fuel-efficient vehicles following the very large increases in gasoline prices. (On the other hand, in the 1970s, governments also enacted laws that required that manufacturers produce cars that met higher fuel-efficiency standards—and SUVs were exempt from those laws in 2003.) It is also likely that industrial users of gasoline would be more price-sensitive than consumers.

3. There are three answers to this question—politics, politics, and politics. Consumers love cheap gasoline, and are very hostile to taxes that increase the price of their gas. Politicians will never forget that, in the early 1980s, the short-lived Progressive Conservative government of Joe Clark was defeated after it proposed an 18-cent-per-litre tax on gasoline that would have benefited both federal finances and the environment.

4. Taxes are more than merely sources of revenue for governments. Taxes are also *incentives* that can change the behaviour of people. Higher taxes on gasoline could encourage energy conservation, while lower taxes on personal and business income would encourage the work effort and business investment that increase productivity.

GLOSSARY

acreage restrictions   A crop supply management program that either forces farmers to reduce their acreage under cultivation, or gives them financial incentives to do so.

administered prices   A term used to describe prices that have been fixed by sellers. See *price-fixing*.

arbitration The resolution of union–management disputes by the decision of a third party; required by law for grievances that the union and employer cannot resolve by themselves; used to settle disputes over the terms of new collective agreements in cases where strikes of essential employees are prohibited.

board of directors A group of people elected by the shareholders of a corporation to provide direction to the management of the corporation.

budget deficit   An excess of government spending over government revenues.

capital equipment   The tools, equipment, machinery, and factories used to increase production per person per hour and thus living standards.

cartel   A formal agreement among producers to coordinate their price and output decisions for the purpose of earning monopoly profits.

coefficient of elasticity   The percentage change in quantity demanded that results from a 1-percent change in price.

collective agreement A contract agreed upon by an employer and labour union, specifying the terms and conditions of employment of the employees for a specified period of time.

collective bargaining   The process through which employers and unions negotiate a new collective agreement.

command system An economic system in which economic decisions are made mainly by the government in a centralized manner.

competitive industry   An industry that consists of many small firms and is easily entered by new competitors.

compulsory conciliation   A procedure, required by law before a strike is legal, in which a government-appointed officer (conciliator) attempts to help a union and employer to reach an agreement on the terms of a new collective agreement.

concentrated industry An industry that is dominated by a few large firms and is not easily entered by new competitors.

consumption taxes   Taxes levied when consumers buy goods and services; for example, sales taxes.

corporation   A business firm that is a separate legal entity from its owners, or shareholders, each of whose liability is limited to the amount of his or her investment in the firm.

Crown corporations Corporations owned by a government and that are ultimately responsible, through a cabinet minister, to that government.

deficiency payments A program for supporting farm incomes under which the government guarantees farmers a target price for a crop by subsidizing all sales of that crop that fall short of the target price.

demand The entire relationship between the various possible prices of a product or service and the quantity demanded at each price, expressed through either a schedule or a graph.

deregulation Policies to reduce the extent of regulation of business by government, with the intention of promoting efficiency through increased competition.

derived demand The demand for a factor of production, which is generated by (derived from) the demand for the good or service that it is used to produce.

ebusinesses Businesses using processes and activities based on electronic information and data exchanges via the internet and the World Wide Web.

economics The study of the decisions a society makes concerning the production of goods and services and the division of these among its people.

economies of scale Lower production costs per unit made possible by higher volumes of production that permit the achievement of increased efficiencies.

effectiveness A measure of how well an economy performs in terms of producing goods and services that are needed and wanted.

efficiency A measure of how well an economy performs in terms of producing high volumes of goods and services at a low cost per item.

elastic demand The term used to describe demand if a price increase causes a reduction in total sales revenue.

elastic supply A situation in which the quantity supplied increases readily when the price rises.

equal pay for work of equal value The concept that the values of different jobs may be measured against each other using a point system that incorporates a variety of criteria, including skill levels, effort, degree of responsibility, and working conditions.

equilibrium price A price determined in the marketplace by the interaction of supply and demand.

equilibrium quantity The quantity sold (bought) at the equilibrium price.

externality An incidental cost, or side effect, inflicted on others by the production or consumption of a product. Also known as *spillover effect*.

fixed costs Production costs that remain constant, regardless of the level of output (for example, rent).

general partners Partners who take an active part in the management of the business and who have unlimited personal liability for its debts.

globalization The growing internationalization of business, trade, and finance that has characterized the period since the early 1980s.

grievance An alleged violation of a collective agreement by an employer.

Gross Domestic Product (GDP) A measure of the total value of goods and services produced and incomes earned in a country in one year.

inelastic demand The term used to describe demand if a price increase causes an increase in total sales revenue.

inelastic supply A situation in which quantity supplied does not increase readily when the price rises.

industrial concentration The degree to which an industry is dominated by a few firms.

individual bargaining The process through which workers deal as individuals with employers in negotiating their terms and conditions of employment.

inputs Economic resources, such as labour, capital equipment, and natural resources, that are used to produce goods and services.

labour The largest single productive input available to any economy, labour includes all of the productive talents of the people of a society, mental as well as physical.

laissez-faire The doctrine or philosophy that from the viewpoint of the public interest, it is neither necessary nor beneficial for governments to intervene in the operation of the economy.

land Short form for all the natural resources available to a society's economy as economic inputs.

Law of Diminishing Returns A physical law stating that, if additional units of one productive input (such as labour) are combined with a fixed quantity of another productive input (such as capital), the average product per unit of the variable input (labour) will increase at first and then decrease.

limited partner A partner who invests in a business but takes no active part in the management of it, and whose liability is limited to the amount invested.

long run The period of time after which the quantities of all inputs can be changed.

Low-Income Cut-Offs Income levels (as determined by Statistics Canada) below which families or individuals spend 56.2 percent or more of their income on food, clothing, and shelter. The 56.2 percent is 20 percentage points higher than the national average of 36.2 percent.

marginal cost per unit The addition to total costs resulting from the production of one more additional unit of output.

marginal productivity (per worker) The increase in production resulting from the hiring of one additional worker.

marginal revenue per unit The addition to total revenue resulting from the sale of one additional unit of output.

marginal tax rate The percentage of any additional income that is earned that goes to taxes.

"market basket measure" Poverty lines based on the cost of a "basket" of goods and services that a family requires in order to live above the poverty line.

market power The ability to raise one's prices; usually associated with a dominant or monopolistic position in the market.

market structure Term used to describe the organization and nature of a market or an industry, particularly whether it is competitive or concentrated in nature.

market system An economic system in which economic decisions are made mainly by consumers and privately owned producers, in a decentralized manner.

marketing boards Government-sponsored organizations of farmers that support farm incomes by restricting the supply of produce, usually through a system of quotas on individual farmers.

minimum wage A legal minimum wage rate set by law.

monopolistic competition A term describing industries that consist of many small firms, where entry to the industry by new firms is easy, and where the products or services of individual firms, while basically similar, are differentiated from each other to a degree.

monopoly A situation in which there is only one seller of a particular good or service.

National Council of Welfare A citizens' advisory body to the Minister of Human Resources Development Canada on matters of concern to low-income Canadians.

natural monopoly An industry, such as public utilities, that by its nature lends itself to a monopolistic form of organization.

non-price competition Competition between sellers based not on price but rather on factors such as product differentiation and advertising.

offer-to-purchase A farm-income support program under which the government establishes the price of the farm produce and undertakes to purchase any unsold produce at that price.

oligopoly A situation in which four or fewer firms account for at least half of the sales of an industry.

opportunity cost The concept that the real economic cost of producing something is the forgone opportunity to produce something else that could have been produced with the same inputs.

output The goods and services produced by a society using its productive inputs.

partnership A business firm owned by two or more persons, with each person bearing full legal liability for the firm's debts.

payroll taxes Taxes paid by employers based on the number of their employees or the amount of their payroll.

perfect competition A term describing industries that consist of a large number of small firms, where entry to the industry by new firms is easy, and where all firms in the industry sell identical products.

perfectly elastic demand A situation in which any price increase above the market price will cause a firm's sales to fall to zero; represented by a horizontal demand curve.

poverty lines Income levels below which families or individuals are considered to be poor.

poverty rate The percentage of any given group that has an income below the poverty line.

price control (ceiling) A legal limit on a price or on increases in a price, which holds the price below its equilibrium level.

price-fixing Agreements among oligopolists to raise their prices above levels that would prevail in a competitive situation.

price leadership A technique of price-fixing in which one firm (the price leader) sets its price and the rest of the firms in the industry follow suit.

price-maker Term used to describe the position of the dominant firm(s) in a concentrated industry, which can influence the price of the product.

price-taker Term used to describe the position of the individual small firm in a competitive industry, which is unable to influence the price of its product and is forced to accept (take) whatever price is determined in the market.

price support (floor) An artificially high price, held above the equilibrium level by the government.

private corporation A private corporation has fewer than 50 shareholders.

private (internal) costs Production costs, such as labour and materials, that are paid by producers and ultimately included in the price paid by the consumer.

privatize The process of selling government enterprises (usually Crown corporations) to private interests.

product differentiation Attempts by individual firms to distinguish their products or services from those of their competitors.

production-possibilities curve A curve that shows the economy's potential output, assuming that economic inputs are fully employed and efficiently utilized.

productivity Output per worker per hour; a measure of efficiency.

profits Those funds left from a business's sales revenues after all expenses have been paid; such funds are therefore available (after taxes have been paid) for dividends to shareholders and reinvestment in the business.

progressive taxes   Taxes that take a higher percentage of high incomes than of low incomes.

proxies   Legal instruments that allow a shareholder's right to vote at shareholders' meetings to be delegated to another person, either with or without specific instructions as to how that vote will be exercised.

public corporation   A public corporation has 50 or more shareholders.

recessions   Situations in which the economy is producing considerably less than its potential output, and unemployment is high.

regressive tax   A tax that takes a higher percentage of low incomes than of high incomes.

resource wealth mentality   The view that society's economic wealth is derived mainly from the sale of natural resources, as opposed to efficiency in the production of goods and services.

scarcity   The problem that, while economic inputs (and thus potential output) are limited in availability, people's wants and needs are apparently unlimited.

shareholders   The owners of shares (stocks) in a corporation; shareholders may or may not have voting rights and their liability is limited to the amount invested.

short run   The period of time during which the quantities of some inputs cannot be changed.

social (external) costs   Costs that are not paid by producers, but rather passed on to society at large.

sole proprietorship   A business firm owned (and usually managed) by a single person who bears full legal liability for the firm's debts.

standard of living   A measure of the economic prosperity of the people of a society, usually expressed in terms of the volume of consumer goods and services consumed per household or per person per year.

subsidies   Payments by the government of part of the cost of a service in order to reduce the cost to the user of the service.

supply curve   A graphical representation of a supply schedule.

supply schedule   A table depicting the relationship between the price of a product and the quantity supplied (offered for sale).

tax credits   Credits that reduce the income taxes payable by Canadians in order to offset a variety of factors that adversely affect their living standards, including dependants, property taxes, and sales taxes.

user fees   Charges to the users of government services.

variable costs   Production costs that vary with the level of output (for example, direct labour and direct material).

World Trade Organization (WTO)   An international organization through which over 100 member nations negotiate and enforce rules for international trade.

INDEX